DISCOVERING THE POSSIBLE

A Title from the Helen Kellogg Institute for International Studies

Discovering the Possible:

The Surprising World of Albert O. Hirschman

BY

LUCA MELDOLESI

UNIVERSITY OF NOTRE DAME PRESS

Notre Dame   London

Library of Congress Cataloging-in-Publication Data

Meldolesi, Luca, 1939–
    Discovering the possible : the surprising world of Albert
Hirschman / by Luca Meldolesi.
        p.   cm.
    Includes bibliographical references.
    ISBN 0-268-00877-9
    1. Hirschman, Albert O.   2. Economists—United States.
3. Economics—United States.   I. Helen Kellogg Institute for
International Studies.   II. Title.
HB119.H57M45   1995
330'.092—dc20   94-42834
[B]   CIP

    ∞ The paper used in this publication meets the minimum requirements
   of the American National Standard for Information Sciences—Permanence of Paper
            for Printed Library Materials, ANSI Z39.48-1984.

From my birth in 1915 to my emigration in 1933, I lived in Berlin and when the Freie Universität of that city bestowed an honorary degree on me some five years ago, I told a story about my childhood or early adolescence—how I found out to my intense surprise and disappointment that my father did not have, what I then thought was a basic necessity for any real person—a *Weltanschauung!* The subsequent history of my life and thought could probably be written in terms of the progressive discovery on my part how right my father had been.

Albert O. Hirschman
Coimbra, March 1993

Contents

viii   CONTENTS

Part 2

Foreword

I first became interested in Albert Hirschman's work in 1982, when my wife, Nicoletta, and I took a trip to Poland to get a better picture of the turmoil there. We arrived a few days before Jaruzelsky's military coup, an attempt to hold back the tidal wave of freedom that only a few years later was to sweep through the whole of Eastern Europe. In that same period, my personal experience had led me to question the intellectual roots of traditional European progressive culture, with its reformist and revolutionary branches, and to seek an alternative approach. I began to appreciate the significance and complexity of Hirschman's contribution, and its relevance to my compelling need for new ideas, while compiling and writing introductions to various collections of his essays.

The present book presents an itinerary of over half a century of Hirschman's work. Its aim is to shed light on the importance and durability of his writings, which are born out of different political, social, and historical contexts and yet remain topical to this day.

It goes without saying that an author that cannot be classified gives rise to an unclassifiable book. My intention is not to provide a biography, intellectual history, or handbook on his scientific works. Rather, the personal and historical aspects of Hirschman's life have been used as a means to trace links between his works, to observe them "in the making," and attempt to pursue their intellectual implications. My hope is to facilitate the task of Hirschman readers by exploring his theories, by discussing the form and style of his works and outlining the lessons that can be learned from them, and, finally, by indicating possible new perspectives from which to view his vast production.

The directness and clarity of his presentation make Hirschman's books deceptively easy to read; there is, however, far more to digest than one might think. I have learned that it is vital to go beyond the first impact if one does not want to risk misinterpreting or missing some element of Hirschman's thought process. My ambitious aim is therefore to train readers to pause and reflect after their first reading, to make the necessary connections and in-depth analyses, and to follow Hirschman in his frequent changes of perspective. In short, to appreciate the extraordinary fertility of his work and accept his challenge to "think better."

Acknowledgments

This book took shape following a long itinerary starting at home base in Italy, moving on to the Institute for Advanced Studies in Princeton, New Jersey, and finishing up in various libraries in Cambridge, Massachusetts, and in Berlin. A long journey through five Latin American countries undertaken in 1990 also contributed to the book's evolution.

I would like to thank, above all, Sarah and Albert Hirschman and Nicoletta Stame, each of whom, in his or her own way, screened the process of my work. For their warm welcome, I would also like to thank Guillermo O'Donnell, Carlos Bazdresch, Liliana Báculo, Ruth and Fernando Henrique Cardoso, José Serra, Javier Villanueva, Miguel Urrutia, Pedro Malan, and all of the other Latin American intellectuals mentioned in chapter 3. Finally, thanks are due to the Ford Foundation, the Italian Education Ministry (now MURST) and the Italian Research Council (CNR) for their generous financial support which made the project possible.

Previous versions of chapter 1 were published in Albert O. Hirschman, *L'economia politica comme scienza morale e sociale* (Naples: Liguori, 1987), pp. 175–210, and in *Revue française de science politique*, vol. 43, no. 3 (June), pp. 379–411. In addition, a version of chapter 3 was presented as a Special Lecture at the international symposium, Hirschman's Work and a New Strategy for Development for Latin America (Buenos Aires, Nov. 13–15, 1989), later revised and published in *Studi economici*, vol. 45, no. 3 (1991), pp. 23–75, and in *El trimestre economico*, vol. 59, no. 1 (1992), pp. 65–106.

Part 1

1

Prologue:
The Origins of Possibilism

Before visiting a famous town filled with works of art, an intelligent tourist will make sure he has a map of the sights worth seeing. He will accordingly plan itineraries that will lead him to discover, with today's eyes, many aspects of the past. These discoveries will doubtless lead him to make detours from his original plan, and to trace links between different periods and elements that would at first sight have seemed unlikely. This is the image that came to mind as my work on this book drew to a close; the trajectory I ended up following—one of the many that exist—had forged its own links and set me on its own logical path.

In this introductory chapter, I will examine Hirschman's formative years in various European countries and analyze how this turbulent, confused, and multifaceted period contributed to the originality of his thought. I will also discuss Hirschman's 1945 book, *National Power,* and deal with the question of how recognition of power disequilibria in "harmless" trade relations allows one to reconsider some aspects of the traditional foreign trade theory and reconcile it (to a certain extent) with observable facts. This will lead to an analysis of the cognitive process that led Hirschman at that early stage to delineate such essential aspects of his theory as the relationship between economics and politics, and the dimensions of possibilism.

In Hirschman's writings between 1946 and 1951, corresponding to the period of the Marshall Plan, the idea of a way out, or a narrow path, between, say, inflation and deflation in Italy began to take shape. One can also see the beginnings of possibilist proposals for increasing collaboration between European countries, such as the proposal for creating a European monetary authority (a problem that has not yet been solved).

Returning to *National Power*, I go on to deal with the industrialization of underdeveloped nations and with the obstacles to this process that were created by the cultural climate prevailing in some European countries. The chapter concludes with an examination of two articles written in 1951–52, which shows how American culture had been successfully grafted onto European roots.

FORMATIVE EXPERIENCES

Let us start with a gnoseological question. How did a German intellectual, molded by the 1930s, see through the abundant but deceptive illusions created by contemporary European progressive culture, and yet remain faithful (at least as a cognitive choice) to the idea that social problems are important and that change is needed?

The possibility is not contemplated by progressives who can think only in terms of the typical antonyms—realism and utopianism. As a matter of fact, Hirschman's recognition of the need for economic and political advancement is rooted in his own experience and in the opportunities afforded him. Such a claim invites us to study the structure and articulation of his experience and life opportunities.

Otto Albert Hirschmann[1] was born in Berlin on April 7, 1915, to a Jewish family. His father was a well-established surgeon in the city. Until the age of 17, he studied at the Französische Gymnasium where he received a solid classical education: Greek and Latin (a key to many other languages), religion and morals, literature and mathematics.

By 1931–32 he was already part of a group working on Hegel's *Phenomenology of the Spirit* and spent a summer writing an interpretation of one passage that Hirschman admits today is incomprehensible. "Perhaps," he observes, "the torment of having to make sense of Hegel had an unintended side effect later in France: to make me fall in love with the French moralists of the 17th century, such as Pascal and La Rochefoucauld; they seemed to me just as deep, but in a marvelously easy going manner" (1984f, pp. 2–3).[2]

Hirschman's interest in social justice can be traced back to this period. He became well versed in the classics of socialism and committed himself, together with his sister Ursula, to the Young Socialist Workers' Association, where, after the advent of Hitler, he organized illegal propaganda. Hirschman remembers the first signs of repression, a wave of arrests: "Then my father died suddenly (of an operation) at the end of March 1933. The shock of this event and the feeling that I was in some danger, made me decide to leave Germany in the early days of April 1933" (1984f, p. 3).

After moving to Paris, the young Hirschman enrolled in the École des Hautes Études Commerciales (HEC) to continue the studies in economics he had already commenced at the Humboldt University of Berlin. The HEC was the *grande école* of business in Paris,[3] where Hirschman spent two "exhausting years." "I had," he recently recalled (1993d, p. 2) "a lot of courses in accounting and in something called 'technology' which was about various sequences of industrial operations invariably starting . . . with 'concassage.' " There were also some good courses on economic geography, money, banking, and (to a certain extent) international trade. At the same time he came into contact with the world of European political émigrés, from Germany, Italy, and (Menshevik) Russia. He gradually let slip his German-sounding name Otto and became simply Albert.

In 1935–36, Hirschman studied economics at the London School of Economics (LSE). But in the summer of 1936 he signed up with the Spanish Republican Army. In January 1937, Hirschman went back to his books, this time at the University of Trieste, where he became an unpaid assistant and graduated in economics at the Statistics Institute directed by Professor Paolo Luzzatto Fegiz.[4]

In Trieste, Albert joined other militant anti-Fascists, sharing his activism once again with his sister Ursula who had meanwhile married his good friend, Eugenio Colorni, professor of philosophy.[5] Hirschman chose not to favor one faction of anti-Fascism over another, but to offer his services, using his German passport and carrying double-bottomed suitcases.[6]

In May 1938, the introduction of Mussolini's racial laws, however, spelled the end of Hirschman's early academic career and precipitated a return to Paris. As the Second World War erupted, he signed up with the French army, fighting until France capitulated in June 1940. With demobilization, Hirschman adopted a new identity: Albert Hermant, born in Philadelphia of French parents.

This was when Hirschman reestablished contact with Neu Beginnen, a group of young, militant Germans with social-democratic backgrounds. A representative of the group in the U.S., Karl Frank, was promoting an Emergency Rescue Committee supported by American universities and personalities (including Eleanor Roosevelt). Its aim was to save from extermination by the Nazis European—mostly German—intellectuals and artists, who were gathering in Marseilles in the hope of a passage to America. Hirschman soon became right-hand-man to an American named Varian Fry, the committee's chief of operations in Europe.

One participant later remembered Hermant as being " 'a demon of ingenuity with a puckish smile.' He traded currency on the black market, obtained forged documents and passports, devised methods for transmitting messages to the outside world by concealing strips of paper in toothpaste tubes" (Bell, 1984, p. 2).[7] By December 1940, Hirschman came so close to being discovered that he too set sail for America.[8]

In a 1990 interview (1990b, p. 153), Hirschman claimed he was basically a self-taught economist. At the Paris HEC in the 1930s, economics as a discipline was still rather primitive. The year spent at LSE, by contrast, was an eye opener. Albert absorbed all he could from professors and engaged in heated discussions with fellow students. On arrival in Italy, however, he was almost isolated as far as economics was concerned.

Nevertheless, if we take his irregular learning path as given, we can consider other aspects of Hirschman's formation which, by softening the blow of what is typically a rigid initiation in the discipline, may have favored the creative development of his thought.

I have already mentioned Albert's flirtations with French culture. I would now like to add that it was during his years at HEC that Hirschman developed an interest in statistics and applied economics—a certain kind of inductive applied economics (intelligently presented factual reconstruction) that was nurtured by the Parisian ambience. It is important to remember that several features, for a series of reasons generally left aside, were peculiar to French economics at the time. These include an inclination towards practical description of economic facts, a fair degree of tolerance for various schools of thought (liberal, historical, social, mathematical, sociological, etc.), and a marked interest in the political aspects of economics (Dumez, 1985; Meldolesi, 1991a).[9] This, together with HEC courses on money and banking held by Henry Pomméry, probably made up the breeding ground of Hirschman's research project on French monetary policy from the 1920s to 1930s, conceived in London and completed as a graduation thesis in Trieste.

Two other elements were also influential: political science and economic geography. "I think that the reason why I got into economics," Hirschman said recently (1990b, p. 153), "was the experience of mass unemployment and political convulsion of the 1930s." When he first arrived in Paris, Albert's intention was to enroll in the School of Political Science (see note 3) where the courses seemed to combine very happily economic with political matters, technical subjects with history and philosophy. Then, for practical reasons, Hirschman opted for another school, but his original idea of creating links between economics and politics was not abandoned: indeed it was to become of primary relevance in his thinking.[10]

Vidalian geography, moreover, was the first social science in France to have a status as a discipline. Once sociologists had exhausted their criticism, it played an important role in the formation of the Annales history school (it is sufficient to mention *La terre et l'évolution humaine* [1922] by Lucien Febvre) and deeply influenced many other social disciplines. Hirschman was introduced to this school of thought while following Albert Demangeon's courses at HEC (see chapter 2, note 21) and furthered his acquaintance by reading many works by André Siegfried, a well-known political scientist interested in geography, economics, and history. The idea of focusing his analysis, as geographers do, on a limited area was already present in various works dating back to his Italian period.[11]

As we have already said, in early 1937 Hirschman enrolled in the faculty of economics at the University of Trieste. A large part of his course at HEC was recognized as equivalent by the academic authorities. Moreover, he brought with him a manuscript that he translated into Italian and presented as a thesis entitled *The Poincaré Franc and Its Devaluation*.

Alongside some statistical-demographic research (see note 4), then, Hirschman found time to study the Italian economy.[12] The young economist was commissioned by a French review to send reports on the Italian economy, about which very little was known due to the lack of statistical data released by the Fascist regime. "Italian finance and economy," he wrote (1938b, p. 1), "are increasingly impenetrable. . . . In order to have an approximate idea of what the Kingdom's financial situation might be, one is forced to make a meticulous compilation of official communiqués from the Council of Ministers or the Grand Council of Fascism, anything but explicit reports from the Ministry of Finance . . . , increasingly cautious research published by Italian newspapers or reviews."

As a result of this research, Hirschman was able to write "Les finances et l'économie italiennes: Situation actuelle et perspectives," an accurate reconstruction of public finance (the budget, deficit financing, capital taxation of corporations), monetary policy, consumption, production, and foreign trade.[13] The overall picture that emerged was of an economy well managed technically, but strangled by policies of economic autarky which, in conjunction with war mobilization, resulted in a bloated public sector, an impoverished population, and suffocated productive and financial sectors.

When Hirschman returned to Paris in 1938, the reports published in the French review helped him open up shop as an expert on the Italian economy. On this basis he was taken on at Robert Marjolin and Charles Rist's Institut Scientifique de Récherches Économiques et Sociales.[14] "Not only had I somehow acquired a 'profession,' " Hirschman commented recalling those years (1990f, p. xxx), "but, to my great relief, I realized I was able reasonably competently to do the job of an economist without first having to judge the absolute validity of Keynes' *General Theory* that I had bought in London the year it was published (1936) and brought back to Italy to study in depth."

As we can see, Hirschman's approach differed substantially from that of the theorizing economist in the British tradition.

His experience led him to undertake, armed with a sharp spirit of observation and an indefatigable curiosity for concrete facts, the patient task of inquiry, using statistical data and historical reconstruction, and scrutinizing the available economic literature.

NATIONAL POWER

Hirschman's writings from the years 1937–39 reveal another characteristic: as well as an extraordinary capacity for hard work, he was also able to focus on one theme and simultaneously launch himself into others. Thus his specialization in Italian matters gave birth to his interest in foreign trade and other connected problems, which eventually led to his writing *National Power and the Structure of Foreign Trade* (1945).

In 1938, Hirschman received a request from John Condliffe to write a report on exchange controls in Italy[15] for an international conference on "Economic Policies and Peace" planned for August 1939 in Bergen, Norway.[16] For this conference he also wrote his first ever piece on foreign trade: a statistical study on the tendencies of foreign trade towards equilibrium and bilateralism (1939c, published in English in 1988 by P. F. Asso).

After he arrived in the U.S., Hirschman was called upon by Condliffe, who had in the meantime become professor of international economics at Berkeley,[17] to take part in a "Project on the Regulation of Trade"; writing *National Power,* however, was of paramount importance to him. After his troubled years in Europe, Hirschman jumped at the (unhoped for) opportunity to realize a project he had long dreamed of. At the University of California at Berkeley he made friends with Alexander Gerschenkron who was engaged in writing *Bread and Democracy in Germany* (1943), a book that dealt with Junker policies and the agrarian transformation from the 1870s to the advent of Hitler, prefaced by the eloquent motto, *Latifundia perdidere germaniam.* Hirschman wrote *National Power* hoping to stir the economic community to reconcile the traditional theory of foreign trade with observable German experience.[18]

With quite remarkable practical and theoretical background for a man of twenty-five, Hirschman had developed "special sensitivity" to the propensity of large and powerful countries to dominate weaker countries through commerce (see Hirschman, 1986b, pp. 6–7). Witnessing Nazi expansion throughout Eastern and Central-Eastern Europe during the 1930s inspired *National Power,* which was written at Berkeley, California, in 1941–42 and published at the end of the war.

The use of foreign trade as a means of political pressure and leverage, was one of the main characteristics of the period immediately preceding the outbreak of the Second World War. Attention had previously been focused on the instruments of power politics, but Hirschman's emphasis was different (v. 1981a, p. 27). He did not wish to dwell on "the diabolical cunning of the Nazis, or on Dr. Schacht's technical innovations such as bilateral-ism, exchange controls and so on," but rather on "the structural characteristics of international economic relations" that can be exploited to exert influence, create dependence and ultimately dominance.[19]

This question received very little attention, "yet its impor-tance is obvious," Hirschman wrote in the introduction, "since it points to an element in the international situation which is not necessarily temporary nor confined merely to the techniques and circumstances of which the Nazis took such good advantage."[20]

Jean-Claude Casanova recently observed (1990, p. 11) that *National Power* presents two typical features of Hirschman's work: it is of uncertain classification and exceptionally long lived. Hirschman was "lucky first time" in finding his path, Casanova claimed, because his experience gave him the opportunity to make a synthesis of different national traditions. He identified an "order of power" in the German tradition, and an "order of the market" in the British tradition. Furthermore, he understood that one does not absorb the other, and that both must be analyzed and linked together from an objective distance.

The book opens with a brief survey of economic thought on the relationship between foreign trade and national power. It then goes on to provide a systematic theoretical analysis, a historical reconstruction of the debate at the time of World War I, and a review of certain safeguards or remedies. In the second part of the book, Hirschman presents statistical inquiries into the structure and tendencies of foreign trade, answering in quantitative terms some of the questions raised in part 1.

Hirschman's cultural and political upbringing pervades *National Power*. Immediate evidence of this is his first-hand knowledge of the classics of European thought, from Machiavelli and Montesquieu, to Smith, Hume, and Fichte. References to these works are made in the brief survey of economic thought that constitutes the basis of Hirschman's argument.

Policies proposed by free traders, protectionists, or eclectics, Hirschman explains, are supposed to be "conducive to more economic power." They have one common characteristic, however: since all nations can pursue what they consider to be the right policies, the latter do not necessarily lead to an increase in relative power for the country concerned. This observation was natural enough for free traders who claimed there was "mutual benefit accruing from commercial intercourse," but not so for protectionists, "who had their eyes fixed exclusively upon the dependence incurred through foreign trade by their respective national economies." Protectionists did not realize that dependence "has a double aspect" (1945, p. 9), i.e., it implies the dependence of other nations on the power in question, as well as the possibility of asymmetrical relations.

The new perspective emerged, however, when J. S. Mill, and others in the liberal camp, showed that "the material benefit derived from international trade is not necessarily divided equally between the various trading nations." Since then, Anglo-Saxon economists have reflected at length on the "ways in which the terms of trade might be altered by changing conditions or by adopting policies favorable to one nation. . . . Thus, although the reasoning of the mercantilist balance of trade theory had been decisively discredited by the criticism of Hume and Adam Smith, some of its main conclusions were rehabilitated, not as a certainty, but as a possibility. . . . It need not surprise us," Hirschman concludes, "that the obvious power implications of these findings . . . , somewhat neglected by English economists, have been seized upon by their German colleagues," though their treatment was far from systematic (1945, pp. 10 and 11).

In the words of Mark Blaug (1985, p. 94), Hirschman has a special talent for "looking at an old problem from a new, unexpected angle." In *National Power*, new light was shed on power and trade because the two were considered in terms of their interaction. Hirschman showed how power is manifested through trade and that trade presupposes power. While the proposals put forward by various schools of economic thought were usually aimed at strengthening the power of a nation, Hirschman worked against the grain, taking national power as given and studying at a theoretical level the characteristics of foreign trade that can be exploited by the politics of power. This is why his book is called *National Power and the Structure of Foreign Trade*, not *The Structure of Foreign Trade and National Power*.

Hirschman assumes there is always a coercive power—either military or peaceful—in one country's relations with another. To expand this power, a nation must take many historical, political, military, psychological, and economic factors into consideration. His analysis in *National Power* was restricted to foreign trade, or, more precisely, to the relationships of dependence, influence, and even domination that can arise out of trade relations.[21]

Foreign trade, Hirschman claimed, has two main effects upon national power. The first—supply effect—consists in increasing the availability of goods or substituting goods wanted less with goods wanted more. This "enhances the potential military force of a country" and, therefore, indirectly boosts the nation's power. Through the second—influence effect—foreign trade can become an instrument of power. A sovereign power, in fact, can always interrupt or cut off trade with other countries. For these other countries, trade with the dominant country "is worth *something*," and they will accordingly grant the latter political, economic, or military advantages in order to retain existing trade relations.

The book focuses on the conditions that increase the power of a dominant country to cut off trade relations and thereby increase its influence, and on the conditions that make it more difficult for subordinate countries to find alternative markets and sources of supply or to dispense entirely with the trade they conduct with that country. The higher the total net gain from trade with the stronger nation and the more powerful its vested social and economic interests, the longer and more painful is the adjustment process imposed by the interruption of trade and the greater are the difficulties faced by a weaker nation.

Therefore, in order to increase its power, the dominant country can simply increase the total net gain of the subordinate country. This does *not* entail, however, a change in the terms of trade in favor of the latter. The sovereign power can modify the composition of its exports and/or select trading partners in such a way that they need the goods urgently, both because they are not able to produce them themselves and because they are poor (and therefore reluctant to become even poorer). The dominating country will also have an interest in choosing partners with restricted mobility of domestic resources—basically agricultural countries—and with a high concentration (in terms of produce and position) of goods exported. These factors make the process of adjustment even longer and more painful.[22]

THEORY AND SOLUTIONS

The analysis presented by the young Hirschman is surprising, in my view, for at least two reasons.

First, it succeeds in demonstrating that "power elements and disequilibria are potentially inherent in such 'harmless' trade relations as have always taken place, e.g. between big and small, rich and poor, agricultural and industrial countries—relations which could be fully in accord with the principles taught by the theory of international trade" (1945, p. 40). In order to appreciate to what extent this theory was before its time, it should be remembered that, not long after *National Power* was published, Paul Samuelson claimed on the basis of traditional assumptions that the countries involved in free commercial exchange not only obtained mutual benefits from it—as the literature on the subject had long claimed—but they achieved equal absolute renumeration of production factors.

Second, although economic literature at the time hardly ever referred to the politics of international trade, the outside world had been all too eloquent. *National Power* dwells at length on this discrepancy between theory and practice and shows how the outstanding features of Nazi Germany's trade policy followed the principles of power politics outlined in the book (1945, pp. 34–40). This clear example of the potential manipulation of foreign trade should perhaps have been backed up by others if Hirschman's intention had been to study the different types of influence and explore the range of possible developments. But this was not Hirschman's aim: "We believe," he wrote, "that by a theoretical analysis we may arrive at a fundamental diagnosis and ultimate cure" (1945, p. 12).

The diagnosis, as we have seen, is the premise that foreign trade can be used as an instrument of national power policy: "so long as war remains a possibility and so long as the sovereign nation can interrupt trade with any country at its own will . . . foreign trade provides an opportunity for power which it will be tempting to seize" (1945, p. 40). The cure, Hirschman thinks, can only be administered by severely restricting national sovereignty.

To put things in perspective, Hirschman provided "a historical background of our problem," surveying the literature on "economic aggression" before and during World War I. Opinions were basically divided between two equally unsatisfactory positions: politicians, historians, and journalists who, with the help of protectionist economists, proposed averting the danger of economic aggression by increased economic nationalism; and free-trade economists who failed to see the reality of the danger pointed out by their adversaries because they answered "on purely economic grounds."

Hirschman criticized proposals put forward on both sides (imposed restrictions on German economic policy, universal free trade) arguing: "The Nazis have merely shown us the tremendous power potentialities inherent in international economic relations, just as they have given us the first practical demonstration of the powers of propaganda. It is not possible to ignore or to neutralize those relatively new powers of men over men; the only alternative open to us is to prevent their use for the purposes of war and enslavement and to make them work for our own purposes of peace and welfare. This can be done only by a frontal attack upon the institution which is at the root of the possible use of international economic relations for national power aims— the institution of national economic sovereignty" (1945, p. 79). The power to organize and regulate foreign trade, Hirschman suggested, must be taken away from single nations and transferred to an international authority able to oversee the machinery of world trade.

In later years, Hirschman described this suggestion as "infinitely naive" (1981a, p. 28), but we should not be taken in by his retrospective irony. Hirschman's views reflect a profound need for transformation after the tragic years of the war and in a sense they inspire his future activities. His experience with the Marshall Plan, the long period devoted to development economics, and his numerous working trips across countries and continents all contributed to building a very personal intellectual itinerary that is supranational in its very nature.

It may be useful, at this point, to go over the main analytical theme Hirschman used to challenge traditional analysis: that is, the gain from trade theory. According to Alfred Marshall, the gain of a country from its foreign trade is given by the difference for that country between the value of the goods it imports and the value of the export goods the country could have produced with the same capital and labor. In this definition, the net gain is subjective, with the result that a country can obtain from the exchange a lower proportion of the physical surplus generated by international productive specialization, and, at the same time, a higher level of satisfaction than its trading partner's. This satisfaction is greater, the less elastic (in the relevant interval), and therefore the more compelling is the demand curve for imported goods compared to the variations of the terms of trade. Thus, Marshall concludes, "The rich country can with little effort supply a poor country with implements for agriculture or the chase which doubled the effectiveness of her labor, and which she could not make for herself; while the rich country could without great trouble make for herself most of the things which she purchased from the poor nation or at all events could get fairly good substitutes for them. A stoppage of the trade would therefore generally cause much more real loss to the poor than to the rich nation" (1923, p. 168).

The theory of trade asymmetry could be considered a development of this observation. Hirschman took it upon himself to analyze some aspects of the theory, arriving at the conclusion that, "All our analysis of the influence effect of foreign trade may then be summarized by the following principle: Given a certain gain from trade of A, and a fixed indifference system of A, create conditions such as to maximize the difference in satisfaction between the indifference curve which B actually reaches by trading with A and B's no-gain-from-trade with A curve" (1945, pp. 47–48). "The entire theory of the gain from trade and of its distribution," he later added (1971a, pp. 8–9), "became therefore relevant for an understanding of the influence and power relationships that arise out of trade."

This leads us to an important point. The theoretical arguments put forward in *National Power* were born outside traditional economic theory; they were generated by politics, not by economics. Yet Hirschman used the theory of foreign trade to support his analysis. In this way, it would seem, Hirschman avoided coming down in favor of one of the two alternatives faced by critical economists this century: to make their contribution from within the context of the dominant school of thought (like Keynes and Schumpeter), or to reject the latter in favor of a past tradition (like Sraffa, and, to some extent, Joan Robinson).

Nonetheless, from the point of view of economic theory, P. F. Asso and M. de Cecco claim (1987, p. 26), Hirschman's analytical work "is of the same type as that conducted by Keynes on orthodox theory and . . . has the same purpose: to help orthodox economists understand considerations and arguments based on philosophical premises that are opposed to theirs." The prewar Hirschman, the two authors continue, was not yet an upsetter of traditional analytic procedures; he was in fact attracted by the power of economic theory. His "principal desire" was to identify stable relationships between variables in order to crystalize his analysis in an alternative model to the traditional one. The result is a mirror image, showing, the authors conclude, a methodological gap between Hirschman's pre- and postwar work.

Hirschman himself provided biographical details to explain the issue. "Until Fascism and Nazism was entirely defeated," he observed (1986e, p. 42), "everything I wrote was in some way forced to link up with that struggle." Therefore it is easy to reach the conclusion that, like Saint-Simon,[23] Hirschman used economic analysis here as a platform for stating a political thesis. Despite the great ferment and intellectual lessons of the 1930s, *National Power* was ultimately forced to link up with an unreasonably narrow logical structure.

When the Latin American Studies Association asked him in 1976 to preside over a meeting entitled "Dependency Theory Reassessed" (Caporaso, 1978), Hirschman was presented with an ideal opportunity to retrieve some of the questions raised in *National Power* as a logical backdrop to his subsequent research. Hirschman admitted his grandparent status vis-à-vis dependency theory but felt he should distance himself from it.[24] With the proposal regarding a frontal attack, he argued, "I invoked a *deus ex machina:* I wished away the unpleasant reality I had uncovered instead of scrutinizing it further for some possibly built-in modifier or remedy" (1981a, pp. 28–29).[25]

It is not just a question of judging how ready a poor country is to accept its subordinate position; understanding if (and how) this position can be modified is also important. On the basis of his observations of United States–Latin American relations, Hirschman answered with an argument reminiscent of Hegel's description of the relationship between lord and bondsman (*Phenomenology of the Spirit*, 1977, pp. 111–19): an asymmetry of political attention in favor of the poor country may correspond to an asymmetry of trade in favor of the rich country.

The poor country will normally try to reduce its dependence, taking more trouble than the rich country (engaged in interests more vital to its foreign policy) is prepared to take to prevent it. A stronger nation will leave its relations with weaker countries in the hands of lower level administrators (heavily influenced by an invasive business community) whose decisions will usually be shortsighted and predictable. It is not therefore able to stand up to the challenge of a small country that is sufficiently resolute.[26]

Foreign trade is only one of the many situations in which relations of dependence create trends in the opposite direction. Take, for example, a country monopolistically producing a specific item: a price increase could well set in motion competing producers in other countries. Or take a foreign firm's investment in the exploitation of an underdeveloped country's natural resources: once the plants have been built, they become hostages of the host country. "In general, trade and investment relations between countries A and B may lead initially to dependence of B on A for reason of the various asymmetries, but to the extent that the economic intercourse increases the resources at B's command it becomes possible for B to pursue, by diversification and other means, a policy of lessening dependence, be it at the cost of some of these welfare gains" (1981a, p. 32).

There are of course many different mechanisms (economic, political, or both) through which these trends emerge. The fact that they are not identified—to the detriment of dominated countries—is not only due to the difficulties of interdisciplinary analysis. To a fair extent, Hirschman claims, it should be attributed to "an intellectual orientation that is both undialectical and what I would call antipossibilist" (1981a, p. 32).

THE BIRTH OF POSSIBILISM

We can now detect a certain logic in Hirschman's development. To start with, Hirschman's political and professional interests were expressed through the reconstruction and interpretation of economic facts. Later, politics led him to recast economic theories which, in their turn, became a platform for his political views. In an even later period—to which we shall presently turn our attention—Hirschman had to deal with the complex interaction between economics and politics on a practical level.

In 1941, Hirschman married Sarah Chapiro, a Russian-Lithuanian student of philosophy and French literature, with whom he had two daughters, Katia and Lisa. In early 1943 he signed up in the U.S. Army, thus obtaining U.S. citizenship. Hirschman was forced to update his views; events moved faster than ever, and the world seen from the U.S. looked rather different than from Europe.[27] There are hardly any biographical writings about this period. All we know is that Hirschman was sent to fight in North Africa and Italy, where he stayed until the end of the war. He spent half of his three years between Siena, Florence, and Rome, working with the Allied Command. He also resumed contact with his sister Ursula and other members of the family, and began visiting the Research Center of the Bank of Italy (Baffi, 1985, p. 6).

When he got back to the U.S., Gerschenkron (Coser, 1984, p. 164) suggested Hirschman take up a position as research economist at the Federal Reserve Board, with the specific task of overseeing the Program for European Reconstruction—the Marshall

Plan. He thus found himself working, "with intensity and occasional enthusiasm," on the problems of reconstructing France and Italy and on schemes for European economic integration.

Looking back over this period, Hirschman says he had to deal with both orthodox and innovative economists. The former proposed stopping inflation in Europe and devaluing currencies against the dollar: ideas Hirschman considers "politically naive, socially explosive, and economically counter productive" (1986b, p. 5). Keynesian innovators, on the other hand, proposed the creative solutions incorporated in the Marshall Plan, justifying them with new doctrines such as a dollar shortage brought about by structural changes resulting from the war (the low level of economic activity in Europe, the great need for reconstruction, the loss of "invisible income" from overseas, the disruption of traditional trade relations with countries from the Eastern bloc). Many of these innovators, however, fast became doctrinarians.

In his recent essay, "How the Keynesian Revolution was Exported from the United States" (1989), Hirschman explained how Keynesian theory had attracted a group of faithful followers in the U.S., partly because of the incredible opportunity in the 1930s and 1940s to verify the theory in practical terms, and partly because it presented (often in a convoluted and paradoxical way) a series of commonsense intuitions long opposed by the profession. At the end of the war many of these economists, having become government officials, flocked to work for the military governments installed in Germany and Japan and in the administration of the Marshall Plan.[28]

Marshall Plan aid was distributed according to estimated deficits in each country's balance of payments. In order to advocate aid, therefore, it was almost inevitable that officials exhibited greater confidence in their forecasts of current account deficits than was warranted. But some Marshall Plan administrators "attempted to *make* their estimates come true by taking a considerable interest in the domestic plans and policies that shaped external accounts of the aid-receiving countries" (1986b, p. 6), especially weaker countries such as Italy, in order to make sure events did not prove them wrong. This kind of authoritarian and oppressive interference induced in Hirschman a sense of aversion, distress, and concern.

Moreover, he remembers, "in my new position in Washington after the war, I found myself in an ironical situation. Not long before I had been a political refugee, with no power at all, who had criticized in my most ambitious work to date *[National Power]* the political use of economic power. All of a sudden I could not but notice that the economic power of the nation to which I had sworn citizenship and which I represented, gave undeserved weight and consideration to my opinions and to those of my colleagues in the U.S. government" (1987e, p. 42).

This is the human condition that sent Hirschman off in search of other landing spots. "As a reaction," he continued, "perhaps at times excessive, I repressed the exercise of any power I may have had. Most of all, I worked hard at *undermining* the certainties of my colleagues (whether they were pro-market or pro-planning) many of whom saw nothing wrong in using their power to the full in order to air their opinions and convictions."

This is not to say that many Marshall Plan administrators did not have the best of intentions. In the case of Italy, for sure, they wanted to create a more prosperous economy and a fairer society. These good intentions, they seemed to feel, justified their authoritarian operations. However, in its practical application the ideological certainty deriving from economic theory was dangerous and often counterproductive.

In my view, it was this field work demonstrating the dangers of an antidemocratic use of economics that led Hirschman, in a more relaxed postwar atmosphere, to modify his claim, put forward in *National Power*, that economic analysis could lead to "a fundamental diagnosis" and "ultimate cure." In order to undermine his colleagues' certainties more effectively, Hirschman devoted himself to a research project on the concrete possibilities of change to be realized with interactive (inductive and deductive) processes between practice and theory (and between economics, politics, and other aspects of society). The research was grounded in his formation as an applied economist, but transcended it because of its more complex theoretical background and its wider context of economic policy. Hirschman thus began to focus on two aspects: the search for adequate proposals to bring about change, and the search for ways of putting them into practice. These were referred to later (1971a) as dimensions of possibilism.

THE WASHINGTON TEXTS

In the articles written between 1946 and 1951,[29] two interesting lines of argument can be identified. The first is contained in the two essays, "Inflation and Deflation in Italy" and "Economic and Financial Conditions of Italy" (1948), which develop Hirschman's idea that it is necessary "to walk on a very narrow path between deflation and inflation." And in the first part of "Disinflation, Discrimination and the Dollar Shortage" (1948),[30] which indicates a path for development until then ignored by theory.

Slaloming, as it were, between orthodox and innovative theories[31] Hirschman observed that *"the causal relationship"* between inflation and the balance of payments deficit *"runs both ways"* (1948m, p. 887). If it is true that inflation increases the deficit, it is also true that the deficit—and therefore U.S. aid covering it—can generate inflation (especially when large quantities of domestic resources are utilized). This relationship was described analytically by comparing the deflationary effect produced by aid (which figures in the model as imports) with the greater inflationary effect brought about by investments. Hirschman's point was that aid contributes to putting investments to good use, and that the relationship between the two must therefore be made explicit.

This is the "narrow path between deflation and inflation." Great caution must be exercised when using disinflation because, if it leads to reduced outlay for essential investments, the remedy is worse than the illness. If, on the other hand, it reduces consumption and unnecessary investments, and gradually increases resources for exports and indispensable investments, disinflation can be an effective tool.

Moving on to the second line of argument, in "Disinflation, Discrimination, and the Dollar Shortage," Hirschman criticizes a contemporary proposal to allow American goods to be discriminated against until the dollar shortage came to an end. Hirschman felt discrimination would hinder the structural changes needed to overcome the existing disequilibrium, especially in countries that exchange complementary goods (such as Great Britain and its partners in the Sterling area). But very different results, he claimed, in a 1950 conference held by the Department of State, would come of a reduction in customs barriers within the industrialized European countries. European industries would be stimulated to greater productive efficiency due to increased adaptability and mobility; improved allocation of resources; better exploitation of economies of scale; and, most important, greater competition, entrepreneurial initiative, and morale among Europeans. This would, in its turn, reinforce the competitive position of European countries in the international market, thus allowing them to overcome the dollar shortage.[32]

The philosophy behind the Marshall Plan, and the central role played in it by the schemes for European integration, perhaps contributed to these early possibilistic views. Two different approaches can be detected in the articles written by Hirschman in his capacity as negotiator for the U.S.: cognitive (regarding trade flows and payment systems among European countries), and propositive.[33] In the latter category, one can see the effort made to present proposals that address specific necessities (offshore procurement, the destination of unused drawing rights, the liberalization of the ECA dollar), and to find a point of common agreement between conflicting interests (such as the platform for the European Payments Union).[34]

In 1949, Hirschman also wrote his first possibilist proposal, circulated privately among friends and colleagues. In "Proposal for a European Monetary Authority," he maintained that it was possible to coordinate "the economic and fiscal attributes of national sovereignty" and build "new institutions in the 'interstices' of the national prerogatives" (1949a, p. 1). The objective is neither realistic[35] nor utopistic, as a frontal attack on national sovereignty (here explicitly rejected) would have been.

Hirschman was not yet proposing a European currency, but he was already wondering if it was not possible to imagine forms of organization that "would result in a closely knit European monetary and financial structure" (1949a, p. 2). His answer consisted in examining the functions of a hypothetical European Monetary Authority that would gradually acquire the power to coordinate monetary and fiscal policies, reserves, exchange controls, service functions, and so on.

THE TRADITIONAL TYPE OF EXCHANGE
AND THE AMERICAN TURNING POINT

At the beginning of the 1950s, Hirschman's research interests began to change. The success (and subsequent withdrawal) of Marshall Plan aid, and the unfruitful nature of the debate on the European payments system, together with a desire to probe deeper into the political and intellectual questions raised by these experiences, perhaps contributed to turning Hirschman's mind in new directions.

Two articles, published in 1951 and 1952, take up a theme first touched on in chapter 7 of *National Power* and testify to Hirschman's development.[36] Part 2 of *National Power,* as we have seen, comprises three inquiries into the structure and tendencies of international trade based on statistics from between the wars whose declared aim was to reexamine in quantitative terms some of the problems posed in part 1. Chapter 5, "The Preference of Large Trading Countries for Commerce with Small Trading Countries," quantifies the trade that directed itself—or was directed—from larger to smaller trading countries. Chapter 6, "Concentration upon Markets and Supply Sources of the Foreign Trade of Small or Weak Nations," assesses the extent of the concentration.[37] Chapter 7, "The Commodity Structure of World Trade," appraises the proportion of foreign trade based on the exchange of manufactures (secondary goods) against foodstuffs and raw materials (primary goods).

Hirschman's objective was certainly to define the structure of trade and thus contribute to the study of power relations. But there was a further aim. "The prevention of industrialization of agricultural countries," Hirschman writes, "has often been founded upon the claim that such an industrialization would put an end to any 'sound' international division of labor, and this view has been an important factor in shaping the economic and foreign policy of various countries," Germany in particular (1945, p. 86).

The study of national power and foreign trade thus led Hirschman to the problem of industrialization in underdeveloped countries.

From a traditional point of view, foreign trade consists essentially in the exchange of primary and secondary goods; from another point of view, international trade is basically the exchange of manufactures against manufactures. These two views had never before been put to the test: chapter 7 of *National Power* provides a series of statistical analyses with precisely that aim in mind. These inquiries distinguish between (bilateral or triangular) exchanges of commodities against invisible items (such as freights, tourism, insurance, etc.), exchanges of primary against primary, and secondary against secondary commodities, and finally exchanges of primary against secondary commodities, defined by Hirschman as being the "traditional type of exchange."[38]

Hirschman thus shows that neither of the two views has a sound basis. He backs up this conclusion in detail, with the statistical analysis first of groups of countries, and then of key countries. The traditional type of exchange is the backbone of foreign trade in only a limited number of countries. Countries whose foreign trade consists mostly in exchanges of primary against primary commodities, or is divided more or less equally between the four classes of foreign trade considered, are at least as important.

On the other hand, in the theoretical debate, the idea that the division of labor between industrial and agricultural countries is the only sound basis for the expansion of world trade has often been the result of, and justification for, the concern of dominant powers over the industrialization of less developed countries.[39] At the end of the century "Germany looked at the rising American industries and at the growth of manufacturing in Russia and Italy and other 'new' countries with much the same alarm as England looked at German competition" (1945, p. 147). This was the beginning of agricultural protectionism, colonial policies, the urge to build a strong fleet, and the policy of hindering or preventing the industrialization of other countries: policies adopted by Imperial Germany that were later brought to their extreme consequences by Nazi Germany.

Of course, Hirschman added, "we do not suggest that the traditional concept of the commodity structure of world trade is alone responsible for the emergence of these policies" (1945, p. 149): power interests certainly played their part. But the traditional view has become a rationalization of these interests in terms of economic analysis and has thus given extra weight and impetus to their pursuit.

"If we refer to a historical parallel," Hirschman continues,

> we may say that it would certainly be wrong to regard mercantilist views on the balance of trade as entirely responsible for the aggressive commercial policies of the seventeenth and eighteenth centuries. But supposed interests play their part in shaping actions, and economic theories play their part in creating interests. In this sense both the mercantilist theory of the balance of trade and the idea that world trade can only be based upon the division of labor between industrial and agricultural countries had a disruptive effect on international economic and political relations. (1945, p. 150)

These important claims provide us with an insight into the general inspiration of the book. Written in a period of widespread pessimism about the future of international trade, *National Power* calls for its expansion, starting with the industrialization of developing countries.[40]

As the Marshall Plan was drawing to an end, almost ten years after writing *National Power*, Hirschman once again took up the question of international trade and industrialization and published two papers, both variations on the same theme, one aimed at an Italian and the other at an American readership. The first, "Industrial Nations and Industrialization of Underdeveloped Countries," was published in English in the review, *Economia internazionale* (August 1951). The second, "Effects of Industrialization on the Markets in Industrialized Countries," was included in *The Progress of Underdeveloped Areas* (1952), a volume edited by Bert Hoselitz collecting the lectures held by a group of social scientists at the twenty-seventh Institute (June 18–21, 1951) of the Norman Wait Harris Memorial Foundation at the University of Chicago.[41]

In the final chapter of *National Power*, Hirschman had examined the evolution of British foreign trade since 1854, showing that in the last decades of the nineteenth century, the share of the total "traditional type of exchange" in the total exchange had significantly declined because Germany and the United States had sold Britain increasing quantities of manufactures. In the

1951 and 1952 articles he took up the theme again, claiming that, in general, the industrialization of new areas has a twofold effect on old industrialized countries: "market destroying" and "market creating." It is easy enough, he claims, to understand how the industrialization of new areas can be harmful for established industrial countries not only by substituting imported commodities with locally produced ones, but also by competing successfully with the older industrial countries in third markets, and even in the market of the very country that originally supplied it with finished goods and capital. Nonetheless, these negative results are more than compensated for by a number of beneficial effects, such as the demand for capital goods necessary for industrialization, and the demand for a wide variety of manufactures arising from the increased income of the new areas.

These claims are backed up by statistical data on the industrialization of a whole group of countries and on the composition of international trade.[42] The statistics show that "*on balance* industrial countries have nothing to fear, and much to gain, from the industrialization of other countries" (1952, p. 273).

At the end of *National Power* (1945, p. 151), Hirschman had already anticipated that "international trade had nothing to fear" from the development of new areas. "There will probably always remain," he wrote, "a fruitful division of labor between the various countries and parts of the world," even if the transitions from one pattern to another "will present many adjustment difficulties which might best be solved by the establishment and extension of effective international controls." In a later article (1952, p. 273) Hirschman takes from Eugene Staley (1944, p. 159) an outline of the economic policies to be adopted in the adjustment process set off by the industrialization of underdeveloped countries. In order to maximize their net gain, the established industrial nations must strive to fulfill three conditions. They should specialize in exports that are likely to benefit from the industrialization of new areas (capital goods, complex consumption goods sensitive to rises in income); develop new, improved processes and products; and maintain a sufficient degree of mobility and adaptability in their economy.

If the economic structures—and the political institutions linked to them—are flexible, Hirschman concluded (echoing to a certain extent his experience in the Marshall Plan), established industrial nations have nothing to fear from the industrialization of new areas. Yet the opposite view prevailed for a long time, often significantly influencing government behavior and policy. How, then, can the two views be reconciled?

"In truth," Hirschman wrote (1952, p. 276),

> the technically more advanced countries have been remarkably inconsistent in their attitude toward the less advanced countries ever since the rise of manufacturing: they have alternatively and often simultaneously helped, feared, and attempted to block the efforts of these countries to acquire industrial techniques and equipment.

Concern about the spreading of industrial methods to other nations was nevertheless to increase with the spread of industrialization in the second half of the nineteenth century. Toward the end of the century, an extensive literature grew up describing the "disastrous dangers of German trade rivalry." And yet, this fear found its most outspoken expression in Germany itself which had hardly joined the small band of older industrialized nations "when it was already intent on slamming the door behind it in the face of any additional new-comers."

One voice, Hirschman continued, was consistently absent, however: that of the United States.[43] As an intellectual American addressing fellow Americans, Hirschman wondered why the United States was "exempt of a fear that has afflicted most other industrial countries" and turned its attention to the problem only to foster the development of underdeveloped countries through the promotion of the International Bank for Reconstruction and Development and of the development loans of the Export-Import Bank, and through the elaboration of Truman's "Point IV Program" on technical aid (see Packenham, 1973, pp. 43–49).

Hirschman's answer is twofold. First, American manufacture exports are mostly investment or consumption goods aimed at high income consumers. Clearly these can only stand to gain from rising income levels in the rest of the world. Second, the United States exports substantial quantities of industrial raw and semifinished materials which are bound to increase with increased manufactory production in other countries (not to mention that

American dependence on foreign supplies of raw materials has always been of a smaller order than in European countries).

The first aspect alone cannot explain the phenomenon. After all, the differences between the structure of foreign trade in Germany and in the United States, though significant, are not all that great. There are other less tangible answers. "The truth," Hirschman writes (1952, pp. 280–81),

> is that German writers took a certain delight in showing that industrial countries were digging their own graves through the export of machinery and industrial techniques. This propensity for discovering apocalyptic historical vistas has been a general trait of German historical and sociological writing since the nineteenth century. It can, for example, also be found in the familiar Marxist analysis which showed how capitalism was preparing its own destruction through the creation of a proletariat and how competition was destined for extinction because of the way in which the competitive struggle led to monopoly.

This extract is, in my view, highly revealing; it helps us understand the distance from traditional European culture that the American experience had already produced in Hirschman. "These numerous prophesies of doom," he added,

> do not teach us so much about the real nature of industrialism, capitalism, and competition as about the state of mind of their intellectual authors, ill at ease in the industrial age, and therefore inordinately fertile in finding proofs for its inevitable dissolution. The fundamental reason why these theories have never gained much credence or influence in the United States is to be found in the absence of the many conflicts and strains—deeply embedded in history—that in Germany and many other European countries resulted in a widespread intellectual hostility toward industrial capitalism. (Ibid.)

The difference between the attitude of Germany and other European countries and that of the United States towards the industrialization of new areas has important roots in the cultural climate of the two continents, in their conflicts and social tensions, in their history. It is thus clear why Hirschman became closer to Louis Hartz whose comparative analysis of American political thought focused on Europe's feudal heritage and who described Marxism as an anticapitalist and antifeudal view linked to the waning of the European "Ancièn Regime" (Hartz, 1955; Meldolesi, 1985b and 1989). In later years (1982a, pp. 1478–1480), Hirschman also described not having a feudal past as a handicap. But in 1952, this was viewed as just positive: in the more dynamic and vital capitalism of the United States, "difficulties of growth" were not necessarily interpreted as "deep-seated cracks fated to bring about the collapse of our whole economic structure." Remedies could easily be found case by case.

As Hirschman put it (1952, p. 281),

> Instead of casting an uneasy eye toward the industrial advances of other countries, we [Americans] have always believed in the possibilities of further economic and technological progress and in our ability to maintain industrial leadership. Moreover, our economic history testifies abundantly to the benefits of vigorous industrial expansion; and a theory maintaining that any further extension of industrialism, be it within or without our borders, is disastrous or even dangerous, is prima facie suspect to us.[44]

2

How to Complicate Economics

This chapter starts with a leap forward to the 1980s, when Hirschman questioned the economic paradigm of the isolated individual, motivated by material self-interest alone. In his view, other previously neglected human characteristics, such as "voice," self-evaluation, tensions between instrumental and noninstrumental behavior, and private and collective interests were equally important. This starting point allows us to apply this view to Hirschman's work and to observe, for example, the delicate balance between moral requirements and scientific production that became clear when Hirschman decided to devote himself, after the success of the Marshall Plan, to the important theme of the development of Third World countries.

The chapter goes on to focus on the Bogotà period (1952–56), when Hirschman was first economic adviser to the Colombian government, then private consultant. In the writings I will be looking at clear traces of themes that later became central to his thought. A few key dualities—between economic policy and decision making, general planning and sector projects, programming and experimentation—had already shifted Hirschman's work onto a different and more complex plane than that traditionally occupied by economics.

In the inaugural number of *Economics and Philosophy,* (1985) Hirschman published an essay entitled, "Against Parsimony: Three Easy Ways of Complicating Some Categories of Economic Discourse." In 1986, moreover, he held a course at the Collège de France entitled "For an Enlarged Economics" and later chose the title *How to Complicate Economics* for an anthology of his work published by Il Mulino (Bologna) in a collection dedicated to "Great Contemporary Economists" (1988).

Complicating economics is a contemporary theme, but its roots can be traced back much further. The need to renew the discipline—or the question of whether it should be renewed—had long absorbed Hirschman's attention. Going back in time, we might consider to what extent the problem was present in his shifting of research interests at the end of the 1960s (see chapter 6). We might examine to what extent the need to respond to the challenge of political catastrophes in the Third World, and to engage in digressions and forays into other fields (voice and exit, passions and interests, shifting involvements) (1981a, pp. vi and 23), led him to the conclusion that parsimony in economic theory could be exaggerated and that "something is sometimes to be gained by making things more complicated" (1986b, p. 143). Going back even further, we can see that Hirschman was already committed to finding a balance between economics and politics and to making the discipline less isolated and self-enclosed in *National Power.*

In this chapter, then, I will examine five theses put forward by Hirschman regarding the reform of the discipline. In order to trace their roots, I will concentrate on the Colombian years and on a few points of contact—generally left unmentioned—linking the writings generated in those years. My aim is to show that the theme of if, why, and how to complicate economics, is in itself a central, though often latent, aspect of the entire body of his works.

Why Complicate Economics?

Was not economics already a moderately complicated discipline, a contemporary reader may well have asked? Naturally, Hirschman's intention was not to make analytical formulas even more complex; it was rather to understand that by working conceptually on the discipline and by providing even its basic categories with more structure, economics could be made more useful and even more accessible.[1] Hirschman set out deliberately to question the parsimonious paradigm upon which traditional economics was founded: that of the isolated individual, motivated by material self-interest, who chooses freely and rationally between alternative courses of action after calculating the anticipated costs and benefits.

In 1977, Hirschman published *The Passions and the Interests: Political Arguments for Capitalism before Its Triumph*. In this important essay on the history of ideas, Hirschman explored theoretical speculations on the political consequences of economic development, starting with Machiavelli and ending up with the eighteenth century view according to which interests were called upon to counteract passions. In the second part of the book, he concentrated on a few salient aspects of the story—such as the doctrine of *doux commerce* of Montesquieu and Steuart—concluding that, since Adam Smith, the traditional analytical distinction between passions and interests was abandoned.

In *The Theory of Moral Sentiments*, Hirschman argued, the father of economics ended up making noneconomic drives feed into economic ones with all their force, thus losing the independence they had previously enjoyed. In *The Wealth of Nations*, Smith's analysis was based on the idea that men are motivated exclusively by the desire to improve their condition. Adam Smith thus inaugurated economics as a discipline: an intellectual breakthrough that nevertheless implied a significant limitation of the field of inquiry.[2]

The history of ideas surveyed in *The Passions and the Interests* shows, in a sense, the "progressive impoverishment of the prevailing concept of human nature over a period of some three centuries," (1981b, p. 288) culminating in the birth of economics. The next intuitive step was that the discipline should gradually be complicated, above all because it was founded on oversimplified assumptions. Criticism was leveled mainly at traditional theory, but also at the schools—Keynesian, institutionalist, Sraffian, Marxist, etc.—which criticized that tradition.

Hirschman's methodology, as we have already seen, was often to create for himself a political focal point (of economic policy, social, or general interest) outside the discipline, and, beginning with research in the field, to recast several aspects of economic theories into new molds, combining them (at times) with analytical elements borrowed from other social sciences. His antidoctrinarian inclination meant that he did not take sides for or against one or another school of thought, thus avoiding heated debate and interminable arguments. He was free to evaluate the heuristic value of the various propositions as well as their relevance to the problems at hand.[3]

His ability to work his way through the net of traditional theoretical reasoning led him to reject its authority over reality. Hirschman showed that it was possible, as in the early Renaissance, to recycle ancient columns and capitals—combining them with other materials for specific, limited, and useful purposes—and in doing so to find new architectural perspectives.[4]

A constant characteristic of Hirschman's work was his lack of respect for the traditional limits of the discipline; this gradually became an "Art of Trespassing"[5] into the realm of social sciences. This is not the place to go into "The Concept of Interest: from Euphemism to Tautology" (1986e). For our purposes, it is enough to remember that as early as 1820, James Mill put forward—as Schumpeter, Downs, Olson, and many others have done this century—an economic theory of politics based on self-interest. But the fact that there might be a gap between a citizen's interests and his personal perception of where his best interests lie gave Macauley the chance to condemn the doctrine as tautological. Motivations other than material self-interest *strictu sensu*—such as in the concepts of enlightened, farsighted, and real interests—and the fact that the eighteenth-century distinction between passions and interests was never rehabilitated further convalidated this criticism.

Hirschman put forward the novel idea that the positivistic and formalistic direction in which economic analysis had moved in the last century was linked, by opposition, to the extraordinary attraction prevalent in philosophy, psychology, and sociology at the end of the nineteenth century towards the nonrational: instinct, the unconscious, habit. Based on the rational pursuit of interest, economics could not incorporate the new discoveries into its analytical system. It therefore reacted by "withdrawing from psychology to the greatest possible extent by emptying its basic concepts of their psychological origin" (1986b, p. 51).

This idea underscored the effect of the intellectual turning point leading to the rise of marginalist economics, which can be linked back to the economics of appearance of Say, Senior, or Bailey (rather than to classical thought, as long-standing orthodox tradition has always claimed). Marginalism presented itself as an intellectual revolution that swept through several countries at the same time, nurtured by the advances made in the physical and mathematical sciences. Moreover, as far as several basic concepts such as equilibrium, efficiency, and the harmony of interests are concerned, neoclassical economics was the child of positivism. It was thus thought to be favored by the escalation of social conflict.

To this interpretative framework Hirschman added the hypothesis that the development of economic analysis in the direction of positivism and formalism was in fact connected to the evolution of other social disciplines. Rather than digging exclusively into the history of economic thought (taking external influences as given), Hirschman's attempt was to understand the development of economics as part of the general progress of ideas.

At the end of the last century, drastic changes took place: several new social sciences such as psychology, sociology, and anthropology were born; ancient sciences such as geography, philosophy, politics, and history were reformulated; and many disciplines were attracted to the nonrational aspects of life. The positivistic culture that gave significant drive to the natural sciences was expressed in physics and mathematics by the deductive method, and in medicine and biology by the inductive-experimental method. Economics was inspired by the former, while in other social sciences the latter prevailed. Thus, differing contents in the social sciences led to different methodologies and mentalities in research.[6]

Hirschman's hypothesis is confirmed by the relatively recent phenomenon, especially in the United States, of economics trespassing into other fields of inquiry. Francesco Forte and Elena Granaglia (1980, p. 7) have shown how there are three threads in the literature: the economic analysis of collective decision making in politics and bureaucracy; the microeconomic analysis of legal and social institutions regarding ownership and relations inside and outside the firm; and the extension of the economic paradigm to fields usually studied by other sciences, such as nonprofit associations, the family, illicit activities, and even association and disassociation between plants and animals (the economics of biology). Civil servants, lawyers, philanthropists, lovers, parents, and criminals—long considered prey to complex passions—and even animals and plants (in theory ruled by mother nature), were all described as "busily 'maximizing under constraints' . . . with the emphasis on grubby cost/benefit calculus" (1981a, pp. 298–99). Thus the economic paradigm, willy nilly, "invaded the most 'sacred' and seemingly disparate spheres of life" (Forte and Granaglia, 1980, p. 43).[7]

Hirschman (1981a, pp. 298–99) saw two sides to the question. On the one hand, these analyses triggered the "compulsion to produce shock and paradox" so typical of the social sciences. Their intention was to show that self-interest lurked behind all these "non-economic pursuits." This fact "was bound to produce moral shock; and, once again, the analysis drew strength from having this shock value." On the other hand, the more spheres of social life outside the traditional areas of economics that were invaded, the more predictable were the results, inevitably "running into decreasing returns."

This might suggest the existence of a possible reverse logical process, because several intrinsic weaknesses in the way society is interpreted by the economic paradigm are revealed. "As a result, it has become possible to mount a critique which, ironically, can be carried all the way back to the heartland of the would-be conquering discipline" (1986b, p. 142).

Hirschman thus reaches a general thesis that is part of a wider trend of thought. In his introductory note "Around *The Passions and the Interests*" (1981a, pp. 287–88), he places this work and other essays linked to it firmly alongside the progressive intellectual works in the United States that were stimulated by the publication of *A Theory of Justice* (1971) by John Rawls. His argument refers above all to micro- and macroanalyses (such as Kenneth Arrow's and John Goldthorpe's) that disavow Adam Smith by demonstrating how "the economy is in fact liable to perform poorly without a minimum of 'benevolence'" (1981a, p. 299).

Some years later, Hirschman's work came closer to that of Schelling, Sen, Boulding, Collard, Margolis, McPherson, Phelps, and Pizzorno, all of whom started taking seriously human actions and behavior that were not dictated by the traditional concept of self-interest: "actions motivated by altruism, by commitment to ethical values, by concern for the group and the public interest, and, perhaps more important, the varieties of non-instrumental behavior" (1986b, p. 52). In the meantime, he also wrote *Shifting Involvements* (1982), a monograph on the way people's involvement oscillates between public and private spheres. Chapter 5 in particular opens with a critique of *The Logic of Collective Action* by Mancur Olson.[8]

"FREE RIDING," THE "INVISIBLE HAND," AND "THE HEART AND THE MIND"

A key element in the theory of public choice (see, for example, D. C. Mueller, 1979) is the concept of "free riding," now an established concept in many finance, sociological, and political science textbooks.

It is an easy concept to grasp for an economist. The logic of collective action, Olson claims, must be revealed through the assumption of self-interest. Groups of people with common interests do not act in the name of these common interests; rather, the individuals that make up the group pursue their own interests and have no real reason to participate individually in the activity of the group. An individual, in fact, can achieve the same results if he lets others become active participants in the collective action: a free rider reaps benefits without contributing to the costs.

If every individual behaved in the same way, however, collective action would be impossible. Olson's answer to this dilemma is that, with the exception of small groups, collective action is based on constriction and induction (through economic benefits). Examples might be the closed shop of the British Trade Unions whereby a job was available only to union members; the state enforcing taxation; agricultural organizations exerting pressure on government agencies or cooperatives; professional orders influencing the supply of services.

This theory denies the existence of a noninstrumental component in the activities of a trade union (or political party) and neglects altogether the bulk of collective action: political passion, participation in demonstrations, ballot casting, everyday conversation about the world at large. Why are people interested in politics then? Why do they mobilize, discuss, go and cast their vote? Olson's theory suggests they should not. Hirschman sarcastically claimed that the success of the book was due to the fact that his thesis was *dis*proved by the turn of events. *The Logic* was published in 1965, "at the precise moment when the Western world was about to be all but engulfed by an unprecedented wave of public movements" (starting in California in 1966). Once these movements had safely run their course, Hirschman concluded, "the many people who found them deeply upsetting could go back to *The Logic of Collective Action* and find in it good and reassuring reasons why those collective actions of the sixties should never have happened in the first place, were perhaps less real than they seemed, and would be most unlikely ever to recur" (1982b, pp. 78–79).

In *Shifting Involvements,* as we shall explore further in chapter 7, Hirschman studied the shift of personal involvement from the private to the public sphere (and vice versa) that takes place in the quest for happiness. In Hirschman's view, it is the product of frustration—i.e., disappointment—that forces the individual to reflect on and modify his behavior by appealing to his "metapreferences" (or "second-order volitions"). Disappointment in the private sphere leads to greater participation in the public sphere. Participating in collective action has a positive connotation in itself; it is not just a cost of a cost-benefit analysis.

The essay, "Against Parsimony," grew directly out of the explanation of political action given in *Shifting Involvements.* In this essay, Hirschman divided activity into the two categories, instrumental and noninstrumental. He also furthered his analysis of the disappointment deriving from consumption (and of the self-evaluation that comes with it), and of the notion of love (or civic spirit). Launching a debate on a reform of the discipline, he proposed "complicating" economic discourse by including two basic human qualities—"voice" (protest, information, communication) which we shall come across in chapter 6, and self-evaluation—and by taking account of two basic tensions inherent in human nature—between instrumental and noninstrumental modes of behavior, and between self-interest and public morality.

An important aspect of the various forms of noninstrumental behavior is that they are subject to marked variations. In politics, as we have said, there is a vast range of possible actions—between active involvement and everyday debate—in constant flux: greater participation in the various forms of collective action implies less dedication to private interests (and vice versa). Throughout the range, however, there is always a "horizontal voice" (as Guillelmo O'Donnell called it) meaning the spontaneous and daily expression of what people think. Near-total privatization is a phenomenon that can only prevail under particularly authoritarian governments that try to suppress any private expression of dissent from official politics.

"An arresting conclusion follows. That vaunted ideal of predictability, that alleged idyll of a privatized citizenry paying busy and exclusive attention to its economic interests and thereby serving the public interest indirectly, but never directly, becomes a reality only under wholly nightmarish political conditions." A shocking result, if we consider the concept of the "invisible hand" that represented the keystone of the doctrine of self-interest, and that was probably used to placate the guilt of all those Englishmen, brought up on the idea that the public good always came first, who were nonetheless attracted to economic activity by eighteenth-century colonial expansion (1986b, p. 53 and p. 39).

In *Morality and the Social Sciences: a Durable Tension* (1981), Hirschman put forward the argument that by birthright and vocation, the bias of social sciences—including politics and economics—was largely "immoralist." By birthright, because they came about through a process of emancipation from traditional moral teachings;[9] by vocation, because the fact that we live in society means we have "considerable intuitive, commonsense understanding of social science 'problems.'" To "*enhance* our considerable, untutored knowledge," Hirschman continued, " . . . social science discoveries are therefore typically counterintuitive, shocking and concerned with *unintended* and unexpected consequences of human action" (1981a, pp. 297–98). This was true both of Mandeville's rehabilitation of luxury, and of Keynes's paradox of parsimony; but it was just as true for the expansionistic expeditions recalled above.

How is one to reconcile this existential incompatibility between moral activity and scientific analysis? It is not enough to reject Adam Smith's self-interest model and realize that a certain amount of benevolence is vital to the efficient functioning of our society; nor is it enough to attempt a head-on attack, concentrating for example on altruism to make amends for the previous disregard of moral values and "generous impulses." The only way to achieve "an effective integration of moral argument into economic analysis," Hirschman argued, is "to proceed rather painstakingly, on a case-to-case basis," incorporating "such basic traits and emotions as the desire for power and for sacrifice, the fear of boredom, pleasure in both commitment and unpredictability, the search for meaning and community, and so on." This task, he concluded, requires "first, familiarity with the technical apparatus of economics; and second, openness to the heretofore neglected moral dimensions whose introduction modifies traditional results" (1981a, p. 303).

This was an uphill struggle. The "mutual exclusiveness of heart and head" was deeply rooted in Western culture: an economist, "groomed as a scientist," must wrestle with himself before admitting the possibility of a new order of ideas. His "trained incapacity" (Veblen) may be so dominating that he will often not even confess to himself the moral inspiration of his inquiry.

Presenting a typical paradox, Hirschman went on to argue that being unconscious moralists was not necessarily such a bad thing. Given the present lay of the cultural land, if a morally sensitive social scientist unconsciously incorporated conditions of a moral order into his work, this could turn out to be particularly effective.[10] Moreover, "once we have become fully aware of our intellectual tradition with its deep split between head and heart and its not always beneficial consequences, the first step towards overcoming that tradition and toward healing that split has already been taken" (1981a, p. 305).

The narrow path that winds between head and heart must carve its course between respect for the rules of traditional thought, and the creation of new ones. Hirschman's intellectual development follows this path, to some extent. Regarding the years of the Marshall Plan, for example, Hirschman recently wrote (1990c) that Charles Kindleberger and his theory about the "structural dollar shortage" represented "an inspiration to those of us whose *hearts* were all on the side of a substantial transfer of wealth from the richest country to the then downtrodden Europeans, but whose *minds* felt nevertheless the need to justify that transfer by technical economic reasoning, rather than by purely ethical considerations."

It is therefore logical to advance the hypothesis that when Hirschman established himself as one of the foremost development economists with *The Strategy of Economic Development,* he actually succeeded in carving a path between the moral need to deal with what appeared to be (and what, unfortunately continues to be today) "the major unresolved economic problem" in a future "Agenda for a Better World" (1986b, p. 34), and the intellectual need to contribute to a workable strategy for solving this problem.

What assessment might we make of Hirschman's point of view in the early 1950s—that is at the beginning of his Colombian experience—compared to twenty years before when he was a leader of the Young Socialists enrolled in the Social Democrat Party in Berlin?

First, his many commitments had led him far away from the political and cultural context of the past. Two passages from the 1951–52 essays shed light on this detachment. One dealt with the industrialization of backward countries and maintained that the Russian people paid an exorbitantly heavy toll in political and human terms for economic progress (1951d, p. 615). This reveals Hirschman's total lack of illusions about the experience of real socialism. The other (see chapter 1) was about prophets of doom, clearly including Marx and the entire revolutionary and reformist Marxist culture in the category.

Second, his critique of the political use of economic power contained in *National Power* did not stop Hirschman from having a role to play in the Marshall Plan. Despite all his difficulties, Hirschman emerged from this experience with a (perhaps over-)optimistic attitude, possibly linked to his discovery and appropriation of possibilism. He returned to his work on international trade in order to add his voice to the cultural trend in favor of the industrialization of underdeveloped countries after the success of the Marshall Plan.[11] He also advocated, with federalist logic, increasing international "entente" in order to develop a division of labor based on differences in historical development and in skills rather than on the distinction between industrial and agricultural nations. "By creating closer forms of economic association," he wrote, "it is hoped that serious divergences of national economic policies can be avoided, that sectional interests can be held in check, and that the special risks of affecting foreign trade can in general be reduced. It remains to be seen to what extent the aim can be achieved through the operation of the economic field alone. Closer forms of political association may be required to convert what is today international trade into the interregional trade of tomorrow" (1951d, pp. 617–18).[12]

Third, in the texts written during Hirschman's Washington period, one can detect a double edge in his attitude, behind the inevitable professional officialdom. On one hand there is his sense of responsibility for his work and his determination not to "follow the stream"; on the other (one might even say for this very reason), there is his willingness to remold his own outlook to correspond (as far as possible) to concrete developments—at the cost of dealing with the same subject many different times from many different points of view.

It might be useful at this point to refer to a surprising passage from Hirschman's essay "Economic and Financial Conditions in Italy" (1948n, p. 3, now in 1987a, p. 331). As if condensing a long mulled-over thought process, he wrote:

> The remaining continuing task of the Italian economy is to lift itself to higher levels of economic activity and investment. Here as always, action implies the taking of certain risks. Even when the national accounts of a country are known with good approximation, it is not easy to indicate the "correct" amount of investment. In Italy, *a priori* deductions, while instructive, can only yield extremely rough guesses and are not able to replace as yet the method of trial and error. While the diagnosis of Italy's position is difficult, the therapy to be prescribed is thus quite likely to be unorthodox. . . . The necessity to walk on a very narrow path between deflation and inflation may suggest new methods of using both foreign aid and counterpart funds. Finally, it must be realized that we cannot possibly hope to solve Italy's problems within three or four years. ERP aid can avoid a deterioration in Italy's position and point the way toward economic development. Unless the Italian problem is seen in this light much time may be lost in looking for a simple formula that "sets things right."

As we can see, Hirschman's criticism of the doctrinarian use of Keynesian macroeconomics is barely concealed, while the declared necessity to walk along a narrow path has as its corollary the need for continuous interaction between thought and historic reality which, in its turn, is the starting point for the discovery of unusual and hidden relationships.[13]

In real life, economic phenomena live symbiotically with many other phenomena. Despite the character of these writings, another peculiarity already visible in Hirschman's texts on Italy before the war (especially in his "Memoire sur le contrôle des changes en Italie," 1939a) emerges: the fact that he builds up his analysis by referring from time to time to noneconomic aspects of reality—history, politics, administration, social factors, etc.—weaving them into his discourse unsystematically, simply, directly, as if this was a perfectly natural thing to do.[14] This opening up of economic analysis to politics and beyond goes hand in hand with the quest for solutions that do not follow the tracks laid down by economic theory.

A fourth aspect is worth considering. There is a way out of the split between head and heart and of the split between the need of a researcher with any ethical sensitivity to be an economist and his desire to construct a socio-moral science (where moral considerations are not "smuggled in surreptitiously or expressed unconsciously," [1981a, p. 306]). The way out is to find, time after time, a (temporary) balance in one's own work, so that both scientific and moral requirements are satisfied. From his detective work on the Italian Fascist economy to his devotion to undermining the certainties of his colleagues on the Marshall Plan, this double requirement has always been a constant in Hirschman's work.

We have a chance to see the further unfolding of this approach if we focus on the links between Hirschman's Euro-American and his Latin American experience in the writings from the Colombian period.

Aquí en el Trópico Hacemos Todo al Revés

Hirschman revisited his experience as development economist in two essays—"The Rise and Fall of Development Economics" (1981), and "A Dissenter's Confession" (1984)—that trod, respectively, objective and subjective paths and referred (mostly) to The Strategy of Economic Development.

In the preface to *Essays in Trespassing: Economics to Politics and Beyond* (1981a, p. v) Hirschman quotes an assertion made by the Russell Sage Foundation, " . . . the discipline [of economics] became progressively more narrow at precisely the time when the problems demanded broader, more political, and social insights," with the purpose of underscoring that the essays collected in the book completely disregard the narrow confines of the discipline. The problem, however, is that these confines do exist in the conscience of many different researchers.

The debate on Hirschman's work runs the risk of becoming almost inadvertently channeled into various professional streams. Hirschman is appreciated by economists above all for his contribution to development economics; sociologists consider his key work to be *Exit, Voice, and Loyalty*, while political scientists are interested in the question of morality.[15]

I do not deny the importance of focusing on different topics and contributing to the debate on the basis of one's own professional experience. It is, however, important to bear in mind that the issues Hirschman deals with require an openmindedness towards new frontiers of knowledge: their implication is that there is no single key for unlocking the complexity of reality. One must rather seek a series of limited, transdisciplinary, and connected results. In the past, mainstream criticism tried to incorporate part of Hirschman's contribution into economics by expunging it of its noneconomic significance and connotations (take, for example, from chapter 3 below the way *The Strategy* was received, which impelled the author to ask people to consider several chapters, including the first, in more detail).

I think it is legitimate, on the contrary, to take interest in the all-round results and in their numerous interrelations. In this chapter and in the two that follow, I shall try to come to grips with the complex, interlocked genesis of *The Strategy* and of *Journeys toward Progress: Studies of Economic Policy-Making in Latin America* (1963).[16]

In early 1952, rather than continuing with his Washington post (or moving to some comfortable international agency), Hirschman decided to take up a position as economic and financial advisor to the Colombian Council for National Planning.

Very little is known about his experience there; nonetheless it was an important step in Hirschman's intellectual development.

For anyone coming from the northern hemisphere, his wife Sarah recalls,[17] the effect was one of horizons suddenly widening. Once they had overcome initial difficulties, their interest in the cultural, social, and anthropological aspects of this new life—mingled with unexpected discoveries, friendly people, and the incredible beauty of its tropical climate—soon took over.

Anyone who knows Colombia will understand. It is easy to imagine Albert and Sarah's pleasure in exploring every nook and cranny of La Candelaria, the colonial quarter of Bogotá near Albert's office; or the family holidays in a choice of warm, cold, or temperate climates. We can sympathize with their interest in the native culture, in colonial baroque architecture, in the craftsmanship of the goldsmiths, in local history, and in that "extraordinary spirit of fervor, missionary zeal, and power" born from the Reconquest of southern Spain from the Muslims and developed in the Conquest of the new continent and the intense proselytism of both church and the state (Hirschman, 1989h, pp. 350–51).

It is true that the conditions in which Hirschman worked in his Colombian period represented an extraordinary tropical greenhouse for the ideas he had brought with him. Perhaps the different kind of commitment required of him (relatively set apart compared to his period in Washington when he was in the spotlight of international economic culture), in addition to the family's natural gravitation towards the community of European origin, protected him from an overly traumatic impact with a social reality that was thwarted at the time by tragic violence[18]— a definite case of the "hiding hand."[19]

And yet, seen from another angle, Hirschman's period in Colombia was anything but easy. Once he had obtained his position through the World Bank, Hirschman had two interlocutors— the Colombian government and the bank—which should have allowed him greater freedom. In the spring of 1953, however, the country's political instability erupted in a coup d'état led by General Rojas Pinilla. To make matters worse, Hirschman ran into increasing difficulties with the World Bank. As he wrote in "A Dissenter's Confession," he had been asked to draw up an ambitious development plan for Colombia, specifying investments, domestic savings, growth, and the extent of foreign aid. "All of this was alleged to be quite simple for experts mastering the new programming technique" (1986b, p. 8).

Hirschman's rebellion, resignation, and subsequent decision to open a private consultant's office in Bogotà were the result. Another result was two sets of essays: the first covers various arguments, while the second contains two particularly illuminating analytical texts.

In the first set, the only essay that springs from Hirschman's work as a government consultant was his "Guide to the Analysis and Elaboration of Recommendations on the Monetary Situation" (written in Spanish). Hirschman himself described its genesis: "coming out of the planning office, I think it is useful to describe in general terms the methods and principles that must be followed in the periodic writing up of information on the monetary situation. This task logically comprises three phases: gathering of statistics, analysis of the situation based on these data, and the formulation of recommendations" (1954a, p. 531).

As a private consultant, by contrast, Hirschman published together with George Kalmanoff the previously mentioned (chapter 1, note 11) *Colombia: Highlights of a Developing Economy*, a presentation booklet on the Colombian economy prepared for the "Inter-American Investment Conference" held in New Orleans in the spring of 1955. He also brought out with Kalmonoff "The Demand for Power in Cali and the Cauca Region" (1956), and *Investment in Central America: Basic Information for United States Businessmen* (1957), a volume prepared after an exploratory journey made by Hirschman in Costa Rica, El Salvador, Guatemala, Honduras, and Nicaragua in the spring of 1955. There are also other unpublished works from the 1955–56 years onward: an inquiry into the salaries of managers in Colombia; the financial situation and prospects for Cali's municipal firms; the demand for domestic gas in Cali and the Cauca Valley, and the paper and pulp market in Colombia (2 vol).

The overall impression is that, while professionally engaged (and becoming a respected member of the small community of economic consultants in Colombia),[20] Hirschman's thinking was breaking new ground in many directions.

The aspects of life in Colombia that so surprised him seem to have conspired in demonstrating that there was no such thing as a single path (or a unique Pareto-optimum). Indeed, a series of observations and some important discoveries may have been stimulated by the spontaneous confirmation in the field, as it were, of previously learned lessons, and by the inquiries into the functioning of the state and the everyday evolution of economic reality that were required by his professional activity.[21] The fertile terrain of the Colombian *cordillere* thus contributed to transforming Hirschman's propensity to speculation and investigation into a quest for hidden rationality, unusual chains of events, and unexpected consequences (1986b, p. 10).

In a recent interview (1990b, pp. 155–56), Hirschman claimed that he always started a book with an observation, an insight he considered worth probing. That observation would then "open up a little bit like a Chinese paper flower that you put into water." In *National Power,* the starting point was a set of statistics—for the extent of Germany's trade concentration in the Balkans had still gone unnoticed. Hirschman's initial interest was simply in the percentages of trade distribution that differed from country to country. "All the other considerations," he maintains, "came out of this first insight."

Of course, preliminary observations are never out of context; they are a part of an appraisal of concrete reality, and of the state of the art. But it is "the capacity to be surprised which is important." This is what engenders research (and the elation that comes with it), and what provides the drive for the author to analyze the initial perception in depth and come up with generalizations. "The talent I have," he explained, "is not just to come up with an interesting observation; it is more a question of going to the bottom of such an observation and then generalize to much broader categories. I suppose that this is the nature of theorizing."

Let us return to Hirschman's rebellion against the World Bank, and to his view that a development plan based on heroic estimates was the last thing Colombia needed: "My instinct," he wrote (1986b, p. 8), "was to try and understand better *their* [the Colombians'] patterns of action, rather than assume from the outset that they could be 'developed' only by importing a set of techniques they know nothing about."

The essay "Economics and Investment Planning: Reflections Based on Experience in Colombia" helps clarify the issue. It was written for a conference on the criteria of investment and economic development held at M.I.T.'s Center for International Studies in October 1954 by a group of economists that supported state intervention by means of aid and development plans in third world countries.

The essay opened by praising the "highly interesting effort" made by individual economists and international institutions to relate various macroquantities of the economy in order to orient economic policy.[22] Hirschman soon made the point, however, that the generalizations one may draw from these macroquantities cannot readily be applied "to the specific problems that confront the practical planner." He went on to claim that there had been too much emphasis on development plans as such, and too little on the search for "a body of principles and meaningful generalizations which would permit the economist to be concretely helpful in the location and elaboration of promising, specific investment projects" (1971a, p. 44).

The "elaboration of 'overall, integrated development programs,'" the author added, "is not essential, and in fact may be harmful." If the economist directs his work mainly to drafting general investment plans, projecting everything ten or twenty years ahead, the risk he takes is to bring into the economic sphere what has been observed by André Siegfried in the Latin American political sphere, namely "the contrast between fine theory and wretched practice" (1971a, pp. 46–47). Hirschman's view was that a commitment should be made to drawing up well-researched sector projects. A low level of investment and low efficiency in most investments were and still are the hallmarks of underdeveloped countries. It was thus vital to act upon both aspects at the same time, focusing on tensions and scarcities that come about during the process of development and not on political priorities laid out by government, local institutions, or even by the economist himself.

If we compare this argument to the one contained in "Economic and Financial Conditions in Italy" there are some surprising parallels to be found. While the Italian essay claimed that a priori deductions concerning the right amount of investment could only result in conjecture, the Colombian article proposed abandoning exercises in projecting investments and in overall planning for development. Similarly, the former claimed it was vital to concentrate on the main sectors in trouble (heavy industry, mechanics, construction, etc.) from within the actual evolution of the economy, while the latter called for economists to focus on sector projects, giving priority to the points of tension that emerge once development is underway. So far Hirschman's experience had been mainly that of an economic adviser. But to take account of sector realities, Hirschman added, a few guidelines should be made available to the economist. The urge to identify this body of generalizations was what led to his writing of *The Strategy*. It was more or less at this time that the Chinese paper flower of the book started opening.

In "Economics and Investment Planning," Hirschman had already proposed some specific criteria for investments, based on the observation of basic characteristics peculiar to underdeveloped economies. From the simple affirmation that these countries suffered from insufficient maintenance of capital goods, one could derive the criterion that priority must be accorded to investments, industries, and technical processes that hardly need any maintenance, or that need regular maintenance (such as airlines). Moreover, contrary to the widespread conviction that backward countries should develop industries able to transform the primary commodities they produce, it was important to realize that often the opposite took place: industries that were potential buyers of national agricultural products began by importing these commodities and only later did they supply themselves from the domestic market (when, that is, those national products had become standardized, due to the inducing effect of their new outlet).

These observations were crucial discoveries. The first concerned the degree of latitude or tolerance for poor performances (see chapter 6), and explained (at least in part) the preference of underdeveloped countries for advanced technology and continuous flow capital-intensive industry. The second (see chapter 3) developed the concept of "backward linkages" and therefore of "linkages"—one of the main concepts in development economics.

Today Hirschman tells us that it was the former that sparked off *The Strategy:* "It was when I looked at Colombian economic development," he said, "—how certain functions are carried out or are not carried out or are poorly carried out—that I made one of my first most basic observations. It concerned the difference in performance of the airlines and the highways. Airlines perform better than highways for the reason . . . that the penalty for not maintaining planes is far more serious and immediate than that for not maintaining highways" (1990b, p. 156, see also chapter 6, note 28). "Far more fundamentally than the idea of unbalanced growth," he wrote in retrospect, "this search for possible *hidden rationalities* was to give an underlying unity to my work" (1986b, p. 9).

In the preface to *The Strategy*, Hirschman declared that while he was writing he drew encouragement from the following statement made by Whitehead (1930, p. 6): "The elucidation of immediate experience is the sole justification of any thought; and the starting point for thought is the analytic observation of components of this experience." In his own case, he writes (1958a, p. v), "the various observations and reflections I had gathered began to look more and more like variations upon a common theme. So I undertook to discover this theme and then used it in reinterpreting a variety of development problems."

Looking for generalizations in sectorial policies, Hirschman happened to come across a few hidden rationalities that, in their turn, prompted him to seek out a general economic principle able to provide a link between these considerations and connected propositions. Hence the idea of "inducement mechanisms," the search for which concerned much of the book (1958a, p. 28). Once the conceptual framework of the book was ready, Hirschman was able to develop his initial guidelines and to identify others.[23]

Planning and Experimenting

The prodigious harvest of Hirschman's Colombian period, however, did not come to an end with *The Strategy*. This is soon appreciated if we look at "Economic Policy in Underdeveloped Countries" (the second essay born out of his Colombian experience and published in 1957) and at the trend of thought unleashed by it, which has so far been neglected for various reasons.

First, it bears no precise reference to a discipline,[24] and came about through successive breakthroughs rather than through a gradual evolution from within. Second, Hirschman proceeded by focusing his attention on one or another aspect of policy making at a time, mostly responding to his own cognitive needs. Third, economists, who are not used to studying the relationship between economics and politics, find the reverse relationship (between politics and economics) even harder.

"At the outset of their mission," Hirschman wrote with surprising frankness in "Economic Policy in Underdeveloped Countries" (1957, now in 1971a, p. 255), economists "are likely to think that the principal problem they are going to be confronted with will be that of determining what ought to be done. . . . But soon they realize that they have little trouble in deciding what to do or rather what to advise to do, while by far the largest portion of their time is devoted to energy consuming and often frustrating efforts to put their ideas and proposals across."

This is how Hirschman launched his first political article on underdevelopment. While "Economics and Investment Planning" made clear the reasons why he revolted against the task that was assigned to him, this essay showed genuine interest in government authorities, and more in general in the cultural and political environment of developing countries. "On the one hand," Hirschman wrote later (1986b, p. 11), "I reacted against the visiting-economist syndrome, that is against the habit of issuing peremptory advice and prescription . . . after a strictly minimal acquaintance with the 'patient.' But, with time, another objective was assuming even more importance in my mind: it was to counter the tendency of many Colombians and Latin Americans to work hand in glove with the visiting economists by their own self-deprecatory attitudes."

Hirschman referred here to the period that followed the publication of *The Strategy,* but the roots of this attitude can be traced further back. In "Economic Policy in Underdeveloped Countries" we read that if these countries have already made important steps forward, a few investment projects are always available, while some fiscal and monetary reforms, and certain institutional changes are clearly useful. The history of technical assistance missions is inevitably linked to their capacity to achieve these goals. But "the huge difficulties of this task are not always properly appreciated," Hirschman wrote (1957b, now in 1971a, p. 256), "partly, I suspect, because, in order to do so, one must catch the experts themselves during their unguarded moments rather than rely on their reports to headquarters; and partly, because the whole tale here is in terms of personalities and of human passions, frailties, and frustrations which the experts, once they are 'back home' are liable to forget easily and completely as physical pain."

As we see, the starting point was still that of an economist struggling with his difficulties, but Hirschman's argument was no longer limited to unwarranted interference by the World Bank. It was a first step towards what Hirschman was later to call "an understanding of the understanding Latin Americans have of their own reality" (1961e, now in 1971a, p. 271). The aim of his article was to demonstrate with a series of examples that, contrary to what a typical economist may think, a few useful generalizations on the subject can be made and that some results can be reached.

The reasons for adopting development plans, Hirschman claimed, complementing the arguments put forward in "Economics and Investment Planning," are well known. A plan expresses an aspiration for better standards of living (and is thereby popular); it is often a necessary condition for obtaining foreign aid; it is a way to demand financial sacrifice at home and to spread out spending requests over a period of time. A plan is a useful restraint that allows central government to force development plans through. This function is not usually the main reason for a plan to be adopted, but the realization that it is useful often becomes one of the main reasons for continuing with it.

Once development plans have been introduced, then, they usefully restrict governments' freedom of choice; however, they can also be over-restrictive. Often, Hirschman explained in "Economics and Investment Planning," plans claim they can establish overall investment programs despite the avowed weakness of investment criteria and the great differences in significance of the estimates regarding the various sectors. Once more accurate studies have been undertaken, it is likely that several elements of the plan have to be radically revised. Thus the initial plan should make clear which projects are final and which require further research (constructing perhaps a scale according to the quantity and quality of the work already undertaken).

After long experience in national economic planning, Hirschman continues (1971a, pp. 259–60), it is high time we recognized that together with a "propensity to plan," governments in underdeveloped countries also have a "propensity to experiment and improvise." This is an irrepressible urge of government, "a force which properly directed can be made to play a beneficial role in the development process." After all, in underdeveloped countries "many dynamic growth sectors remain to be discovered; many patterns of social organization conducive to economic progress remain to be identified; and much flexibility in programming economic development must be preserved to enable governments and investors to take advantage of changing trends in world markets."

The Two Functions of Government

An economic adviser is required, on the one hand, to make a good job of the sector projects, and on the other, to take into account the country's decision-making problems and to study their evolution. This is, in my opinion, the fountainhead of the *The Strategy* and the source of the spring that flowed on to *Journeys Toward Progress*.

One way of navigating this stream is to show how the dualities we have come across so far—between economics and politics, between the two analytical essays produced during the Colombian period, between a general plan and a sector plan, and between the propensity to plan and the propensity to experiment—can be connected to the concluding section of *The Strategy* on the functions of government.

The argument is introduced in the text by the amusing image of Charlie Chaplin as a glazier employing Jacky Coogan to throw stones into shop windows and thus provoke requests for repairs. "The ingenious twist consists here in combining, *under a single command,* the disequilibrating and the equilibrating functions. From our point of view, the story's only blemish—which, incidentally, accounts for its hilarious quality—is the fact that the unbalancing act is destructive rather than constructive. Otherwise we find in it a perfect illustration of what we conceive as the two principal roles of governmental economic policies in the course of the development process" (1958a, p. 202).

In order to be efficient, government action should promote development by means of vigorous thrusts forward that create incentives and pressures aimed at stimulating further initiatives. At the same time, it should prepare to alleviate shortages and ease the bottlenecks brought about by development, for example, in public administration, education, and the health system.

Thus, Hirschman continued, the subdivision of government actions into inducing and inducted (or unbalancing and balancing) can prove useful to government authorities if they wish to have a clearer perception of their own role in the development process. "In this respect," Hirschman concluded, referring implicitly to "Economics and Investment Planning,"

> the contemporary fashion of drawing up comprehensive development plans or programs is often quite unhelpful. For the very comprehensiveness of these plans can drown out the sense of direction so important for purposeful policy-making. A plan can be most useful if, through its elaboration, a government works out a strategy for development. While the choice of priority areas must of course proceed from an examination of the economy as a whole, it may be best, once the choice is made, to concentrate on detailed concrete programs for those areas, as in the first Monnet Plan for France's postwar reconstruction. (1958a, p. 205)[25]

As we can see, the dialectic between the two government functions was being compared to that between the two functions (general and sector) of the plan. These functions must be both economic and political to support the decision-making process. Hirschman's argument can thus be extended almost naturally to that presented in "Economic Policy in Underdeveloped Countries." A rigid and comprehensive plan does not only crowd out sector projects and indications of which way to move; it also denies governments' propensity to experiment, which should, rather, be recognized and gradually disciplined. It is not wise, Hirschman argued, to identify the propensity to plan "with everything that is sensible and virtuous" and the propensity to experiment "with all that is unreasonable and sinful." He proposed, rather, looking reality in the face: "Would it not be better to proceed in accordance with the prescriptions of any elementary textbook in psychology and provide healthy and constructive outlets for both propensities?" (1957b, now in 1971a, p. 259).

Almost as if he wanted to exemplify his outlook, Hirschman proceeded to explain the recurrent nature of inflation (with the difficulty of maintaining a surplus budget, and the political and fiscal advantages of moderate inflationary pressures, etc.). He dealt with the typical oscillations between unique and multiple exchange rates (and import controls), and between a general budget and taxes linked to specific spending (where different needs force governments to move away from one condition in order to have access to the other until the complexity of the system convinces them to move back again). He also explained the cycles in development administration, characterized by the creation of new semiautonomous institutions (to tackle new functions or, rather, to deal with those already in force) which are later restricted in their freedom of action.

The aim of all this was not to "understand all and forgive all," but to understand in order to improve the technical assistance offered to interested governments. Just as in *The Strategy* the recognition of two government functions was aimed at improving government action, so the conclusion of "Economic Policies in Underdeveloped Countries," was to use the propensity to change, and not only to plan, to further a country's development. Thus, when the propensity to experiment is indulged, "it does not come as a revolt against intolerable restraints but as an action that is foreseen as well as regulated. Economic policy of underdeveloped countries will then continue to fluctuate, but the limits of these fluctuations should gradually become narrower and the oscillation between these limits slower, as experiences with diverse policies are assimilated" (1957b, now in 1971a, pp. 268–69).

3

How One Thing Leads
(or Does Not Lead) to Another

The Strategy of Economic Development (1958a) is one of the most important works on development economics since the war, but it is also little understood. As the debate surrounding the book shows, and with the partial exception of the Latin American literature, it is usually interpreted from the restricted point of view of "established academic patterns." In contrast to this tradition, I will suggest that it is necessary to reinterpret the volume in the light of Hirschman's Colombian (and pre-Colombian) experience, and to take into account the subsequent evolution of his ideas.

Backward countries, Hirschman claimed in *The Strategy*, experience a tension between a desire for development and a resistance to change that is one of the main reasons for their condition. The leitmotif of the book is that this tension needs to be broken down and put to productive purposes by means of inducement mechanisms. This line of interpretation sheds light on a series of significant, though often neglected, aspects of *The Strategy*. These include: the slack paradigm, unbalanced growth, oscillations, and the special relationship—of close separation—with theoretical economics. Attention is also focused on the parallel analysis of economic and political decision making induced by disequilibria and on the limits (and even contraindications) that Hirschman discovered in the key notion of sequence.

In this chapter, then, I will take the reader on a lengthy itinerary based on the theme of how one thing leads to another. I will show how Gershenkron fathered Hirschman's concept of development, discuss linkages and their generalization, look at the theory of micro-Marxism, which is ultimately shown to be rather non-Marxist. The aim behind an itinerary of this kind is to follow the author's ideas as they are conceived, sketched out, molded, worked, and used in different contexts.

By now we have encountered the better-known side of Hirschman: renowned in many countries in the Northern and Southern Hemispheres since the end of the 1950s as an idiosyncratic economist and social scientist, and an authoritative exponent of a "flexible yet rigorous" progressive viewpoint.[1] At this point, I can no longer limit myself to isolating and combining some of the basic elements of a viewpoint in formation. I must provide those aspects and useful links that will contribute to an understanding of Hirschman's widely read books.[2] In this chapter, then, I will abandon the aim of providing a comprehensive analysis, in favor of selecting certain meanders of thought. I will take as given Hirschman's main ideas, focus on some of their lesser-known characteristics, and set off from there on an adventurous but problematic trip.

PSYCHOLOGY AND CHANGE

The Strategy of Economic Development was written during the years 1956–58, while Hirschman was visiting research professor at Yale University.[3] For a long time, anyone asking him how the ideas contained in the book came about met with the answer that he had gone to Colombia knowing nothing and having read nothing about development economics; an advantage, he claimed, because it allowed him to observe reality without prejudice. On his return he then read up on development literature and soon realized that his experience as government adviser and private consultant had led him to form a personal angle that differed from the prevailing point of view.

This was a "nice line and not *notably* untrue," Hirschman later admitted (1986b, p. 5) self-mockingly. A good story that contains a half-truth. When he arrived in Colombia he had little knowledge of the (limited) development literature available at the time, but he did have relevant experience from his years in Europe and California, and in Washington with the Federal Reserve Board.[4]

This story is indicative of Hirschman's independence and of his insistence on considering the lessons of reality more significant than those of economic theory. The argument could be taken in many different directions, but for my purposes it is enough to mention Hirschman's encounter with psychoanalysis and with Eugenio Colorni.

A few friends have left us an image of Colorni—who was killed by the Nazi-Fascists in 1944 a few days before the liberation of Rome—as passionately involved in discussions which dug into the hidden and less rational sides of life (Rossi, 1975, pp. 187–91; Spinelli, 1984, pp. 296–301).[5] Hirschman, in his turn, was described by his sister Ursula (1993) as having always been rather reflective, even as a child. While still at school he had come across the three great de-mystifiers of the German-speaking world—Marx, Nietzsche, and Freud. Neither Freud's ideas nor his research project ever convinced Hirschman fully. Although, of course, he recognized the existence of the unconscious (and Freud's gift for compelling humanity to face it), he saw no reason to delve into its tangled web—almost as if he had foreseen Popper's problem of the necessary falsifiability of social theories. This view is one of the things Hirschman fruitfully discussed with Colorni.[6]

Thus, while Colorni was open to criticism and debate, with a tendency to explore his own soul (and that of those around him) in order to provoke intimate revolutions, Hirschman was rather working on the opposite direction: that is, referring pulsions and tensions as far as possible to reason and making use of their constructive stimuli.[7]

Keeping this in mind, let us look at one of the concluding pages of *The Strategy* (1958a, p. 209), in which Hirschman claimed that development draws strength from the very tensions it creates. "It is perhaps the pervasive influence of psychoanalysis," he added in a note, "that has kept us from seeing this point. For Freud, difficulties, conflict, and anxiety were mainly pathogenic agents; their constructive and educational functions in individual development have been rediscovered only recently" by psychologists, regarding individual development, and by anthropologists, regarding social cohesion. This claim rings a bell: for Hollis Chenery, in fact, (*American Economic Review*, 1959, p. 1064), Hirschman's theory of development was "more applied psychology than economics."

Hirschman stated clearly the destructive reactions that may arise from the tensions examined in the book, but, as in the case of the "propensity to experiment," (see chapter 2) he did not think it was feasible or even desirable to suppress tensions altogether. He advocated, rather, breaking down into "a series of smaller and more manageable" parts, this "grand tension" to which underdeveloped countries are subjected due to their "universal desire for economic improvement oddly combined with many resistances to change."

Studying and making constructive use of specific tensions, Hirschman argued, would not only contribute to fighting the ineffectiveness of the many political proposals formulated a priori without taking account of real conditions. It would also help prevent the brutality that can suddenly take over where proposals leave off, turning the mirage of development into a nightmare. Futility and brutality, Hirschman continued, quoting a passage from Paul Tillich, "are manifestations of 'the inability of the neurotic to have a full encounter with reality' "; "many under-developed countries are showing today that their policies need not be confined between these sterile alternatives." The pressures and tensions created by the development process, Hirschman concluded, "do not necessarily frustrate it, but can be made to help it along. To sharpen the realistic perception of this third way has been the aim of this book."

The Strategy grew out of work in the field and was the result of a cross-fertilization of experiences, disciplines, and cultures during the course of a complex itinerary across three continents.[8]

Take for example chapter 1, which opens with the idea that the results of the search for the *primum mobile* (belonging to the theories of the missing component) paradoxically refute the logical basis for such a search. From this critique Hirschman was able to reach a fundamental proposition in his argument: "development depends not so much on finding optimal combinations for given resources and factors of production as on calling forth and enlisting for development purposes resources and abilities that are hidden, scattered, or badly utilized" (1958a, p. 5).[9]

Further on he outlined the psychological foundations of this economic "slack." The idea of progress in underdeveloped countries, Hirschman argued, appears in two ways. One is "group

focused," the other is "ego focused." The former is incompatible with differences in treatment and opportunity, with social
mobility, and with self-improvement—all called for by the modernization of the economy. The latter is incompatible with the
continuous and collaborative commitment required by industrial
production. Development policy is thus intended to gather and
productively engage resources and talents kept at bay (as it were)
by these motivations, produced by the country's history. To this
end, as many specific tensions as possible must be put to use.
A central theme of the book was to discover the inducement
pressures or mechanisms and the binding or pace-setting factors
suited to this purpose.

Thus Hirschman took a step away from economics and politics as they were usually understood: that is, as theoretical foundations and consequent prescriptions. In *The Strategy,* analysis and
policy are born hand in hand, as a fulcrum of scientific, political
and ethical needs; moreover, they are subject to a two-way relationship in which recognition of the slack involves searching for
inductive mechanisms, while these mechanisms eventually bring
about a retrospective reaction to psychological motivations.

The first aspect of this relationship dominates Hirschman's
argument in *The Strategy,* while its opposite is revealed when he
claims that sectors and regions that enjoy a suddenly high rate
of economic growth tend to modify their behavior by adapting to
new requirements. "In other words, there is reason to think that
the 'protestant ethic,' instead of being the prime mover, is often
implanted ex post as though to sanctify and consolidate whatever
accumulation of economic power and wealth has been achieved"
(1958a, pp. 185–86).[10]

Hirschman later realized that the theory of cognitive dissonance—drafted in the 1950s by an influential group of social
psychologists—was relevant to his argument, and wrote "Obstacles to Development: a Classification and a Quasi-Vanishing
Act" (1965). Instead of escaping the web of discussions on the
obstacles to, and prerequisites of, development by stressing their
contradictory procedure (as in the beginning of *The Strategy),*
this article took up the issue as raised by Gerschenkron (1962,
chapter 2) and classified obstacles according to their reliability.
This permitted real obstacles to be distinguished from presumed

ones. It also yielded a discussion on the inverted sequence of the theory of cognitive dissonance whereby (fortunately) changes in belief, attitudes, and even personality can be produced by certain actions rather than being prerequisites for them. Thus, Hirschman suggested in this article, whoever lags behind and stumbles upon modern behavior (such as the quest for personal profit, taking on entrepreneurial risk, promotion according to merit, long-term planning, calling democratic elections) may well experience an unpleasant dissonance with previous convictions. This might induce him gradually to close the gap, making it narrower and narrower. As a consequence, Hirschman claimed (1971a, p. 325) in a phrase that pulls many threads contained in *The Strategy* together, "the art of promoting development may therefore consist primarily in multiplying the opportunities to engage in these dissonance-arousing actions and inducing an initial commitment to them."[11]

But Hirschman's argument did not stop here. Working subsequently on *Exit* (1970), and in particular on the effect of severe initiation or of high entrance fees on loyalist behavior, Hirschman observed that in this case the client or component of the organization has a marked interest in hiding from himself the fact that the purchased commodity, or organization, has deteriorated. There is a limit, however, beyond which the interested party will actively respond in order to modify the situation and demonstrate that he was not wrong after all in paying such a high price (moral and/or material) for membership.

This result implied modifying the theory of cognitive dissonance, because two paths for reducing the existing discrepancy were revealed: the first was to modify one's ideas; the second was to change reality. An individual may for example perceive an organization's boring ventures as interesting at first. Later, however, if any possibility of modifying them presents itself, he will commit himself more than others will to making the ventures more interesting; that is, he will try to reduce or close the gap between his perception and reality by acting upon the latter. This hypothesis of inverted behavior was discussed in an appendix of *Exit* (written together with Philip Zimbaldo and Mark Snyder of Stanford University) and supported in the book by a few historical observations (such as those on ideology and American practice in chapter 8). Hirschman was convinced, to the point of maintaining the view in his introduction to *A Bias for Hope* (1971a, p. 31), that an important task of possibilism was to indicate the way to free oneself of cumulative sequences such as that in the theory of cognitive dissonance.

Some aspects of this theory, Hirschman explained referring to *Exit*, imply an unreasonable denial of human choice and freedom. The theory predicts, in fact, that if we engage in a certain action, our beliefs will adapt themselves to it. This makes renewed recourse to the same type of action probable, leading to further reinforcement of the new belief, and so on. A useful way of escaping this sequence is to concentrate on the unintended consequences of human actions (with which we shall be dealing in chapter 5). This unexpected but benign stick in our wheel fortunately reopens the analysis to more fruitful interactions between thinking and acting. The same question was taken up again ten years later in *Shifting Involvements*. The results of the theory of cognitive dissonance were reinterpreted from the point of view of disappointment,[12] while the individual's behavior was explained in terms of the theory of metapreferences (see chapters 5 and 7).

What then is the moral of these developments? Must we assume that the psychological springboard for *The Strategy* has been superseded? Although the book certainly differs from more recent works, its limits, and those of other books that followed, have been gradually identified in order to build new frameworks of thought partially linked to those of the past. By looking back in this way, it is possible to appreciate the significance of each contribution within the specific logic that gave life to it.

A SINGULAR INCOMPREHENSION

In chapter 2 of *The Strategy*, Hirschman criticized the use of the economics of growth for dealing with underdevelopment, focused on investment activity and on the ability to invest, and anticipated some aspects of his own strategy (corresponding to the two Colombian discoveries). In chapters 3 and 4, "Balanced Growth: A Critique" and "Unbalanced Growth: An Espousal," he compared and contrasted his point of view with those of a group of "senators" of development economics.[13] These two chapters received the greatest scrutiny and became a standard reference in discussions and teaching on the subject of balanced growth.[14]

The controversy undoubtedly contributed to the initial success of the book, but in the long run it gave rise to a one-sided reading.[15] "It is remarkable," Hirschman wrote in the 1961 preface to the paperback edition, "how the question of balanced versus unbalanced growth, together with the analysis of linkages . . . seems to have caught the exclusive attention of many readers. I should like to plead for a correction of this bias."[16]

The issue seems implicitly to contain another. Chenery's comment that Hirschman's theory of development belongs more to applied psychology than to economics, in fact, continues: "Since in this view capital and other input limitations are illusory, the economist is left with nothing to economize, except the elusive quality of decision-making" (Chenery, 1959, p. 1064). Here one can clearly see the difficulty—even embarrassment—in which economists used to economizing scarce factors of production found themselves when dealing with this book, based on the idea that scarcity, in the form illustrated by the theory, simply does not exist.[17]

Another example is Hla Myint's detailed analysis in the *Review of Economic Studies*, "The Demand Approach to Economic Development" (1960). In this article, Myint accurately reconstructed several topics discussed in *The Strategy*, but insisted on defining the many inducement mechanisms which Hirschman distinguished both on the demand and the supply side as being part of a "demand approach," whereas these mechanisms are as important on the supply side as internal pressures in the firm, forward linkages, or permissive sequences of unbalanced development.[18]

This brings me to a general observation. If we widen our horizons and take into consideration a whole group of reviews rather than just the two mentioned earlier—e.g., Frank (1960), Hoselitz (1960), Kindleberger (1959), Knox (1960), Sen (1960), and Yamey (1960)—the tone becomes more constructive. The effort made to interpret the book led to a few specific contributions. Moreover, the sensation produced by all these writings, including a letter by Roy Harrod,[19] is that the book represented a significant intellectual event, suddenly erupting out of the blue, which required careful assessment. The gap between perceiving the importance of Hirschman's contribution and actually coming round to his view was still great, however.

Hirschman, as I have already mentioned, used to speak of economists' "trained incapacity" (1981a, p. 304). It is already clear from the episodes we have examined that if an economist restricts himself to operating within the intellectual boundaries of the discipline, he can only actually come to grips with the elements in Hirschman's work that are compatible with his own way of thinking.

In order to understand a little more, it would be useful to go into the analytical side of the matter.

"The traditional approach," Amartya Sen wrote in his perceptive review of the book (1960, p. 592), "is to take a certain supply of resources as *given* and to discuss how to allocate them in the most efficient manner. Professor Hirschman, on the other hand, assumes that the supply of resources will vary with the 'inducement mechanisms.' He does not, therefore, worry about the problem of inflation, or of balance of payments, arising out of a high level of induced investments and activity." The emphasis Hirschman placed on the variability of supply of productive factors should not prevent us from paying attention to the constraint of productive capital equipment and foreign exchanges.[20]

This statement can be turned right around: Hirschman's aim was not to sweep away previous economic knowledge; he suggested, rather, not to forget the variability of supply of productive factors when considering productive capital equipment or available foreign exchanges. "My principal assumption," Hirschman wrote to Chenery (1959c), "is that underdeveloped economies are *squeezable* and my principle contention is that there are special techniques of resource mobilization which are not necessarily the same as, and should complement, the techniques of the efficient use of given resources. I do not understand why the former techniques are necessarily the concern of the psychologist and only the latter the province of the economist," as Chenery seemed to imply.

The idea of slack (and therefore of squeezability) suggests concentrating on techniques of resource mobilization. When these techniques are put into practice, the level of relaxation in the economy is affected, as are, ultimately, subjective behavior and motivations. A cognitive and normative path is thus outlined in the text, which takes the alternative between balanced and unbalanced growth as its starting point, but which transcends the typical mental context of such a controversy.

Let us look in detail at a passage in chapter 4 in which, after remarking on how Scitovsky betrays "a certain impatience" with the process that brings the economy from one point of equilibrium to another, Hirschman suggested focusing on the very process of interaction that takes place "up and down and across the whole of an economy's input-output matrix." "In other words," he wrote (1958a, p. 66), "our aim must be to *keep alive* rather than to eliminate the disequilibria. . . . That nightmare of equilibrium economics, the endlessly spinning cobweb, is the *kind* of mechanism we must assiduously look for as an invaluable help in the development process" by means of growth in the ability to invest.

Hirschman did not, of course, deny the working of market forces, as studied in economic theory. He linked it, rather, to the complementarities of productive activity, and focused on the ability of investment to promote other investments either through the demand deriving from the complementary commodity or through the slow induction generated by complementarity in the uses of different commodities. The latter, less rigid form of complementarity was taken into careful consideration because the opportunities for profit arising from the initial development move are powerful levers for subsequent development: they must be "carefully nursed, maintained at some optimum level, and if necessary created consciously" (1958a, p. 69).

At this point an economist could well cling to the (human) need to lead the argument toward more familiar ground. If nothing else, for every unbalanced situation, it is always possible to imagine a (classical or neoclassical) set of equilibrium prices—not an altogether useless exercise since markets tend to "redress the balance" as Hirschman explicitly pointed out.

Such a mental exercise may be useful for a long-term historical reconstruction,[21] but it cannot explain the growth paths that have actually been followed since the pressures born from disequilibria are no longer taken into account. Moreover, it is important to understand that theoretical equilibrium prices, imagined on the basis of an unbalanced situation, would not usually be the same as the prices that would establish themselves in the economy in the event (itself unrealistic) that other factors did not interfere. This is because the slack that exists in the economy and the various intensities and pressures of disequilibria generate a whole spectrum of possible solutions. Finally, it is clear that in these complex conditions, entrepreneurial behavior is not as automatic as theory supposes. The result (however positive or negative), crucially depends on the abilities and discretionary choices of different (public and private) operators.[22]

Traditionally, economists have no mental framework to deal with this point of view.[23] As well as the technique of "partial equilibria," (see note 15) that of macroeconomics must also be set aside ("to look at unbalanced growth," Hirschman stated in a conference [cited in 1961a, p. ix], "means, in other words, to look at the dynamics of the development process *in the small*"). All that is left then, if we restrict ourselves to the main approaches, is general equilibrium and classical economics. Both, however, are a different part of the restricted logic that Hirschman was inviting us to abandon.[24]

It is not only a matter of agreeing with the notion, supported at the time by development economists (Hirschman, 1981a, pp. 5–6), that orthodox monoeconomics could not be applied to underdeveloped areas. Hirschman considered himself a "dissenter" even when regarding the "new orthodoxy."[25] He left aside all the models (Keynesian, classical, neoclassical) that visualized development as a transition from a traditional (ahistoric and vaguely defined) society to a modern one (see 1981a, pp. 87–88), and wrote an innovative book that put forward a strategy of intervention in order to interact positively with the "images of change" produced by the history of these societies. In doing so, Hirschman implicitly abandoned the postulate at the basis of the whole economic discipline that the pursuit of material self-interest is man's only motivation, and decided to "complicate economics."

The result was a book that has been discussed at length but not always understood; a book that continues to attract flocks of readers because it offers a concrete view of the problems of growth, almost magically opening up the narrow intellectual boundaries into which economic thought had been confined by the discipline.

The *loci classici* of the book were obviously Colombia and, more generally, Latin America, where the book was received favorably from the start.[26] Widely debated and taught, *The Strategy* was a source of inspiration for intellectuals dedicated to the economic and civic development of their countries. To this day it is a reference point for three generations of Latin American economists and social scientists in universities, research institutes, and government.[27]

With such concrete issues in mind, the book was read for the specific solutions offered by Hirschman (inverted sequences, linkages, trade policies, latitudes in performance standards, role of disturbances, geographic transmission of growth). With the passing of time, the controversy over balanced growth (which never received a great amount of collective attention in Latin America) naturally lost some of its impact. This did not mean however that the economist's cognitive difficulties all of a sudden vanished miraculously; rather, they reemerged in specific issues or took on a different trajectory.

An important review of the book by Celso Furtado (1960) is typical in this respect. He wrote that *The Strategy* "reflects much more the desire to understand the reality of underdevelopment and late development than the concern for subjecting reality to pre-established academic models"; he culled the sense of the book's opening perfectly, and observed, quite rightly, that Hirschman was not concerned with the circumstances in which dynamic centers that are able to gather and enlist abilities and resources wrongly considered scarce, either rise or decline (this was to be a theme in *Journeys*, dedicated to Celso Furtado and Carlos Lleras Restrepo who ideated dynamic centers such as SUDENE and INCORA). Nevertheless, having reviewed some of Hirschman's ideas on balanced growth, planning, inflation, and the balance of payments, Furtado concluded that "a great deal of what is said in the book" had already been said by Latin American economists, especially by Raul Prebisch's ECLA.[28]

Aside from a few specific similarities,[29] a legitimate question might be whether Furtado did not fall into other forms of pre-established academic models (see note 31). Conceived as a reaction to the visiting economist syndrome (see chapter 2), one tacit objective of *The Strategy* was probably to fight the self-deprecatory attitude of Latin American intellectuals.[30] Hirschman's caution—reticence even—with regard to the Latin American literature was dictated perhaps by his desire not to compromise (for the sake of polemic) the impact of his arguments, and to deal with the subject at greater length elsewhere, as indeed he did in "Ideologies of Economic Development in Latin America" (1961) which made specific reference to the work of ECLA.[31] The fact that this self-deprecatory attitude is today explicitly opposed by Gert Rosenthal's ECLA (1990) must be a source of great satisfaction for Hirschman.

ECONOMICS AND POLITICS

To get back to the point, Hirschman's analysis proposed abandoning the calm backwater of ex ante theorization. If I am not mistaken, however, this clashes with the *psychological* need of a typical economist—to whatever school he belongs—to hang on for dear life to as many or as few theoretical certainties as he has laboriously collected.

Adopting Hirschman's idea of the economist's "trained incapacity" and a line of argument contained in *Exit, Voice, and Loyalty* (1970a, chapter 7), I would like to specify that probably this attitude comes from a special case of loyalty with "severe initiation" (in the sense that entry into and exit out of the discipline are the result both of the decisions of individuals and of recognition by the profession). Since initiation heightens loyalty, intimate change can only come about after inner struggle. Habit of mind can only be modified gradually by working unconventionally both inside and outside the discipline with true freedom of thought.

In his work, in fact, Hirschman leaps with sagacious naturalness, from aspects of psychology and anthropology,[32] to politics, geography, and history, in a construction that always allows for interaction between thought and reality. He was careful of the economic side of his construction, however. He maintained direct contact with the concepts and with the language of the discipline, adopting it for his own purposes. Thus the economist-reader who is attracted (perhaps in a contradictory fashion) by the contents of the work, finds its gates wide open, but may feel bewildered by the change required of him once he is inside. Once the secret is revealed, however, he will not find it so difficult to follow Hirschman as his ideas unfold.

This fact is particularly important when it comes to understanding the relationship between economics and politics woven into the work.[33] When Hirschman spoke of unbalanced growth, he proposed—among other things—overcoming the "overly narrow view of the adjustment process that has long dominated economic literature." Traditionally, he continued, economists argue over the question

> whether, in any disequilibrium situation, *market forces acting alone* are likely to restore equilibrium. . . . But as social scientists we surely must address ourselves also to the broader question: is the disequilibrium situation likely to be corrected at all, by market or non-market forces, or by both acting jointly? *It is our contention that nonmarket forces are not necessarily less "automatic" than market forces.* Certainly the almost monotonous regularity with which interventionist economists have come forward—and with which authorities have acted—when the market forces did not adequately perform their task testifies to the fact that we do not have to rely exclusively on price signals and profit-maximizers to save us from trouble. (1958a, pp. 63–64)

The problem, as Hirschman saw it, is that the desire to survive politically is no less strong than the desire for profit, with the result that when there is a shortage (of electricity, or classrooms, etc.) brought about by unbalanced growth, social pressure to do something about it usually induces some corrective measures. This does not necessarily ensure that equilibrium is restored—as economists would like; it does, however, leave room for an analysis of the combined reactions to disequilibria of market and nonmarket forces produced by economic growth.

Furthermore, this view is a vaccination against a fairly common line of argument which claims that one should first choose an economic objective, then demonstrate that it cannot be accomplished through the action of market forces, and finally declare that the state is undoubtedly in a position to achieve it. Hirschman described this as a "non sequitur." The fact that private entrepreneurs cannot or will not accomplish a given objective does not necessarily mean that public authorities can or will (1958a, pp. 54 and 65).

The missing interaction between economics and politics helped identify two opposing tendencies (which, from a different angle, Hirschman explicitly dealt with in his recent monograph, *The Rhetoric of Reaction*). One, criticized in *The Strategy,* relied on public intervention and aimed to show that market forces were not able to achieve set goals. The other, which became popular later, stemmed from distrust of the state and theorized its inefficiency in order to give absolute precedence to market forces. This is clearly a second non sequitur which, like the first, can be solved only with a specific analysis of the reactions of market and nonmarket forces to the issue at stake.

The passages quoted above play a significant role in the corpus of Hirschman's work, because they sowed the seeds for *Journeys Toward Progress* (1963a, p. 4). Through them, we can "transit" as it were from one volume to the other, as we did in chapter 2 with the two analytical articles from the Colombian period.

For most economic theories, Hirschman claimed in his introduction to *Journeys,* the public decision-making process is considered either entirely outside the economic field of inquiry, or else an automatic subproduct of classical inputs such as capital, labor, etc. If one looks more closely, however, the private decision-making process has never been properly analyzed either. According to formal price theory, an entrepreneur springs into action "as soon as his calculations tell him there is profit to be made": ability to calculate and entrepreneurial motivation are taken for granted.

Along the same lines, Hirschman continued, referring to *The Strategy* (1963a, p. 3): "the feeling that ebbs and tides of decision-making play a considerable role at *all* stages of development had led me earlier to investigate a variety of mechanisms (imbalances, linkages, and the like) which make for the tides, i.e., which squeeze out extra doses of entrepreneurial and managerial decision-making in the course of the development process. This leading theme of my previous book was by no means limited to private decision-making." The desire to document this claim is what led to the writing of *Journeys.*

Thus, between the non sequitur of those who "believe in the plan" and the non sequitur of those who "believe in the market," Hirschman tried to build a realistic, unified view based on the actual reactions of economic forces and of the public administration. I do not mean by this that he had to weave together too many relationships; I mean that he had to cut the coat of his analysis according to a different cloth from the one traditionally used by economics and politics. Although *The Strategy* and *Journeys* are grounded respectively in these two disciplines, the volumes are unclassifiable, linked to one another to such an extent that neither can be considered a typical product of their respective social science.

As a result, the concept of economic policy in *The Strategy* was more concrete, far-reaching, and complex than it is in contemporary economics. It was more concrete because it got closer to actual behavior; more far-reaching because in order to get closer it widened the spectrum of human affairs taken into consideration, naturally extending its scope from society to the state; more complex because it was not based on a value judgment about the primacy of planning or market forces. The book tried to create an interaction between analysis and policy by studying the reactions of public and private decision makers to changes in their economic and political conditions in the light of the goals to be achieved. These goals can be pursued only if a corresponding strategy can be drawn up; if, that is, sufficient productive and/or democratic forces can be mobilized. Hirschman therefore set up a two-way relationship between intention and comprehension, between "heart" and "head."

Sequences and Oscillations

In the introduction to *A Bias for Hope,* a collection of articles on development and Latin America published in 1971, Hirschman underscored two main features of his work: political economics[34] and possibilism. Generally, he explained, economists and political scientists are at ease only in their own disciplines. Links with the adjacent social science (too obvious to be disregarded) are often dealt with in their work, as an obligatory step.

As soon as they launch into their analysis, however, these links are promptly forgotten.

Is there an alternative method? On the one hand, Hirschman claimed, there is no such thing as a *passe partout* for the finer political dimensions of economic phenomena: each one requires an ad hoc discovery, facilitated by a "certain turn of mind" and by a few heuristic expedients (a "blessing in disguise," a "reversed sign," "cumulative disequilibrium"). On the other hand, he maintained, there is a much more skillfully constructed alternative to the primitive models used by economists and political scientists: the Marxist concept of historical process. The interaction described by Marx between the development of productive forces and relations of production can be translated into economic and political factors. Beyond a certain threshold, growth in the former is impeded by lack of change in the latter, which generates transformative social forces and conflicts.

Hirschman added at this point that he was unaware of being so close to this construction when, in *The Strategy,* he launched the idea that political forces are no less automatic than economic ones, and showed repeatedly "how such forces are likely to arise when market mechanisms by themselves would cause shortages of social overhead capital, or would lead to regional imbalances or to other types of disequilibria, which required—and were likely to entrain—the intervention of political action" (1971a, p. 17). The fact that this correspondence was not pointed out was due largely to the modest scale of the mechanisms surveyed compared to the huge canvas painted by Marx.[35]

Hirschman was writing in a period of rediscovery of Marx, and perhaps used him as a vehicle of communication,[36] a way of being understood. With today's hindsight, however, it may be worth establishing whether his joining forces with the Marxian concept of historical process had a solid foundation or whether it was merely a fruitful match.

The question arises spontaneously as a result of Hirschman's qualifications in the introduction to *A Bias for Hope.* It is likely, he argued, that on a small scale, political changes are less revolutionary than on a larger scale. They are probably also less clearcut, more fragmentary, and less durable. His focus thus shifts to the amplitude, length, and frequency of interaction cycles and to the efficiency of their economic and political sequences (aspects which are usually different in dependent countries which are forced to smuggle in changes furtively and less comprehensively). Furthermore, the specific agents of change are different every time and cannot be identified with the industrial proletariat. The more one reads, the more the picture looks like Hirschman and not Marx.[37]

The question is still open (and will be taken up again later in the present chapter). In the meantime, the net of Hirschman's arguments allows us to trawl a fair intellectual catch. Take, for example, the anything-but-Marxist idea that there is a *choice* between economic and political action. Or again, the mistaken perception of opportunities by economic decision-makers placed here at the very foundation of "one particular (and perhaps particularly interesting) class of economic-political sequences." Still again, take the principle of oscillation presented as an alternative to the thesis of optimal combinations (typical of economics). The former, Hirschman maintained, can produce better results; it can "permit one to acquire a feeling for the right amplitudes of the many swings that do occur anyway in the real world" and make the search for new economic and political sequences easier (1971a, p. 26).[38]

It is worth wondering if this view of the principle of oscillation might not help us understand more about *The Strategy*. Following an indication in the text, let us look therefore at chapter 5, "Investment Choices and Strategies"[39] in which the author demonstrated how he preferred development to take place because of a shortage (rather than excess capacity) of Social Overhead Capital (SOC).[40]

While a shortage of SOC creates a compulsive sequence, excess SOC only creates a permissive, and therefore weaker, sequence. Evidently, both bring into play economic-political oscillation: in the first case, growth triggers social pressures and forces the authorities to make decisions (loosening the bottleneck and inducing new developments); in the second case, the construction of SOC ordered by the authorities has only an inductive effect on productive activities (which in its turn has a weaker influence over new investments).

Nevertheless, the argument contains no institutional assumption regarding the way SOCs and DPAs (Directly Productive Activities) are organized. The latter could well be (wholly or partly) in public hands, while the former could be (partly) substituted by private activity (see 1958a, pp. 88–89 and 95).

The notion that political forces are not necessarily less automatic than market forces tends to put the two kinds of forces on the same level (and therefore to analyze them together); yet it invites one to take the differences into account as well.

These characteristics can be put into action in succession, thus making the path easier. From a starting point of unbalanced growth, one can talk initially of the correspondence between the behavior of economic and political forces and consequently develop several aspects of development strategy in contrast to the prevailing ideas in economics. Following this, one can consider the differences in behavior between the two kinds of forces independently and incorporate them by means of the specific economic and political oscillations they produce. In this way, these variegated oscillations take their place next to those "fanciful digressions" evoked in the book (on chain sequences, on assembling a jigsaw puzzle, on putting the cart before the horse, etc.) to make the concept of efficient sequence more palpable and to apply it to a variety of necessarily different situations.

To use a variation of Hirschman's metaphor of the Chinese paper flower, it seems to me that the construction of *The Strategy* bears a resemblance to a folded paper cutout; only when it is opened can we see what the linked figures represent.[41]

BLOCKAGE AND DEVELOPMENT

Hirschman's anti-authoritarian way of thinking rarely allows absolutes. The concept of sequence (permeating notions of unbalanced growth, oscillation, linkages, etc.) was accordingly subjected to a series of limitations and counterindications.

The notion of unbalanced growth assumes that the advancement of one activity (sector, zone) effectively induces progress in another.[42] In *The Strategy*, Hirschman showed that this effect can be either altogether lacking or insufficient (such as in permissive sequences or when the effect of propagating regional development does not make up for the effect of polarization). It was soon clear, however, that economic development can in fact lead to serious political regression (a bitter lesson of the Latin American coups during the 1960s and 1970s). Equally, the reestablishment of democracy can be accompanied by a crisis or a slowing down in development. The creation of imbalance on one side or the other triggers off some forces that work to alleviate it, and others that work to aggravate it.

A perhaps unexpected side product of *The Rhetoric* was a critique of the principle "one thing at a time" (1990d).[43] In *The Strategy,* at the end of chapter 6 ("Interdependence and Industrialization"), he had already remarked that a sequence can lead to a cul-de-sac, and that the industrialization of developing countries can be blocked at the stage of finished consumption goods by the political opposition of those industrialists who have worked until then with imported materials and who, for many reasons, are often adverse to substituting them with domestically produced materials.[44] In his recent critique on the offensive of conservative thought during the 1970s and 1980s and the serious regression of the welfare state in the United States and Great Britain, Hirschman again picked up the theme of the risk of being blocked. He claimed that a society that has long promoted individual liberties can find itself in trouble when it has to create (or contribute to the progress of) a welfare state, because the stress placed on individual acquisition and responsibility can become an obstacle when it becomes necessary to underscore the community ethic of collective solidarity.[45]

Hirschman's conclusions were that the notion of sequentiality cannot be a uniform, overall solution to the problem of development; that latecomers enjoy a certain compensation compared to some advanced countries for not having gone too far along the path of individualism; and that—as Hirschman, following Alexander Gerschenkron's example, had always maintained—there is no absolute best way for all situations.

Hirschman advanced these conclusions in order to avoid the possibility of *The Strategy*'s being "canonized." We should therefore return with new awareness to the notion of linkage as it was presented in that book. In *The Strategy,* the danger of a block of industrialization was raised with reference to a sequence that gradually works its way through the triangularized matrix of the economy, starting with the "last touches" applied to imported commodities. "Whereas the first steps are easy to take by themselves," Hirschman claimed, "they can make it difficult to take the next ones" (1958a, pp. 118–19). This observation emphasizes the author's preference for more propulsive sequences that trigger robust forward and backward linkages and that gather together abilities and resources of all kinds.

The option advocated by Hirschman—undoubtedly the most popular among readers of *The Strategy* (1986a, p. 15)—was not based on a mere evaluation of economic forces and consequences (as is usually understood by economists). It also rested on the ability of these forces and consequences to challenge the political resistance of industrialists who are already operating. In the light of Hirschman's recent observations, however, we cannot exclude a priori the possibility that even these strong disorderly sequences, complete with powerful linkages, might be in a position to block future development. This possibility means I must widen the scope of my analysis to make sure that no conscious or unconscious restraints (on different levels) are being imposed on the pursuit of desirable goals.

The observations contained in *The Strategy* on the counterforces created by every step in the industrialization process acquire greater emphasis when one realizes that overall Latin American industrialization was indeed tightly staged (1958a, pp. 110–13; and 1968b, now in 1971a, pp. 91–96). If, therefore, the progression of industrialization—from last touches, to consumption goods, to intermediate commodities and machinery etc.—represents the prevailing model, the resistances associated with it should be overcome rather than being entrusted to external shocks (such as perturbations in the balance of payments, or the inflationary tensions described in *The Strategy*).

Overcoming resistances was one of the aims of a well-known article, "The Political Economy of Import-Substituting Industrialization in Latin America" (1968), in which Hirschman dealt in particular with the resistance to tariff protection for new industries. He contrasted this resistance with some positive effects generated by the same cycle of import substitution including new investment opportunities for industries already installed, the possibility of creating vertically integrated industrial groups, technological contiguity (where it existed),[46] and the influence of geographical and social distance on industrialists' behavior.

My goal, Hirschman wrote (1971a, p. 114), is to shed light on a "highly complex 'field' of forces and counterforces," a field which, considering recent criticism, should probably be extended further. It is not just a matter of taking into account all the (positive or negative, direct or indirect, economic or political) effects of the sequence on itself. It is also a matter of connecting the sequence to external sectors and social spheres to which it can confer constraints and from which it can receive impulses (as in the case of socio-political forces or of the *técnicos* that overcame resistances to the development of an automobile industry in Brazil and Mexico: see 1971a, p. 108).

Halfway through the 1970s, when referring to Hirschman's works, Guillelmo O'Donnell advanced the idea that the emergence of authoritarian regimes in the major Latin American countries was largely due to the difficulties of deepening the industrialization process. Hirschman, on the other hand, in "The Turn to Authoritarianism in Latin America" (1979) criticized this idea, recalling that his 1968 essay "The Political Economy of ISI" had questioned the very concept of "exhaustion" of import-substituting industrialization. He also added, however, that he now realized that the ideas contained in his essay on the tightly staged nature of industrialization in Latin America, on resistance to the dynamic of backward linkages, and on the reality of an easy and exuberant starting phase, "could lend support to the idea that the deepening of industrial structure in the direction of intermediate inputs and capital goods represented some crucial threshold" (1981a, p. 107).

This was clearly not Hirschman's aim. Perhaps the fact that he himself raised the issue of the "ambiguity" of his writings indicates more than the fact that O'Donnell's point had just made him think again. It might have been a hint (by means of a rather bitter surprise mechanism) that the obstacle generated by a sequence, already noted in *The Strategy,* implicitly undermines the general applicability of one of the book's main theses, and that if sequences can impede rather than induce advancement, this observation must be presented as an explicit caveat.

This was a first step, on the basis of which—after further encouragement—Hirschman's later work developed. Thus, as in the case of the interaction between economics and politics, Hirschman's more recent development inspires us to reread and extend our interpretation of his previous work.

Linkages and Unusual Paths

Hirschman claimed this "case against 'one thing at a time' contradicts or qualifies a central proposition" of *The Strategy* (1990d, p. 119). In my view it also represents an evolution within that very line of thought. We can keep it in mind as we look back at the long path trodden by Hirschman since he called for tangibly observable industrialization processes (in Colombia and elsewhere)[47] and proposed the sequential concept of linkages as an alternative to the idea that industrialization was destined to failure if it was not developed simultaneously in many key sectors.

Take, for example, the inquiries and field surveys undertaken during the Bogotà years, or his study of the paper and pulp industries in Colombia (to which, in his capacity as private consultant, Hirschman devoted two volumes [see chapter 2]). His time there germinated many reflections on creative disorder and the propulsive efficiency of sequential processes. It was also the probable breeding ground for the idea of substituting the analysis of external economies (typical of the theory of firms and of partial equilibria) and that of complementarities and cumulative causations (drafted by the "new orthodoxy") with the analysis of linkages; and of attributing to linkages a central role in his effort "to describe how the development path ought to be modified" so as to maximize the advantages clarified by these concepts (1958a, p. 100).

In *The Strategy*, linkages are presented as if they were intimately connected to input-output analysis. This allowed the reader, Hirschman later explained (1981a, pp. 63–64, and 1986b, p. 58), to visualize the process of industrialization better and to endorse the image of linkages compared to corresponding images contained in other attempts. On the other hand, though, the close links with Leontiev's model suggested a rather mechanistic interpretation of industrialization and hinted that it was easy to measure backward and forward linkages. This was mostly an illusion because, while input-output analysis is by definition synchronic, linkages need time to take effect.[48]

The delicate relationship between *The Strategy* and economic theory can thus be seen. While input-output synchronicity is supported by the general equilibrium analysis, in fact, Hirschman's concept of linkages cannot (and would not) claim the same ascendancy. Despite the partly illusory nature of the juxtaposition (and the difficulties that empirical controls, requested by the author himself, ran into [see 1958a, p. vi]) it cannot be denied, however, that close contact with the technical corpus of economic knowledge also played a role.

For example, it called attention to forward and backward linkages (which soon entered the vocabulary of development economics). It facilitated access to a certain way of considering the strategy of economic development. It also provided an intellectual way out from the absolutist a priorism prevailing in economic theory, as in the case of those economists with a historical orientation who came up with the most enlightening use of the concept of linkages by examining the development sequences of single industries and countries at close quarters (see 1981a, p. 64).

The juxtaposition of linkages and input-output was presented in the text as "a mental experiment," useful for studying unusual growth paths that differ from those followed by developed countries. "Following Gerschenkron," Hirschman wrote later (1986b, p. 15),

> I saw originality and creativity in deviating from the path followed by the older industrial countries, in skipping stages, and in inventing sequences that had a "wrong way round" look. It was surely this attitude that permitted me to ferret out the backward and forward linkage dynamic and to acclaim as a dialectical-paradoxical feat what was later called, with disparaging intent, import substituting industrialization.

Here we come across another thread in Hirschman's tapestry, since he began to take an interest in the problems of economic development at the beginning of the 1950s, participating in a conference in which Gerschenkron decided to present his famous article, "Economic Backwardness in Historical Perspective" (see chapter 1, note 41). It is tempting, then, to look at *The Strategy* as if it were a kind of dialogue with Gerschenkron, and ask oneself whether the seed of Hirschman's search for hidden rationalities (which, as we have already said, provides unity to the volume) might not have been sown under that influence. Anyone agreeing with Gerschenkron that "the only generalization one can make about the development of latecomers is that they will not follow the sequence of their predecessors" (Hirschman, 1962a, now in 1971a, p. 184) will necessarily want to turn his attention to specific processes, to little understood or underestimated sequential solutions and action schemes that work "the wrong way round" to what one would expect.

CLOSE ENCOUNTERS

When it is claimed that development depends on drawing together and enrolling productive resources and available abilities by means of a "binding agent"—as Hirschman does in *The Strategy* (1958a, pp. 7–8)—the idea emerges that the development process of latecoming countries is bound to be less spontaneous than was the case in the countries where the process first occurred; and that the process comes about as a result of their "relative degree of backwardness" and of their desire and determination to make up for this fact. "Once economic progress in the pioneer countries is a visible reality, the strength of the desire to imitate, to follow suit, to catch up obviously becomes an important determinant of what will happen among the nonpioneers." Like Gerschenkron, Hirschman saw development as the result of a deliberate attempt to catch up on lost time (and not as a way of making up for objective scarcities or specific prerequisites).

The general affinity between the two authors must not lead us to forget their divergences, however, starting with their differing interpretations of the launching of the development effort. In Gerschenkron's view, as the gap between backward and pioneer countries increases, so do the advantages to be reaped from economic progress, so that backward countries are pushed to make the needed development effort. Using an ironic image (1958a, p. 9), Hirschman objected that "the underdeveloped country is thus pictured in the role of an Oblomov who can bring himself to leave his beloved bed and room only if the outside weather is irresistibly splendid."[49]

The image allows us to turn our backs on the postulate of perfect knowledge typical of economics, and to enter a more realistic world in which the launching of development is not—like Minerva—the product of Jove's mind, but results from a learning process and from abandoning erroneous views. In *The Strategy*, observations on group and ego-focused psychology are brought in to help, thus inaugurating a reflection on the dyscrasia between motivation and action (and therefore between action and result) which later took on a central role in Hirschman's work.

As we have already pointed out, the industrialization of Latin America started out with relatively small plants administering last touches to imported inputs. It concentrated on consumer goods rather than producer goods, often to satisfy the demands of populations suddenly deprived of their habitual supplies by a balance-of-payments crisis or by war. It developed at significant rates but never assumed the essential features of "the great spurt" theorized by Gerschenkron.

Consequently, Hirschman's strategy aimed mainly at strengthening the process underway by means of inducement mechanisms. It continuously fell back on the initial problem of how to utilize still dormant abilities and resources for productive purposes, thus exploiting the tension between development goals and the mistaken interpretation of how to achieve them.

This leads us to a third point. The idea that underdeveloped areas required a development effort that was deliberate, intensive, and guided took root in the West during the Great Depression and the World War. It became clear in those years that industrialization was on its way to assuming an important role in development policy, and that many backward countries, long-time producers of primary export goods, would perfect this activity (1981a, p. 10). Gerschenkron's analyses of industrialization in nineteenth century Continental European countries were part of this realization.[50] But as far as economics was concerned, the decline of traditional orthodoxy (which relied entirely on the free market) soon led to a new orthodoxy, to which the thesis of balanced growth and that of the "big push" belonged.[51]

Given the limited investment ability of underdeveloped countries ex ante, Hirschman came to fairly negative conclusions about both. Alternatively, he thought of breaking down the grand tension between backwardness and development prospects. As he put it in a letter of August 18, 1959, to André Gunder Frank (in 1986b, p. 27) his aspiration had been to break Paul Resenstein-Rodan's "big push" or Harvey Leibenstein's "minimal critical effort" down to "a series of smaller steps."[52]

To sum up, the clear, not always visible, water of an important tributary that runs into the delta of *The Strategy* was indeed fed by the source of Hirschman's dialogue with the economic history of Gerschenkron. Their convergence in terms of general outlook—on the absence of a unique development path, and on the necessity of discovering original processes in order to influence their course in the desired direction[53]—stimulated Hirschman to move in a new direction, once again distinguishing similarities from differences, and eventually identifying a few key features of industrialization and of economic policy in backward countries.

Two of these were the linkage theory and the role of imports in industrial development. Arguing in terms of fixed coefficients and foreign trade, Hirschman considered the investment stimuli that (due to industrial interdependence) result from the birth of specific input markets and from the availability of domestic products (backward and forward linkages). He showed that the formation of specific input markets played a crucial role in various industrialization processes and could be modified and even created deliberately to reinforce these processes, and that its thrust was significantly strengthened by the availability of domestic products. He also explained the important function of imports (before they are swallowed up) to create and explore markets; the negative role of protectionism that severely restricts imports; and the necessity of promoting exports in order to allow the whole process to be reproduced.[54] Thus underdeveloped countries, wrote Hirschman with his usual taste for paradox (1958a, p. 122), "tend to develop a comparative advantage in the articles they *import*."[55]

Moreover, in his article on import-substituting industrialization, Hirschman went into the variations and traits characteristic of industrial development in late-latecoming countries (thus distinguishing them from the latecomers studied by Gerschenkron), and drew a series of socio-political conclusions. This kind of industrialization, he argued, is imitative in nature; it does not usually have the inspirational and turbulent thrust of the "great spurt" and does not generate the same political turmoil that took place in other industrialized nations (a fact that caused much disappointment in Latin America).

After an "easy" first stage, Hirschman maintained, this kind of industrialization does not "exhaust" itself, as is often wrongly claimed.[56] What is true, rather, is that every cycle of substitution sets off resistances to the opening of the following cycle. Moreover, other important difficulties come up on the export side since their development would require well-established industries, and favorable economic policies, as well as the firms' acceptance of risks and additional costs for opening up access to foreign markets. Viewed this time from the foreign trade point of view, the danger of being blocked comes up again, and with it the need to extend the area of intervention and integrate sequentialism with simultaneity (by launching, for example, a program of trade policies, promotion of exports, inter-American agreements, and international cooperation).

It is not by chance, it seems to me, that after so many vicissitudes, during a period in which oscillations in the spirit of the times are pushing many Latin American countries to deal with the problem of liberalizing their economies, the idea has been aired of going back to *The Strategy* as a logical starting point for devising new policies aimed at launching a full industrial recovery of the continent (in the recent symposium at Buenos Aires [see 1992, ed. Simon Teitel]).[57]

An Un-Marxist Marxism

This exemplifies a typical procedure of Hirschman's. The metaphor of the Chinese paper flower thrown into the water and opening up gradually suggests that as each new petal unfolds, it has its place in the design, and its own contribution to make. It is able to reveal the (cognitive) impulse of the already unfurled petals, redefining their message which is as yet hidden or unperceived.

The 1965 article on obstacles to development took up *The Strategy*'s starting point from a different angle, developed its argument by means of the theory of cognitive dissonance, and connected the results of the strategy of development to the art of modifying individual and collective behavior. Similarly—as we have just seen—the 1968 article on the industrialization of Latin America defined the features of the continent's development along the lines sketched out in *The Strategy*. It then identified a complex field of pressures and counterpressures for growth, developed an economic-political analysis that heralded the introduction to *A Bias for Hope*,[58] and laid the foundations, from this point of view, for a more general reading of the seminal text.

Each time Hirschman seems to discover in his own arguments a new aspect that appears worth exploring, and develops an adequate methodology for doing so. It is like a constant treasure hunt for new and worthy elements,[59] generally spurred on by a personal need not to repeat himself. Starting with an initial observation, generally born from a surprising event, his argument gradually unfolds into a progressive generalization of the theme in question.

The first text on linkages that moves explicitly in this direction was Hirschman's preface to Judit Tendler's *Electric Power in Brazil* (1968). The main contribution that could be made to our knowledge of economic development, Hirschman suggested, was through detailed inquiries that offered, in addition to solutions to specific dilemmas, clearly outlined clues as to their typical structure. These studies, he added, show in minute detail the variegated influence of technology on the choices of individuals and of societies. They lend support to the "microtechnological" point of view as an alternative to the current of social thought that ran from Monstesquieu through Marx to Wittfogel and McLuhan.[60]

This opinion was echoed in several later texts. It makes one think that it was his reflection on other authors[61] that gradually led Hirschman to explore the analytical potential of linkages in a wider field—that is beyond the specific problem of industrial development dealt with in *The Strategy*.

As far back as 1963 Melville Watkins had already connected the effect of linkages on the thesis of "staples" developed by Harold Innis and other Canadian historians, according to which the development experience in a "new" country is modeled—in terms of its transport structures, kinds of settlements, economic activities—by the staple goods it exports to the world market. The growth of these exports, Watkins explained, generates an increase in income and, through the consumption linkage, induces the production of local products to substitute previously imported goods.

This text highlighted the versatility of the linkage concept: born from policy requirements, it proved useful for historical interpretations; proposed with industry in mind, it became applicable to agriculture and mining; theorized originally for production, it extended to consumption (and then to taxation [Pearson, 1970]).

It is easy to appreciate why Hirschman drew together notes, references, and ideas on this theme over the years, writing finally "A Generalized Linkage Approach to Development with Special Reference to Staples" (1977) which contains an outline of a book that never actually saw the light.

Once they had been christened, consumption linkages (already physically and spiritually present in *The Strategy*, chapter 7) played an increasingly important role. Unlike backward and forward production linkages, they can be decidedly negative (in the sense that, for a long period, increased exports of staples can be accompanied by the progressive destruction of established artisan activity.)[62] Consumption linkages depend on income level and on its distribution, and induce investment (and disinvestment) in various productive sectors, both industrial and agricultural.[63]

Fiscal linkages allow us to focus on the role of the state. Direct taxation (usually by means of export duties in the case of staples produced in "enclaves" such as plantations, mines, and oil seams) can be added to the argument, together with indirect taxation (by means of duties on imports bought with the income from exports of staples produced over wide areas by many domestic producers who are not taxed directly for administrative or political reasons). The state's ability to tax and to invest can therefore usefully be compared.

Taken together, production, consumption, and fiscal linkages help fix the boundaries to a whole field of thought and contribute to the identification of a few main features of the *crecimento hacia afuera* of various countries. From the outset they underscore the existence of very different experiences, of development and underdevelopment paths that correspond to linkage bundles of different staples[64] and of the constellation, force, speed and reliability of linkages that had already been activated. Just as new colors on a painter's palette open up the possibility of a whole range of variations and tonalities, so the evaluation of different combinations of linkages allows us to grasp much of the complexity of development. This is what led Hirschman to make new distinctions, interpretations, and methodological clarifications, and finally to come up with the well-known thesis of "micro-Marxism."

The argument we have already encountered concerning the microtechnological approach and the Marxist concept of historical process comes to the fore here. As in Marxism, Hirschman argued (1981a, p. 89), a linkages-based view takes a few characteristic features of the commodities produced, their production processes, and the technologies adopted as a starting point for understanding social and political events. But it does so "on a much smaller scale, in much more minute detail, and for a much more limited time frame." This is particularly useful when it succeeds in showing that significant differences in social-political development can be traced to relatively modest or little considered differences in the structure of productive forces (such as in the case of the countries of the periphery during the so-called period of export-led growth, from around 1850 to 1920–30).

On the other hand, Hirschman continued, Marx also moved in the direction of "micro" when he dealt with specific events and concrete national experiences. Even in a well-known page from the preface to *Capital,* after suggesting that the most industrially advanced country presents a picture of their future to those that follow, he claims that the evolution of Germany and continental Europe will be different from England's due to the absence of factory laws and to the presence of a variety of social and political residues of feudalism; that is, differences in the superstructure.

In this regard, Gerschenkron and Hirschman himself "were to be more Marxist than Marx" (1981a, p. 90). Gerschenkron did not invoke feudal residues to explain the difference between the development pattern of England and that of Germany and Russia. He focused, rather, on the different rates of growth in agriculture and industry and the diverse roles of consumption and capital goods in industrialization. Likewise, in analyzing the industrial expansion of late-latecomers, Hirschman showed that the "tightly staged" pattern of their industrialization, the importance of national or foreign minorities in this process, and the absence of industrial products for exports, could explain several outstanding features of political development in these countries: such as the weak influence of the industrial bourgeoisie, the weight of export sectors (agricultural and mineral), the role of the *técnicos*, the independence (in both its positive and negative sense) of the political class, and the often volatile nature of the economic policies pursued.

The degree of real affinity between Hirschman's micro-Marxism and Marxism as such has still to be established, however. My impression is that the kinship between the two is fairly remote (more than might appear at first sight). This is so because, although he seeks to identify the social and political influence of the bundle of features of commodities and productive processes, Hirschman tacitly abandons a crucial aspect of Marxism, that is the element of determination that is usually attributed to this influence.[65] In the Marxist view, if I am not mistaken, it is only possible for the direction of the relationship between productive forces and production relations to be reversed (as it is in the passage from the preface to *Capital* quoted earlier) if the traditional direction of the relationship remains the main one and, in the final analysis, the determining one.[66]

In the last section of the article "A Final Puzzle," where Hirschman's micro- and ultra-Marxist (more Marxist than Marx) theses go one step further, we find further confirmation. On the basis of a comparative discussion on the sociopolitical consequences of the production of various staples, Hirschman claimed, it would seem evident that the heavy, unskilled labor in tropical climates required by sugar-cane production, in addition to the availability of free land close to the plantations, the need to keep the labor force together during the unproductive season, and the possibility of exploiting it for minor tasks, conspired with Europe's post-Renaissance hunger for sugar to create a special affinity between sugar cane and slavery. "Generalizing from this historical example," he added (1981a, p. 94), "it is possible to conjecture that the emergence of a new mode of production is more intimately tied to the availability, at the proper time, of a specific economic activity with a strong affinity for that mode than is realized later on when the mode has become ubiquitous and dominant." Probably, he pointed out, this is also true for the textile industry and the industrial revolution.

Having advanced this culminating idea that a specific economic activity can give birth to a new production mode, however, Hirschman went on to introduce two qualifications. The first suggested that "it is easy to claim too much for the connection between the characteristics of a specific staple and the socio-political environment." This connection depends on the exact conditions of production and is therefore closely bound up with a particular time and place (thus, for example, coffee production in Colombia could have a completely different meaning from future coffee production in Uganda). The second stated that "there is not necessarily a one-to-one correspondence between a staple and its socio-political environment." The environment can in fact be different—as in the case of Cuba, where the seasonal labor force for sugar-cane harvesting is provided by city youths who temporarily relinquish their usual pursuits.

Thus Hirschman's micro-Marxism "takes a rather un-Marxist turn,"[67] leaving the reader as puzzled, amused, or disappointed as if it were a conjuring trick.[68] Granted, as in the case of economics, bringing in Marxism can create misunderstandings and end up being misleading. And yet one should also look at the other side of the coin. Comparisons often help one put things into focus, elaborate on and develop one's ideas, and communicate them more effectively. We have observed this repeatedly with economics, with Gerschenkron's economic history, and with the psychological theory of cognitive dissonance. It is a process that Hirschman spontaneously duplicated in his many comparisons with elements of political science, anthropology, and other fields.

4

Journeys and Reforms

Journeys toward Progress: Studies of Economic Policy Making in Latin America (1963) maintains that political shortcomings do not pose an insurmountable obstacle to the continent's progress and that Latin American policy making "is endowed with considerably more sense and rationality than it is usually given credit for." In fact, the stories of drought in Brazil's northeast, of land reform in Colombia, and of inflation in a Chile reconstructed during the book suggest that, to start with, winding bumpy roads may actually favor the progress of collective learning.Underlying each of these stories, however, it is possible to detect a deep-seated "failure complex," or, as Hirschman coined it, "fracasomania"— an almost pathological insistence on declaring past policy to be inadequate or doomed to failure.

In his book, Hirschman stressed the importance of a cumulative learning process, of building on past experience. In the three stories, he explored the intermediate area of social transformation that lies between peaceful reform and revolution. Social violence is a form of protest; it puts pressure on the authorities and takes the fulfillment of direct needs into its own hands. Similarly, crises capture collective attention, uncover established interests, and stimulate understanding and action. Furthermore, new problems can shed light on the solution to previous ones. These three elements can be utilized as powerful pressures to reach the desired results.

The chapter will go on to deal with the matter of "making reforms pass," and will review the actions of the two "reform-mongers," Celso Furtado and Carlos Lleras Restrepo, to whom *Journeys* is dedicated.

PROBLEM SOLVING

The Strategy of Economic Development presented a well-argued and reasonable set of proposals to the governments of under-developed nations. Hirschman was well aware, therefore, that these proposals would have to undergo a public decision-making process in those countries. Once the book came out, he began to explore this aspect.

During the early part of the 1959–60 academic year, Hirschman coordinated a study group on Latin America organized by the Twentieth Century Fund. He asked participating economists to refrain from judging and prescribing solutions and to identify, instead, the reasons why "Latin Americans support, adopt and change certain economic policies."

The contributions of the study group were collected in the volume *Latin American Issues: Essays and Comments* (1961) in which "Ideologies of Economic Development in Latin America" was published. This essay was both Hirschman's first contribution to the history of ideas, and a bridge between *The Strategy* and *Journeys*. Criticizing as it did the arguments put forward by ECLA, it stoked the polemical fire of *The Strategy*. With the search for "an understanding of the understanding that the Latin Americans have of their own reality" (1961e now in 1971a, p. 271), it also picked up where "The Economic Policy in Under-developed Countries" (1957) left off (see chapter 2) and indicated an agenda for his subsequent work.

Gerschenkron, Hirschman argued, used the concept of rel-ative economic backwardness not only to explain the specific characteristics of the industrialization of France, Germany, and Russia in the nineteenth century, but also to show how each spurt of development was accompanied by a set of ideas concerning the cause of the delay and the remedies for overcoming it; the greater the delay, the more radical the theories. Unfortunately, this gen-eralization does not seem valid in the case of Latin America. In the nineteenth century the problems of survival and consolidation in South American countries meant that political organization drew more attention than development. This brought about a peculiar divergence between ideology and reality, and inaugurated an era of introspective exploration into the Latin American "character" which degenerated into an "extraordinary orgy of self-denigration, self-laceration and pessimism" (1971a, p. 275).[1]

The main thesis of the essay, (inspired by the work of Victor Urquidi, Edmundo Flores, Octavio Paz, and Carlos Fuentes on Mexico and especially by the work of Celso Furtado and Gilberto Freyre on Brazil) was that the aim of economic development is not just to increase per capita incomes. In Hirschman's words, it also involves a " 'conquest of decision centers,' which were previously in foreign hands and a new ability to strike out on one's own, economically, politically, and intellectually. For this reason, the quest for development is also a quest for self-discovery and self-affirmation" (1971a, p. 304).

When Hirschman realized how difficult it was to make useful generalizations about the Latin American decision-making process, he proposed that the Fund conduct a study based on detailed observation of the sequences of policy making that had taken place around some recurring economic policy problems. The outcome was "a hazardous expedition into the vast no man's land stretching between economics and other social sciences such as political science, sociology and history" (1963a, p. ix).

Together with Charles Lindblom, an expert in policy making who was consultant for the project, and his wife Sarah, research assistant, Hirschman set out in the summer of 1960 on an extended trip to five Latin American countries (Mexico, Colombia, Chile, Argentina, and Brazil). The team conducted interviews with numerous government officials, political, business and labor leaders, intellectuals, and economists, many of whom had played an important role in the events Hirschman intended to reconstruct.

Of the five country studies originally planned, only three were actually published after a second trip made in the summer of 1962 to check on questions that had arisen while researching and writing, and to update the "problem stories." These chronicle the story of Brazil's attempt to strengthen the socioeconomic position of its drought ridden and stagnating northeastern provinces since the long and cruel drought of 1877–79; Colombia's attempts over some thirty years to improve patterns of land use and land tenure by means of reform and peasant action; and Chile's experience with recurring inflation since the second half of the nineteenth century. These "Three Problems in Three Countries" make up part 1 of *Journeys toward Progress;* part 2, "Problem-Solving and Reformmongering," is devoted to theoretical generalizations.

In an article presenting *Journeys* (1963b), Hirschman explained that the book grew out of a question without an answer.[2] Today, thanks to the historical swing that has taken place in the meantime, we can examine the various answers presented in *Journeys* with more detachment.[3] We can also appreciate Hirschman's moderate optimism—another dimension of his possibilism—which seeks solutions to complex, recalcitrant, and seemingly unmanageable political problems. The very title of the book, as Celso Furtado noted,[4] emphasizes the idea of possible positive change.

Journeys is also a lesson in democratic politics:[5] failings in the political framework, Hirschman claimed, should not become an obstacle to change. The three "problem stories," then, became Hirschman's "empirical lantern," used to shed light on how "a society can begin to move forward *as it is, in spite of what it is and because of what it is*" (1963a, p. 6).[6]

Hirschman took advantage of his experience as a "participating observer" of American, and later Colombian, decision making. In a subsequent note (1981a, pp. 139–40) he remembered how, in the early 1950s, (during his Washington years), many institutions in the United States were closely studied by the country's social scientists, who were surprised by the success of these institutions and anxious to understand why. Later, Walt Rostow (1958 and 1960) put forward the idea of an American "style." Defining "national style" as the way in which a country typically deals with its circumstances and problems, Rostow had in mind a country's reaction to the historic challenges it has encountered. In a conference on the topic, a sharp division arose between those who—like Rostow and Millikan—defined the American style as an "acutely pragmatic national style" and those who—like Kaplan and Hofsteadter—stressed the rigid moral absolutism of the United States.

Disagreements of this kind—Hirschman argued—(1963a, p. 228–29)—cannot fail to arise when national style is discussed without reference to specifics. A country's decision-making style depends on the historical and cultural background of the community as well as on the nature of the problems that need solving.[7] Of course, different societies prioritize their problems differently, and an author's decision to signal one problem rather than another changes his results because it leads to the identification of certain structural characteristics and exits and not others. Hirschman's decision to work on more than one problem at a time, however, produced good results:[8] it made the work more varied, allowed Hirschman to reach more general conclusions, and, unexpectedly, permitted him to better identify the characteristics of each problem by comparison with others.

Economic development forces governments to face a variety of problems, and its success in promoting development depends on how these problems are dealt with. Hirschman thus decided to identify some general notions about the way in which political issues are selected, and to study how the state handles them repeatedly over a long period of time.[9]

It was important to distinguish between pressing problems and problems selected by political authorities: solutions proposed for the former were appraised according to their ability to bring about some sort of relief, while this was not the case for the latter kind of problem. The ratio of the former to the latter is an index of a state's autonomy in dealing with the various kinds of pressures. In *Journeys,* Hirschman presented his concept of a state that, without altogether denying traditional *étatism,* responds above all to collective and sectoral pressures. Public authorities in *Journeys* are prevalently engaged in dealing with problems that they have not chosen: pressing problems related to emergencies such as drought, violence, and economic crisis.

A second important distinction that Hirschman made was between privileged and neglected problems. The mechanism available to citizens and pressure groups to compel governments to take action, Hirschman pointed out, are very different from one society to another and from one problem to another (for example, violent demonstrations are more likely to arise from price increases than from a high infant mortality rate). If the only mechanism is protest, many important problems are left aside.

In many underdeveloped countries, in fact, the links between the public and authorities (elections, political and trade union forces, independent press, etc.) are fragile or nonexistent. Other paths leading to the neglected problems must then be found. One path—indicated in all three studies—is to link them to the problems on which policymakers wish to act.[10] Ideology, Hirschman claimed, can serve as an "in-between structure" designed to forge a link between two distinct problems (1963a, p. 232).[11]

A third distinction concerned the motivation and the understanding of problems. When motivation systematically races ahead of understanding, he claimed, it is all too easy to make mistakes. The revolution of increased expectations, and the desire to rush into solving all their problems as rapidly as possible puts the country on a path of complicated development, paved with exaggerated requests and with "brand new" institutions.[12] The typical *rage de vouloir conclure*,[13] supported—if not actually instigated—by unscrupulous foreign experts, in no way eases the process of understanding and problem solving.

To begin with, the winding and bumpy roads—exemplified by Paul Klee's "Highways and Byways" on the book-cover illustration—may favor nonetheless the process of collective learning because shifts from one policy to another can contribute to bringing problems into focus, glaring mistakes can serve as lessons, and attempted policies can provide useful elements for subsequent ones. Even the "failure complex" can serve a purpose for a limited time: the expectation of failure reduces resistance to change, and the total rejection of past efforts sets the stage for a commitment to new solutions.

Fracasomania and Ideology

Let us look at the other side of the question. Faced with a pressing problem, policymakers are motivated to act in order to pacify, or occasionally to suppress, protest. This is Schumpeter's "adaptive response," and is likely to be faulty, given the low level of initial understanding. There will then be an attempt to deal with the problem by scouting around in search of ideas and suggestions; a few local and a great many imported solutions—some useful, some misleading—will subsequently be tried out. These are not truly "creative responses"—to use Schumpeter's words again—but "pseudo-creative"; they are more apparent (and ostentatious) than real.[14] The overhasty and therefore unsatisfactory application of these responses will eventually lead to their being replaced by different, though equally pseudo-creative, cures. This pattern makes for "wide swings" in policy making, and when "rival ideologies compete for the policy-makers' attention" (1963a, p. 241), an *"ideological escalation"* can take place.

The desire to know more about this negative side of the matter was an important spark for Hirschman's new endeavor. His objective was, first of all, to document "one of the most pronounced common characteristics" of the three stories, which is, "an almost morbid insistence on declaring past policy-making to have been a series of halfhearted, piecemeal efforts, doomed to failure" (1963a, p. 243). Thus, Colombians never acknowledged any significant results in reforming land reform; Chileans never disclosed the positive aspects of their anti-inflationary policies, and Brazilians seemed to be afflicted by amnesia when they proclaimed the futility and almost the nonexistence of their previous efforts in the northeast.[15]

In *Journeys,* then, Hirschman began to explore what was to become a recurrent theme: that of Latin Americans' "fracasomania," as he later baptized it in his essay on import-substituting industrialization. In part 1 of another article written in the same period, "Underdevelopment, Obstacles to the Perception of Change, and Leadership" (1968) Hirschman came back to the same theme and tried to identify the obstacles to the perception of change which exist in underdeveloped countries.

The starting point of this article was the distinction between real and apparent changes based on one or more highly demanding tests (such as a radical redistribution of wealth or reaching the per capita income of a developed nation). This indicates a country's reluctance to admit that change has been brought about; Hirschman claimed this could be linked to one or more obstacles to understanding. First, there is the difficulty of distinguishing between the cultural characteristics of the country, which can (and often should) retain a collective identity during the modernization process, and those features which should change. It is all too easy to interpret the persistence of a "little tradition" (which is often harmless or even useful) as a lack of change.

Second, comparisons with developed nations create expectations in latecomers that similar cumulative change will come about. These expectations are often frustrated (take, for example, the case of the social and political consequences of industrialization) thus creating a deforming prejudice in perception, accentuated by the consequent inability to perceive other aspects of change. Moreover, changes in dependent countries often take place furtively, in order not to disturb the relations (pressures, potential threats, etc.) to which the country is subject. It is an ingenious defense mechanism which can, nevertheless, deceive public opinion and scholar alike.

Third, Hirschman claimed that "the age of self-incrimination" had recently been substituted by the related "age of the *action-arousing gloomy vision*" (1971a, p. 351).

Hirschman thus arrived at a generalization of his key observations from the Colombian period—the "visiting economist" syndrome and the tendency towards self-deprecation (1986b, p. 11). Social scientists from the North who emigrated towards warmer climes, he explained in "The Search for Paradigms: Hindrance to Understanding" (1970), have produced a deluge of laws, models, and paradigms which give us a Latin America locked up in an iron cage, with its own citizens reduced to mere stereotypes. Latin American social scientists themselves, he added, have made an important contribution to this headlong rush toward the all-revealing paradigm.

The social and economic reality of the continent had until then been explained on the basis of some model or paradigm in such a way as to show that current trends were producing stagnation or deterioration and disaster. The gloomy vision—Hirschman observes—lays down "excessive constraints on conceivable moves of individuals and societies." Moreover, it "creates more gloom than action"; and can even be "positively harmful" in that it becomes "an invitation *not* to watch out for possible positive developments" (such as growth in one particular export or domestic product). Frequently, the propensity to see gloom and failure everywhere is the result of the illusion that development is necessarily accompanied by social justice and freedom. Finally, its roots may lie in the fact that "one has come to expect his country to perform poorly because of its long history of backwardness and dependence" (1971a, p. 352).

The theory of cognitive dissonance was then applied to underdevelopment: evidence that the country is doing better contradicts previous knowledge and is often ignored, while evidence that confirms the country's backwardness is picked up, underlined, and even favorably accepted, because no change is required in the previous cognitions to which one has become comfortably adjusted. "This is so," Hirschman explained, "because people who have a low self-concept and expect failure apparently feel some discomfort when they suddenly perform well, as psychologists have shown" (1971a, p. 353). Difficulties in perception and gloomy vision form a vicious circle reinforced by the conservative bias of collective psychological processes.

Hirschman addressed the subject once again in the new 1973 preface to *Journeys* and in the essay that reexamined the entire content of the book, "Policy-Making and Policy Analysis in Latin America—A Return Journey" (1975), in which we find a connection between fracasomania and the condition of dependence.

Following prolonged relative backwardness, Hirschman explained, it is generally expected that the country will continue to produce mediocre results. Furthermore, long intellectual dependence generates a lack of communication between generations of scholars and precludes the formation of cumulative knowledge in loco, due in part to the scant cumulative understanding of the decision-making process. Political partisanship and factionalism, reinforced by other causes of fracasomania, also produce a negative effect.

"Lack of learning," Hirschman concluded (1981a, p. 157), "is by no means the most serious consequence of fracasomania and of the inability or refusal to perceive change. In a government intent upon transforming a country's economic structure, these traits can lead to complete mishandling of the political situation, from ignoring and needlessly antagonizing groups that could be won over to underestimating the strength of others that cannot. It is precisely such mishandling that marked the careers of the Goulart and Allende regimes."

We can thus begin to see a typical itinerary take shape. In *The Strategy* and related texts, Hirschman focused on indirect ways to correct behavior that is incompatible with the needs of development (triggering processes of cognitive dissonance which, through the practice of change, transform behavior and hence mentality). In *Journeys*, on the other hand, he concentrated on the underlying rationale of the Latin American style of policy making and pleaded *sotto voce* for a change in that style. In later years, closer examination of the causes of fracasomania (and of the way cognitive dissonance works) caused Hirschman to plead his case a little more loudly and to question the cumulative nature of sequences described in the theory of cognitive dissonance. Direct changes in mentality and behavior thus took on increasing importance in his work and formed the bases of his subsequent theses on the authoritarian turn of events in Latin America and on how to favor the return to democracy.

Let us look more closely, then, at the most recent phase of Hirschman's itinerary. In "Industrialization and Its Manifold Discontents: West, East, and South" (1992), the author reviewed (old and new) proposals put forward in his work from the viewpoint of disenchantment with industrial development. Several advanced western countries form a logical backdrop for an analysis of the dissatisfactions arising out of two very different types of industrialization: the Eastern European kind based on central planning and heavy industry, and the Latin American kind, entrusted (especially at the beginning) to market forces and to consumer goods production.

In this article, fracasomania took on a new aspect: it was no longer seen as driftwood from the past, nor as a product of backwardness and dependency generating hindrances to perception, gloomy vision, and political disasters. It was described, rather, as an explicit dissatisfaction, or—more precisely—as a variety of resistances, criticisms, and anxieties which arise out of development. Disappointment was linked to the fact that development in Latin America, unlike in East Europe, concentrated on consumer goods. Thus, as we saw with import-substituting industrialization, industrial growth in Latin America was considered to be exhausted, incomplete, mutilated, and truncated.

Hirschman underscored the contrast with Gerschenkron who interpreted the industrial development of France, Germany, and Russia in terms of relative backwardness, where social reaction was seen as being motivated by dissatisfaction with insufficient industrialization. The thesis Hirschman put forward was that dissatisfaction was produced *by* industrialization.

Returning to *The Strategy*, one can trace the point of departure of this argument. The dominant tension in underdeveloped nations is no longer simply produced by a desire for change and a resistance created by images based on the group or on the individual. Present reality also expresses keen dissatisfaction for the achievements of contemporary change.[16] Furthermore: the relationship between desire and resistance (plus dissatisfaction) acquires particular significance because cognitive dissonance is recognized as fulfilling its own reinforcing effect in the change or permanence of the status quo. Direct intervention thus becomes a reasonable choice—for example, in the form of a campaign against the obstacles to perception, gloomy vision, and their political effects—which could favor the recognition and galvanization of direct and indirect positive processes (see chapter 5).

However, the lessons of the past, economic difficulties, political advances, and changes in the international scene gradually seem to persuade Latin American public opinion to adopt a different attitude towards the economic and political development of the continent. It is quite natural that Hirschman never tires (1986a, 1987b, 1990a) of registering the symptoms of this change in attitude, which include a new willingness to exchange ideas and to be mutually persuaded, a different evaluation of the past, ECLA's change of heart, and the emergence of "a more doubtful attitude" leading to a more open, eclectic, and skeptical investigation.[17]

As we have said, Hirschman's interest in fracasomania grew out of a policy problem and eventually led him to supply the counterpoint to Gerschenkron's thesis. It would seem that, for Hirschman, the ideologies of economic development are inherently contradictory: they can favor the process of industrialization, but they can also put a brake on it through resistance, anxiety, and frustration bred by the very same ideologies. In any case, ideology has a strong impact on economic and political life.

Gerschenkron, on the other hand, thought that ideology could not play a central role. In 1970, the organizers of a symposium on "Comparative Economic Systems" communicated the topic of his paper which was supposed to be on "Ideology as a System Determinant." Gerschenkron responded to this "mysterious title" by arranging his observations under the following headings: "Theoretical Systems and the Meaning of Ideology," "German Agriculture, Industry, and Ideology," "Ideologies of Industrialization," "Marxian Labor Movement in Central Europe," and "Soviet Russia."

This is where the two friends parted ways. Reinterpreting some of Gerschenkron's arguments from a different angle, Hirschman (1971b) maintained that dominant ideologies definitely have a significant role to play in economic systems; that, as historical experience shows, different ideologies usually lead these systems onto diverging paths; and that the tensions between ideologies and systems can be relieved both by watering down the ideologies and by adapting economic systems to them. Ideology, Hirschman concluded, is not a mask so much as a Nessus shirt that burns whoever wears it.

BASIC MATERIAL FOR A MANUAL

Let us return now to *Journeys*. Unaware of the events looming on the horizon,[18] Hirschman had decided to deal with the matter of progress by starting with the political and ideological atmosphere of the time.[19] The debate at the time raged between the two extremes of effortless and painless reform and total revolution. The three stories in *Journeys* threw light on a vast intermediate area which Hirschman considered worth exploring.

Hirschman argued that it was all too easy to underestimate the difficulties of change brought about by measures considered nonantagonistic (such as technical assistance or health). It was equally easy to overestimate difficulties when confronted with openly antagonistic proposals for shifting wealth and power from one social group to another. Hirschman referred to the authority of Kautsky, Laski, Galbraith, Baran, Edwards, and Sorel[20] to show that, in revolutionary thought, a shift in power relations is a prerequisite for putting such antagonistic measures into practice. This notion (1963a, pp. 254–55) "draws immense strength from the very limited human ability to visualize change and from the fact that it makes only minimal demands on that ability."[21]

On the other hand, he continued, reformers are also to be blamed because, instead of investigating concrete ways to bring about change, they endorsed the link between reform and electoral success (or, more naively still, between reforms and pressures from international experts with offers of financial aid). Hirschman thus concentrated on the "many intermediate stations" between these contrasting extremes with the aim of broadening the boundaries of the possible and with them those of collective freedom. "We shall attempt to show," he wrote (1963a, p. 256), "how elements of both reform and revolution are present in the sequences of policy-making which we have studied. In the process we hope to provide basic materials for what may eventually go into a reformmonger's manual."[22]

Leafing through this manual in the making, we see that the first chapter is entitled "Violence as an Ingredient of Reform." To qualify as revolutionary, violence must be centralized. But in the history of the Colombian countryside it has always been "scattered, local, and decentralized" (1963a, p. 257). For an entire century, peasants have occupied (at various times) land that was not theirs. In the end, this forcible appropriation of large areas was sanctioned by the state, to the extent that, Hirschman claimed, "The willingness of the peasants to occupy uncultivated lands—a kind of entrepreneurial spirit—has powerfully contributed to reform legislation." In Brazil's northeast, decentralized violence "appears in a different guise." It was "unloosened by nature itself which through its droughts, periodically chases hundreds of thousands of *nordestinos* from their homes in search of food, water and work." Violence thus erupted in the form of looting food stores in the cities to spur on relief funds as rapidly as possible.

Hirschman distinguished this form of violence from revolutionary violence due to the fact that it is not immediately countered by the aggrieved party. It is "unilateral, sequential *temporarily unrequited*": at a later date, in fact, the state may forcibly evict the squatters and punish those responsible for the uprising. Or again, nothing may happen for a long time, leaving the situation suspended between repression and political intercession. When this takes place, Hirschman claimed, reforms are sanctioned and social violence is forgotten.[23]

Unlike the "decisive clash" usually associated with revolutionary violence, this is "akin to guerilla warfare," Hirschman argued (1963a, p. 258). The groups practicing it "now advance, now retreat, now lie low and now come forward with a new thrust" to take advantage of the opportunities offered by the evolving situation. Chilean inflation presented a similar picture. Typically, inflation results when demands for additional money on the part of one social group do not meet with immediate resistance, but are countered "indirectly after some time interval by similar demands on the part of other groups." There is reluctance to agree, but also reluctance to disagree to the point of reaching a breaking point.[24]

A final characteristic of this form of violence is that it does not only exert a function of protest and pressure on the authorities; it is a "direct problem-solving activity." The Colombian peasant who occupies land, the northeastern refugee who loots stores, and the Chilean worker who demands a wage increase through strikes are all taking action first and foremost to solve their own problems. These individual decentralized actions signal a problem and set in motion a political process which can produce positive results (in terms of land reform, regional development or redistribution of income). Sequences are set in motion by powerful pressures; conflicts come to the fore and solutions are found following very different patterns from those set out by reformist and revolutionary tradition. Thus, Hirschman concluded, "instead of the sequence: revolution (centralized violence) – redistribution of land, . . . the Colombians invented a highly disorderly sequence: decentralized violence and illegal redistribution of land – legalization of redistribution." (1963a, p. 260).

This "first chapter" of Hirschman's manual-in-the-making shows how the results of this research put traditional rigidity of thought to the test and invoked a more flexible approach. The two "chapters" that follow, "Crisis as an Ingredient of Reform," and "The Emergence of Problems as an Aid to Reform," confirm this view.

Emergency situations or crises represent an important stimulus toward the solution of problems: they concentrate attention, they make it possible to attack well-entrenched interests, they stimulate action and hence learning on a problem into which insight has been low.[25] A wide range of possibilities is thus opened up. Popular imagination, however, Hirschman pointed out, believes that the perception of common dangers will bring the "warring parties 'to their senses'" and result in an equitable solution to the problem "'just in time' i.e. just as the revolution was about to take over." Reformers and revolutionaries, despite their contrasting conceptions, both assume that a total solution exists: "the idea that a national union born out of national emergency is sufficient to solve the country's problems in a comprehensive and integrated fashion is almost as tenacious and powerful a myth as that of 'total change via revolution'" (1963a, p. 263).

The three "problem stories" show that the myth is unfounded. Indeed, Hirschman argued, "situations do not suddenly change from normal to emergency or crisis." Events are marked by "bitter and protracted battles, unexpected switches, and narrow margins of victory." The same emergencies gather for a long time and various groups become "alerted and sensitized" to them, gradually and unevenly. Rather than a "Unique Comprehensive Reform," Hirschman concluded, a "series of attempts at dealing with the problem through changing coalitions" are more likely.[26]

The third "chapter," "The Emergence of New Problems as an Aid to Reform," deals with the possibility of an "'extraneous' second problem B" helping "decision-making on problem A" (1963a, p. 265). Supporters of both causes, Hirschman argued, reinforce one another's problem-solving potential in a mechanism he called "logrolling." Should these problems be seen as interrelated, solving or attenuating one is expected to improve the other. In this case "the backers of one reform will support the other *in their own interest* rather than merely in the expectation of having the favor returned to them." For example, the worsening of the balance-of-payments' deficit in Colombia in 1957–58 induced officials from the Central Bank and Ministry of Finance to support a series of measures on land ownership in the hope that it would have a positive effect on the balance of payments. Similarly, reformers of Brazil's northeast, who in the late fifties intended to reorganize the public works program, found allies in groups from the central and southern parts of the country concerned about the inefficient management of federal funds.

Hirschman pointed out that there are a wide variety of antagonistic and nonantagonistic measures; but typically, policymakers are almost totally absorbed either by one or the other. "The situation reminds one of the well-known psychological experiments," he went on, "where a subject is shown a composite picture in which he perceives either an elegant woman or an old witch . . . and can perhaps learn to switch from one to the other and back, but can never perceive both together" (1963a, p. 268). In later years, Hirschman made further attempts, in various contexts, to penetrate the psychological process behind the shift from one perspective to the other (see the tunnel effect, 1973b, and the disappointment and rebound effect, 1982b; see also chapter 7). In *Journeys*, his aim was to analyze how the switch from an antagonistic to a nonantagonist perspective took place in the context of the three stories.

In the case of droughts in the Brazilian northeast, relief aid and investment funds obtained from abroad were initially seen as being nonantagonistic, that is, as corresponding to the interests of all major groups in the region. However, as the problem was tackled nonantagonistically over an extended period of time, some antagonistic factors inevitably turned up (such as the differential impact of the drought on landowners and rural laborers, or the obstacles to irrigation under existing systems of land tenure). The antagonistic aspect thus captured the collective attention.

Similarly in Colombia the theme of outright land reform became dominant "after experiments with colonization and land taxation were discovered to be unsatisfactory" and after entirely nonantagonistic policies had been in use. In Chile, again, the idea that structural changes largely of an antagonistic kind were required to deal with inflation emerged "with the strength of a fundamental new insight" after protracted use of "merely" monetary measures.

The inside history of the three problem stories (which corresponds to a psychological history of their participants) helps to explain the switch from one perspective to another. Keeping in mind the idea of alternation and oscillation, Hirschman (1963a, p. 270) denied that antagonistic remedies were intrinsically more persuasive than nonantagonistic ones: "the discovery that nonantagonistic remedies are available after antagonistic measures have held sway should in principle be greeted as just as stunning an intellectual discovery as the opposite feat." To perceive that two groups with wholly divergent interests actually have some important interests in common, Hirschman quipped, necessitates about as much imagination as to notice an opposition of interests between groups which, until then, had been considered "partners travelling along the same road toward common objectives."

Hirschman quoted some elements from the stories to illustrate his point, such as the idea of "mutual sacrifices" to solve the problem of Chile's inflation. However, he had great difficulty in finding a "good and effective example" of a shift from the antagonistic to the nonantagonistic perspective. "We are dealing with societies," Hirschman explained (1963a, p. 271), "where existing social order had not been seriously disturbed or questioned at the point of departure of our stories. . . . Only later was this assumed harmony questioned, and the discovery that an antagonistic treatment might be required came as a blinding insight after so long a period of firm belief in, and practice of, the non-antagonistic therapy."

This seems to me an illuminating clarification. The three stories were written as antagonistic perspectives were being discovered in the late fifties and early sixties. I think that *Journeys* was born from Hirschman's observations of the reawakening of a composite antagonistic movement. The shift in perspective that took place, and the social and political energies that were released, make this reawakening particularly interesting and instructive.

The Contriving of Reform

In order to understand the lessons of *Journeys* more clearly, then, we should take into account the years in which the book was written—a period which Hirschman later defined as "exuberant" (1981a, p. 39). In my opinion, we should also (retrospectively) underscore the distinction between the political situation and the intellectual opportunity afforded Hirschman. The political situation soon proved to be unfavorable, while the intellectual opportunity was peculiar. The forces set in motion and the potentialities glimpsed during that period of hope allowed Hirschman to focus on political processes that are often hard to grasp. This is the most hidden aspect of *Journeys*, which can only be revealed through a close reading of the stories, focusing, in particular on their conclusions.[27]

I therefore propose a short detour into Brazil's northeast and into Colombian agrarian reform to catch two "master reformmongers," Celso Furtado and Carlos Lleras Restrepo,[28] "red-handed." In doing so, we must leave aside the great natural and human attractions of Brazil *sertâo,* and of the Colombian *Cordilleras,* and concentrate on the question of how to engineer a significant change in traditional institutional structures without being noticed.

One characteristic of northeast Brazil is the irregularity of its dry spells. The region is compared, not to other arid zones, but to countries such as Italy and Japan, where people make a living cultivating the slopes of a volcano that erupts unpredictably every now and again. Under these circumstances, local populations refuse to concern themselves too much with the possibility of catastrophe; if disaster does come they expect government to step in. In Brazil, government action has mostly been motivated by extended periods of drought (and favored by preexisting programs). In addition to emergency aid, important public works projects—such as roads and dams—were also implemented in order to foster development in the region and employ large masses of labor that had become available because of the drought. Hirschman reconstructed the "jerky character" of government action since the Great Drought of 1877–79 which, he writes, seems to be "molded on the jerky behavior of nature" (1963a, p. 16). We thus learn about the Inspetoria (later called DNOCS), spurred on by Epitacio Pessôa (the only northeasterner ever to become president). We also follow the important decisions and action of the thirties, and the ups and downs which follow the construction of dams.

The long sequence of official efforts met with formidable difficulties. The effects of government action on the position of the various social groups were very different and the sequential solution of building dams in order to exert powerful pressure in favor of irrigation continued to meet with strong opposition. ("The large açudes of the Northeast," as a preamble of one of the numerous irrigation bills states, "serve even today mostly to reflect poetically the beauties of the moonlit nights of the sertâo," [1959, in Hirschman 1963a, p. 47].)

The crisis brought by the 1958 drought emergency, among other "ingredients of reform," made the government "receptive to the idea of a radically new attack." The emergency presented by the record exodus from rural zones, Hirschman wrote, was dealt with in the usual way by airlifts of food stuffs and intensification of public works. The remarkable efficiency of the operations, however, was marred by the fraudulent practices of some DNOCS functionaries and "drought industrialists." Moreover, during the 1958 electoral campaign, DNOCS funds were appropriated to contrast the advancing opposition. These elements caused President Juscelino Kubitschek to send Colonel Orlando Ramagem on a mission to the northeast: his report "painted an extraordinary vivid, somber, and alarming picture of economic, social, and administrative disintegration [of the zone] and concluded by stating that the crisis endangered Brazil's national security" (1963a, p. 72).

This is when the reformmonger, Celso Furtado, made his appearance. In his search for new solutions for the northeast, Kubitschek turned to the National Bank for Economic Development, which was a "natural home" for a group of economists who favored structural changes guided by "a new, managerial and efficient state." In 1959, Furtado, a native of the northeast and intellectual leader of the group, produced in record time "a basic analysis of the region's problems and a plan for action" which Hirschman considered "a highly skilled document" (1963a, p. 73). He painted "a picture of disparity, injustice, and institutional bias" (because inflation and an overvalued exchange rate boosted industry in the center-south and depressed the northeast's exports of natural resources). Furtado proposed a comprehensive development program which aimed to develop a few specific lines of economic policy rather than limit itself to simple programming exercises.

He reasoned that the northeast needed new dynamic exports to flank sugar and cotton crops. It could count on its main comparative advantage, cheap labor, if this "asset" were not held back by the high price of food. Furtado proposed striking out in three directions: to use dammed-up waters and the irrigation basins; to colonize the humid lands and the tropical rainforests of the nearby state of Maranhâo; and to make better use of the rich lands of the *zona da mata* along the Atlantic coast. With each of these proposals Furtado raised highly delicate issues: irrigation encountered problems of expropriation; colonization of the Maranhâo had already been attempted (and later abandoned) in the nineteenth century; the fertile lands of the *zona da mata* were controlled by sugar cane producers.

Nevertheless, it was easy for Furtado to criticize the construction of dams if this was not followed up by utilizing the water. Similarly he could show that the colonization of the Maranhâo was taking place spontaneously in parts. Finally, he intended to establish a link between critics of the *monocultura latifundiaria e escravocrata* of sugar, and firm advocates of the status quo, with the argument of an efficient use of the richest lands—a central theme that he was able to bring into the debate for the first time.

"The competence, freshness, and vigor of the Furtado Report" Hirschman continued (1963a, p. 78), "and the promise of its new approaches made a profound impression. Its inescapable conclusion was not only that agencies working in the Northeast had failed to carry out satisfactorily their assigned tasks, but that a number of crucial policy lines had yet to be tried and mapped out." A new superagency thus began to take shape; the task of the Superintendency for the Development of the Northeast (SUDENE) was to supervise and coordinate existing agencies and promote new initiatives.

Furtado's report, "A Policy of Economic Development for the Northeast," was an important meeting point between analysis, policy, and policy making, and its author proved himself to be both "an outstandingly able economist and economic historian," and "a good politician" (1963a, pp. 73 and 82). It was this dual dimension that caught Hirschman's interest, confirming as it does his view that an intellectual proposal may lead the way to the political solution. Furtado's "tactical gamble" paid off, because, under conditions of political crisis, it activated the logrolling mechanism among the various groups interested in northeast intervention and created a vast coalition in its favor.[29] By attacking entrenched interests and glaring abuses, Furtado's proposals advocated "changes in power positions of administrative agencies and social groups *within* the Northeast," (1963a, p. 81) and launched a political battle characterized by bargaining and alliances. The victory of SUDENE and Furtado depended on a composite coalition made up of: reform governors, popularly elected in 1958, who sat on SUDENE's board of directors; strong, social backing due to unrest, violence, peasant leagues, and drought emergencies; Catholic bishops in the northeast, some senators from the south in favor of reform and the president himself.

This should be kept in mind when, towards the end of *Journeys,* Hirschman posed the question: "the Reformer—Naive or Wily?" His answer is that to start with, he is "a naive and pathetic figure" because he sets out after his reforms "blissfully unaware that the ruling class will never allow this or that antagonistic measure to pass or be effective." However, because he acts and learns from his mistakes and from the resistances he meets with, he often ends up as a "wily individual from whom the revolutionary may well learn a trick or two" (1963a, p. 271).[30] At the end of the Brazilian story, Furtado is presented as precisely that: a highly skillful reformer maneuvering himself around domestic and international situations, transforming the problems of the northeast from the unwanted stepchild of both national and international development agencies to their pet; supporting the need for profound change in traditional relationships; advancing on more or less antagonistic ground, with the strength of his composite coalition behind him to generate "controlled" social transformations.

THE LOGIC OF THE REFORMMONGER

The case of land use and land reform in Colombia[31] provides further evidence that could be used to answer the question, How to pass reforms?[32]

Reformers, Hirschman explained, had tried to achieve better utilization of land by means of a territorial tax and the colonization of public lands. They soon discovered, however, that colonization made only marginal returns and that the tax stirred up opposition without generating support. The switch to land reform can partly be explained by these negative experiences: although it is a more antagonistic measure than taxation, campesinos and even small and medium-sized landowners usually lend their support. Moreover, large landowners will not fight hard against reform because each one thinks either that it will never be applied, or that it will never involve him directly. "Taking full advantage of such constellations, our 'naive' reformer has by now turned into a master tactician who manages to slip through a workable reform" (1963a, p. 272). The man, of course, is Carlos Lleras Restrepo.

After Hirschman's Colombian period, he always maintained relations of friendship and cooperation with Colombian progressive intellectuals, politicians, and entrepreneurs. Carlos Lleras Restrepo was (and still is) a prominent leader. A member of the Liberal Party, a *grand commis de l'état* since Bretton Woods, minister, vice president, and then president of the Republic, Lleras has unquestionably had an outstanding role in Colombian political life since the war.

"Reform," Hirschman wrote (1963a, p. 122), "requires a special combination of circumstances, a sequence of moves in the course of which the ruling groups acquiesce to, or even connive in, the nibbling away of their own privileges. Viewed in this fashion, reform is a feat of contriving which has a chance of being accomplished only if liberal use is made of some of the more wily arts of bargaining." Hirschman was referring to the years that he was in Colombia (that is, the "second phase" of the story, see note 31). His argument is all the more true of the third phase that was brought about in the mid-1960s by renewed fear of the peasant movement and *El incendio agrario* as *Semana* called it. Some leading politicians maintained that land reform was the only alternative to revolution. "Carlos Lleras Restrepo may have shared this belief or, as an expert politician, he may have sensed a unique opportunity to shake the National Front government.[33] . . . In any event, he now took hold of the situation with unique determination, tenacity and intelligence" (1963a, p. 143).

Lleras encouraged political leaders from different parties to put their opinions on the agrarian issue in writing; Lleras drew the conclusion that their points of view were not unbridgeable. He therefore decided to set up a National Agrarian Committee "in which all political tendencies, as well as the Church, the Army and various interest groups were to be represented." After a brief but intense period of work, the committee produced a unanimous report and proposed a bill that was immediately brought to the Senate. Here it was discussed and amended before being passed on to the House, which was able to ratify it just in time—that is to say, shortly before the presidential elections brought about a change in legislative voting procedure that would inevitably have kept the bill from passing.

What are the secrets of "revolution by stealth," as Hirschman called it with a mixture of admiration and disbelief? Since it was not difficult to reach a consensus on the order of priority which the future land reform was to follow,[34] the principal fights were over the exact price and the manner of payment for expropriated lands. The collective fascination with this bargaining process may have helped other important political decisions to be pushed through. Examples were the creation of the Colombian Institute of Agrarian Reform (INCORA), and the approval of laws against the *minifundio* and *latifundio,* in favor of irrigation, and for the reutilization of uncultivated land.

The beginning of modernization in the agriculturally richest and best located farm areas had reduced the original size of the problem and had made it possible to stage a successful attack on the more backward elements of the agrarian structure: semifeudal residuals that continued to exist within a modernizing society and that could not be easily dissolved by market forces alone.[35] Such an unnatural and improbable event as the breakup of large estates—a centuries-old system of land management—was made possible by two principal pressures: social agitation in rural areas and the observable fact that low levels of agricultural production had reoccurring negative consequences on inflation and on the balance of payments.

Hirschman claimed that the action of the peasant movement had a prevalently indirect effect, while the political circumstances of the National Front (in particular the danger of unpopularity for the Liberal Party, and the Conservative Party's desire to sweeten the pill of the shift of power) played an important role. In becoming the champion of the reform, Lleras was thus responding to basic political realities and pressures of public opinion and he consequently invested most of his energies at a parliamentary level.

This leads us back to the matter of "reformmongering." The tactic of "divide and reform" corresponds to an idea of Helio Jaguaribe's, according to which social conflicts represent not indomitable class struggles, but contrasts within each class that divide dynamic sectors from static and parasitic ones. Reforming action, moreover, becomes easier when economic development is already under way and when the antagonistic part of the proposal can be limited—for example by putting pressure on absentee landlords and neutralizing (or involving) modernizing landlords. While deterioration usually leads to action, it is also true that action may be stimulated when the problem begins to recede. This was the case in the struggle against colonialism, as well as in Colombian land reform.

Hirschman later claimed that in writing *Journeys* he pieced together significant episodes featuring decisions that seemed from the viewpoint of cultural climate or socio-political structure, a priori unlikely. From these episodes he drew "a number of fairly low-level generalizations about the conditions which permit these 'surprising' or 'out of character' policy decisions to be taken" (1975, now in 1981a, p. 158). But this understatement (typical of the author) must not deceive us. He was not only interested in the cases themselves; he also attributed great value to the surprise effect that they created. "While I may have been excessively intent on making discoveries of the 'out of character' sort," he added, "I was thereby reacting against most previous analysts who seemed to be determined never to be surprised by anything."

This confirms the distinction between political circumstances and intellectual opportunity. While the significance of the stories may seem limited considering the Latin American political situation at the time, the role they played in Hirschman's research was decisive. Hence Hirschman's insistence on the fact that "the gist of the book is in the details of these stories, in the detours and byways which are testimony to the 'ingenuity, originality and flexibility with which backward countries try to solve the specific problems of their development' as Professor Gerschenkron put it once" (1963b, p. 40; see also 1963a, p. 1). The point is that he had succeeded in reconstructing the three stories and in becoming a witness to the processes inherent in them.

This seems to me an interesting aspect of *Journeys*. Evidently, some events of the period put Hirschman on the right path: they convinced him that it was possible to write an unusual book based on stories that presented decisions that were a priori improbable (and therefore surprising) into which he could instill the knowledge of policy making in Latin America (and other continents) that he had accumulated over the years. He was thus able to demonstrate that the state reacts to political and social stimuli in such a way that is no less automatic than that between entrepreneurs and the market. This, in its turn, allowed him to identify the functions of the various protagonists in the story (conservatives and progressives, in society and in public management), and the complexity of the political and social processes at work.

"In fine," the author wrote concluding his book (1963a, p. 275), "the roads to reform are narrow and perilous, they appear quite unsafe to the outside observer however sympathetic he may be, *but they exist.* Having become acquainted with their twists and turns throughout this book, we emerge with a heightened consciousness of the difficulties facing Latin American policymakers; but also and foremost, with a new appreciation of the many unsuspected and unorthodox opportunities for manoeuvre and advance."[36]

5

Possibilism and Social Change

In this chapter, I will consider some issues which branch off from *Journeys*. The first deals with political leadership, a vital quality for Hirschman. Mentioned at the end of *Journeys*, Hirschman later reproposed the theme in order to analyze leadership ability. Skill and the better known aspect of charisma, in Hirschman's view, form a combination that turns out to be contradictory: ability involves a correct evaluation of the situation, beyond collective perceptions and beliefs; while charisma expresses and represents exactly those kinds of mass feelings.

The second is the matter of the unintended consequences of human actions—a key instrument of possibilism that is explicitly discussed from *Development Projects Observed* (1967) on, but that is already present in *The Strategy* and *Journeys*. In the introduction to *A Bias for Hope* (1971), unintended consequences are proposed as a means of kindling perception and imagination in order to increase alertness when confronted with dialectical processes. These take on a primary role in Hirschman's methodology, encouraging Hirschman to propose his own cognitive style as an alternative to the coercive and senseless theorizations that hamper the understanding of social phenomena.

I will go on to examine some important features of Hirschman's approach: the role of story-telling, the history of events alongside that of longer periods of time, the importance of uniqueness together with that of regularity, and the constellations of events that characterize both large-scale changes and less dramatic ones.

I will then turn to Hirschman's political development in the 1960s, examining some short articles written during the same period as *Journeys* which testify to Hirschman's commitment to developing mutual understanding and collaboration between the two Americas.

SKILL AND CHARISMA

By means of a process that will become almost customary in his later works,[1] in the last page of *Journeys*, Hirschman unexpectedly introduced a theme. Partly new, this theme was consigned to further research. There was much talk in *Journeys* of Latin American reformmongers needing to gain new allies. This of course, Hirschman added, meant maintaining old allies as well: if he is on the left, the reformer will postpone for as long as possible, and might even avoid, any break with his old radical friends. Thus, while he pursues change by negotiating new alliances, he will not stop agitating for change.

The ability to negotiate, in fact, presupposes the ability—be it exceptional or limited—to agitate for reform. Although Hirschman spoke at length about the former quality, he did not say a word about the latter. In order to create a majority to pass reforms, past allies—both reformers and revolutionaries—are needed as much as new ones. Leadership is not only skill: it is also agitation and hence the ability to convince, and to exercise influence over others.

Thus almost imperceptibly, with an objective and captivating narration that recalls Gustave Flaubert's *L'éducation sentimentale*, Hirschman reshuffled the cards on the table. "These two tasks are of course so different," he wrote (1963a, p. 275), "that they are best performed if they can be dealt out to *several* principal actors who feel quite independent of each other, in the manner of the struggle for Italian unification which was able to draw on the highly diverse talents of Cavour, a master contriver, and of Mazzini and Garibaldi, who filled the role of conspirators and agitators. But sometimes there is only one chief actor who, to be successful, must combine both roles . . . —a highly risky assignment, though perhaps also rather an entertaining one!"[2]

The theme was taken up again in "Underdevelopment, Obstacles to the Perception of Change, and Leadership" published in *Daedalus* (summer 1968) as part of a symposium on "Philosophers and Kings: Studies in Leadership" organized by the American Academy of Arts and Sciences.

Encouraged by a series of factors—the quality of the participants, the presence of various fields of study, and the gallery of leaders analyzed, such as Gandhi, Nkrumah, Ataturk, De Gaulle, and Bismarck—Hirschman used this occasion to exchange ideas and put the issue into focus. He wrote the first section of the essay (see chapter 4) on his return from one of his Latin American trips. He later added a second, rather brief, section linked to discussions at the meeting.

Research into the obstacles to the perception of change in underdeveloped countries had been surprisingly prolific; this success troubled Hirschman and led him to wonder what good leadership required. It is at this point that the argument was overturned: while leadership is needed to overcome the obstacles to perception of change, the reverse is also true, since the ability to sift out erroneous beliefs and evaluations is a vital feature of leadership. It thus became clear that representing the prevailing perceptions cannot be the only attribute of leadership,[3] making it possible for Hirschman to cut short the Weberian discussion of the question (partly reflected in "The Theory of Charismatic Leadership" by Robert Tucker presented at the symposium) and to address the aspect of skill.

It is not surprising (for readers of *Journeys*) that Hirschman called upon Carlos Lleras Restrepo to illustrate this point. Elected president in 1966, but lacking the two-thirds majority needed to pass important legislation, Lleras and his administration seemed doomed to *immovilismo*. But during his first year in office, the President frequently demonstrated his determination to push for important socio-economic reforms, so much so that he was able to create the majority required. "Here is a leader," Hirschman commented (1971a, p. 339), "who excels at perceiving opportunities, takes great pleasure in his special powers of perception, acts successfully on what he perceives, and strengthens his claims to leadership as a result."

"In recent theorizing on leadership," Hirschman continued (1971a, p. 341), "we probably have had an overemphasis on the charisma component—and in recent practice, we certainly have had an overdose of it and a corresponding underdose of skill, particularly in the Third World." A minimum of skill, he argued, is indispensable if leadership is to be successful (while he made no mention at all of a minimum of charisma). Revolutionaries and reformers would do their jobs better if they trained themselves to overcome obstacles to the perception of change and sought to take advantage of the opportunities that arise.

Hirschman's analysis was more balanced than it was in *Journeys*. Using an indirect approach, he underscored two contrasting components of leadership: skill requires a stronger than average ability to perceive change, while charisma is partly based on a rejection of such perception. The two requirements, he explained, are often at odds with each other and the most effective leaders are those, who, in one way or another, can deal with both.

Hirschman was not very interested, however, in delineating the various ways in which these two characteristics have gradually been combined in the history of politics. After having paid homage to Lenin's ability to rouse people to action, the article dealt with the disjunction between the two characteristics, referring again to the division of labor between Garibaldi and Cavour during the Risorgimento, and explaining that charisma may prevail during a period of mobilization, while the need for skill grows with that of political administration. He also showed that various authors (including Dankwart Rustow, Stanley and Inge Hoffman—all present at the symposium—and Machiavelli) recognized the need for, and the difficulties of, such a sequence. Finally, he came very close to posing the question of the degree of oscillation between the two characteristics.[4]

Thus the problem of relative predominance and of conciliation between the two aspects of leadership remains open. During the Mexican Revolution, for example, Hirschman argued (1971a, p. 340, and pp. 347–49) with reference to *Zapata and the Mexican Revolution* by John Womack, Jr., the passage from a more charismatic leadership to a more skilled one came about fortuitously through the death of Zapata and the emergence of his secretary, Gildardo Magaña, as commander-in-chief.

Gildardo, Womack maintained, had learned the art of mediation; not that of compromise or transaction, but the ability to detect why various positions are in conflict, and to recognize potential areas of agreement and conciliation. His success as a skillful negotiator of ever new alliances, is contrasted by Womack with the disasters created by the rigid and sectarian Palafox who had preceded Magaña at the head of Zapata's secretariat. By alternating struggle and negotiation and by backing Obregón at the right moment, Magaña was able to transform Zapatista guerrillas into local administrators and members of the national coalition.[5]

A second example is the experience of Carlos Lleras Restrepo. During preliminary research for the continuation of *Journeys* (which became part of "Policy-making and Policy Analysis in Latin America—A Return Journey") Hirschman made a survey of Colombian economic planning under the presidency of Carlos Lleras (1966–70). For the first time in its tempestuous history, the Planning Office—to which the author had lent his services between 1952 and 1954—functioned properly. Using cost-benefit analyses, it played an important role in advising on basic economic policy decisions and even more in contributing to public investment choices. But there is another side to the argument: "There is no doubt that the delegation of decision-making to a body of 'cold' experts had a sizeable political cost for President Lleras, the magnitude of which he probably did not perceive correctly" (1975, now in 1981a, p. 163).

Lleras lost the nomination of the Liberal Party for a second mandate. A first reason for his defeat was ascribable to enmities that Lleras incurred by curtailing traditional pork-barrel spending. Hirschman then mentioned an indirect, negative effect of the success achieved; the international financial availability, which rewarded the procedures and the competence of the Planning Office, relieved the pressures for necessary fiscal reforms. Finally, he asserted, "these orderly procedures in which the government took such pride may have made it impossible to attack some of the more basic tasks which the Colombian economy faced . . . , such as urban reform or vigorous prosecution of the land reform. Making progress in these conflict-ridden areas would have required a readiness to manoeuvre and to surprise which was not easily compatible with the orderly decision making in which the principal policy-makers were revelling."

One may put forward the hypothesis, then, that Lleras lost the battle not only from the point of view of skill but also of charisma, since he underemployed his ability as a political leader to represent collective passions and interests. By relying too much on the "propensity to plan," to the detriment of the "propensity to experiment" (see chapter 2), he may have been captured by a kind of technocratic fascination.

POSSIBILISM AND UNINTENDED CONSEQUENCES

While still professor of International Economic Relations at Columbia University, Hirschman had planned another research project: a study on some investment projects financed by the World Bank. This research was conducted in 1964–65, initially in Washington, D.C., and then, with Sarah Hirschman's active collaboration, in the eleven countries in which the projects were located. The work was published by the Brookings Institution in 1967 under the title of *Development Projects Observed.*

Development project is a term—the author explained in the introduction—that denotes purposefulness, a specific location, something qualitatively new, and even the expectation that a sequence of further development will be set in motion. The study of these privileged elements of the growth process belongs to development economics (and will be discussed in the following chapter). However, by concentrating his attention on different field work from that examined in *Journeys,* Hirschman might also have wanted to develop some threads of the previous research. It is this collateral effect described in the well-known prologue to *Development Projects:* "The Principle of the Hiding Hand," that is of interest here.

Let us briefly recall Hirschman's argument. Starting with the poetic example of the flowering of bamboo, the raw material of the Karnaphuli paper mill in Pakistan, and of the unexpected availability of alternative raw materials, Hirschman suggested that every project is accompanied by two kinds of potential developments. The first is a series of unsuspected threats; the second, a series of unexpected remedial actions that can be taken whenever the former become real. If the planners of a project knew the difficulties awaiting them, they would probably never become involved in it and, therefore, they would never reach the alternative solutions that often make their project valid. The reason, Hirschman explained, is that creativity always comes as a surprise, so that when success clearly depends on it, we dare not rely on it: that is to say, we underestimate our creativity. Consequently, the only way to mobilize our creative resources is to imagine the undertaking as being simpler than it actually is: this is the benign function of the "hiding hand."

This phenomenon makes it possible to reinterpret certain aspects of human behavior: "Mankind always takes up only such problems as it *thinks* it can solve" (not that it can solve—as Marx claimed). When one is actually grappling with these problems, Hirschman explained, they are generally found to be more difficult than expected; by that time, however, one is already committed, and so one reacts and may at times be successful.

My impression is that this idea unlocks a general aspect of Hirschman's work. As we have seen, the problem examined in *The Strategy* is to set in motion not only development but also a mechanism of reaction and personal change. Likewise, in *Journeys*, we found a problem-solving process that passes through involvement and learning. Reformmongers and leaders embark on their projects, generally helped by the hiding hand, and fight to overcome unexpected difficulties. When Hirschman finished "Underdevelopment, Obstacles to the Perception of Change, and Leadership" (after having published *Development Projects*), he undoubtedly thought his leader, up against problems of charisma and skill, had underestimated the troubles ahead (as well as his own creative skills and those of others).

The effort of identifying ways of thinking that are useful for decision making was intended to remove the surrounding haze as much as possible, bringing the self-deceptive process to manageable proportions. "The hiding hand," Hirschman wrote in *Development Projects* (1967b, p. 35), "does its work essentially through ignorance of ignorance, of uncertainties, and of difficulties. Therefore, if we wish to avoid immoderate use of it in making project decisions, our first task is to become aware in some detail of the uncertainties that affect projects and of the resulting difficulties they may have to encounter and overcome."

Let us turn now to the introduction of *A Bias for Hope*.[6] The first section deals with the political dimensions of economic phenomena, while the second reveals a preoccupation with processes of social change that is expressed in certain hopes and convictions: in a word, in politics. Its intention is thus to contribute to improving the reality that surrounds us.[7]

In the introduction, Hirschman explored the idea of two "opposite types of endeavors" coexisting on an equal footing: the search for regularity, balanced relations, and uniform sequences on the one hand and, on the other, the study of multiplicity, creative disorder, and the uniqueness of a specific event.[8] "Upon inspection," Hirschman wrote at the end of *Development Projects* (1967b, p. 186), "each project turns out to represent a *unique constellation* of experiences and consequences, of direct and indirect efforts." In a later essay he added: "large-scale social change is a unique, nonrepeatable and ex ante highly improbable complex of events" (1971a, pp. 359–60). A basic need, therefore, encouraged Hirschman to make use of both the unique and the general, the unexpected and the expected, the possible and the probable. Responding to this need, he committed himself with perseverance and tenacity to widening the limits of what is, or is perceived to be, possible, thus widening the discretionary margins of the process of change.

This fundamental bent can be seen clearly in the seven essays Hirschman addressed to rich and developing countries.[9] Referring to developing countries (as in "Obstacles to Development" and in "Underdevelopment, Obstacles to the Perception") he found "an exceptionally good hunting ground for exaggerated notions of absolute obstacles, imaginary dilemmas, and one-way sequences. The essence of the possibilist approach consists in figuring out avenues of escape from such straitjacketing constructs in any individual case that comes up." For this purpose, the author added (1971a, p. 29), it is useful to master some conceptual devices, such as the blessing in disguise, cognitive dissonance, and the unintended consequences of human action. An analysis of the first two notions[10] led the way to the third general foundation of possibilism.

Just as the principle of oscillation is examined at the end of the first part of the introduction, the notion of the unintended consequences of human actions is theorized at the end of the second.[11] Hirschman traced the ancestry of the concept to Vico, Mandeville, Adam Smith, and others. It was cast—he explains—in a particular mold in order to show that activities such as the pursuit of material gain have a beneficial effect on the functioning, stability, and rationality of the existing social system. And the fact that, until then, many critics of this view were social reformers made it difficult to exploit its potential for understanding and foreseeing change. Thus, Hirschman concluded, "the idea that change . . . is something to be wrought by the undeviatingly purposeful actions . . . is certainly far more widespread than the view that change can also occur because of original side effects of human actions which might even have been expressly directed toward system maintenance" (1971a, pp. 34–35).

Hirschman illustrated his argument with an episode from the recent history of Peru, where a military government which had gained power in 1968 decided to expropriate the large sugar cane plantations along the coast as part of its land reform program. Two explanations were often given for this. In the 1950s, the technical training of upper-echelon Peruvian officers was supplemented by a course in citizenship. Although this was meant to maintain the status quo, it allowed officers to learn about modern theories on social integration and development. During the 1960s, moreover, these officers conducted an antiguerrilla campaign. It is generally agreed that the experience left its mark. Instead of setting in motion the sadly familiar psychological mechanism of progressive brutalization, these officers decided to change the status quo, which they considered to be at the root of such cruelty.[12]

Hirschman united in this episode the basic devices of possibilism. First, there was the blessing in disguise of the fact that the country's intellectual elite was so restricted. This made it inevitable that the officers should be placed in the hands of the very few Peruvian social scientists, almost all of whom were oriented towards progressive ideas. Second, the example shows the limits of the theory of cognitive dissonance (see chapter 3) and of all cumulative notions—such as Mydral's process of circular causation, Merton's self-fulfilling prophecy, reinforcement and feedback processes, etc. According to Hirschman, this was "an undialectical and, what is worse, unperceptive and unimaginative way of thinking." Conversely, "one important way of rekindling perception and imagination and of developing an alertness to dialectical, as opposed to purely cumulative, social processes is to pay attention to the unintended consequences of human actions" (1971a, p. 34).[13]

The fact that the history of change is regarded as a process guided by free will, or as one in which men (and ruling classes) continually outsmart themselves in their effort to reproduce and preserve existing order, has to do with our perception. In the real world, after all, these two processes are usually linked, since the former may come to the fore after the latter has done the spade-work or, alternatively, the latter may silently advance while the former is in the limelight. The Peruvian story contained elements of both these situations. Once again, Hirschman was dealing with the switch from one aspect to another, with sequence and oscillation.

Concluding *The Passions and the Interests* (1977b, pp. 130–31), Hirschman showed how discoveries symmetrically opposed to the unintended consequences are also possible and valid. On the one hand, social actions may produce unintended effects; on the other, they are frequently undertaken to produce effects that then fail to materialize. It is the existence of such illusory expectations that plays an important role in social decisions. Exploration and discovery of them therefore "help render the social change more intelligible." Unlike unintended effects that actually take place, unintended effects that fail to materialize can only be understood by going back to the expectations expressed at a given moment in time, because when these expectations are not met, they will very often be forgotten and even repressed so as to claim the legitimacy of the order that had arisen in the meantime.

Continuing to generalize from the idea of the "hiding hand," Hirschman based *Shifting Involvements* on the paradoxical idea that *"men think they want one thing and then upon getting it, find out to their dismay that they do not want it nearly as much as they thought or do not want it at all and that something else, of which they were hardly aware, is what they really want"* (1982b, p. 21). This plethora of unrealized aspirations are related to private and public happiness and underlie shifts from private interest to public action, and vice versa.

According to standard economic theory, individuals display specific preferences through their choices. The formation of and the changes in these preferences, usually shelved by theory, are dealt with in the process triggered by unrealized expectations and the experience of disappointment. Hirschman used his analysis of the decision, discussed in *Shifting Involvements,* to pass from one style of life focused on private pursuits to another dedicated to the public good (or vice versa) to talk about a more general phenomenon: man's ability to reflect on past experience and his consequent decision to confirm or change the preferences that guided him (see Hirschman 1982b, 1984e, and chapter 2).

These devices of possibilism thus sharpen our perception of the paths that lead to change. Naturally, we cannot expect them to reveal new, previously undetected paths: "they are only meant to help defend the right to a non-projected future as one of the truly inalienable right of every person and nation; and to set the stage for conceptions of change to which the inventiveness of history and a 'passion for the possible' are admitted as vital actors" (1971a, p. 37).

THE COMPULSION TO THEORIZE AND THE LESSONS OF HISTORY

"The Search for Paradigms as a Hindrance to Understanding" (1970), now included in the authoritative reading on the methodology of social sciences edited by P. Rabinow and W. M. Sullivan (1979), contained an explicit rejection of the tendency towards compulsive and mindless theorization. In the academic world, Hirschman wrote (1971a, p. 342), "the prestige of the theorist is towering," and in the United States, the social sciences are forced into making intellectual shortcuts by a hegemonic power. Revolutionaries, moreover, are encouraged to theorize by the strength that derives from the conviction of holding the key to reality. Searching for an alternative, Hirschman concentrated on the types of cognitive style that hinder or promote understanding. He introduced his argument by referring to two books by young scholars from the United States: *Patterns of Conflict in Colombia* by James Payne and *Zapata and the Mexican Revolution* by John Womack, Jr.

Hirschman went straight to the heart of the problem. "Within the first few pages of his book," he wrote (1971a, pp. 343–44), "Payne presents us triumphantly with the key to the full and complete understanding of the Colombian political system. The rest of the book is a demonstration that the key indeed unlocks all conceivable doors of Colombian political life, past, present, and future."

Payne claimed that, with the help of questionnaires and interviews, he had discovered that politicians in Colombia are motivated primarily by status considerations rather than by genuine interest in the programs and policies. Starting with this paradigm, he drew up thirty-four hypotheses covering all possible aspects of the Colombian political scene. His results showed Colombians to be selfish, ambitious, unscrupulous, unprincipled, and never "on the brink of anything." His conclusion was that it was futile to anticipate any change through industrialization or agrarian reform. To this Hirschman retorted: the Colombians "will just have to go on living in their self-made hell while Mr. Payne, after his seven-month diagnostic visit . . . , has returned to his own, so much more fortunate section of the hemisphere" (1971a, pp. 345–56).

Hirschman's black humor hardly soothed his indignation, although Payne's book is certainly not the only example of extreme views. His argument would not have had the same strength if Hirschman had not been able to count both on his own experience, and on Womack's remarkable book. "Strongly repelled" by Payne's book, he found Womack's way of telling the story of Zapata and the Zapatistas "extraordinarily appealing."

Womack's book is a study of social history: "not an analysis but a story, because the truth of the revolution in Morelos," Womack claimed (1965, p. x), "is in the feeling of it, which I could not convey through defining its factors but only through telling of it. The analysis that I could do and that I thought pertinent I have tried to weave into the narrative, so that it would issue at the moment right for understanding it." "And indeed," Hirschman commented (1971a, p. 344), "what is remarkable about the book is the continuity of the narrative and the almost complete, one might say Flaubertian, absence from its pages of the author who could have explained, commented, moralized, or drawn conclusions. Yet whoever reads through the book will have gained immeasurably in his understanding not only of the Mexican revolution, but of peasant revolutions everywhere, and Womack's very reticence and self-effacement stimulate the readers' curiosity and imagination."[14]

Later in the text Hirschman returned to Womack's proposition that "the truth of the revolution in Morelos is in the feeling of it." After defining it as "at first sight rather shocking" (1971a, p. 360), he maintained that perhaps Womack was talking not only about the truth, but also about the main lesson of the revolution. Womack's book was free of paradigms; he succeeded in transmitting a knowledge of the Mexican Revolution by telling a story with a minimum of analysis. The book was an antidote to many of the models and paradigms that social scientists felt obliged to build.

But Hirschman's objective was clearly not to prefer stories to models: without paradigms, he often remarked, one cannot even begin to think. He used the example of *Zapata and the Mexican Revolution*, rather, to plead for a change in cognitive style. "I would suggest," he wrote with reference to Latin America (1971a, p. 354), "a little more 'reverence for life,' a little less straitjacketing of the future, a little more allowance for the unexpected—and a little less wishful thinking."[15]

"The cognitive style," he added, "that is, the kind of paradigms we search out, the way we put them together, and the ambitions we nurture for their powers—all this can make a great deal of difference." In this sense, Womack's book is proof of the need to change style.

A question regarding the meaning of *Zapata and the Mexican Revolution*, however, remains unanswered. At the end of his essay, when illustrating his own "cognitive pleading," Hirschman suggested that "large scale social change typically occurs as a result of a unique constellation of highly disparate events and is therefore amenable to paradigmatic thinking only in a very special sense" (1971a, p. 354).[16]

Large-scale changes over a brief period of time, he explained, are unpredictable and nonrepeatable. They are unpredictable and ex ante highly improbable because their success depends on the surprise effect, and nonrepeatable because "forewarned is forearmed." The unique and opaque character of history as it accelerates has often been remarked upon, and is made clear in Womack's book. As the anthropologist Max Gluckman observed (1965, p. 286; cited in 1971a, p. 358), since scientific method cannot deal with unique complexes of multiple events, "the accounts of the actual course of events which produce change therefore necessarily remain historical narrative."

"The architect of social change," Hirschman explained later on (1971a, p. 360), "can never have a reliable blueprint. Not only is each house he builds different from any other that was built before, but it also necessarily uses new construction materials and even experiments with untested principles of stress and structure. Therefore what can be most usefully conveyed by the builders of one house is an understanding of the experience that made it at all possible to build under these trying circumstances" (1971a, p. 360). It thus becomes clear how a historian like Womack can reveal, on the one hand, the uniqueness of such events and suggest, on the other, that the most valuable lessons can be learned from history.

From the possibilist viewpoint, therefore, large scale change is seen in terms of short-term history, and casually oversteps the artificial barriers that separate the human sciences. To avoid being ensnared by rigid logic, however, we may remember that possibilist interest in short-term history does not rule out medium and long-term history; that important analytical lessons may be drawn from large scale changes; and that historical reconstruction may play a significant role in related fields.

Hirschman later stated (1986b, p. 171) that he was happy with the "turn of the wheel" that brought the history of events back to the forefront. This was a reaction against the history of the *longue durée* which had dominated French (and international) historiography for quite some time. "Following in detail the process of a revolution," he explained, "gives us a strong feeling . . . for the many might-have-beens of history, for narrowly and disastrously missed opportunities as well as for felicitous and surprising escapes from disaster." Rejecting a mistaken need for completeness,[17] Hirschman's insistence on events, details, and micro-aspects, came from the fact that he was attracted by possible change (political, economic, cultural).

Nevertheless, this passion did not stop Hirschman from becoming involved (in "Ideologies of Economic Development in Latin America") in a history of ideas of that continent after independence, nor from dealing (in *Journeys*) with three long-term and intractable problems. In *The Passions and the Interests* he showed how the prevailing concept of human nature had been gradually impoverished over three centuries. He then examined, in *The Rhetoric of Reaction*, the two-hundred year period during which the rhetoric of reaction developed. Thus, (see note 21, chapter 3), a dominant interest in the detailed history of events often finds its logical alter ego in historical theses based on the long term.[18]

On the other hand, as in *Journeys*, Hirschman does not back away from the lessons that can be learned from large-scale changes. Although each change is unpredictable and nonrepeatable, by comparing them, and focusing on where they converge and diverge, it becomes possible to understand them more deeply and to generalize. This is true not only for the Latin American style of policy making, but also for the democratic outcome of the revolutions. Hirschman analyzes the latter by taking up some general comments made on a paper by Samuel Eisenstadt (1980b, now in 1986b). He develops an approach that leads to some fortuitous and, a priori, rather unlikely combinations, which are, however, less discouraging than simply prescribing "overriding preconditions for redemocratization."

Hirschman's argument, reminiscent of Womack's work, was that the improbable sequence "conjures up the image of a rare conjunction of circumstances *such as we are familiar with from history.* The mere fact of finding or imagining such a conjunction gives confidence that, even if this particular one cannot be repeated or translated into reality, there must be some other similarly farfetched ones that history has up its sleeve. For history is nothing if not farfetched—unfortunately, one must add, in the direction of both good and evil" (1986b, pp. 174–75).

Finally, historical reconstruction, even in terms of large-scale social change, certainly does not mean that theoretical elaboration is unnecessary. On the contrary, the latter is often largely dependent on the former. The careful investigation of facts and historical (and literary) narration is a significant element in many fields of social and economic change. This can be seen in the micro-Marxist approach in those historical studies that provide the most illuminating contributions to the subject of linkage,[19] or in Hirschman's small book, *Getting Ahead Collectively* (1984), with its account of grass-roots experience of development.

Almost without realizing it, we have returned to the general comments made in the introduction to *A Bias for Hope:* to the relationships between uniqueness and regularity, factual reconstructions and models, and to a possibilism that focuses on proposals and identifies ways out. Whoever is interested in large-scale change—Hirschman wrote in "The Search for Paradigms" after citing Althusser and Lenin[20]—must be on the lookout, ready to grasp whatever rare clues appear on the horizon. He must be possessed, as Kierkegaard said, by "the passion for what is possible."

Large-scale changes, exceptional both for their nature and for their "specific weight," make us strongly aware of the need to consider uniqueness, and to develop possibilism. As soon as the individual lesson has been learned, however, we realize that it has a general meaning. Cognitive reflection on exceptional events may help us focus more successfully on the vaster and more pedestrian reality that surrounds us.

A SMALL POLITICAL CONTRIBUTION

Journeys did not only address scholars and Latin American governments. Hirschman stated more than once that he had North Americans in mind. He intended to show them that the Latin American reality was much more complex than they imagined and that the decision-making style of its governments sometimes led to positive results. But this was only the tip of the iceberg.

Although Hirschman was a member of the progressive camp, he had often expressed reservations about the theories underlying progressive thought, especially when some of its representatives used economic theory, in an a priori way, to deduce "revealed" prescriptions that could be imposed on other countries. I am thinking in particular about the 1954 conference on investment criteria and economic development (see chapter 2). On that occasion, Hirschman faced a group of Keynesian economists, most of whom identified with *A Proposal: Key to a More Effective Foreign Policy* by Max Millikan and Walt W. Rostow. This proposal was intended to give the United States foreign policy a new expansionistic direction based on aid, some reform, and development planning. Together with *The Stages of Economic Development* by Rostow (1960), *A Proposal* had circulated widely, becoming the basic text of the so-called "Charles River Approach" to foreign aid. This approach emerged at the end of the 1950s, as a united effort by M.I.T.'s Center for International Studies and the Harvard-M.I.T. seminar on economic development.

The group of economists that headed these initiatives began by criticizing notions of traditional aid tied to projects, which had prevailed during the postwar period. They maintained that development depended on an adequate overall investment and on corresponding fiscal, monetary, and exchange policies. They proposed to increase aid considerably, linking grants to development programs agreed upon together with the recipient country. Furthermore, they did not insist that the recipient countries had to "put their houses in order" by adopting orthodox economic policies and by opening their economies to foreign investment (as happened during the Eisenhower era and later during the Reagan era). On the contrary, these economists saw the need for a certain amount of reform in land ownership, in the role of the public sector, in political institutions, and in education. Such measures, included in the development plan, were supposed to favor economic growth by giving the recipient countries the social stability and the degree of democracy required.

These ideas may appear seductive (to such an extent that they attracted the attention of important sectors of progressive public opinion). However, they suffer from an irremediable double handicap. On the one hand, they expect the impossible from Latin Americans—easy well-mannered reforms intended to create a favorable climate for private investments. On the other, they propose a dizzying increase in donor country interference in the domestic affairs of the recipient country. What is more, this interference would occur in very broad sectors of its economic, social, and political life, where the administrative knowledge and experience of the donor country is very limited.

Having already battled at length with integrated intrusive plans of every kind, Hirschman observed with anxiety the increasingly authoritative stance of this approach, which would become dominant with the Kennedy administration.[21] As professor, it was logical that he should examine the problem more closely.

Alongside "Ideologies of Economic Development," *Latin American Issues* (1961) contains a short political text, "Abrazo versus Coexistence," that pleads the case for deemphasizing the link between the United States and Latin American countries.[22] According to this text, if we want development in South America we must learn to live with its drive towards self-assertion: North

America's current insistence for a total consensus on ideas and objectives is unrealistic and is seen by Latin Americans as a demand for conformity and subordination. Explicit recognition of the differences between the two zones, less emphasis on inter-American solidarity and stronger institutional structures in South America, on the other hand, would make it possible to increase significantly the spheres of collaboration. These spheres might include prices of natural resources, production projects, the formation of a Latin American common market, etc.

This political alternative to the "Charles River Approach" was elaborated on in two short articles written during the same period, "Second Thoughts on the Alliance for Progress" (1961) and "Critical Comments on Foreign Aid Strategies" (1962). In these articles, Hirschman expressed his bewilderment regarding the evolution of United States policies in Latin America. Although he approved of increasing aid and changing some aspects of traditional behavior (regarding nationalized companies, social development projects, and, more generally, reform), Hirschman insisted that the situation had been misunderstood. He referred to the difficulties of integrated plans, the dangers of reformist neophytism, and the likelihood that all this would give rise to abuse and resentment. In order to change the image presented by the United States, he suggested placing the Panama Canal under international control, starting up a new policy of investments (including their gradual withdrawal when desired), reducing obstacles to imports from Latin America, and developing a policy of aid based on cooperative projects of undisputed worth.

Hirschman also criticized "A Positive Approach to Foreign Aid" (1961), a well-known article by John Kenneth Galbraith. The thesis of the article is that a successful aid policy must be directed towards countries with a suitable level of education, a substantial degree of social justice, a reliable apparatus of public administration, and effective understanding of what development involves. Hirschman, however, asserted that this contained a *reductio ad absurdum* of the concept of aid as the missing link of development (already criticized in *The Strategy*). He suggested that an intelligent policy of aid, tailored to meet the needs of a variety of situations, might give better results than a single formula applied in all circumstances, as was the case with overall development plans.

SEARCHING FOR AN ALTERNATIVE

What can be said about this "small political contribution" at the beginning of the 1960s? First, it is not hard to accept the idea that it lies at the very roots of *Journeys,* along with the other motivations discussed above. There is no doubt that the "journeys towards progress" were also conceived to show the architects of an impossible "Alliance for Progress" how complex the situation was. (We must probably choose between *"alianza e progreso,"* Hirschman wrote in "Second Thoughts" [1971a, p. 182].) It is also true these journeys were intended to force North Americans to recognize the diversity (and dignity) of the decision-making style of their "cousins in the South."[23] Indeed, in the brief text presenting *Journeys,* "How Policy Is Made" (1963), we see an explicit effort to "keep together" the battle on both fronts.[24]

In this work of *trait-d'union* between the two Americas, the brief political articles of 1961–62 take on an important role, and are authentic expressions of those years. In "Critical Comments," for instance, Hirschman recalled the themes of the three stories of *Journeys,* maintaining that providing development aid was a way of becoming involved in the recipient country's battle against backwardness, obstacles, etc. Initially—he wrote, echoing his own experience—the important thing was to participate. Then, little by little, as one gets to know the problems of the country, it is possible to come up with a few hypotheses on the most promising sequences for dealing with them.

However, a problem remains. What do we do if we reach the conclusion that no further progress is possible unless we turn out a corrupt government or distribute land by agrarian reform?

"Naturally," Hirschman replied (1962, now in 1971a, pp. 186–87), "if the situation is the one depicted in Communist textbooks where the government is entirely the expression of one homogeneously reactionary and parasitic ruling clique . . . the best thing for the United States Operations Mission to do is to join the rioting students or the back-bush guerillas. But ordinarily reality is not that simple: the government in question may be unwilling to decree . . . certain reforms that the United States Mission thinks are desirable; at the same time it may be anxious to undertake a variety of unexceptionable tasks of economic development."

In this case, Hirschman argued, financial and technical aid is justified provided we realize the difficult game in which we are involved. The peripheral tasks of development can wage a kind of guerilla warfare against the supporters of reaction. Instead of intensifying the government's prestige and conservatism, foreign aid may weaken it and accelerate reforms. But "in order to be able to use aid in this fashion and not to be unduly surprised by the explosive consequences, one should devise ways of giving aid in a fashion that does not imply a wholesale endorsement of the programs, objectives, and values of the recipient government." Hence, "not to underwrite a development program . . . need not mean the absence of an overall design, or resignation to having just a collection of random projects. It may be a deliberate choice to remain aloof from full cooperation while giving support to certain aspirations."

These brief essays of 1962–63, along with the stories of *Journeys,* move from problem solving to reformmongering. It is clear that Hirschman was advancing along the path of possibilism and social change, part of a collective aspiration which unfortunately met with defeat. In this sense, these contributions are particularly pervaded "by certain common feelings, beliefs, hopes, and convictions, and by the desire to persuade and to proselytize which such emotions usually inspire" (1971a, p. 27).

Later on, this kind of direct approach and language was no longer valid. As an analytical-explanatory device Hirschman resorted to a naive disregard for sociopolitical realities and vested interests (1971a, pp. 28–29). Criticizing the policies of rich countries toward developing countries, he refused to be a part of the realistic-incrementalist camp. However, he also avoided utopian pitfalls. He felt obliged to elaborate his proposals "in concrete institutional detail thereby deliberately creating the optical illusion that they could possibly be adopted tomorrow by men of good will." They would be accessible (and useful) if favorable political conditions were created.

This is the thinking behind two essays: "Foreign Aid: A Critique and a Proposal" (1968) and "How to Divest in Latin America and Why" (1969). These returned to some ideas from the short articles of 1961–62 and transformed them into elaborated possibilist proposals. The former (written with Richard Bird) maintained that foreign aid is "as Janus-faced an institution as can be found." Although it redistributes the income of the rich to the poor (and can accelerate the development of the latter), it is often used as a means of political policy to increase the influence and power of the former.

This is the origin of Hirschman's criticism of the fundamental concepts of the "program approach."[25] He introduced, as an alternative, a proposal capable of overcoming some of the most obvious difficulties that actually occur.[26]

His ingenious solution was based on the involvement of individual taxpayers in the donor country. Upon request they would receive a tax credit (equal to 5 percent of income tax) to be devolved to one or more World Development Funds, created for this purpose. These funds would offer financial assistance to public and private investors in developing countries. Such a mechanism would allow for a gradually increasing transfer of resources that could in time become considerable; it would stimulate public interest by placing international development on a people-to-people basis; it would institutionalize the flow of aid by providing it with continuity and greater independence vis-à-vis the economic and political interests of dominant powers; and it would be devised in such a way as to exert pressure toward the efficient management of the funds collected. While taxpayers would receive only a symbolic compensation (sizable enough to make them opt for the tax credit), the development funds, as private independent organizations, would be managed by a small professional staff, dedicated to the transfer of available funds on condition that the projects selected be partly financed by other investors, whether public or private, national or foreign. The funds (about 10) and the recipient countries would compete, in their respective spheres, on the basis of the results obtained in development, while an international advisory board could carry out limited functions of overseeing and general guidance.

Regarding foreign investments, Hirschman had maintained in *The Strategy* that they could encourage the country to fling itself into unbalanced growth. Together with aid, this might permit the country to overcome certain imbalances that emerge during the growth process, and might allow those sectors with a higher potential for rapid growth to fully exploit this potential.[27] He now resumed the argument to maintain that foreign investment, like a great many human inventions, is highly ambiguous: we need to sharpen our wits to exploit the advantages it offers and, at the same time, reduce its negative effects. On the positive side of the scale he placed the availability of resources, technology, skills, international relations, and the teaching function it fulfilled; on the negative side, together with the risk of economic plunder and political domination, he mentioned a series of aspects that tend to prevail when development reaches a certain threshold. "Foreign investment," Hirschman wrote (1971a, p. 229),

> can be at its creative best by bringing in "missing" factors of production, complementary to those available locally, in the early stages of development of a poor country. The possibility that it will play a stunting role arises later on, when the poor country has begun to generate, to a large extent no doubt because of the prior injection of foreign investment, its own entrepreneurs, technicians, and savers and could now do even more along these lines if it were not for the institutional inertia that makes for a continued importing of so-called scarce factors of production which have become potentially dispensable.

Moreover, development policies in the country need the strong, influential, and even militant support of the business community. But this cannot be provided by foreign investors who are so "mousy" because they are guests in a host country (and thus afraid of running up against natives' feelings and interests), and because local political authorities might not look kindly upon the strengthening of their market and power position. For all these reasons, Hirschman proposed the rediscovery of "the lost art" of liquidating and selectively nationalizing private foreign investments so as to encourage, on a selective basis, new investments as well.[28]

POLITICAL DISASTERS AND POLITICAL ORDER

"The Charles River Approach," maintained Arthur Schlesinger, Jr., who had been personal adviser to President Kennedy for foreign policy (1965, p. 589), "represented a very American effort to persuade the developing countries to base their revolution on Locke rather than Marx." This assertion provided grist to the mill of those who followed Louis Hartz and the exceptionalist school in considering this approach to be inspired by the liberal American tradition.[29] But even if one interprets it as a typical product of postwar development economics which had its political moment in the 1960s, when it influenced the Kennedy administration (and later, the Johnson administration) and became a part of their ideology,[30] the fact remains that the expectations of economists, and of politicians, were soon to face the harsh reality of the facts.

Those who expected economic development, helped by some social reforms, to favor the expansion of democracy, could not remain indifferent to the sequence of coup d'états that took place in Latin America.[31] This was particularly true when the 1964 takeover in Brazil created a collective shock and made it clear that an "authoritarian turn of events" was taking place in the subcontinent. (The partitioning of Pakistan and the Nigerian civil war placed the hypothesis of a general political reversal in the Third World firmly on the agenda.)

How could this sequence of political disasters be explained? Development economists had very little to offer. Their professional inclinations led them to think that economic development could promote only good.

This helps explain why an initial answer to these questions came from political science, rather than from economics. Already in 1965 Samuel Huntington had published "Political Development and Political Decay," an essay that, together with two subsequent books—*Political Order in Changing Societies* (1968a) and *Military Intervention and the Unlessons of Vietnam* (1968b)—inaugurated an approach that was destined to have a certain success just when the hardening of American policy pushed the Vietnam War towards tragedy.

It is generally maintained, Huntington reasoned, that economic modernization leads to democracy, to national unity, to the rationalization of the political system, and to political participation. In practice, only the last of these trends materialized. Instead of the other three, developing countries witnessed an erosion of democracy, ethnic conflicts and civil wars, as well as the gradual decay of organizations inherited from the colonial period, and a weakening of those political organizations originating from the fight for independence. The only real consequence of modernization, he concluded, is the growth of mobilization and political participation—through urbanization, communications, education, universal suffrage, etc. In its turn, this undermines the existing organizational and institutional reality; so that, despite every expectation, it generates political decay.

In this analysis, the relation between economic and political development as traditionally regarded by economists of development is simply turned upside down. The resulting opposition (as Hirschman explained at the beginning of his introduction in *A Bias for Hope* [1971a, p. 2]), exemplifies the respective inability of economists and political scientists to cross their own disciplinary boundaries to produce a genuinely interactive analysis.

Huntington defined political development as the institutionalization of organizations and procedures. This process was represented by adaptability, complexity, autonomy, and by the coherence these produce. By adopting, against his will, an economist's approach (according to whom, in turn, capital goods, natural resources, entrepreneurship, etc., were indispensable to economic and political development), he asserted that *only* institutionalization of the political system in backward countries could allow them to achieve real economic and political development. This thesis was explored systematically, and Huntington expressed the desire for "a new CIA style, more capable of building governments than of subverting them" (1968b, p. 28).

The reverse of the traditional relationship between economic and political development thus gives rise to a newly unreasonable relationship. "The conjecture that economic growth would lead to the lowering of political tensions and to greater cohesiveness," Hirschman wrote in his introduction to *A Bias for Hope* (1971a, p. 16), "has been increasingly disputed by those who hold that growth tends to have destabilizing political effects. On the basis of the latter view . . . : first there is economic growth, then this growth leads to adverse political developments which in turn cause economic decline so that economy and society revert to the low level from which they started out. Such models . . . are really quite primitive. It is odd that they should have been taken so seriously and tested so doggedly."

It is easy to see why even the introduction to *A Bias for Hope* is Janus faced. It was not only a methodological outline and interpretation of Hirschman's work for Latin American countries. It also responded to the ongoing debate in the United States. Furthermore, it represented an attempt to deal with the difficulties faced by development economics itself.

Political disasters had, in fact, left their mark. As Hirschman recalled later (1981a, pp. 20–23) they could not but give pause to the group of social scientists who had created development economics after the war, urged on by the need for a better world.

When it became clear that instead of leading to an improvement of political and social conditions, economic growth might entail a sequence of events that even leads to the loss of civil rights, the self-confidence of these economists was damaged. Some of them retired from the scene, others devoted their efforts exclusively to specific technical problems, while others became involved in a criticism of economic performances—and later dealt with distribution of income and basic needs.

"There is of course much to be said," Hirschman added, "for this new concreteness in development studies, and particularly for the concern with the poorer sections. Nevertheless, development economics started out as the spearhead of an effort that was to bring all-around emancipation from backwardness. If that effort is to fulfill its promise the challenge posed by dismal politics must be met rather than avoided or evaded." This statement was published in 1981a (p. 23). Only then could the author imply that he was finally able to deal with the matter.

Part 2

6

Exit, Voice, and Latitude

In this chapter I will start examining a new phase in which Hirschman moved beyond the threshold of development economics and into the wider sphere of the social sciences. This phase was heralded by *Exit, Voice, and Loyalty.* I will suggest some reasons for the unexpected and durable success of the book, such as the fact that economics and politics are analyzed in a single setting, and Hirschman's talent for creating communication channels between different areas of culture.

I will also examine some of the more ingenious theories contained in *Exit,* and attempt to trace the development of the concept of voice; how the early idea of voice as demand, appeal, or protest was gradually complemented by the ideas of voice as benefit, information, and communication, and of vertical and horizontal voice.

I will then go on to survey a few themes of the present debate, such as those of exit and voice in trade relations between firms (with reference to hierarchy and different market economies) and in spatial mobility; and those of latitude in performance standards. I will reconstruct the history of the latter from the Bogotá years to *The Strategy* and *Development Projects* to show how an observation on competition between highway and rail transport in Nigeria led to the complex notions of exit and voice.

THE GENESIS OF THE "HYDRAULIC MODEL"

We have now reached the third phase of Albert Hirschman's work,[1] which is also marked by a new career.[2] After having worked for many years as economist and professor of economics, Hirschman was appointed Professor of Social Science at the Institute for Advanced Study at Princeton, N.J., in 1973 (and works there still, although he has long since reached the status of emeritus).

The reasons why this change occurred in the late 1960s are rather complex. As had happened at the end of the Marshall Plan (see chapter 1) there was a sense of dissatisfaction that something had come to a close.[3] In this case, however, there was perhaps an even stronger desire to extend a path that had already been discovered to other fields. Unlike those development economists who had been obliged to reconsider by historical events, Hirschman could find the reasons, methods, and ideas he needed to continue with his work in his own experience. This is what makes the texts we have just examined so significant, and where the new path that would successfully address some of the key issues of the time was gradually defined (see 1981a, pp. vi, 23–24 and 95–105). This is the source of the "luck," as Hirschman called it, that led him to discover a particular aspect of his own work that could be expanded on a much vaster horizon. I refer to the genesis of *Exit, Voice, and Loyalty* (1970) and to the observations on rail transport in Nigeria in *Development Projects Observed* (1967).

Hirschman attempted to explain this change of direction on several occasions. In his preface to *A Bias for Hope* (1971a, p. ix) he wrote: "After eighteen years and three books almost wholly concerned with development and Latin America, the focus of my interests may shift (as it did in my most recent book)," *Exit, Voice, and Loyalty*. Furthermore, in his preface to *Essays in Trespassing* (1981a, pp. v–vi) he observed that the arrangement of the volume "makes plain that my interests have moved away from the exclusive concern with development issues," while the essay entitled "The Rise and Decline of Development Economics" was given an introductory role partly because it helped to explain this shift of interest. "It is not so much," he stated, "that the 'decline' made me move on to greener pastures; rather, I came to feel that progress with some of the major puzzles in economic-political development requires considerable detours and forays into other areas."

Finally, in his preface to a collection of essays selected from the two works just mentioned, for publication in Germany (1988a), Hirschman wrote that his intellectual itinerary could be accounted for in several ways.

In the 1950s and 1960s, I evolved a view of my own, often considered as highly idiosyncratic, about the problems of economic development. The process of explicating and defending my position forced me to elaborate a number of more general ideas about the process of social change, the relation of economics to politics, and other topics, ideas that then lent themselves to being tried out in a wider arena. The other reason I moved from the particular and foreign to the general and familiar is well-known to anthropologists. Characteristics that I initially believed to be specific to a country like Colombia or to a group of similarly situated countries, turned out in the end to be far more general and universal than I had thought.

We can see several aspects of the complex change we have just described: a personal inclination, undoubtedly encouraged by the success of *Exit;* a need stemming from his work and the possibility of it being fulfilled; a generalization process that proceeds by leaps and bounds; an increasingly aware anthropological approach. If we add to this the difficulties encountered and the solutions found case by case, we begin to see the path ahead.

Besides *Development Projects Observed,* which concludes the trilogy devoted to development and marks the turning point for this change, Hirschman's new direction led to four monographic works—*Exit, Voice, and Loyalty* (1970); *The Passions and the Interests* (1977); *Shifting Involvements* (1982); and *The Rhetoric of Reaction* (1991)—two books of essays—*Essays in Trespassing* (1981) and *Rival Views of Market Society* (1986)—and a travel report, *Getting Ahead Collectively* (1984). These widely-known texts concern political-economic theory, the history of ideas, social analysis, progressive project design, etc. The central issues dealt with mainly lie in fields other than economics and development policy as such, even though they are connected to them. On the one hand, the latter provide inspiration for the new phase and, on the other, the new phase allows Hirschman to return to these fields frequently and to achieve new results.[4]

These texts address issues in a wide-ranging field that might be defined generically as social science. They operate mainly at high levels of generalization, identify new dualisms that yield to original approaches, use new or neglected information, and reveal connections concealed by interdisciplinary barriers. In short, the point of view whose gradual growth we have observed is now brought to maturity.

It is well known that "responses to decline in firms, organizations, and states" (to quote the subtitle of *Exit*) provided the spark behind Hirschman's insight into the working of Nigerian railways, contained in *Development Projects*. One critic remarked that "there must be a lot of assumptions hidden there somewhere." "After a while," Hirschman wrote in his preface, "I decided to pursue these assumptions into their hiding places and was soon off on an absorbing expedition" that lasted a full year "in leisurely meditation."[5] The book, therefore, was the unpremeditated result of a spontaneous observation.

In attempting to explain the inefficiency of Nigerian railways, Hirschman analyzed in *Development Projects* some of its specific causes: tribal, economic, socio-political and organizational. The railway administrations' prolonged inability to make up for some of the service's most outstanding shortcomings, despite the competition of highway transport, still had to be explained. He reversed the prevailing trend of thought and remarked that "the presence of a ready alternative to rail transport makes it less, rather than more, likely that the weaknesses of the railways will be fought rather than indulged. With truck and bus transportation available, a deterioration in rail service . . . can be lived with for a long time without arousing strong public pressures" to offset it (1967b, pp. 146–47).

This is the groundwork for what Hirschman subsequently called the "basic seesaw pattern" of exit and voice (1986b, p. 91) or the "hydraulic model" (1993b, p. 176): deterioration generates complaint pressure which is funneled into voice or exit; the more pressure is released at the exit, the less pressure is left to stir up the voice.

As we shall see in *Development Projects*, the Nigerian railways case-study illustrates the weakness of public-owned companies in sectors subject to competition, such as transport or education. However, when Hirschman analyzed the logical grounds for this more deeply, he realized he had come across "a manner of analyzing certain economic processes which promised to illuminate a wide range of social, political, and indeed moral phenomena"

(1970a, p. vii). Broadening the field of reference allowed him to transfer the analysis from underdeveloped to developed countries, and to propose it in general terms.[6] This is what shapes the presentation of the book, which resembles a minitreatise. It proposes the notion of deterioration in the performance of individuals, firms, and organizations, and discusses the theoretical background and specific features of recovery mechanisms. Only then does it lavishly apply his Nigerian observation.

Unlike political scientists, Hirschman stated at the beginning of the book, economists have paid little attention to recoverable deterioration, even though it is a highly significant aspect of reality. The reason is theoretical: they assume a standard rational behavior and argue that a firm that loses ground in the competitive struggle will simply be replaced.[7] On the contrary, behavior can change over time, and there is generally room for recovery from many types of deterioration under both monopolistic conditions and "normal" (i.e., imperfect) competition. It thus becomes important to focus our attention on response and recovery mechanisms, as represented by exit and voice.

As is often the case with Hirschman, this argument conceals two already familiar theses (from *The Strategy*): the presence of slack in society (bearing out the key proposition that development depends on the ability to squeeze out unused or underused resources), and the notion that nonmarket forces are not necessarily less automatic than market driven ones (which gave rise to *Journeys*).

As stated in *Exit* in very general terms, slack is a typical characteristic of human societies that produce a surplus above subsistence levels: their deterioration falls within the natural order of things.[8] Once this unpleasant truth is discovered, it may spur the search for ways and means to avoid the phenomenon (as in *The Strategy*). But at a later point, it may actually represent a hidden blessing: economic slack makes it possible to overcome market misfortunes (Cyert and March) and political slack contains resources that can be mobilized in times of crisis.

Taking stock of both these aspects, *Exit* assumes that deterioration might occur or slack be created continuously, like the effect of a sort of human entropy. Furthermore, since the aim of the book is both to study the recovery response to this phenomenon and to combat economists' and political scientists' respective biases against the other discipline's approach, exit and voice are considered in such a way that neither one necessarily becomes less automatic than the other in the face of deterioration.

Exit also returns to the need to keep economic theory both at arm's length and within reach. On the one hand, Hirschman translates his concepts into the language of traditional analysis (and even enriches it [1970a, p. vii]). On the other, he formulates these concepts more accurately and facilitates their dissemination. This intellectual tension is revealed to be very useful when producing an integrated analysis in which economics and politics have equal weight.

To illustrate this line of reasoning, let us return to the example of Nigerian railways. Public enterprise, Hirschman affirmed in *Development Projects* (1967b, p. 147),

> has strangely been at its weakest in sectors such as transportation and education where it is subjected to competition: instead of stimulating improved or top performance, the presence of a ready and satisfactory substitute . . . merely deprives it of a precious feedback mechanism. . . . For the management of public enterprise . . . may be less sensitive to the loss of revenue due to the switch of customers to a competing mode than to the protests of an aroused public that has a vital stake in the service, has no alternative, and will therefore raise hell. Put differently: . . . the chances for action being taken against intolerably bad service . . . are better when it is supplied in conditions of monopoly.

For economists, the scandalous conclusions reproposed and developed in *Exit* could not pass without comment. Gordon Tullock objected, in a review of December 1970 (pp. 1194–95), that in the case under scrutiny, the lack of competition "would simply have meant that more money was extracted from the taxpayer to support good service to the noisy customers." Evidently, the idea that nonmarket forces are not necessarily less automatic than market forces was only half accepted; that is to say, by the railway management but not by the treasury. In fact, the review assumed that the railway deficit might double, but not that the treasury might respond to such a down trend. Probably Tullock—like Williamson (1976) or Lindbeck (1988, p. 307, n. 1)—did not find it easy to adopt the outlook represented by the set of reasonable assumptions that we have just examined and that support the analysis made in *Exit*.

THE CAUSES OF AN UNEXPECTED SUCCESS

If demand is a function of quality, Hirschman explained, deterioration of the latter causes the exit of some customers; this activates the response of management. Generally speaking, to favor recovery, there should be neither too much nor too little elasticity of demand in relation to quality. In other words, customers should reflect a mix of inert and alert individuals. The latter's exit triggers a feedback mechanism; the former, unexpectedly, represent a necessary damper on time and money, reducing instability and allowing management to recover.[9]

On the other hand, the recovery mechanism for voice is also most effective if the reaction is neither too great nor too small and if the customers' reaction to deterioration lies somewhere in between the two extremes. Voice may be residual or complementary in relation to exit, and may thus enhance the recovery mechanism activated by exit.[10] Voice may also be seen as an alternative or substitute for exit, in the sense that the decision to use either voice or exit implies an assessment of the expected outcome of the two actions, which leads to a preference for one over the other. If the most informed and active individuals decide to opt for exit, this atrophies the possibility of using voice. This "hydraulic" proposition undoubtedly plays a central role in the analysis, and paves the way for an itinerary that produces a complete circle of situations, eventually reverting to the point at which voice hinders exit.

It is not easy to evoke the impact that these ideas had on social science milieux. In the United States, the widespread practice of community action and the considerable interest in the search for more participatory political and social systems co-existed, at that time, with an opposite trend. In the wake of some of the key texts of neoconservative thought—such as Tiebout on the exodus toward the suburbs or Friedman on education—emphasis was placed on "the power and rationality of *individual* decentralized activity in various newly emerging or to-be-organized markets" (Hirschman, 1981a, p. 211). At the same time (see chapter 2), Mancur Olson was expressing his criticism of community action.

Thus, while the two rivaling factions ignored each other or barely coexisted, divided as they were by disciplinary and ideological barriers, *Exit* suddenly proposed a way of solving problems by combining politics and economics.[11] Its extraordinary success stemmed from its capacity to open a communication channel between the two camps: between the effectiveness and perfectibility of the democratic political process and the power of market-driven mechanisms. The book "hit some sort of sensitive nerve": it unleashed a very lively debate and soon became a standard reference in the intellectual environment.[12] This gave rise to a momentum of hope which was, however, partly fueled by the illusion that economics and politics in general could be reshaped—a common interdisciplinary aspiration of the time. Hirschman was only too aware of this danger: it probably motivated his decision to avoid any "clarion calls" for an integrated social science and concentrate his efforts (in his introduction to *A Bias for Hope*) on a more pedestrian review of the building blocks that already existed between economics and politics, focusing his attention on the political significance of the finest aspects of economic relations (see chapter 3).[13]

Which aspects of *Exit* attracted so much attention? First, the book was able to clarify some poorly-understood economic and political phenomena. Together with the Nigerian railways, Hirschman analyzed public education (whose recovery potential through voice is drastically reduced by the decision of the most active and informed individuals to send their children to private schools) and the stock market, where the selling of shares in the face of a deteriorating corporate situation perpetuates bad management. Later in the book, he also discussed the case of the postal system whose inefficiencies are made more tolerable by the existence of other forms of communication, as well as the case of some Latin American countries which, in order to safeguard their daily routine, encourage the exit of political enemies and potential critics. In all these cases—as, undoubtedly, in many others—this "special difficulty in combining exit and voice" (the title of the fourth chapter) can be explained by the phenomenon itself, by the specific features of existing alternatives and, thus, by the concrete disincentivating effect that exit can have on voice.

One of the main attractions of the text lay in its ability to translate this reasoning into economic terms. The ingenious application of demand curves, consumer surplus, price, quantity and quality selection, etc., allowed for technical and explanatory clarity, and reassured those readers who felt the need for a "scientific" presentation.[14] Another attraction was the sometimes paradoxical overturning of traditional knowledge in the fields of competition, monopolies, and political parties. We only have to think of the concept of a "lazy" monopoly backed up by competition in its propensity for deterioration (chapter 5); or of how the tendency of political parties in a two-party system to converge towards the center, suggested by Hotelling and Downs, can be contrasted by the voice of their own militants who appreciate politics in a different way (chapter 6).[15]

Another noteworthy theme of the book is "a theory of loyalty" (chapter 7) involving situations in which both voice and exit play an important role. Loyalty acts as an informal barrier to exit and activates voice; the latter, in its turn, is considerably strengthened by the credible threat to exit. Taken together, these notions confirm and enhance the economic policy idea that inspires the book, according to which specific artificial barriers (of an institutional, procedural and economic nature, etc.) can check exit and strengthen voice. This normative notion underlies the analysis of the cases outlined (to which loyalty with severe initiation and the difficult exit from public goods and high-ranking positions are now to be added). This approach does not lead to the traditional search for "the" optimal combination. Rather, Hirschman underscores in his own way the possibility of such unstable balances between exit and voice that one induces the action of the other, thereby obeying the logic of sequences and alternations.[16]

THE DEVELOPMENT OF VOICE

Exit leads the reader along an ever-changing path, starting off from a single source and gradually finding appropriate solutions to different situations. However, the debate that followed, and contingent events, soon convinced Hirschman that some important elements were still on the drawing board: "the theme I had come upon," he wrote (1981a, p. 212), "was richer than I had suspected and it simply proved impossible to exhaust it in one sitting."[17]

He was mainly concerned with the concept of voice. "In *Exit, Voice, and Loyalty*," as he had written in the introduction to *A Bias for Hope* (1971a, p. 6, note 8), "I allowed myself to be imprisoned by the traditional notion that the use of voice is always costly. My case for the potential superiority of voice over exit would have been considerably strengthened had I realized that in certain situations, the use of voice becomes acutely pleasurable and should therefore no longer be computed as a cost, but as a benefit."

Returning to the book, it is clear that voice is considered in terms of expected outcome, of cost (in time and money), and of the influence that it might be expected to exert. Furthermore, whereas exit is an individual action that is easy to exercise, voice often requires group action, and is therefore subject to the well-known difficulties of organization, representation, and free riding. "The presence of the exit alternative can therefore tend to *atrophy the development of the art of voice*. This is a central point of this book," Hirschman concluded (1970a, p. 43).

However, as soon as it is recognized that, under certain conditions, voice becomes gratifying per se, the relationships analyzed up to now take on new meanings. It is therefore necessary to consider a range of different situations: at one extreme, the use of voice is thought of as a benefit; at the other, voice is practically stifled by exit and the free riding behavior of the subjects involved. This is a dichotomy that, in the years of *Exit*, could not help but influence different social sciences. In fact, while economists continued to focus on the problem of free riding, political scientists had to acknowledge the "participation explosion." "The latter phenomenon," Hirschman affirmed (1971a, p. 5), "is clearly the obverse of the former" and can only be explained by admitting that, in this case, participation in a movement in order to obtain the desired policy is the next best thing to the policy itself.[18]

This thesis was expanded in two other texts (written for two meetings on *Exit* organized in 1973 and 1975, respectively [see n. 12 and 21]) that Hirschman considered "essential additions" to the original book (1981a, p. 212).[19] He concluded that when there is a large component of public interest, voice will be important per se: this is shown by consumer reaction to health hazards in the food industry; to problems of safety in automobiles; to the environment, or to racial discrimination (for example), for institutional investors. Investors, such as big private universities in America, can voice their opinion on these topics and thus activate a "recuperation mechanism," which would otherwise be missing, in the working of the exit-based stock market.[20]

Alongside the idea of voice as benefit, Hirschman also proposed the notion of voice as information.[21] In *Exit* (1970a, p. 30) voice was only petition, appeal and protest; it is now integrated with a second, much vaster dimension present in most daily economic activities. Voice as information is needed to reduce uncertainty and ignorance among consumers and producers, to make organizations work, to handle labor relations and disputes, to deliver public services, etc.[22]

This line of thought became even more generalized when Hirschman considered voice as communication necessary for markets to work. "Commerce," he wrote in 1986b (p. 87), "*is* communication, and is premised on frequent and close contact of the contracting parties who deliver promises, trust them, and engage in mutual adjustment of claims and complaints—all of this was implicit in the eighteenth-century notion of *doux commerce*. Adam Smith even conjectured that it was man's ability to communicate through speech that lies at the source of his 'propensity to truck and barter.' "

In this last work, when discussing some of the problems underlying voice formation (1986b, pp. 82–84), Hirschman also adopted Guillermo O'Donnell's distinction between horizontal and vertical voice. O'Donnell (in 1986) had looked for a point of convergence between exit-voice and private-public polarities (see chapters 2 and 7) in order to explain the experience of Argentina in the late 1970s. He had claimed that the political power that had organized the coup in that country had repressed horizontal voice as a side effect of its terrorist methods. Without even being totally successful, it had imposed an isolated, self-contained life onto its citizens, closed within the private sphere of family and work. It had thus seriously weakened spontaneous self-expression, daily exchange of opinions, and the worries and criticisms that are freely revealed in democratic societies (and that are often recorded in opinion polls).

This notion played an essential role in Hirschman's thought. First, it provided the voice concept with the solid foundation that it had lacked. Horizontal voice is the breeding ground for different forms of vertical voice: the well-known difficulties of expression that interfere with the latter, however, do not exist for the former which, with its self-generated momentum, constantly recreates the conditions needed to mobilize and organize the citizens' voice.[23]

Second, the notion of horizontal voice makes it possible to further criticize an economics-based view of voice. This view does not even admit the existence of horizontal voice, which fulfills a need that is almost as natural as breathing. Finally, this line of thought also leads to a radical criticism of economic theory insofar as it refers to a society exclusively based on exit and, thus, without horizontal voice. Such a society would be difficult to achieve, even for the most rigid dictatorships (see chapter 2).

As early as 1974 (now in 1981a, p. 214), Hirschman wrote that the conclusion of *Exit*, "an essay in persuasion on behalf of voice," had been "too timid." Evidently, voice played a much more important and extended role than initially foreseen.

This emphasizes the fact that exit and voice, as personifications of economic and political modes of action, are simultaneously present in numerous activities usually attributed to either the one or the other mode, to such an extent that they cannot be analyzed in terms of the traditional fields of economics and politics. Nor can this analysis be built up from one of them (e.g., by crossing its boundaries or finding a meeting point halfway). On the contrary, Hirschman discovered a viewpoint that lies outside and (in a certain sense) above the two disciplines, while enabling himself and the reader to communicate with them both.

ASPECTS OF AN ONGOING DEBATE

After the debate surrounding *Exit*, which started in the United States and invaded half the world (especially in the political and social sciences), Hirschman probably thought the time had come to review the results obtained. He agreed to make the exit-voice dichotomy one of the three main entries he wrote for the new Palgrave Dictionary,[24] and wrote a text that recalls the essential elements of his thought. He defined general steps forward and showed how the exit-voice could be applied to a great variety of fields: trade unions, the market-hierarchy antinomy, public services, spatial mobility, political parties, marriage, and the development of adolescents. "With this imaginative use of the exit-voice concept," he concluded (1986b, p. 99), "the outer limits of the sphere of influence may have been reached."

But, the expansion of exit-voice was far from being over. It regained momentum shortly after, in the wake of the major international political events of the late 1980s. Two fields of application seemed to enliven the debate more than any other:[25] the exit-voice combination in intercompany market relations, and spatial mobility.

In the discussion on *Exit* at the American Economic Association (1975, see note 21), Oliver Williamson presented "The Economics of Internal Organization: Exit and Voice in Relation to Markets and Hierarchies," in which he reiterated his well-known preference for hierarchical organization, expressed at that time in *Markets and Hierarchies* (1975).

Ten years later, when responding to such arguments, Hirschman pointed out that hierarchy did not necessarily outperform the market when there was a need for a continuous, straightforward dialogue between the contracting parties.[26] This is true both because market relations between independent companies can successfully discourage fraud, and because control dodging and shelving practices can undoubtedly lurk within the folds of hierarchy.

Incomplete information, a prolonged apprenticeship of one company to another, and the possibility of opportunistic behavior, he argued, actually require contracting firms to consult, and to keep a close watch on, each other. *"But this need for voice does not necessarily imply that hierarchy is in order.* Whether voicing is done best within the same organization or from one independent firm to another is by no means a foregone conclusion (Granovetter, 1985, p. 33). Moreover, when the two parties are independent and resort a great deal to voice, the possibility of exit often looms, and the implicit threat of exit may carry as much clout as that of sanctions in a hierarchy" (1986b, p. 86).[27]

In this text, Hirschman also hinted at the differences that exist in the industrial setups of different countries: for example, subcontracting is more widespread in Japan than in the West, while in Italy it spread during the 1970s (Sabel, 1982). The significance of different forms of market relations was soon to attract considerable interest.

This interest is partly due to the unexpected aftermath of the fall of European "real socialism" following the democratic revolutions of 1989–91. Declining interest in the age-old opposition between capitalism and socialism was compensated for by greater attention to different forms of market societies: comparisons between how the American, Japanese, and German economies functioned thus gained new ground. In this respect, Susan Helper (1991) showed how subcontracting in the American automobile industry is essentially based on exit (on numerous competing suppliers kept at arm's length to strengthen the bargaining power against them). In Japan, on the other hand, it centers on a small number of suppliers, and on their relationship, based on trust and information, which fosters the introduction of technological progress in design and production. This is what gave rise to the current generalization expounded by Ronald Dore, who compares the Anglo-Saxon and the Japanese-German style of conducting market economies as centered, respectively, on exit (keeping options open) and on voice (making commitments to each other and using voice first of all in case of disputes).

The second topic of debate was spatial mobility or emigration. In one important way, this relates to the broader theme of the state, which, although present in the title of the book, was dealt with only briefly in *Exit*. Chapter 8, "Exit and Voice in American Ideology and Practice," which actually discusses the problem of resignation among officials who disagree with public policies, is nonetheless conceived primarily from the bottom up. From this angle the issue of immigration and internal exit is pivotal in the American historical experience, with tangible consequences that can still be seen today (Meldolesi, 1985b).

Moreover, voice and exit are discussed in *Exit* from the point of view of customers and members of organizations and states faced by qualitative deterioration. Hirschman himself recognized

(1974; now in 1981a, pp. 224–25) that the book is not addressed "directly and systematically to the possible manipulation of exit and voice as 'management tools.'" "Fortunately," he added, "Stein Rokkan had since made a considerable contribution in this area" through "Dimensions of State Formation and Nation Building: A Possible Paradigm for Research on Variations within Europe" (1975). At this point Hirschman reached a conclusion which became increasingly important in the light of the events that followed. While in *Exit* (1970a, p. 124), manipulation of exit or voice is studied as a safety valve with a view to encouraging the least dangerous type of reaction in perpetuating power, "Rokkan," Hirschman wrote, "is probably right in asserting that, particularly during some initial phase of organization, attempts to restrict exit and to choke off voice tend to go hand in hand and to feed on each other."

This partial recognition of the joint role of exit and voice in a nonresidual relationship is the first step in a process that leads up to the present. Recently, Hirschman (1993b, p. 187) went back to the exit-voice debate that developed in Germany after the fall of the Berlin Wall. He wrote that the simultaneous repression of exit and voice implemented in 1961 with the construction of the wall,

> was to have its counterpart twenty-eight years later, when exit and voice exploded jointly and brought down the whole edifice of the German Democratic Republic. In a first cut, the event of 1989 looks like the exact inverse of what happened, or failed to happen, after August 1961. The inability of the G.D.R. . . . to prevent a large-scale flight of its citizens to West Germany via Hungary, Poland or Czechoslovakia signalled a novel, serious, and *general* decline in state authority. It was thus taken to imply a similar decline in the ability and readiness to repress voice.

LATITUDE IN PERFORMANCE STANDARDS

As we have seen, *Exit* was not planned. It was the new shoot of a vigorous plant; a work that sailed against the cultural and political tide, and created debate among social scientists from different backgrounds and with different convictions. The book and the wide range of related literature met a need of our time, and we continue to refer to them to solve urgent problems, whether large or small.[28]

Casanova (1990, p. 12) stated that *Exit* "is a totally unclassifiable masterpiece: is it a book on economics, is it a book on politics, is it a book on philosophy? The term that would suit it best is the nineteenth century French expression: it belongs to the 'political and moral sciences.'" This may be linked to that "bias for voice" that characterizes *Exit* and the texts that stem from it: we only have to consider the many multifaceted voices (complaining, informative, communicative, horizontal, vertical) that, if properly used, can produce many-fold positive effects in our societies. This democratic and propulsive vocation, which reemerges in other key contributions to the career initiated by *Exit,* fulfills a deeply felt need. It is part of an active search for viable solutions in the most diverse fields.

Before following Hirschman's thought any further, however, I should like to tackle an issue that has been deliberately left on hold. In "A Dissenter's Confession" (1984; now in 1986b, p. 20) Hirschman stated that he had "only now" and "with much surprise" noticed that the concept of latitude in performance standards—discovered at the origin of *The Strategy* (see chapter 2)—has a real affinity with the concept of voice.[29]

To understand this link, we should remember that "Economics and Investment Planning" (1954) contains not only the first ideas on backward linkages, but also an embryo of the concept of latitude; the notion, that is, of the defective maintenance of existing capital. This elementary empirical observation refers to the reality of underdeveloped countries.[30] It led to Hirschman's criterion that priority should be given to investments, industries, and technical processes that do not require maintenance or that need it because "its absence carries with it a very high penalty, that is, leads to accidents or an immediate breakdown rather than to slow deterioration in the quantity or quality of output" (1954, now in 1971a, p. 58).[31]

In chapter 8 of *The Strategy,* Hirschman claimed that the maintenance of capital encounters difficulties as it is a preventive activity phased at time intervals. In primitive societies, ritual is used to set deadlines and tasks that, because of their very nature, might be postponed. Similarly, for capital maintenance to be actually performed, people must be made to act as though they had to fulfill this task at precise intervals, trying to overlook the fact that delaying such an activity might not be important. People "must organize this fiction, submit to it and set up a signalling system to enforce it" (1958a, p. 141).[32]

On the other hand, Hirschman continued, if one resorts to expedients based on scheduling or the use of machines that are not provided by the production process (such as changing the oil of the car every five thousand kilometers) in order to organize maintenance efficiently, this suggests that it is the very absence of signals that creates the difficulty. Transferring such an observation to productive activities, he found himself contrasting machine-controlled with operator-controlled operations, and process-centered with product-centered industrial activities: the so-called "Hirschman Hypothesis," as named by the lively debate that developed around this issue.

It is undoubtedly a very attractive notion. It makes it possible to question the traditional criterion of capital extensiveness (namely specialization in labor-intensive productions) put forth by development economics for investment planning in underdeveloped countries. It also makes it possible to show that the frequently recurring bias for advanced technologies and for continuous process, capital-intensive production in underdeveloped countries "need not necessarily be regarded as flowing from a quest for prestige and economic megalomania" (as Gerschenkron had already written, 1952, p. 25).

Furthermore, this concealed rationality has even broader consequences: the push towards efficiency caused by the narrow latitude in poor performance can change the behavior of workers and indirectly spread into the economy and into society. This starts off a new induction process (and one of cognitive dissonance). It was a reliance message, Hirschman recalled (1986b, pp. 19–20) that countered Weberian literature on cultural obstacles to development, and that was later confirmed by the wide ranging sociological survey conducted by Inkeles and Smith, 1974.[33]

ELEMENTS BEHIND A REFORMULATION

This brief reference to the notion of latitude does not yet enable us to look more closely at the real affinity with the problems raised in *Exit*. We must now turn back to *Development Projects*. In contrast to his approach in *Journeys,* Hirschman scanned through the development of some projects in different sectors, drawing out differences and analogies in their dynamic, and tracing them back to their typical structural features.[34]

First, he distinguished between the reaction of the people in charge to external developments and actions that depend on their freedom to make decisions. He then differentiated the concept of latitude from uncertainties such as technology, the human factor, funding, excess and inadequate demand. Hirschman's digression on research and development strategy juxtaposed the principles behind such strategy and those behind investment planning. He then expressed a viewpoint that recalls the dual propensity of governments in underdeveloped countries to plan and experiment, discussed by Hirschman in 1957 (see chapter 2). This view is developed in chapter 3, "Latitude and Disciplines."

We learn, for example, that site-bound projects are given preference because it is easier to convince public opinion of their appropriateness, but that they are generally on a larger scale than non-site-bound ones and that their relative decision-making process becomes laden with emotional factors and nationalistic pride. We learn that decision making for site-bound projects is faster but more likely to be mediocre; that non-site-bound projects tend to be subjected to delays, pressure, and decision reversals, but that they enjoy a broader latitude and can represent an opportunity for constructive political compromises, rational choices, creative sequences, etc. As if by magic, each aspect seems to call into play another that tends to counterbalance it. It is thus logical that one feels the need for some point of reference.

Proceeding in this way, the discussion on latitude reaches a different viewpoint from that in chapter 8 of *The Strategy.* What is particularly striking is the ambivalence (if not ambiguity) of the different characteristics examined. Hirschman claimed that he had applied the concept of latitude to new space-time dimensions and that he also intended to expand and qualify the concept in its original sphere (relative to the problem of corruption, the quantity and quality of the product, private and public spending); but he went on to add (1967b, pp. 126–27) that he was by then "a long way from the attractive simplicity" with which this notion had been presented in *The Strategy*. Compared to the original formulation, we now have, typically, a logical rebalancing based on a series of concrete facts.

"As a result of a more thorough exploration of the concept," Hirschman concluded, "we have now acquired a more qualified or perhaps an ambivalent position: while lack of latitude retains the great advantage of determinateness, of preventing mere slippage, of accelerating decision making, and in general of providing project directors and managers with firm discipline and guideposts for action, the presence of latitude has in some situations been shown to foster training in rational decision making or the adaption of imported models of economic behavior to local conditions and requirements."

BEHIND VOICE AND EXIT

Exploring the function of a wide latitude beside that of a narrow one, the capacity for decision making and learning beside the capacity to bind, Hirschman thought that he had lost in simplicity but gained in realism. Furthermore, he probably thought that, with *Development Projects,* the relevant process of elaboration and generalization had run into decreasing returns and that therefore it was no longer worth insisting on it. Here again he made quite a hasty evaluation, since the theme was destined to continue its trajectory underground, and then to emerge as exit and voice.

This process is illustrated by Hirschman's work after observing Nigerian railways; and by the chapter in *Development Projects* in which the ambivalence of uncertainties and latitudes is used to focus on the dilemma of project design. If the project is implemented after having accepted a number of preexisting negative attributes, the opportunity to stimulate change in them is lost. However, if the intention is to produce change, project implementation becomes haphazard. The art of project design evidently consists in avoiding this antinomy and in deciding which characteristics are changeable (trait-making) and which are not (trait-taking). "It turns out," Hirschman wrote at the end of the discussion (1967b, p. 139), "that latitude and lack of latitude can both be valuable in facilitating that learning or acquisition of needed skills and traits which we have called here trait-making.

But, each has been shown to have specialized functions: latitude is attuned to gradual learning, whereas lack of latitude has a special affinity to the changes that take place through discontinuous commitments to new values and types of behavior."

At this point Hirschman introduced the example of Nigerian railroads as an example of failure; it was a project that was implicitly trait-making but in an unrealistic way, since it would have required energetic treatment to deal with some typical management pathologies—such as tribal antagonisms, nepotism, corruption, and Nigerianization.

However, instead of linking the lack of change in such social, economic, and human traits to the structural features of the project (railways, Hirschman explained in *The Strategy,* are halfway between the narrow latitude of airlines and the wide latitude of roads [1958a, p. 142]), he preferred to discuss an option between railway and highway transport. He thus showed that these characteristic traits of the Nigerian situation heavily penalized the efficiency of railways compared to highway transport, and that the expansion of the railway network worsened this discrepancy. This led to the empirical observation that the existence of a possible alternative to rail transport actually reduces, rather than enhances, the probability of offsetting the railways' shortcomings.

In this case, therefore—as in the discussion on use value and exchange value that opens Marx's *Capital*—the connection between latitude as constraint and latitude as choice-making capacity internal to the project is reflected externally in the relationship between railways and highway transport: the former are less constrained precisely because it is possible to choose the latter. Hence, the voice of train passengers is silenced by the exit of the more active and enterprising fellow travelers.

In conclusion, while the exit and voice concepts developed independently from that of latitude, a textual analysis would appear to suggest that the former arose almost spontaneously from the development of the latter. Retracing the path that leads from "defective maintenance" to the formulation of *Development Projects,* we can thus refer voice and exit respectively to narrow and wide latitudes for poor performance. In all these charactertistics, the propensity towards deterioration must be fought: in *Exit,* this propensity is regarded as a general characteristic.

The delay in recognizing this connection can probably be traced back to two things. First, the path from *Development Projects* to *Exit* crosses the border between backward and advanced countries: this innovation inaugurated a new phase in Hirschman's work which was later consciously pursued in both directions. Second, given the nature of his task, Hirschman may have drawn heavily on the "hiding hand" (see chapter 2, note 20, and chapter 5). He probably felt the psychological need to protect his creative effort against interference from preexisting ideas.[35] This produced an innovative intellectual structure that, in hindsight, fit into a vaster area of research.

In the first part of this work we saw how the idea of linkages gave rise to a line of research that Hirschman later referred to "as one thing that leads or does not lead to another." However, Hirschman also claimed that latitude in performance standards is the forerunner of a long sequence of ideas that is reincarnated in *Development Projects, Exit, The Passions and the Interests* (and also in *Shifting Involvements*). This approach, "even more basic than the first," was named "how one firm or productive operation can be made to *endure* as an efficiently performing unit of the economic system" (1986b, p. 18).

A final comment must be made. The two lines of thought just mentioned play such an important role in Hirschman's work that they could be regarded as the *cardum* and *decumanum*—or, to stick to Bogotá, the *calle* and *carrera*—of the Hirschman *polis*. We see both lines of thought lead into the poorer and richer parts of town. Considering Hirschman's work, we can thus adopt a four-entry table, with the two main research subjects and the two worlds they refer to as our entries. We can discover it gradually, tracing the connections and intersections as we progress.

7

Passions and Involvements

Another key work of Hirschman's, *The Passions and the Interests*, is examined in this chapter from the viewpoint of the new phase originated by *Exit*. I will compare closely the themes of the book with those of *Exit* in such fields as emigration, capital flight, and the ambivalent concept of latitude. The comparison will underscore how *The Passions* probably derived from Hirschman's desire to develop this new phase by drawing on a wider historical context, one that he felt had been unjustly neglected. We shall see how Hirschman elaborated his historical canvas further by combining traditionally noncommunicating approaches; and how he tackled problems that contemporary social scientists had been unable to solve.

I will go on to show how Hirschman dealt with the problem created by the political disasters that took place in some Latin American countries (and elsewhere), and how his analytical baggage (with the development of the tunnel effect and of the two functions of government) was enriched. I will also show how Hirschman evaluated and interpreted the rise and fall of development economics.

Turning to the events that led up to *Shifting Involvements*, the chapter will outline its intellectual trajectory, examine some of its most important results, and focus on the swings between public and private spheres.

The chapter comes to an end with an analysis of Hirschman's recent essay on the fall of the Berlin Wall, to show how Hirschman was able to draw inspiration from that event for an important theoretical breakthrough.

INTERESTS AND VOICE

At the beginning of the 1970s Hirschman started working on a new research project on Latin America (see chapter 5). But then he changed his mind and devoted himself to writing a digression on the history of ideas. The result was *The Passions and the Interests* published in 1977.

The adventure of *The Passions* required a considerable investment in terms of "human capital." Its scope was very wide ranging and it drew upon recent and remote reading lists, adding a host of new material. The first draft dated back to 1972–73 when Hirschman spent his sabbatical year at the Institute for Advanced Study in Princeton. The following year he had to put his work on hold in order to resume teaching at Harvard. But then he became a member of the Princeton Institute, and thus acquired a position that would prove congenial to the new phase of research he was embarking upon.

"A glance at developments in Brazil from 1968 on," Hirschman wrote in "Policymaking" (1975, now in 1981a, p. 143), "left no doubt about what should have been obvious anyway: economic growth, social progress and 'liberty'—or more simply the respect for human rights—do not necessarily advance jointly." In particular, it appeared that some varieties of economic growth are fully compatible with social and political retrogression. The sense of shock produced by this experience could not fail to have its effect on the intellectual climate of the time.

The social sciences, however, were incapable of shedding light on these new collective perceptions. Hirschman thus came up with the idea of knocking down some of the intellectual barriers of his day and revisiting the seventeenth and eighteenth centuries, an age of economic expansion in which economics had not been separated yet from politics as a discipline in its own right. "As a result, philosophers and political economists could range freely and speculate without inhibitions about the likely consequences of, say, commercial expansion for peace or of industrial growth for liberty" (1977b, p. 3).

Hirschman's new enterprise was thus spurred by his desire to go back to the path he had trodden in *Journeys* and forge a solution to the problems raised by the political disaster in Brazil and elsewhere. But another motivation was to range beyond the narrow outlook of contemporary social sciences in order to provide a backdrop to his new work since *Exit*. The debate developing out of *Exit* shed light on general issues that Hirschman felt could be explored by reviving an intellectual point of view largely forgotten. Hirschman undoubtedly sensed that such an enterprise would widen the scope of his work.

Moreover, it seems to me that Hirschman's choice of subject matter in *The Passions* corresponded to his cognitive approach. His attempt was to understand a reality that is much more complex than is generally believed by looking at things from a different angle; to venture out where others had not trodden; to record phenomena which were not visible to all, and follow paths which might lead to new, uncharted territories. This, in my view, explains the extraordinary reconstruction in the first part of the book of how interests were called upon to counteract passions.

In this chapter I make no attempt to explore the vast terrain uncovered in *The Passions*. For my purposes, it is sufficient to keep in mind this broader framework (which gave shape to the theses on economics mentioned in chapter 2), and to focus on some of its consequences.[1] The one linked to the political situation is explicit, while the other, connected to Hirschman's new research interests, is implicit, and as such will be dealt with in terms of analogies with, and differences from, *Exit*.

Working at *The Passions*, Hirschman explained in "A Dissenter's Confessions" (1986b, p. 22), "I found that I was by no means the inventor of these concepts of latitude or discipline and of their uses, but that I had some illustrious predecessors, such as Montesquieu and Sir James Steuart!" This comment was made in reference to the principal theme of *The Passions*: the almost bizzare idea that the commercial and industrial expansion of the market would serve to restrain, for various reasons connected to the complexity of the modern economy,[2] and through various mechanisms, "the 'passions' of the sovereign" (1981a, p. 99).

This was expected to lay down the conditions for a more human and less arbitrary government. "And it is fortunate for men," Montesquieu stated in the phrase used by Hirschman as an epigraph to the volume, "to be in a situation in which, though their passions may prompt them to be wicked, they have nevertheless an interest in not being so." Narrow latitude is the result of the pursuit of "interest" and the development of the market.

Hirschman claimed there was a "straightforward connection" between *The Strategy* and *The Passions* on this point.[3] Looking, however, at Hirschman's new phase, I would like to investigate the relationship between the seemingly unrelated books *Exit* and *The Passions*. Both books dealt with the basic inquiry of how "one firm or productive operation can be made to endure" despite, in *Exit,* the tendency towards deterioration and in *The Passions,* the sovereign's *coups d'autorité.* The world of exit and voice and that of passions and interests, however, look far apart. In the former, narrow latitude stems from voice whereas, in the latter, it stems from interests. Furthermore, although it is possible to draw a parallel between exit and interests, it is less easy to do so for voice and passions. In Hirschman's work voice has a basically positive connotation while passions do not.

It is nevertheless possible to find a brief sequence of ideas that might facilitate a comparison of the two works. To this end, it is necessary to go back to the discussion of the state (chapter 6) in which exit and voice are shown working together rather than as alternatives. Hirschman was "rather stunned" to read Rokkan's analysis of Europe's political development in the Middle Ages in terms of exit and voice. He was intrigued by his thesis according to which the effort to maintain public authority over the exit of men and commodities in Central Europe resulted in the imposition of a much lower level of voice than would have been healthy. He thus drew the conclusion that liberalization and widening of participation might not be possible unless exit and voice controls were eased jointly. Rather than describing the reinforcing effect of exit on voice in such a circumstance—as he did later—Hirschman returned however to the image of the hydraulic see-saw and explained that if controls on exit were not reduced, the voice response mechanism would be too strong.[4] This led Hirschman to consider nineteenth century trans-Atlantic emigration as a safety valve that, by releasing voice, allowed European states to develop modern, representative governments (1974, now in 1981a, pp. 225–26).[5]

Hirschman returned to the theme of the state from the point of view of exit and voice in a 1978 essay, "Exit, Voice, and the State," based on what might be called an informal encounter between the approaches taken by *Exit* and *The Passions* to the exit of movable property. In this essay, Hirschman described how Montesquieu and Steuart believed that the flight of capital represented a salutary restraint on arbitrary government action, but stressed that this is not the case in the many countries in which capital flight hinders necessary reform.[6]

If we read this essay with narrow latitude for poor performance in mind, it is clear that, for Montesquieu and Steuart, capitalist interests constrain government passions, while in many countries the exit of capital prevents voice from demanding reform. Apparently the two mechanisms face each other without actually meeting. Yet, one does not necessarily exclude the other— Hirschman writes for example (1981a, p. 257)—"Occasionally these various exits [of capital] do occur, according to the eighteenth-century script, in response to the arbitrary and capricious actions of the sovereign. But . . . exit of capital often takes place in countries intending to introduce . . . some social reforms designed to distribute the fruits of economic growth more equitably." Exit thus plays a positive or negative role according to whether the role of government action is negative or positive.[7]

One of Hirschman's major findings in his study of eighteenth-century political theory was that interests, or the market, were not championed for economic gains as much as for their civilizing potential. Together with restraining a sovereign's passions, trade made people more courteous, cautious, and upright, bred more civilized customs, and molded better citizens. In this field, Claus Offe observed (1988, p. 17), traditional liberal political theory (the principal theme of *The Passions*), may be considered as a voice for exit; that is to say, a search for consensus on the desirability of freeing some categories of actors and actions from the need for consensus.[8]

On the other hand, in "A Dissenter's Confessions" (1986b, p. 20), Hirschman wrote that voice is a response mechanism that should be placed alongside competition. Now, if we consider competition (the market, interests) within the context of traditional liberal political theory, we can see that *Exit* was based on a reversal of this argument. In this case, pleading in favor of voice can be seen as counterpoint to the liberal tendency to favor exit.

The attraction for Hirschman of Montesquieu and Steuart's doctrine also lies in the ambivalence of the process they highlight and, consequently, in the possibility that further observations might push the doctrine in new, unexpected directions. Take, for example, the thesis that resentment brought about by fear of downward mobility can lead to a strong government (Adam Ferguson), or that the need to insure regularity, tranquillity, and efficiency that stems from trade can become a cause of despotism (Ferguson, later developed by Alexis de Tocqueville). These examples disclose "very similar ambivalent feelings about the meaning of economic progress for freedom," Hirschman argued (1977b, p. 122). On the one hand, they move along the lines indicated by Montesquieu and Steuart; on the other, they prove that the result can turn out to be quite the opposite. There is a case not only for "taming" or actually "chaining" the *coup d'autorité* of despotic governments, but also for repressing popular participation, as well as for undermining the authority and discretionary powers of democratic governments.

The basic ambivalence that interested Hirschman was therefore that economic expansion can both advance the political arts and be responsible for their deterioration. This ambivalence led him to "come up against the limits of latitude concept" (1986b, p. 22).

In certain conditions, then, economic expansion is compatible with both dictatorship and democracy. There is no comparable ambivalence in the world of exit and voice: voice is the expression of narrow latitude and can be either too soft or too loud regarding possible recovery. After reading *The Passions*, however, it is easier to imagine changing the model and considering different types of voice, looking at both disgregation and recovery mechanisms.

Hirschman's interest in the intrinsic ambivalence of the relationship between economic development and the political system also lay in its convergence with history, and, in particular, with the political disasters that took place in some underdeveloped countries during the 1960s and 1970s. As we shall see later on, in order to explain this turn of events in Latin America, Hirschman reformulated a theory first advanced in *The Strategy*, and discussed the possible (positive or negative) interplay between what he called the "accumulation" and "reform" functions. Similarly, the weakening or hydraulic relationship of exit and voice was gradually complemented by its opposite, i.e., the reinforcing relationship, and leads, therefore, to multiple results. For instance, Hirschman reformulated an observation he had already made in *Exit* according to which for voice to have weight the threat of exit must be credible. "Parents who have been passive," he wrote, referring to education (1986b, p. 89), "because they were feeling powerless and fearing reprisal may feel empowered for the first time once they are given vouchers that can be used 'against' the schools currently attended by their children, and they will be readier than before to speak out with regard to desirable changes."[9]

In "Rival Views of Market Society," a follow-up to *The Passions* that lent its name to a new collection of essays (1986b), the theory of *doux commerce* was discussed from the point of view of breeding "gentle manners" in people. The theory was reformulated in an indirect and ambivalent form thanks to the contribution of Durkheim and Simmel, and combined in a *tableau idéologique* with the contrasting theses of self-destruction, and of "feudal-shackles" and "feudal-blessings." Hirschman's conclusion was that economic growth both creates and destroys the moral fibre of society and that inherited social bonds can play either a negative or positive role.

Similarly, voice can either create or destroy appropriate forms of behavior (and can in turn be affected by these effects). This parallel is outlined in the new preface (1992e) to *Rival Views of Market Society* in which Hirschman stated that his essay (together with "Against Parsimony: Three Easy Ways of Complicating Some Categories of Economic Discourse," discussed in chapter 2) are well suited to the analysis of different types of capitalism; and in which Hirschman discussed the several types of exit-voice relationships in and between firms, which characterize some forms of capitalism (see chapter 6).

This preface is confirmation that *The Passions* and *Exit* have some points in common. *The Passions* grew out of Hirschman's desire to give momentum to the new phase by providing a broad historical background that might shed light on the issues that interested him. It was a general framework that lent itself to further expansion (as in "Rival Views") by linking traditionally disconnected theses. It was also a logical tool for loosening some of the tangled arguments which social sciences had failed to tackle, and a stimulus to fan out the exit-voice perspective in different directions.

UNDERSTANDING DISASTERS

One of the best known aspects of *The Passions* is its relationship with development economics. In 1973, Hirschman published "The Changing Tolerance for Income Inequality in the Course of Economic Development." Its very title seems to allude to the issue of latitude (or tolerance); but this is clearly a retrospective observation. Actually Hirschman followed a path in the opposite direction to that which had led him to *Exit.* Inspired by the results of *Exit* he tried and tackled a problem which had been haunting him for years, that of political disasters in underdeveloped countries.

The paper (1973b, now in 1981a, pp. 39–40), represented "an effort to understand both where we were right and where we went wrong." It was grounded in Hirschman's "strong feeling and insistent recollection of one participant observer that the intellectual enthusiasm in the fifties and early sixties reflected elements of real hopefulness that were then actually present in many developing countries." However, he argued, "the precarious and transitory nature of that . . . phase" had not been correctly perceived at the time. This observation led him in turn to introduce what he called the "tunnel effect." Tolerance of growing inequalities in income distribution produced by a quickly developing economy is often quite substantial at an early phase; it is based, however, on the expectation that such disparities will narrow again. If this does not occur, "there is bound to be trouble and, perhaps, disaster."[10]

The tunnel effect (whose logic is also investigated in Michael Rothchild's mathematical appendix to the original text published in the *Quarterly Journal of Economics*) is essentially the result of the passage of time, without the aid of any particular outward event.

This is very treacherous for rulers, who are "lulled into compla-
cency" by their observations of the "easy early stage." Hirschman
used the tolerance-intolerance duality, and the transition between
the two, to illustrate his point.[11]

Highly segmented societies, Hirschman explained, have a
narrower latitude, or tolerance, for income disparities than homogeneous ones, though the latter will be more prone to violent
social conflict if their tolerance level is overstretched (as it was in
Argentina, France, and Italy). On the other hand, societies that
have shared an "intensive historical experience," epic deeds such
as the creation of the United States or the Mexican revolution,
generally have a broader latitude. Hirschman later added a further
point (1979b, now in 1981a, p. 130): the more rapid the growth
the greater the inequalities in its wake; at the same time, however,
tolerance is prolonged by the expectation that one's own turn will
soon come.

Disasters induced by economic development can thus occur both where tolerance for disparities is narrow and where it
is broad. Hirschman put Nigeria and Pakistan (very segmented
countries where "hopeful expectation" has been greatly limited)
into the first group. In the second group, we see Brazil and
Mexico (Hirschman refers to the authoritarian regime in Brazil
after 1964 and to the use of military force to crush the Mexican
student movement). The ruling parties and policymakers in these
countries, in fact, failed to realize that the safety valve of tolerance
would soon cease to operate.

"The Changing Tolerance" is therefore an important first
key to understanding political disasters. In addition to the social
side of the problem, however, it was also important to clarify the
political side. An interesting debate concerning the turn to authoritarianism in Latin America was sparked off in the mid 1970s
by an essay of Guillermo O'Donnell's (1975) that examined the
economic events that had contributed to the turn. A part of the
debate was collected by David Collier (1979) in a book which
included Hirschman's article "The Turn to Authoritarianism in
Latin America and the Search for its Economic Determinants."
The main economic interpretations of Latin American authoritarian rule, the essay pointed out, are based mainly on the belief
that some of the economy's intrinsic exigencies have sometimes
been "blatantly ignored by the rulers or ruled or both," making

regime changes more likely. Latin America, in this sense, did not fulfil Montesquieu and Steuart's expectation that economic development would compel rulers to defer to these exigencies.

The fact that Latin American policymakers have "a particularly low propensity to defer" and "sometimes seem to revel in violating the most elementary constraints of the economic system" (1981a, p. 100) could be traced back to specific characteristics of the "late late industrialization" in Latin America (with high levels of state intervention, little regard for the international market, and an exuberant start-up phase that prompted illusions and extravagant ventures).

This observation paved the way for a critical survey of possible approaches for explaining the turn to authoritarianism. Hirschman surveyed several economic determinants (such as O'Donnell's deepening thesis, the transition to more orthodox economic policies, and accelerating industrial growth through increased income inequality), and concluded that there was no single and specific structural economic difficulty behind the turn to authoritarianism. There was, however, an evident relationship between this turn of events and a general awareness that the countries were facing serious economic problems without being able to solve them.

Hirschman went on to outline further connections, bringing political[12] and cultural factors into his discussion, and stressed the role of ideology, the number of unresolved issues, the widespread frustration, the sense of desperate predicament. The final sections of the article were devoted to "a more general framework" set up in an attempt to discover some "real economic and political factors that might be encompassed by a more general analysis" (1979, now in 1981a, p. 123).

This is seen to be a three-phase process. Hirschman's research for *The Passions* led him to discover the ambivalence of the concept of latitude when applied to the political system. In order to explain the turn to authoritarianism, he collected a number of concrete aspects of Latin American reality and analyzed them from the point of view of unbalanced (economic and political) growth.

At the end of *The Strategy*, Hirschman defined two principal government functions (the "unbalancing" and "balancing" functions) that must be accomplished in the course of economic development. In "The Turn to Authoritarianism," his intention was to examine the interaction of economic and political aspects; the two functions of government thus become reformulated as the "entrepreneurial" and the "reform" functions. "How well these two functions are performed and coordinated is crucial for both economic and political outcomes of the growth process" (1981a, p. 125).[13]

Social and income inequalities arising from or widening during the growth process are an important part of the picture, just as are geographical and sectoral imbalances discussed in *The Strategy*. They require political action in order to be corrected. Therefore reform function has an essential role to play in sustaining growth after a powerful yet disequilibrating push by the entrepreneurs. The latter, Hirschman claimed, are generally unaware of the need for reform to complement their action and are often strongly opposed to the function being performed. Whether the equilibrating function is undertaken from above or from below, it is performed by social and political forces whose appearance "on the stage at the right time and with the right strength is not in any reliable fashion coordinated with the entrepreneurial function and its performance. In fact, while the performance of both functions (in some proper sequence) may be 'objectively' essential for the growth process, their protagonists are more often than not determined adversaries, and, perhaps must be just that if they are to achieve their respective purposes" (1981a, pp. 125–26).[14]

Hirschman argued that in Latin America the ideological forces behind the industrialization process were weaker than those in the European countries analyzed by Gerschenkron. Furthermore, "major intellectual voices" there, after supporting the entrepreneurial function for about a decade, suddenly rallied behind the reform banner and demanded redistribution. This reversal, Hirschman claimed, left strongly entrenched social groups "without any ideological fig leaf."

Another feature Hirschman linked to the tunnel effect was the fact that the reform function arises at "widely differing dates and with very different lags behind the entrepreneurial function." If reform is attempted too early, he claimed, it tends to have a paralyzing effect on entrepreneurial forces, while if it appears too late, it can lead to violence. The outcome thus depends on the "degree and nature of the hostility between the protagonists of the two functions." In Colombia, the ability to recover and maintain some degree of pluralistic stability depended on the fact that a few members of the country's oligarchy succeeded in taking on the role of reformers while others continued to pursue their entrepreneurial activities. Communication between the two groups "was often strained, but was never quite cut off."[15]

Unfortunately, this was not the case in most other Latin American countries. Reformers who now and again took over government in this or that country often had no affinity with the traditional elites that performed the entrepreneurial function. Their reforms were neither perceived nor accepted as having a modernizing function, and were "not particularly helpful to their intended beneficiaries." The *desencuentro* that separated the reforming and the entrepreneurial elites, Hirschman claimed, could be responsible for "the intellectual ferment" at the time, for the ideological reversals, and for the policymakers' low propensity to defer to the normal constraints of economic growth.

ANTAGONISM AND PASSIONS

As with the microfeatures of the interaction between economics and politics analyzed in chapter 3, this investigation of some macrofeatures fills out Hirschman's development. We have seen how Hirschman extended and partly reformulated a basic thesis of *The Strategy* in order to analyze the tragedy of authoritarian regimes. In "The Turn to Authoritarianism," we have also seen how he stressed the importance of convergence in addition to divergence, and of empathy in addition to separation: a notion that became increasingly important in his later work. These results, moreover, probably led Hirschman to reconsider his "basic growth pattern" and to accept, as he did at the end of "A Dissenter's Confession," the existence of an antagonistic element in unbalanced growth. Thus Hirschman was able to apply his concept of sailing against the wind to the postwar development of advanced Western countries,[16] thereby suggesting that some features of his economic and political analysis in *The Strategy* could be applied to Western societies as well as to developing countries.

This observation brings us back to the four-entry-table mentioned at the end of chapter 6, in which two major lines of research—"how one thing leads (or does not lead) to another" and "how an enterprise manages to endure"—and two different worlds of reference are put together. As we have seen, the line of research pursued in *The Passions* concerned the durability of market society, aimed at growth and democracy, and referred to industrialized countries. However, some aspects can equally be applied to underdeveloped countries with corresponding local problems.[17] This conjunction of two major lines of research enabled Hirschman to make a macroanalysis of how one thing leads to another from a different point of view. It also allowed him to extend his analysis to the developed world.

This became the springboard for another well-known contribution. Hirschman's research in *The Passions* led him to criticize some aspects of economics. One could reasonably expect, therefore, a critical assessment of development economics, and an explanation of the subdiscipline's history. This was the aim of a famous essay, "The Rise and Decline of Development Economics," that was published as an introduction to *Essays in Trespassing* because it helped explain Hirschman's shift of research interest and the origins of his new phase.

Generally speaking, postwar progressive economists took for granted the fact that economic growth would eradicate underdevelopment. The political disasters of the 1960s and 1970s proved them wrong, and obliged economists to reconsider their theories. The discipline never really set itself to the task of understanding the real reasons behind these difficulties, however (see chapter 5).

How was it possible—Hirschman wondered—for a group of Western social scientists who had just lived through World War II to have entertained such great hope for the economic development of underdeveloped countries? Hirschman's answers drew on *The Passions*. Economists, he claimed, were convinced that these less developed countries were not all that complicated, and that their major problems would be solved if only their national per capita income could be raised. "At an earlier time," he wrote (1981a, p. 24), "contempt for the countries designated as 'rude and barbarous' in the eighteenth century, as 'backward' in the nineteenth and 'underdeveloped' in the twentieth had taken the form of relegating them to permanent lowly status. . . . With the new doctrine of economic growth, contempt took a more sophisticated form: . . . the underdeveloped countries were expected to perform like wind-up toys and to 'lumber through' the various stages of development single-mindedly. . . . In sum, like the 'innocent' and *doux* trader of the eighteenth century, these countries were perceived to have only *interests* and *no passions*. Once again, we have learned otherwise."

SHIFTING INVOLVEMENTS

Hirschman's realization of the extent of Western contempt for underdeveloped countries may have put an end to the direct fallout of *The Passions* on development economics but at the same time it reiterated the need to reform contemporary socioeconomic thinking.

In Paris, in June 1978, Hirschman was struck by the manner in which many observers celebrated the tenth anniversary of the May 1968 student revolt. They noticed that the political enthusiasm that had run riot over half the world had gone, but simply recorded without explaining it the radical change of climate that had taken place. During the 1970s, after overwhelming concern with public issues—such as war and peace, greater equality, participation in decision making—people withdrew into their own private worlds. Social studies seemed to have difficulty in coming to grips with this phenomenon.

Hirschman thus decided to study whether modern societies are predisposed to these kinds of oscillation, and in what way. The results of his research were presented in a lecture in honor and memory of Joseph Schumpeter in December 1979. This decision may have had an influence on the path Hirschman then followed.[18] Hirschman was in fact convinced that, as for the business cycles theory, the theory of cycles of collective behavior, to be convincing, had to prove that each phase necessarily stemmed from the preceding one. He thus decided to shelve the "exogenous" perspective that prevailed in contemporary literature and to construct a full-fledged "endogenous" theory. Despite his effort to explain the swings from one phase to the next, he reached, however, the conclusion that these swings were not as accountable for, nor as subject to, generalizations as social science would like them to be. Since social scientists are notoriously overambitious, this might not have concerned him. He decided, nevertheless, to point this problem out in his preface to *Shifting Involvements, Private Interest and Public Action* and wrote, with a touch of self-irony, that he had at times felt he was writing "the conceptual outline of a *Bildungsroman* (with, as always in novels, a number of autobiographical touches mixed in here and there)" (1982b, p. vii).

In the motivations for awarding the Talcott Parsons prize to Hirschman in 1983, the American Academy of Arts and Sciences stated that *Shifting Involvements* "takes as its starting point certain problems in the theory of consumer choice, characteristically turns these into an account of political participation, and ends by arguing that the two are actually a single social process, governed by hope and disappointment. What seems to be at first some small, if unconventional idea about 'changes in preference,' is shown to have unimagined facets and, in the fashion characteristic of Hirschman's work as a whole, it uncovers a larger idea that illuminates the way we live." This admirable synthesis, written with the guidance of Clifford Geertz (The American Academy, 1983, pp. 7–8) may help us focus on the reasons why *Shifting Involvements* was not really understood at the time.

The book "takes disappointment seriously"[19] and tries to come to grips with the logic of a world in which people think they desire something and, once they obtain it, find to their dismay that they actually desired something else. In order to study the phenomenon, Hirschman explored the path leading from private consumption to collective action and back again, playing upon the "small, if unconventional idea" that consumption represents both a satisfying and a disappointing experience. He recognized that other important types of shift exist (such as the one from income maximization to the quest for different kinds of individual happiness, through the family, friends, etc.) but supported his choice on the basis of two arguments. "First, a beginning had to be made somewhere; the task I had set myself was so novel and arduous that I could not aspire to breaking ground everywhere at once. Second, and more important, the occasional movement of large numbers of people into the public arena tends to have such momentous historical consequences that this particular shift, even though it may be undertaken only by a small fraction of a country's total population, is of particular interest for the understanding of social change" (1982b, p. 22).

Perhaps these two arguments should be linked together since the importance of collective action does not explain why private consumption was used as a discriminator, rather than other experiences such as work, study, family life, etc. In this case—as often happens—Hirschman's choice seems to have been dictated by the convergence of personal inclination[20] and analytical opportunity. One consequence was that he lost contact with a large area of collective experience and thus reduced the range of his interlocutors.[21]

I therefore propose to interpret *Shifting Involvements* as a text on the cycle between private interest and public action in which the former is tackled starting from consumption. His methodological approach—in which Hirschman focuses his attention on a specific observation and then allows its wider potential to unfold— is by now familiar. In this case, the spark was probably kindled by *The Joyless Economy* by Tibor Scitovsky (1976), "the first book," Hirschman told the Oxford University Press in 1977, "to make a serious attempt at incorporating basic psychological concepts and insights into economics in general and into its unsatisfactory theory of consumption, in particular."

Let us take a closer look. In trying to explain "why a whole generation of young Americans became disaffected and disappointed with the way of life and high standard of living of their parents' generation" (1977, p. vii), Scitovsky had come across the findings of experimental psychology on human desires and satisfactions. He started with the idea that the arousal of the nervous system can be either too high or too low: at one end there is strain (hunger, thirst, etc.), at the other, boredom. He concentrated on boredom, which he considered typical of affluent societies, and on the stimulations that might assuage this condition.

Hirschman took up this argument from the point of view of the disappointment arising from consumption. Only the possession of money, he argued with Simmel,[22] is totally "immune to disappointment" because money is "absolutely devoid of quality" and therefore conceals nothing. All other commodities and services carry with them a certain disappointment potential. Satisfaction for commodities that vanish as they are consumed is short-lived—as is disappointment; while disappointment with durable goods is prolonged. A satisfactory purchase is transformed by habit into a comfort and, in time, the purchaser might regret having bought it. As for services, the high degree of variability in quality and efficacy, makes them good candidates for becoming a source of disappointment, especially when their supply is on the rise causing a temporary decline in quality. (This problem was also discussed separately to explain the crisis of the welfare state and its recovery potential: 1980a, now in 1986b.) In contrast with Scitovsky's view, Hirschman claimed that novelty too can be disappointing and give rise to hostility. This is a surprising result of Hirschman's detour (chapter 3) into the work of Adam Smith, Jean Jacques Rousseau, and the physiocrats, which he recently revisited when he discussed the discontent produced by industrialization (1992b).[23]

This development of the consumption theory in *Shifting Involvements* suspects that an acquisitive society, founded on increased consumer durables together with service and product innovations, can unleash a vast and ever-increasing disappointment potential. These analytical results (and findings in the history of ideas) linked to the rejection of consumerism are, without doubt, important. If they are interpreted, however, as a means for change (and considered incapable of stimulating as such a new type of behavior in favor of collective action), there is nothing to stop the reader from thinking that comparable dissatisfaction and frustration might arise from other areas of life. These different areas may influence each other in a snowballing process that beyond a certain point may acquire the force of an avalanche.[24]

Hirschman started out by explaining preference changes in elementary terms drawn from traditional economic theory. He then went on to ask himself why anybody looking for happiness in the private sphere, and finding only disappointment and frustration, should not orient his quest towards public action. That is to say, why shouldn't he move from exit to voice?

The private-public dichotomy, as he explained in his introduction (1982b, pp. 7–8), has no correspondence with the medieval dichotomy between the active and the contemplative life. Hirschman examined, rather, two forms of active life that clearly became separated only after the economic development of the seventeenth and eighteenth centuries. For the first time, the pursuit of individual material interests was legitimated and even considered preferable—from the point of view of society—to intense involvement with public affairs, a "privileged arena for the more dangerous *passions* of men such as ambition, envy, and the reckless pursuit of glory and power." The dichotomy examined in *Shifting Involvements* therefore has a great deal in common with the principal theme of *The Passions and the Interests,* but its purpose is not historical: it attempts, rather, "a *phenomenology* of involvements and disappointments" (1982b, p. 8).

On the other hand, the logical basis of Hirschman's inquiry is linked to that of *Exit, Voice, and Loyalty. Shifting Involvements,* Hirschman explained in the first chapter of the book (1982b, pp. 19–24), developed out of analogy with, and separation from, economic consumer theory; it concentrated its research efforts on the reaction to disappointment, just as *Exit* studied the reaction to deterioration. Moreover, its philosophical grounds correspond to those of *Exit,* developing as they do from the human faculty of making mistakes which is part and parcel of the capacity to produce a surplus in excess of mere subsistence. As the aim of the book was to better understand public action—one may add—it was also an investigation into the bias for voice that is expressed so clearly in *Exit.*

If now we return to the central chapters in *Shifting Involvements,* we can better appreciate Hirschman's contribution. A first achievement was in terms of exit-voice theory "a rather remarkable result" (1982b, p. 65). The two terms of the dichotomy are usually considered as alternating: exit mainly represents private interest and voice, public action. However, in the shift from one sphere to the other, exit is often *reinforced* by voice (both private complaints arising out of the dynamics of a consumer experience, and collective action in the general interest). The book thus underscored Hirschman's tendency to create a complementary exit-voice relation; a tendency that, as we shall see shortly, manifested itself clearly in his essay on the collapse of the Berlin Wall.

It is also important to keep in mind that it was in this book that Hirschman advanced his theory of metapreferences.

He put together Harry Frankfurt's theory of second-order volitions, Amartya Sen's theory of metaranking of preference or-
dering, Thomas Schelling's two-stage sequence, and even (in a
footnote) Fyodor Dostoyevsky's *Notes from the Underground,* in
order to gain support for abandoning the assumption of a single,
all-inclusive system of preference propagated by traditional economic theory. A disappointing experience, Hirschman argued,
deflates private-oriented ideology: it contradicts its promise of
happiness in the private sphere and its self-sufficient attitude
regarding participation in public life. In so doing, it highlights
different preference systems and life styles, and paves the way
to change.

Finally, chapter 5 of *Shifting Involvements* contains the "better understanding of collective action" that we came across both
in "How to Complicate Economics" and in the formulation of
the voice concept. In this chapter, many important points are
explored. These include: Hirschman's critique of Mancur Olson's
The Logic of Collective Action; the notion of the rebound effect
that overestimates the expected benefits and underestimates the
expected costs of the new action; and the key concept of the fusion
or confusion between striving for, and attaining, public-oriented
activities, arising from Hirschman's view of participation as the
best possible achievement (apart from winning the struggle).[25]

FRUITFUL CONVERGENCES

For the purposes of this book, I shall not dwell on the return
journey from the public back to the private sphere analyzed in
Shifting Involvements. Nor will I discuss other themes such as the
various causes of disappointment with public action, our impoverished capacity to imagine social change, overcommitment, and
addiction to politics—all of which Hirschman analyzed through
observation and introspection. It is sufficient to recall that in
Shifting Involvements Hirschman completes his theory of the cycles
of collective behavior, which he explicitly subjected to public trial
in the preface.

It was however the idea of the private-public cycle itself that
was the main attraction of the text and put Hirschman on the
same wave length as many of his readers. Guillermo O'Donnell

(1986) perceptively applied it to the history of Argentina at the end of the 1970s, and drew from it the distinction between horizontal and vertical voice. I too (1987a) attempted to develop some aspects of it within the logical framework of the Italian experience. The conclusion is therefore that the issue raised undoubtedly exists but that Hirschman's analysis is perhaps still in the making. From this viewpoint some recent contribution by the author may be observed.

Hirschman stated that his enterprise was justified by the heuristic value of some of its byproducts. This led him to write "Against Parsimony: Three Easy Ways of Complicating Some Categories of Economic Discourse" (1984e) and to reinforce both his critical and propositional approach.

However, the potential of the book's central theme was echoed in the contemporary essay "Rival Views of Market Society." According to the *doux commerce* thesis Hirschman wrote, the constant practice of commercial transactions builds up trust, empathy with others, and other *doux* sentiments; however, as Montesquieu already knew this practice permeates all spheres of human life with the elements of calculation and instrumental reason. The moral basis of a capitalistic society is constantly depleted and replenished at the same time: "An excess of depletion over replenishment and a consequent crisis of the system is then, of course, possible" (1982, now in 1986b, p. 139).

Beyond the alternation of different social phases,[26] *Shifting Involvements* made a determined normative effort. Take, for example, the persistence with which Hirschman returned to the theme of asymmetry in favor of the private sphere that characterizes our societies. Private activities, unlike public ones, can almost entirely fill our lives; they are far more stable, and are given public acknowledgement (1982b, pp. 97 and 127–28). The problem of strengthening voice rather than exit—already dealt with in *Exit*—returns here in the form of the desirable strengthening of public rather than private action.

In his conclusions to *Shifting Involvements,* Hirschman stated the "moral" of his story. He had long been convinced, in fact, that some pattern of change from one life style to another "is not only inevitable but outright useful and desirable"; "some movement back and forth between the public and private life can be wholesome for individuals as well as for society as a whole. But such oscillations can obviously be overdone. That this is the case in our societies *is* the moralizing claim implicit in my story" (1982b, pp. 131 and 132).

"Western societies," he continued (1982b, pp. 132–33),

> appear to be condemned to long periods of privatization during which they live through an impoverishing "atrophy of public meanings," followed by spasmodic outbursts of "publicness" that are hardly likely to be constructive. What is to be done about this atrophy and subsequent spasm? How can we reintroduce more steady concern with public affairs as well as "genuine public celebrations" into our everyday lives? How can we learn to take up public causes with enthusiasm, yet without the frenzy and the millenarian expectations that guarantee failure and massive disappointment?

Shifting Involvements provided no answers to these questions. Hirschman limited himself to endorsing the theory (that dated back to Eugenio Colorni) according to which "to achieve a better understanding of pathological behavior means, to some extent at least, to bring it under control" (1982b, p. 134). Further investigation into the phenomenon was needed alongside the search for "more straightforward remedies." This seems to find confirmation in Hirschman's subsequent work, which, in a more encouraging vein, soon after[27] applied his sailing against the wind theory to the behavior of developed countries.[28]

In early 1983, Hirschman set off on another journey through six Latin American countries to see some "grassroots development" projects. This inspired the book *Getting Ahead Collectively, Grassroots Experiences in Latin America* (1984), of which the first section of chapter 4 was also published separately with a Newtonian title: "The Principle of Conservation and Mutation of Social Energy" (1983).[29] In this book, Hirschman described how, together with his wife Sarah, he listened to and collected together the stories of people who were directly involved in spontaneous collective efforts towards grassroots development and how he found that most of them had previously participated in other, more radical, collective experiences. "It is as though the protagonists' earlier aspiration for social change," he wrote (1984c,

p. 43), "their bent for collective action, had not really left them even though the movements in which they have participated may have aborted or petered out. Later on this 'social energy' becomes active again but is likely to take some very different form."

These observations on the field led Hirschman to formulate the principle we are now discussing: social energy can be stored and then reused, often in a different form. Individuals who have been through intense political experiences are capable of taking up arms again and again in the course of their lifetime. Similarly, movements behind these struggles should also be assessed, taking such important consequences into account.[30] Hirschman said in an interview in 1987 that these active individuals have the function of "recharging society's batteries."

These ideas can thus be traced back to *Shifting Involvements*,[31] with the difference that they portray a more optimistic picture than the one that emerged from the earlier book.

LESSONS FROM A HISTORY OF BERLIN

It seems to me that reconsidering with hindsight the principal theme of *Shifting Involvements* is a particularly useful exercise in the light of Hirschman's most recent and significant development regarding the exit-voice theory: "Exit, Voice, and the Fate of the German Democratic Republic: An Essay in Conceptual History" (1993).[32]

Only six days after the crumbling of the Berlin Wall, Germany became involved in a debate on the interpretation of ongoing events in terms of exit-voice. Hirschman came across this debate during his sabbatical in 1990–91 at the Wissenschaftkolleg of Berlin. "I came to feel," he wrote (1993b, p. 175), "that the exit-voice perspective could indeed be of help in seeing some of the events in a new light and that it could itself be enriched by its encounter with a complex historical testing ground," such as the one provided by the history of the Democratic Republic of Germany.

Detlef Pollack, a sociologist of religion from the University of Leipzig, held that in 1989 Germany, exit (the emigration westward) and voice (protest demonstrations against the regime) reinforced each other and together caused the fall of the regime.

This spectacular example of collaboration between exit and voice, Hirschman thought, could be used to provide strength and prominence to the many observations that he had made in the past on the complementarity of exit and voice.

The essay shows that in the history of the G.D.R. (in line with that of Poland, Czechoslovakia, and Hungary) the exit-voice relationship was mainly antagonistic. Escape plans, the hope of success, television as a form of evasion, and authorized or, rather, establishment-manipulated emigration had a stifling effect on voice, on top of its intrinsic weaknesses (lack of independent national traditions, heritage of the Nazi experience, Soviet military occupation).

This analytical approach is at a certain point combined with that of the mutual strengthening of exit and voice. As Stein Rokkan had pointed out almost two decades earlier, Hirschman explained that the decision to erect the Berlin Wall in 1961 was correctly perceived by the population as a turning away from both exit and voice. The decision was to split the city into two noncommunicating halves. As such, it was an extreme show of state power and revealed the G.D.R.'s determination to use this power indiscriminately against "enemies of state." The effect was to suffocate voice, which was soon reduced to silence.

Today we can look back on this tragic negative mutual strengthening of exit and voice with greater detachment, since the "divine surprise" of 1989 later had the opposite effect: the G.D.R.'s failure to contain the westward flight of its population (via Hungary, Poland, or Czechoslovakia) in the spring of 1989 was interpreted as a simultaneous decline in its capacity to stifle voice. The result was to prompt the mass demonstrations that ultimately destroyed the regime.[33]

Hirschman went on to explain that new exit opportunities created a sense of empowerment in the population. People reconsidered their situation and succeeded in getting involved in trying to bring about change directly. The exit-voice combination thus became truly powerful. Reinforced by high levels of emigration and a gradual rebirth of voice, the mass demonstrations of Leipzig, Dresden, and Berlin were characterized by an inner dialectic and even an interplay—documented by Hirschman with fascinating details—between supporters of voice and of exit, which led to their merging and, finally, to revolt.

Just *how* exit stimulated rather than depressed voice still remains to be explained. First on Hirschman's list was a failure in the recovery mechanism usually activated by exit. The authorities had done away with this option claiming—with bloodcurdling rhetoric—"we do not shed a single tear over those who leave." The increasing number of escapees to the West, in fact, deeply shocked better informed public opinion and even affected some quarters of the leadership. It was too late to remedy matters but in time to avert large-scale repression.

If one accepts the fact (as *Exit* did not) that citizens have at least two levels of loyalty, another explanation could be that the less loyal opted for exit while the more loyal, beyond a certain degree of deterioration, came down in favor of voice.

Hirschman's strongest argument, however, was that exit transformed itself into collective action. Thousands upon thousands of individual decisions, made in private, in silence, on tiptoe, were transformed by a social event of overwhelming importance due to the uncontainable number of these decisions, the importance attributed to them by world media, and the shock they left in their wake. The rising wave of politicization was mirrored by the crescendo of spontaneous slogans yelled out in the demonstrations.

In his conclusion, Hirschman stated that the 1989 uprising represented a reversal of trend. A "disastrously characteristic" tendency of German history was, in fact, its propensity to withdraw from the public arena into a strictly private sphere. It is interesting to note that the reversal came about in a different way from that postulated in *Shifting Involvements*. While it is generally thought that the swing from public to private "is supposed to have come all too easily to Germans, particularly when they were confronted with distasteful and repugnant events in the public domain" (1993b, p. 201), the opposite swing was not set off by disappointment. It was, rather, the success and, consequently, the satisfaction of exit that unleashed voice.

Second, Hirschman considered the 1989 movement as a contrast to the long series of failed revolutions in Germany's history since the Reformation. He also expressed regret that the event is referred to as a "turning point" rather than a "peaceful revolution," revealing the Germans' instinctive need to down-scale matters in order to mitigate the differences with the past.

If we return to the perspective of *Shifting Involvements*, a change of emphasis is clearly noticeable. Mass movements are important in and of themselves, due to the effects (direct or indirect, immediate or delayed) that they produce and to their long-term repercussions. In broader terms, collective actions, both small and large, are important outlets that must be "tolerated or fostered" (1982b, p. 118), nurtured and directed towards effectively achieving their various consequences. The task of studying useful ways of exploiting the energy of movements thus presented itself once again.

Finally, in a conclusive remark on method,[34] Hirschman stated, self-critically, that he too had contributed to the pastime of making mountains out of molehills as he "collected conclusive evidence for the existence, in many realms, of a fundamental antagonism between private exit and public voice" (1993b, p. 202).[35]

This seems to be important, too, in view of the concrete consequences that can be derived from it. "In some momentous constellations, so we have learned," the author continued, "exit can cooperate with voice, voice can emerge from exit, and exit can reinforce voice." As this is caused by the greater power that people feel they have acquired through new exit opportunities, it is possible for similar influences to affect different, maybe smaller constellations. Large-scale politicalization processes such as the one that took place in 1989, could open our eyes and give us faith in our ability to encourage the more prosaic social activities that surround us.[36]

8

Democracy:
Doubts and Intransigence

This exploration of Hirschman's works leads us, finally, to the question of intransigent rhetoric and democracy. In this chapter, I will show how Hirschman identified the various conservative and progressive rhetorical arguments that compromise democratic discussion; I will explore the motivations, method of construction, and unexpected developments of his research from the crux of the book to his advice to reformers. I will look into how Flaubert influenced his writing, and focus on the concluding observation of *The Rhetoric of Reaction,* in which Hirschman claims how important it is to be free of intransigent rhetoric, and connect his claim to a few theses concerning the genesis of the democratic process and democratic deliberation. I will examine contributions made by Dankwart Rustow and Bernard Manin, in addition to some shorter pieces written by Hirschman in conjunction with *The Rhetoric.* The chapter closes with a few conjectures on the democratic personality, the culture of doubt, and—by extension—on the inspiration of the author.

The question What can we do? dominates every article in the local newspaper of Fontamara, the poorest backwater of Marsica, Abruzzi, where Ignazio Silone set his memorable story of social struggle under Fascism. The same question presents itself punctually to every generation, and often within a single generation. Silone's book provides no answer; nor, of course, does Hirschman's work, though—as we have seen on more than one occasion—he does make a deliberate point of providing his

187

readers with useful tools for understanding what can be done in the most varied circumstances. This could be one reason why, as Jean-Claude Casanova described it (1990, p. 12), Hirschman not only has an extended circle of established friendships, but also "friends he does not know; that is to say, people who ask themselves, when dealing with an event: What would Hirschman think of this?"

These are some of the thoughts that came to mind as I turned to Hirschman's most recent intellectual "production line" which resulted in *The Rhetoric of Reaction: Perversity, Futility, Jeopardy* (1991), a study of two hundred years of both reactionary and progressive rhetoric devoted to what one should not think. His most ambitious conclusion, Hirschman explained in a passage from a later article that I would like to adopt as my lode star, was to

> show how discussions between reactionaries and progressives—each with their own brand of intransigent arguments—are dialogues of the deaf and contraptions to avoid that genuine deliberation and communication between contending groups that is supposed to be characteristic of democracy. What is such truly democratic debate really like? Of that we unfortunately still lack both deep knowledge and "thick description." In the meantime, then, it may be useful to try indirect approaches: mine consisted in identifying a number of specific arguments and rhetorical practices that endanger the debate itself and therefore have no place in a democracy. Hence, the title of my concluding section: "How *not* to argue in democracy." (1992c, pp. 10–11)

The Rhetoric came about after the Ford Foundation decided to bring together a group of citizens to produce an authoritative statement regarding the "Crisis of the Welfare State" in 1985, not long after Ronald Reagan's reelection. Hirschman, a member of the group, informs us (1993e, p. 303 and 1991, pp. x–xi) that he was "intensely unhappy" about the direction the country seemed to be taking but did not see the need to launch a head-on attack on the reactionary mentality and personality, as was fashionable at the time in the progressive camp.

The explanation he provided—that a head-on attack could have worsened matters by leading "to an undue fascination with a demonized adversary"—was probably the conclusion of an in-depth reflection. Apart from the reasons we have already encountered, such as his marked preference for indirect strategies and desire to take part in a debate without getting caught up in its coordinates, there were two further reasons for Hirschman to seek a new approach. The first was the observation that the reactionary wave created logical traps into which the direct answers provided by the progressive camp unfortunately tended to fall (see, for example, those listed in note 4, chapter 1: 1991, p. 173). This was, if nothing else, a matter of redressing an imbalance of arms. The second was the idea that we do, and can, know very little directly about the democratic nature of a debate because, like happiness, it is a "final aim" that normally "eludes a direct quest" (see note 33).

Hence Hirschman's decision to go against the flow; that is, to attempt a "cool" examination of "surface phenomena"—the discourse, arguments, and rhetoric of reaction[1]—in the hope of being able to show that "discourse is shaped, not so much by fundamental personality traits, but simply by the *imperatives of argument,* almost regardless of the desires, character, or convictions of the participants. Exposing these servitudes might actually help to loosen them and thus modify the discourse and restore communication" (1991, p. xi).

This decision is—typically enough—an attempt to find a way out of a difficult situation through a process that explores paths contiguous to those previously trodden. Take, for example, fracasomania, ideology, and unintended consequences, discussed in chapters 4 and 5. These are referred to several times[2] and often come to mind while reading *The Rhetoric.* In fact, the more the argument develops, the clearer it becomes that Hirschman has found in the analysis of rhetoric a new way of dealing with a question he has cultivated at length. It could thus be said that the book is halfway between the corpus of works that led to *Journeys* and that which led to *The Passions.*

Let us go back, then, to the spark that set off Hirschman's research: Ralf Dahrendorf's opening statement to the working group which recalled the three dimensions of citizenship—civil, political, and social—identified by T. H. Marshall, and claimed that the latter had run into considerable difficulties which the

English sociologist had not foreseen. Hirschman, struck by this observation, decided to go further and generalize Dahrendorf's criticism. "Is it not true," he asked (1991, p. 3), "that not just the last but each and every one of Marshall's three progressive thrusts has been followed by ideological counterthrusts of extraordinary force? And have not these counterthrusts been at the origin of convulsive social and political struggles often leading to setbacks for the intended progressive programs as well as to much human suffering and misery?"

Hirschman opted to deal with the counterthrusts rather than the thrusts, keeping in mind Whithead's well-known observation: "The major advances in civilization are processes which all but wreck the societies in which they occur"—and questioning the appropriateness today of the qualifying "all but" (1991, p. 3).[3] Moreover, he had no intention of embarking on yet another "broad and leisurely" historical narration, but chose to focus on a few common rhetorical arguments that can be traced to each of the three reactive movements following the three thrusts mentioned earlier.

The obstinately progressive nature of the modern age, he argued, is such that anyone trying to oppose one of the characteristic collective thrusts is reluctant to launch a head-on attack. He will try to claim, rather, that the progressive action is destined to fail. In analyzing the principal ways in which reactionaries criticize and attack the three progressive thrusts, Hirschman came up with another triad: the "perversity thesis" (according to which any attempt to impel society in a given direction will have the effect of pushing it the other way); the "futility thesis" (according to which attempts at social transformation will simply be unavailing or futile); and the "jeopardy thesis" (according to which the cost of the proposed change is too high because it jeopardizes a previous, precious conquest).[4]

Hirschman concentrated for a time on the history of "reactionary" ideas, selecting the most significant formulations, and reconstructing by means of hypotheses and elements of fact the evolution of the three theses. He separated them conceptually, compared them, and showed how they are often combined in a contradictory, rare, or irregular fashion; he studied, with his habitual tenacity and irony, their characteristics, their repetitive or innovative arguments, fields of application, intellectual attraction, genesis, and trajectory. He then ascribed an order to his exposition: the perversity thesis—the most constant, shocking, and destructive of reactionary objections—is followed by the futility thesis which is colder, more intellectually refined, and more injurious to the agents of change. Finally, after these extreme, simple, and univocal arguments, came the jeopardy thesis, more respectful of common sense, moderate in its criticism of change, versatile, and polyhedric. The path Hirschman traced grew in interest and significance, and culminated in a synoptic table and a study of the interactions between the three theses.

These results do not, however, cover the whole of the book. While the manuscript was in progress over a period of more than three years, Hirschman had no thought whatever of writing chapter 6, entitled: "From Reactionary to Progressive Rhetoric." On reaching his conclusions regarding the jeopardy thesis, however, he realized that this thesis could be reversed by the thesis of mutual support between a new reform and previous conquests. The path was thus left open for Hirschman to outline a typology of "progressive," as a counterpart to "reactionary," rhetoric. This unexpected development radically transformed the volume, even suggesting the jacket design on which Hirschman chose to depict the prophet Daniel admonishing Jonathan sternly and possibly intransigently. Doubt was also cast on the very title of the book: his publishers retained *The Rhetoric of Reaction* for the original English edition, but the Italian, Brazilian, and Mexican editions bear the more fitting *Rhetorics of Intransigence*.

The whole episode has a paradigmatic quality: the *"unexpected consequences of their own thoughts,"* as Hirschman described it (1993e, p. 307), adding, "it is not easy to cite examples . . . expressly acknowledged and assiduously explored by their authors within one and the same book"—nor even within his own books, one could say. The "combative élan" behind *The Rhetoric* bears some similarities to that behind *National Power;* in the former, however, the results were modulated as the volume was being written, while in the latter, as in other texts, this took place at a later stage.

We could date the turning point back to summer and fall of 1988. At the beginning of September, Hirschman took part in a colloquium in his honor at the University of Bielefeld. He read Claus Offe's introductory remarks claiming that Hirschman had not even provided us "with the outlines of a project of a 'progressive' nature," annotating in the margin "Wait till I finish!" as if a project of this kind was in fact taking shape at this time. Furthermore, in a letter dated September 15, he told Offe that his criticism was premature, remarking: "My work in this field is very much in progress, and maybe I will come up with something!"[5]

In "*The Rhectoric of Reaction:* Two Years Later" Hirschman declared that he had conceived the book as a "tract." On the basis of the first five chapters, in fact, the book was received by sympathetic and unsympathetic critics alike as an "anti-conservative, or perhaps neoanti-conservative manifesto" (1993e, p. 303).[6] There is, however, a more noble connotation of the word "manifesto," as the outline of a new project. My hypothesis is that as Hirschman cleared the way for a critique of progressive rhetoric—the "real crux" of the book, as Otto Kallscheuer wrote in *Die Zeit* (1992)— he opened up a path in that direction which adds another significant dimension to the whole corpus of his work.

TOWARDS OPEN SEA

Chapter 6 of the book covers less than a fifteenth of the pages devoted to reactionary rhetoric. Like the Flaubertian page that concludes *Journeys* (see chapter 5), it is, however, highly evocative.

Hirschman showed that the doctrine of the dictatorship of the proletariat is a mirror image of the jeopardy thesis (since it claims that social progress must be pursued even at the cost of sacrificing liberties). He also presented the idea that the progressive thesis of mutual support between new and acquired rights (or "sinergy illusion") is nothing more than the obverse of the reactionary jeopardy thesis; and that progressives are usually more aware of the dangers inherent in inaction than of those inherent in action stressed by the jeopardy argument, so that they tend to propose the opposite thesis of "imminent danger" which impels them to action.

Later on in the chapter, as a counterpart to the futility thesis and the social laws that sustained it, Hirschman summoned Karl Marx and his proudest intellectual assertion: that of having come upon the traces of the "economic law of motion of modern society." Concluding his excursus into progressive rhetoric, Hirschman contrasted the perversity thesis with the logic of the enlightenment and of utopianism—that is, the fiction of building a new society according to the dictates of reason, which is always "someone's idea of what 'reason' commands" (1991, p. 160).

Hirschman later elucidated some of his reasons for writing chapter 6 (1993e, pp. 304–5). First of all, there was the "sheer fun" of pursuing his argument in an unexpected direction; then there was the sense of moral duty to go ahead "once the idea had crossed my mind." Nor did he exclude "intellectual tastes" as a factor, savoring, for example, two contrasting aphorisms: the proto-Romantic Vauvenargues's "Great ideas come from the heart," and Paul Valéry's counterpronouncement, "Our most important ideas are those that contradict our feelings." "Vauvenargues," Hirschman wrote, "presides over the first chapters and then gives way to Valéry as patron-saint of the last two."[7] Recalling Hirschman's discussion of the lasting tensions between heart and mind in the social sciences (see chapter 2), one can see how this is reflected in his own experience.

There was a fourth reason: the hope of concluding the book "on a broad and positive note." Otherwise, he noted, "I would probably have finished with the somewhat gratuitous advice to the practitioners of reactionary rhetoric to 'plead their cause with greater originality, sophistication, and restraint' which I had proferred at the end of my *Atlantic* article"—a reduced version of "Two Hundred Years of Reactionary Rhetoric: The Case of Perverse Effect" (The Tanner Lecture in Human Values, April 1988).[8] Actually, chapter 6 makes some concluding remarks of the Tanner Lecture more convincing; it clears away others; while it advances the idea of getting rid of rhetorical arguments that compromise democratic debate.

Coming to the last chapter of *The Rhetoric,* and keeping in mind the conclusions contained in the Tanner Lecture (see note 8), we can thus focus on three key points.

The first is the Flaubertian touch. The *bêtise* of the useless repetition of contrasting rhetorical arguments forms the basis of a reasonable presumption as to their logical defects and of an intellectual suspicion as to their use and abuse. "Far from diluting my message," Hirschman pointed out (1991, p. 166), "the preceding chapter on progressive rhetoric further strengthens this point. By demonstrating that each of the reactionary arguments has one or more progressive counterparts, I generated contrasting *pairs*[9] of reactionary and progressive statements about social action." These "extreme statements in a series of imaginary, highly polarized debates . . . stand effectively exposed as *limiting cases,* badly in need, under most circumstances, of being qualified, mitigated, or otherwise amended."

The second is that, aside from the bashful annotation above (and the mention at the end of the usefulness of the volume), there is no real place in Hirschman's conclusions for advice to his users—what we could call, after the example of the Tanner Lecture, a user's handbook in rhetoric.[10] Hirschman was clearly convinced it was not worth insisting on this point, although he changed his mind soon after.[11]

The third is the new conclusion on the rhetorics of intransigence and the need to create a democracy-friendly environment. This was echoed in the preface where Hirschman quoted from a short story expressing "concern over the massive, stubborn, and exasperating otherness of others"[12] to maintain that modern democratic societies have a tendency to raise walls of incomprehension, puzzlement, and mutual rejection between groups of citizens, and in particular between opposing political poles. Rhetorics of intransigence, practiced by both reactionaries and progressives—the "two identical impertinences" as Hirschman called them after Flaubert—are a fast-setting cement for erecting these walls.

Far from wishing to send the Montagues and Capulets to the devil, Hirschman's suggestion to "move public discourse beyond extreme, intransigent postures of either kind" carried the hope that a big enough hole could be made, as a consequence, in the wall to reinstate communication and set into motion a process of deliberation more democracy friendly (1991, p. 168).

THE REFORMER AND THE COMMISSARIAT

The influence of chapter 6 can be deduced with hindsight from an important subsequent development.

Hirschman was invited by the French government's Commissariat Général du Plan to participate in a colloquium on the topic of "Social Justice and Inequalities" (November 12–14, 1992; third meeting—"Putting the Principles of Justice into Practice"). In contrast to the fact that progressive rhetoric had by and large been ignored by critics, the Commissariat explicitly asked Hirschman to use chapter 6 as the starting point for his contribution. "I must presume," he wrote in his address (1992c, p. 3), "that my friends at the Plan found this chapter particularly intriguing, in part perhaps because they hoped to derive some practical use from it for the time when they will wish to present in public policy proposals arising out of their current thinking. . . . At that point, they may wish to avoid the kind of intransigent rhetoric that is the butt of my criticism."

In Hirschman's address to the colloquium, then, we find an interesting summary of practical advice for reformers: the user's handbook we mentioned earlier. In brief, taking up the concluding argument from the Tanner Lecture, Hirschman claimed that reformers should be aware of the principal objections—linked to the perversity, futility and jeopardy theses—that are likely to be raised against their proposals. They must also try to minimize the vulnerability of these proposals by studying the effective damage they could produce. They must not, however, become "unduly skittish" while doing so, nor "endlessly search for all conceivable perverse effects."[13] Finally, they should refrain from typical reformist rhetorics such as the thesis of the disastrous situation, that of history being on their side, and that of the synergy between different reforms.

The alarmist thesis of impending disaster (or revolution) that can only be averted if certain progressive programs are adopted has been very much in fashion this century, but fortunately, with the decline of communism, its influence has waned. The thesis which claims that a certain progressive policy should be adopted because "such is the 'tide' of history" is similarly unattractive at present, and should not be too difficult to discard.[14] Hirschman was thus left with the third thesis—that of mutual support and synergy between proposed reforms—which he asked his friends to use sparingly.

Reformers, he stated, must be aware of the fact that they spontaneously tend to view things through the rose-tinted spectacles of mutual support between reforms rather than through the darker lenses of the jeopardy thesis. If reformers fail to explore the existing possibilities themselves, or develop elements of contrast between the proposal and past reforms, "they will be ill-equipped for useful discussions with their conservative opponents" (1992c, p. 18).

What is more, he continued, the conviction that there are no real obstacles to reform can easily be transformed into the conviction that "nothing *should* stand in its way." Those who hold this opinion can thus turn against the worthwhile aspects of reality when, against all expectations, these very aspects become obstacles to progress. "The advocates of some reform will then be tempted to act in accordance with the maxim, 'the end justifies the means' and may well *prove the jeopardy thesis right.*" The highly popular synergy thesis, Hirschman concluded, "disregards the complexity of the societies we live in and is injurious to democratic deliberations whose essence is tradeoff and compromise" (1992c, pp. 16–17).

What we have seen here is a whole discussion on progressive rhetoric and reformers that springs from the idea underpinning *The Rhetoric*—that is, Flaubert's repeated rhetorics. Hirschman developed his conclusion out of his advice to reformers, and was inspired by the vital need to create a more democracy-friendly environment. Writing chapter 6 was not a turnabout in argument, as he suggested at the end of *The Rhetoric*, but produced a multifaceted and unexpected development of the various aspects and themes analyzed in the book.

My point is as follows: just because Hirschman's critique turned to progressive rhetoric, it did not mean that he chose to withdraw from his *démarche*, as the very readers Hirschman wanted to reassure might have feared. On the contrary, it further qualified Hirschman's choice and committed him to the progressive camp, as his address to the Commissariat showed and as we shall see even more clearly in the second part of this chapter.

THE GENESIS OF DEMOCRACY

We have established that exposing, and even ridiculing, the repetitiveness of contrasting arguments can open up communication channels between opposing groups; but it is still not entirely clear why Hirschman attributed such importance to this.

Anyone interested in answering this question has only to turn to Hirschman's brief concluding thought in the last two pages of the book. Is this intended to clear the way for further research? Or is it a trick to attract our attention? Or could it be a signpost for an intellectual path to follow?

The final alternative seems to be the most promising because it allows us to deal with this significant section of the conclusions to *The Rhetoric* without making doubtful conjectures (and without passively awaiting further developments in Hirschman's research). I shall therefore attempt to snoop behind the scenes, taking Hirschman at his word when he claims that his argument should be linked to two recent and valuable insights, "a historical one on the origins of pluralistic democracies, and a theoretical one on the long-run conditions for stability and legitimacy of such regimes" (1991, p. 168). To these two threads I would like to add a third, indicated in a few collateral texts which complete the arguments presented in *The Rhetoric* and expand the intellectual breadth of the work.[15]

The three threads which I shall try to unweave, although linked to relatively recent cognitive results, correspond to basic guidelines long recognized and developed by the author. Taken together they go back as far as Hirschman's adolescence; the two prophets depicted on the book jacket, in fact, had made a deep impression on the sixteen-year-old Hirschman visiting Bamberg Cathedral.

That the historical insight stemming from Dankwart Rustow goes back a long way is obvious: a young German intellectual living through the turbulent events described at the beginning of this book could hardly avoid pondering over the nature of the democratic system. There are signs of this meditation in many of Hirschman's writings: in his reactions to the political disasters in Latin American countries, for example; in the *Bildungsroman* approach in *Shifting Involvements* (such as chapter 6 on universal suffrage); or in a few sensitive points in *The Rhetoric* (see 1991, pp. 5–6, 77–80, 146–48).

In the painful years following the military coup in Brazil (1964), Hirschman probably gave priority to this subject matter. This is where, if I am not mistaken, Hirschman's path met that of Dankwart Rustow. In 1967, the professor at Columbia University published *A World of Nations: Problems of Political Modernization*, which referred several times to Hirschman's work (regarding, in particular, unbalanced growth, obstacles to development, cognitive dissonance, and journeys towards progress). Moreover, in 1970, Rustow published "Transitions to Democracy: Towards a Dynamic Model." Hirschman commented on the importance of this article in his introduction to *A Bias for Hope* (1971, p. 30). The historical insight quoted in *The Rhetoric* should in fact be traced back to this essay and to the first chapter of Bernard Crick's *In Defense of Politics* (1964).

Rustow's "Transitions to Democracy" presented a fairly innovative argument. Countless explanations of democracy are provided by the socio-political literature of North America, Rustow argued: some underscore socio-economic conditions (such as high income and high literacy rates); others stress the psychological component that permits wide consensus; still others place their emphasis on the reconciliation of conflicts. The various authors, however, have two aspects in common. First, they all raise the same kind of questions and answer them using similar data, culled mostly from current information. Second, the issue at stake is not so much how a democratic system comes about, as how a democracy can best preserve its state of health. Rustow claimed, by contrast, that it is important to investigate the genesis of democratic regimes—not least because it is of considerable interest for the vast majority of nations who are trying to secure or consolidate democracy.[16]

By changing his observation point, Rustow thus looked at his subject from a new and unexpected angle. He left aside some of the traditional restrictions and focused on historical periods characterized by the advent of democracy (periods spanning more than one generation but still relatively brief, to facilitate his task). He eliminated from his survey cases in which the impulse for transformation was due to external factors (immigration, foreign political or military influence, etc.), and subjected two concrete situations to close scrutiny in order to draw up a few general conclusions to verify against the history of other cases. Rustow was thus able to outline a very different universe from the one usually studied, made up of twenty-three countries; and to build his argument from an analysis of Sweden and Turkey he knew in great detail.

There was one background condition—national unity—and three phases to his model: those of preparation, decision, and habituation to democracy. Let us suppose that the majority of citizens has no mental reservations as to the community to which it belongs—taken implicitly for granted; in this case, Rustow argued (1970, p. 352), "I hypothesize that . . . the dynamic process of democratization itself is set off by a prolonged and inconclusive political struggle." To give it these qualities, Rustow continues, the protagonists must represent well-entrenched social classes, and the struggle must have "profound meaning for them." The "particular social composition of the contending forces . . . and the specific nature of the issues," however, "will vary widely from one country to the next and in the same country from period to period."

This is where a key trait of Rustow's argument made itself clear: concentration on a few stylized aspects of transitions to democracy that recur within a context that is otherwise inventive and changeable.[17] In turn-of-the-century Sweden, for example, there was contention between peasants, workers and petit bourgeoisie, and an alliance of state bureaucrats, landowners and industrialists over taxes, military service, and the vote. In Turkey during the 1960s, there was a similar conflict between the rural world and the heirs of the Kemalist military bureaucracy over whether to develop agriculture or industry.[18] The seriousness of the issue at stake and the prolonged nature of the struggle, Rustow continued, generally cause the protagonists to rally around two different banners. This polarization (tempered by national pride that disincentivates mass expulsions and genocide)[19] can lead either to the victory of one group over another, or to a gradual retreat into the ranks. If neither of these eventualities takes place, the road is clear for democracy.

"What concludes the preparatory phase," Rustow wrote (1970, p. 355), "is a deliberate decision on the part of political leaders to accept the existence of diversity in [national] unity and, to that end, to institutionalize some crucial aspect of democratic procedure." In Sweden, it was the Great Compromise of 1907 that led to the adoption of universal suffrage and proportional representation; in Great Britain the process started in the seventeenth century and was not completed until the nineteenth. Many more examples could be cited in addition to these: in all of them a single decision or several decisions are consciously made by the political leadership[20] for a wide variety of reasons.[21]

These decisions, moreover, must be assimilated by the two rival groups and by the citizenry at large; the habituation phase of the model can then begin. "A distasteful decision, once made, is likely to seem more palatable as one is forced to live with it. . . . Festinger's theory of 'cognitive dissonance' supplies a technical explanation and experimental support. Democracy, moreover, is by definition a competitive process, and this competition gives an edge to those who can rationalize their commitment to it, and an even greater edge to those who sincerely believe in it." On the other hand, "a new political regime is a novel prescription for taking joint chances on the unknown:" if it proves viable, it is "a proof of the efficacy of the principle of conciliation and accommodation" and encourages political forces to adopt democratic procedures when dealing with questions of primary importance (1970, p. 358).[22]

Making connections, on several occasions, with Hirschman's work,[23] Rustow stated at the end of his analysis that his genetic point of view was an alternative to the prevailing functionalist belief in the theory of consensus.[24] "It is often thought," Rustow quoted from Bernard Crick (1964, p. 24), "that for this 'master science' [i.e., democratic politics] to function, there must already be in existence some shared idea of a 'common good,' some 'consensus' or *consensus juris*. But this common good is itself the process of practical reconciliation of the interests of the various . . . aggregates, or groups which compose a state; it is not some external and intangible spiritual adhesive. . . . Diverse groups hold together, firstly because they have a common interest in sheer survival, and secondly, because they practice politics— not because they agree about 'fundamentals.' "

It is interesting to see how Hirschman commented on this analysis hot off the press in his introduction to *A Bias for Hope* (see chapters 3 and 5). Having stated that the idea of cognitive dissonance was so congenial to his thinking that he put it into practice in *The Strategy* before he had become acquainted with the social psychologists that first theorized it, he went on to add that "similar critiques of . . . the one-way nature of certain sequences can now be found elsewhere in the social sciences." One example was the critique of the seemingly self-evident notion that, "a consensus on basic values and political procedures is a precondition for the establishment of a viable democratic system."

According to Rustow, Hirschman quipped, "the causation has often run the other way—democracy has come into being as a result of an accidental but prolonged standoff between forces originally quite bent on crushing each other; and what basic consensus about political decision making is later found to prevail in these cases can be shown to have been the consequence of democracy, rather than its cause" (1971a, p. 30).[25]

However, bearing in mind my comments in chapter 3 about the multiplicity of sequences, the criticisms contained in *Exit* regarding cognitive dissonance (taken up once again), and more recent critiques of the one-thing-at-a-time theory, it is easy to see how Rustow's model might clear the way for a new branch of research.

This is hinted at in Rustow's essay when he states that post-war Turkey made the decision to embrace democracy before a real conflict between major social groups broke out. This decision led to changes in government (and to a "drift back into authoritarian practices") interrupted in 1961 by the military coup. "These developments," Rustow claimed (1970, p. 362),

> are not unconnected: Turkey paid the price in 1960 for having received its first democratic regime as a free gift from the hands of a dictator. But after 1961 there was a further evolution in a more appropriate sequence. The crisis of 1960–1961 had made social and political conflict far more acceptable, and a full range of social and economic issues was debated for the first time. The conflict that shaped up was between the military on one side and the spokesman of the agrarian majority on the other—and the compromise between these two allowed the resumption of the democratic experiment on a more secure basis by 1965.

This example was used to demonstrate the primacy of the sequence described in the model but it could also launch a historical search for other, perhaps inverted sequences; even for counterindications or blocks that might be set in motion by the same sequences.

This project is particularly important now, because of the peculiar features of the democratization process unfolding today (in East Europe, Latin America, and elsewhere), highlighted by Rustow in his recent work (1990, 1992).

POLITICAL DELIBERATION

Rustow also shed light on some reasons for the fragility of the democratic system. The prospects of democracy can be damaged, he wrote (1970, p. 359), if urgent political questions are not successfully addressed during the delicate habituation phase, and if continually surfacing key conflicts are not efficiently quelled. For more than twenty years, Hirschman must have thought this was an important clue to a complex problem that would help him reconsider political aspects of his experience; take up new research (such as that on the tunnel effect); get down to the cultural and political roots of the turn to authoritarianism in Latin America; and warn coming generations of the sometime destructive consequences of "shifting involvements."

While devoting his attention to these tasks, outside developments—first and foremost the process of redemocratization of Latin America—led him to embrace a more optimistic view of the future.[26]

The turning point, in my view, can be traced back to *Getting Ahead Collectively* (1984), a report on an inquiry conducted by Albert and Sarah Hirschman into 45 programs of grassroots development. A thrill of emotion can be detected, above all in the last chapter, "What Does It All Add Up To?" as if hesitation had been thrown to the winds to be replaced by an understandably confident hope. Hirschman outlined a series of positive results achieved by the vast movement of grassroots development in Latin America: the role of social activists, solidarity, the weakening of authoritarian forces, the reinforcing of democratic ventures, and the increasing recognition of the basic economic rights of all citizens.

Not much later Hirschman wrote, or "succeeded in writing" as he himself confessed with satisfaction, "Notes on Consolidating Democracy in Latin America" (1986). This concise yet densely-filled paper was presented to a meeting of political scientists held in São Paolo in December 1985, which makes it contemporary with the early stages of *The Rhetoric*. My impression is that the article launched a parallel argument which only joins up with *The Rhetoric* later, while Hirschman was writing chapter 6 (see note 33).

These "Notes," succinctly written in a series of numbered paragraphs as if the author were presenting a political agenda, started off on a gloomy note. "The point of departure of any serious thought about the chances for the consolidation of democracy in Latin America," he wrote, "must surely be pessimism. The principle reason is simply that the historical record is so desperately unpromising" (1986b, p. 176). As a matter of fact the "pervasive characteristic of *any* political regime" in these countries is instability.

Nevertheless, in a passage reminiscent of the beginning of *The Strategy*, Hirschman argued, "There is little point in looking for the root cause of this instability. Its strength and duration suggest that all kinds of convergent, interrelated factors are at work, from culture and social structure to economic vulnerability. It is correspondingly futile to lay down 'preconditions' for consolidating democracy." It was this logical inversion that opened up an unexpectedly possibilist argument as to what can be done against all odds.

"We must train ourselves," Hirschman claimed (1986b, p. 177), "to be on the lookout for unusual historical developments, rare constellations of favorable events, narrow paths, partial advances that may conceivably be followed by others, and the like." The question for Hirschman was how to train oneself to think about these matters. He suggested three ways: to "envisage the possibility of a disjunction between political and economic conditions"; to move forward by sailing against the winds; and to try to understand which good things go together.

Hirschman thus grafted a new idea onto his by now familiar method of searching for a solution to a complex problem. The climate permitting a birth or rebirth of democracy, widespread popular participation and grassroots support, he argued, "may be favorable for introducing democratic values of tolerance and openness to discussion not only into the political process, but into everyday patterns of behavior among groups and individuals" (1986b, p. 179). Hirschman then went on to discuss the complementary contributions of two political scientists: Adam Przeworski's "Love Uncertainty and You Will Be Democratic" (1984), and Bernard Manin's "Volonté générale ou délibération? Esquisse d'une théorie de la délibération" (1985).

Focusing on the propitious moment in which democracy is experienced as an attainment, Hirschman shifted the emphasis of progressive policy from *content* (such as the battle against drought, agrarian reform, and the struggle against inflation discussed in *Journeys*) to a cluster of problems usually catalogued as the *form* of democratic procedure. There is probably a moral to this shift (further developed in *The Rhetoric*): the true advancement of progressive policy, Hirschman seemed to suggest, is not the result of any particular social achievement per se. It is due rather to the real consolidation and development of democracy that it becomes self-propulsive, transforming the collective thrusts of modern capitalist society into lasting achievements.

A basic difference between democracy and authoritarian regimes stressed by Przeworski—we read in "Notes on Consolidating Democracy"—is the uncertainty of the deliberative process which, in a democracy, depends on the outcome of popular elections. In order to let "love of uncertainty" come into existence, citizens must acquire a certain measure of patience: "the defeated party," Przeworski wrote, "must be willing to wait for the next election instead of beginning to plot a coup."

Hirschman then turned to the problem of political deliberation, referring to Manin's view that, "a genuine democratic political process implies that many of the people participating in it have only an approximate and somewhat uncertain initial opinion on various issues of public policy." Despite their starting positions, both voters and policymakers must be amenable to developing their views in the course of the debate. Thus the deliberative process—with its interplay of information, argumentation, and persuasion—concerns all participants and indirectly legitimates the democratic functioning of which it is a part. "To Przeworski's acceptance of the uncertainty of outcomes," Hirschman commented, "Manin thus adds as a characteristic of democracy a degree of uncertainty on the part of citizens about the proper course to take" (1986b, p. 180).

"For our purposes," Hirschman wrote, Manin's analysis is "illuminating." This statement obliges us to reflect a little further, considering that Manin's article was the springboard for the conclusion to *The Rhetoric.*

The issue of democratic deliberation acquired an important position in the contemporary stage of Hirschman's itinerary. The reason is undoubtedly the one given at the end of *The Rhetoric* when Hirschman referred to his two insights about democracy, traceable respectively to Rustow and Manin. "A democratic regime," he wrote (1991, p. 169), "achieves legitimacy to the extent that its decisions result from full and open deliberation among its principal groups, bodies, and representatives."

Hirschman was convinced, in other words, that one of the main roots of the fragility of democracy lies in the deliberation process. This "fertile obsession" became the driving force behind his work. We shall see this more clearly by calling in a digression contained in *Journeys.*

Two Texts Compared

As we have seen, the three stories contained in *Journeys* gave Hirschman the opportunity to refine the possibilist art of making one's way against obstacles of all kinds. These studies on policy making were also, of course, studies on the difficulty of deliberation over the three problems raised in the stories. This was made clear at the end of the book when Hirschman—casting aside his initial reserve—probed the possibility that formal reasoning could contribute to his argument. In "Models of Reformmongering," Hirschman presented models of parliamentary deliberation. He obviously did not intend to end the book on a schematic note. His aim was, rather, to settle sideways some aspects of the book in a stylized form in order to go back over the vast documentary evidence presented, to raise new, originally unperceived questions, and to trigger off further consequences.

Hirschman proposed exploring the extensive area that lies between the traditional polarities of pacific reform and revolution.[27] He thus created a scheme according to which moderate reform can be approved if the reformmonger manages to convince, first, the progressive camp that the chances of radical reforms being enacted are very slim and that the only choice is between the status quo and moderate reform; and, second, the other camp that the chances of maintaining the status quo are almost nil and that their only choice is between moderate reform and radical reform cum revolution.

This exercise in persuasion becomes more realistic if one modifies the assumptions on the basis of the events chronicled in the first part of the book. Hirschman's first model—"Engineering Reform with the Help of the Perspective of Revolution"—was thus inspired by the Colombian experience of land reform; the second—"Engineering Reform through Logrolling and Shifting Analysis"—by Chile's experience with inflation.[28]

Rereading these models with the issue of deliberation in mind, one cannot but notice the striking contrast between their incredible complexity and the simple stylization of the logical and formal structures presented. This should be enough to convince us of the enormous difficulties faced by democratic deliberation when dealing with largely inflexible, preconstituted political stands.

Nonetheless, when he came to discuss the various kinds of solutions, Hirschman distinguished between, on the one hand, majority formation and agreement over mutual sacrifices (usually considered intellectually attractive and morally respectable), and, on the other, logrolling and shifting alliances (usually considered the stuff of politicians). When the former are not available, the functioning of democracy vitally depends on the latter. In this case, if decision makers harbor well-defined prejudices (for social, ideological, or cultural reasons) which do not allow them access to legitimate commercial relations, the political system will have to give way to shifting alliances and therefore to transformism, if not to the betrayal of previous agreements: "a society relying on this mechanism is likely to exhibit political instability" (1963a, p. 290).

"The author," Hirschman added (1963a, p. 292), "has even come across a term which has been specially and whimsically coined to describe this behavior: he was told once by a Colombian that 'here in Colombia *somos todos toderos*—we are all allists (specialists in everything)'—the implication being both that 'we'—i.e. the people that count—have a finger in every pie, and also that even in the absence of this particular infrastructure, we like to acquire and exhibit strong opinions on every issue."[29]

So we see that Hirschman had already studied the problem of political deliberation, but within the coordinates of *Journeys,* that is, of how a society can move forward despite, and because of, what it is.[30] The analysis of political instability that arose at the end of the book was an additional topic that was soon to become dramatically contemporary. Twenty years on—as we have just seen—continues to hold our attention.

In these modified circumstances, then, it is this particular aspect that explains Hirschman's interest in Manin's article. In order to appreciate to what extent, we must try to visualize his reaction to a text (1985, pp. 83–86) that—after challenging the correct but abstract claim made by Sieyès, Rousseau, and Rawls that unanimity is a fundamental principle of democratic legitimation—maintained: "A legitimate decision does not represent the *will* of all, but is one that results from the *deliberation of all.* It is the process by which everyone's will is formed that confers its legitimacy on the outcome, rather than the sum of already formed wills. . . . Legitimate law is the *result of general deliberation,* and not the *expression of general will."*

"Deliberation," Manin continued in a series of affirmations worth quoting fully,

> is individual in the sense that everyone reasons for himself, finding arguments, and weighing them. Because the aim of the deliberative process is to broaden the participant's information and enable them to discover their own preferences, that process requires a multiplicity of points of view and / or arguments. . . . Deliberation requires not only multiple but conflicting points of view because conflict of some sorts is the essence of politics. The parties . . . will

try to refute the arguments of the positions of which they disapprove. New information emerges as each uncovers the potentially harmful consequences of the other parties' proposals.

The parties . . . also try to persuade each other. They argue. Argumentation is a sequence of propositions aiming to produce or reinforce agreement in the listener. In this sense, it is a discursive and rational process. Yet, in contrast to logical proof, argumentation does not result in a necessary conclusion that the listener cannot reject. . . . The listener remains free to give his agreement or withhold it. . . . Thus argumentation is particularly suited to the nature of a political debate. . . . Political deliberation and argumentation . . . constitute processes of education and of training in themselves. They broaden the viewpoint of citizens beyond the limited outlook of their private affairs. . . . Ascertaining a failure does not refute a political principle, it merely creates a *presumption* against it.

Here Manin launched his conclusion:

The process of the formation of the collective will is the essential moment of political decision making. It does not consist in totaling up previously formed intentions or wills. Individual intentions, individual wills are decided progressively in its course. A diversity of points of view and of arguments is an essential condition both for individual liberty (for individuals must have a choice among several parties) and for the rationality of the process (for the exchange of arguments and criticisms creates information and permits comparing the reasons presented to justify each position).

The interest of this passage lies not only in its lucid validity. The need for a collective will that is not completely and definitively formed—one of Hirschman's key concerns—is not the core of Manin's argument, but only an important side effect. Hirschman, however, transformed it into one of the crucial issues of democracy. It was as if Hirschman had suddenly discovered, by reading Manin, a missing link in his own long and complex thought process.

TOWARDS A CULTURE OF DOUBT

This impression is corroborated by two short articles among a set of autobiographical pieces, written for various honorary degree ceremonies,[31] that further develop his ideas concerning the alternative between the culture of intransigence and that of doubt.

In the Turin piece that inaugurated this new line, Hirschman described the most fundamental lesson he learned in Trieste in 1937–38. Colorni and a few of his friends, Hirschman wrote (1987c, now in 1990b, pp. xxx–xxxi), "were highly committed politically as antifascists. And yet they did not adhere rigidly to any one ideology and they were very wary of claiming they had an answer to every economic, social, or political problem of the time." They were, in fact, far from being *todero*. Colorni

> cultivated and had a taste for an intellectual style in which nothing was given except his own doubts. . . . It was precisely this spirit of experimental curiosity that Colorni and his friends applied to the philosophical, psychological, and social matters that stirred them into action. . . . They did not consider their participation in highly risky political activity the price to pay for the freedom of thought they practiced, but its simple, natural, spontaneous, and almost cheerful counterpart. Their attitude has always seemed to me to be an admirable way of viewing political activity and of conjugating public and private life.

Here then, for the first time, Hirschman departed from his initial plan. It is not true that we do not know at all what a democratic debate looks like. Hirschman outlined the basic requisites for the development of democracy-friendly behavior in this very text. "The coexistence of a commitment to public life and an open intellect," Hirschman claimed, are the "ideal microfoundation for a firmly democratic society"—a brief mention, but enough to evoke a few key aspects of Colorni's teachings and the long-term role they played in Hirschman's work.

In the second piece, the Berlin Festvortrag, Hirschman recalled an episode that I have chosen as an epigraph to this book. In the late twenties, Albert—aged about 13—began to ask himself various "philosophical and semi-religious questions." "One day," he wrote (1988b, pp. 1–2), he and his father "had a conversation where I must have asked him questions to which he frankly avowed not having the answers. I cannot remember at all the nature of my questions, but distinctly recall running from that conversation to the other end of our apartment to report everything to my sister and to exclaim: 'You know, Daddy has no *Weltanschauung* (vision of the world)!' "

"It is possible that I remember this moment," Hirschman added, " . . . because it encapsulates and portends a *Problemstellung* (cluster of problems) that was to remain with me for the rest of my life—to the point where I am just now, some sixty years later, writing an essay on whether it is good or bad to be outfitted with a complete set of firm opinions."

This account allows us to trace even stronger connections between the three brief pieces written in parallel to *The Rhetoric*. In "Notes" (1986b, p. 181), in fact, Hirschman wrote: "Many cultures—including most Latin American ones I know—place considerable value on having strong opinions on virtually everything from the outset, and on winning an argument, rather than on listening and finding that something can occasionally be learned from others. To that extent, they are basically predisposed to an authoritarian rather than a democratic politics." In his Turin piece he had tried to outline an alternative recalling his encounter with Eugenio Colorni and friends. Later, he turned to the theme of firm opinions in general terms at a session of the yearly meeting of the American Economic Association on the quality of life organized by Thomas Schelling.[32] He had constructed a brief (but pioneering) theoretical analysis on how this problem has tormented humanity (at least since Dante) and on why this originally aristocratic cultural heritage is in fact harmful to the good functioning of democracy. With the addition of a clarifying reminiscence, finally, he transferred this analysis to his native city. In his honorary degree acceptance speech at Berlin's Frei Universität,[33] he raised more explicitly the question of *Weltanschauung*, calling it a research on the "microfoundations of a democratic society," that is, on the "construction of a democratic personality" rather than the authoritarian one described by Adorno (1988b, p. 9).[34]

Thus, by excavating beneath the problem of the fragility of democracy, Hirschman realized that he had to deal with the alternative between a conception of the world and the abandonment of that conception; and that he had to link this to a further dichotomy between the culture of intransigence and the culture of doubt.[35]

This point of view was supported by the economic analysis offered to the American Economic Association (1989b, pp. 77–78). Having opinions, Hirschman wrote, is a good that is "not nearly as well behaved" as those of having clean air and a good atmosphere, recently discovered by economists: in fact satisfaction does not increase indefinitely as its availability increases (at a decreasing rate). This point is of course Bernard Manin's thesis (and that of Amy Gutmann and Dennis Thompson, 1989) according to which democratic deliberation demands that opinions be partly unformed.

Given the basic need for identity in our culture, the forming and acquiring of opinions has considerable utility to the individual. At the same time, if carried beyond a certain point, the process has dangerous side effects—it is hazardous for the functioning and stability of the democratic order. Might not individuals, Hirschman asked, "learn to value both having opinions and keeping an open mind, to mix the delights of winning an argument with the pleasures of being good listeners?" This would enrich their personalities with strong opinions that are not borrowed but shaped through "intense confrontation with other views"—that is, through democratic deliberation.[36]

What can we deduce from this survey of Hirschman's papers and preoccupations?

First, on the basis of Hirschman's written work, we can form "some idea"—however approximate—"about the human type one would wish to foster in a democracy," (1989e, p. 393). One important quality is patience. A further group of qualities is linked to the problem of political deliberation and personality formation. Some of these, such as leaving aside rhetorical clichés and being open to other people's views, freeing oneself of prejudice, modifying one's opinions, educating oneself and others, accepting useful compromises, etc., are basic requisites. There are other, more subtle but nevertheless indispensable, qualities: an inquiring spirit nourished by intellectual perplexity (doubt); a practical, experimental mentality aiming for concrete results, "intellectual openness, flexibility, and readiness to appreciate a new argument, perhaps even pleasure in embracing it" (1989b, p. 77); and cheerful self-irony. Finally, other essential qualities are: participation, commitment, and a sense of both public interest and collective responsibility.

Second, we can now understand Hirschman's conclusions to *The Rhetoric* (1991, pp. 169–70) more clearly. If it is true, he argued, that democratic deliberation needs to be seen as an opinion-forming process in order to acquire long-run stability and legitimacy, then "the gulf that separates such a state from democratic-pluralistic regimes as they emerge historically from strife and civil war is uncomfortably and perilously wide."

This inference can be traced back neither to Rustow nor to Manin; it arose simply from the link between their contributions made by the author. It was this connection that triggered Hirschman's central observation. "A people that only yesterday was involved in fratricidal struggles," he noted, "is not likely to settle down overnight to those constructive give-and-take deliberations. Far more likely, there will initially be agreement to disagree. . . . Or, if there is discussion, it will be a typical 'dialogue of the deaf'—a dialogue that will in fact long function as a prolongation of, and a substitute for, civil war." In "democratic politics as usual," Hirschman concluded, even in the most advanced democracies, debates "with each party on the lookout for arguments that kill are only too familiar."

The message of *The Rhetoric* is that to rise above this world of permanent belligerence is to everyone's advantage. This is true in particular for progressives: in an era generally favorable to them, it is to their advantage to make the democratic system increasingly self-sustaining. However, Hirschman concluded, "There remains a long and difficult road to be traveled from the traditional internecine, intransigent discourse to a more 'democracy-friendly' kind of dialogue. For those wishing to undertake this expedition there should be value in knowing about a few danger signals, such as arguments that are in effect contraptions specifically designed to make dialogue and deliberation impossible" (1991, pp. 169–90).[37]

FINALLY: TRIESTE

It is hard to get away from Hirschman's books. The ideas he has given shape to linger in our minds: they encourage us to

observe reality more sharply, more sympathetically, more ironically; they help us to understand ourselves and one another; they
provide both balance and incentive. It is worth our while, then,
to return briefly to an event made eloquent by the debate over
democracy: Hirschman's encounter with Colorni in Trieste in
1937–38.

The site is significant: Trieste is, in Colorni's words, "one
of the cities in which there is most dissatisfaction, where people
grumble most" (Corlorni, 1937, now in Solari, 1980, p. 119). In
this epoch, Trieste's frontier position, together with the cultural
and political sensitivity of its working class and liberal bourgeoisie,
made it a particularly lively city to live in. Hirschman, as I mentioned earlier, fell immediately for the spontaneous, lighthearted
style of Eugenio Colorni and his friends. "It was," Hirschman
wrote (1990f, p. xxxi), "as if they wanted to prove that Hamlet
was wrong; to show that doubt can actually *motivate* action rather
than exhausting and enervating it."

Albert was then 22 years old; Colorni was 28, with a long
and precocious intellectual history behind him. This experience
led him to develop a few nodal points which formed the basis
of his ingenious work program (Colorni, 1975, pp. 165–72).
Eugenio's disposition made him a natural point of reference. He
nurtured and stimulated people's ideas even before they were fully
formed; he offered approaches, expedients, indications for developing the widest variety of intellectual activity; his psychological
insights were outstanding. At the same time, he was bursting with
his own sagacious ideas, such as the rejection of systemic logic,
and the search for new discoveries.

In 1937, Hirschman recounted (1990f, pp. xxx–xxxi), "I
had already shed some of my previous uncertainties, but because
of my German education, I still felt I was lacking a complete
Weltanschauung." It would seem that Colorni's criticism and
example had a liberating effect. Hirschman realized that political
commitment did not necessarily need to be based on previously
formed and totalizing certainties. On the contrary, if we start out
with doubtfulness (as Colorni put it, referring to the beginning
of Goethe's *Faust* [1938, now in 1962, p. 411]), we can draw
specific elements of knowledge from our intimate perplexities

about reality, which in their turn induce us to act with greater awareness of the issues at stake.

The two brothers-in-law shared the intellectual and political passion for sharpening their skills in perception and analysis in order to cast doubt on ideas that do not correspond to reality, and then to discover new, more solid, alternatives. The admirable example of intellectual openness and commitment to public life probably led Albert to wonder just how Eugenio was able to develop and put into practice his talents.

This is not the place to go into Eugenio Colorni's work in detail. For our purposes, it is sufficient to recall that while he was still at high school he came across Benedetto Croce's work on aesthetics and later tried to reformulate the Hegelian system contained in these texts. He discovered, however, that this process of formulation and reformulation was a serious obstacle to comprehension. Colorni's radical conclusion was that this is true of every conception of the world; of every overall model, system or construction that tries to superimpose itself on the extraordinary richness and complexity of reality. Hence the need for a point of view that goes beyond absolutist constructs and disciplinary barricades in order to comprehend specific, limited matters without losing sight of the whole. Clearing the way for this enterprise—an alternative to Cartesian specialist rationality—Colorni decided to go back to the origins and study Liebnitz. His quest was thus to find those forms of thought that allowed one to trace the widest variety of human and natural phenomena to rationality.

Colorni proposed adopting Kant's reasoning in order to renew interest in discovery—an individual cognitive act that frees the subject of those anthropomorphic illusions which had previously thwarted comprehension—and thus forge the spirit of the discoverer. Colorni was interested above all in the philosophy of science and psychology because he considered these two disciplines particularly instructive in promoting his project. In conversations with friends and family, however, he advanced hypotheses and proposals in all possible directions.

Meeting Colorni almost every day, Albert was undoubtedly taken by his extraordinary inclination for independent research, and by the way he applied his sharp wit to solving problems, including those of a political nature.[38] At the time, Hirschman witnessed Colorni's concrete conclusions rather than the logical path that led to them, but, during the course of his long intellectual career, Albert was often to stop and wonder at that volcano of ideas. In 1970, in dedicating *Exit* to him, Hirschman claimed he had learned from his friend how "small ideas can take seed," thus acknowledging Colorni's influence over the formation of that process of surprise-discovery-theorization-generalization we have seen so often in Hirschman's work.

In my opinion, however, Colorni's sway does not end here. I think, rather, that after a prolonged process of learning,[39] cultural transposition and shift in experience, Colorni's spirit and some of his formulations have actually been reincarnated in the work of Albert Hirschman.

NOTES

1. Prologue: The Origins of Possibliism

1. On arrival in the U.S. in 1940, Hirschmann's two first names were inverted. In 1942, moreover, when he enrolled in the U.S. Army, the final -n of his last name was dropped.

2. This "falling in love," which extended to Montaigne, Diderot and "the whole eighteenth century" (1990b, p. 155) is perceptible in the first chapter of *National Power and the Structure of Foreign Trade* (1945) and is further expressed in *The Passions and the Interests* (1977).

3. At the ceremony in which he was awarded an *honoris causa* doctorate from the Institut d'Études Politiques de Paris (April 27, 1989), Hirschman said that when he first arrived in Paris in 1933 his intention was to carry on with economics although at the time the choice was considered a *brotlose Kunst* (breadless art) compared to law or medicine. He wanted to enroll in the École Libre de Sciences Politiques, but was dissuaded by Michel Debré with the argument that political science prepared above all for careers in public administration or the diplomatic corps. Since access to these careers was in effect barred to a political refugee, Hirschman opted for the HEC which would give him access to the private sector. It was no easy decision. "In the Students' Hand-Book," he explained, "I read that the HEC was a seed-bed ('pépinière') for businessmen. I remember this metaphor distinctly because I had to look up the word 'pépinière' in the dictionary, and once I knew I was no better off because I had no desire to be transformed into a 'pépin' (sapling) of that sort. After all, not long before in Berlin I was a militant Young Socialist" (1990e, p. 16).

4. Two articles belong to this period: "The Fecundity of Italian Women According to Age and Number of Offspring: Observations and Comments" (1937), and "Notes on Two Recent Tables Regarding Marriage Rates in the Italian Population" (1938a).

5. Colorni first met Albert and Ursula in Berlin (where he helped them with their political activity). The friends met again in Paris, and Ursula, seduced by Colorni's "didactic vehemence and iconoclastic intelligence, moved to Italy to marry him" (Spinelli, 1984, p. 322).

217

6. Though reconstructed from a biased point of view, some ideas on Hirschman's activity can be gleaned from Bertelli, 1980, pp. 66–81.

7. Daniel Bell may refer here to Varian Fry's memoirs, *Surrender on Demand,* published in 1945 (second edition, 1992) which mentions the nickname "Beamish" given to Hirschman by his companions because of his capacity to *se debrouiller* (get through) with a smile. More of Beamish's activities were recently recollected by Franco Ferraresi (1990, pp. xxvi–xxviii), when Hirschman was awarded an honorary degree in political science by the University of Turin. A fascinating television documentary—*The Exiles* directed by Richard Kaplan—in which Hirschman, among others, took part, relates the exodus of European intellectuals to the United States.

8. "Asked in a questionnaire of which achievement in his life he was most proud, Hirschman listed his work with the Italian anti-Fascists and with Varian Fry first, before his academic work on development in Latin America, and his books and articles" (Coser, 1984, p. 163).

9. The same can be said for statistics. In its French version, this was a practical science that never lost sight of its concrete applications, even when the form in which it was expressed was technically complex (Desrosières, 1985). With this background, it was easy for Hirschman to take up the study of statistics in Italy.

10. In his "Remerciements" after having received his honorary doctorate at the Institut d'Études Politiques de Paris, Hirschman described how he had always felt regret when walking past the Institute. "Now you know," he said (1990e, p. 16) "why this ceremony has a particular flavor for me. Sweet revenge! The sweet flavor of revenge. Of course I had to wait 56 years for it, but after such a long period in the antechamber—unlike in the famous Kafka story—the doors (in this case of Science Politique) have been opened to me. Thank you very, very much for making this happy end possible."

11. The most explicit example, however, is "Colombia: Highlights of a Developing Economy" (1955). In the manner of a geographer, Hirschman provides a map of Colombia, a brief chapter on population and climate, another on national income. He then adds a group of chapters devoted to various sectors of the country's economy: agriculture, manufacturing, energy, cement, construction, transport, foreign trade, monetary reserves, expenditure, consumption, money supply, and banking.

12. "From a practical point of view, it was then that I acquired that minimum self-confidence that allowed me to make it" (1990f, p. xxx). The early evolution of Hirschman's thought starting with his graduate thesis is discussed in Coppa, 1992.

13. "I liked this detective work," Hirschman recently wrote (1990f, p. xxx) with a touch of nostalgia, "especially when I managed to dig out information the Fascist Authorities wanted to hide."

14. On April 15, 1935, together with the Paris University Statistics Institute, this Institute started publishing a quarterly bulletin called *L'activité économique* which continued the work previously published by Lucien Mach and Michel Huber in *Les indices du mouvement des affaires*. The aim of this new venture, Charles Rist wrote in the first number, is to give "in the most condensed form possible, with the only aim of constant precision, an overview [of the economic situation of each country] from which the reader can draw whatever conclusions he thinks most appropriate. We also add a few concise comments on essential events of the previous three months, providing our readers with some comparative elements for placing the temporary economic constellation in a world context." Hirschman's short reports on the Italian situation appeared in numbers 15, 16, and 17 (dated Jan. 31, Apr. 30, and July 31, 1939, respectively) when Robert Majolin was head of the editorial staff.

It may be useful to remember that Charles Rist, director of the Institute, was a very influential figure in French economics between the two wars. He coauthored with Charles Gide an important history of economic thought, and was for many years editor of the *Revue d'économie politique* that brought together various currents of economics, often at odds with the official line. Immediately after the war (1945, p. 1), Rist still claimed that a descriptive economic sociology was needed alongside economic theory.

15. This was the origin of Hirschman's "Memoire sur le contrôle des changes en Italie" (1939a, now in 1987e), a highly detailed and meaningful documentation of the diverse aspects of the question: the origins of control, its administrative organization, payment mechanisms, commerce and trade policies, currency, the economy, and economic trends.

16. This was, more precisely, the XII Session of the "Permanent Conference of Advanced International Studies" organized by the Institut International de Coopération Intellectuelle of the Society of Nations. The meeting never actually took place. J. Condliffe's opening paper and A. Piatier's summary on exchange control were both published in 1940. Most of the other contributions, with specific studies on 82 different countries, were only ever circulated in manuscript form.

17. Condliffe recommended Hirschman for a Rockefeller Fellowship which is how he got his entry visa for the U.S. (Coser, 1984, p. 164).

18. Hirschman decided not to enroll in a Ph.D. program in economics (as advised by many associates) but to concentrate on finishing the volume to which a professional and academic aim was attached.

19. Perhaps what Hirschman meant here is that having already dealt with exchange controls and bilateralism he now felt the need to analyze the underlying problem.

20. The book had a limited circulation, but it was later reprinted in 1969 and 1980. "The political dimensions and side effects of foreign trade and investment are still very much with us," Hirschman wrote in the new introduction, "two obvious examples are the relations of the United States with Latin America and of the Soviet Union with Eastern Europe" (1981a, p. 28). Retrospectively this might explain some of the doubts surrounding the book when it first came out (see reviews by Stinebower 1946, and Oliver 1946). *National Power* refers explicitly to Germany but it analyzes foreign trade globally and includes therefore other powers as well (see Asso and de Cecco 1987, Asso 1988, and the vast literature cited by them). Moreover, it was published at precisely the time when the United States was taking over leadership of the Western world.

21. Moreover, the "opposite line of causation"—from political to economic asymmetry—is not analyzed. It is true, however—adds the author—that the adoption of economic policies in order to increase a nation's power often presupposes the existence of an "initial power disequilibrium in favor of that nation" (1945, p. 13).

22. Again, from the point of view of the dominant country, if subordinate countries, faced with a stoppage of trade, are able to forward their trade to other shores, further measures can be added to the ones we have just examined to make this adjustment as difficult as possible. Generally speaking, the difficulties inherent in the adjustment depend not only on the absolute amount of exports to the dominant power, but also on its "weight" in relation to the total foreign trade of the subordinate country. Therefore it is an elementary principle of power politics to carry out foreign trade with smaller rather than larger countries.

23. The separation between economics and political science that took place in the Western world at the turn of the eighteenth century (See Dumont 1977 and Hirschman 1977b), urged Count Saint-Simon to claim that in order to build up a social organization favorable to industrial development, the principles of economics must lay the foundations for politics. This type of relationship has been taken up—from many different points of view—to this day, producing many different results. Take Bazard, Enfantin, Prudhon, Marx, Walras, etc. Of course, this

denies Saint-Simon's basic assumption (economics as a discipline did not discover the "general political principle" or the "class of interests" on which political science should be founded). But it also explains—paradoxically—the persistence of a form of mind that still torments us (Meldolesi, 1990a).

24. The author, as we have seen, was initially content with the identification of the potential for influence, dependence, and domination inherent in international trade relations. "In this respect," he wrote (1981a, p. 29), "my treatment had . . . a great deal in common with that of many dependencia theorists: they too tend to rest content with the demonstration that dependency relations are deeply entrenched in the structure of the international system." He was now trying to show that this system can be subject to changes. In so doing, Hirschman took the final step away from his previous theoretical consciousness, and invited some of his old friends to do the same. (See Fernando Henrique Cardoso and Enzo Faletto's preface in the 1979 American edition of *Dependencia y desarrollo in América Latina*, 1969.)

25. In *Beyond Economic Man*, Hirschman explained, "Harvey Liebenstein has reminded us of Tolstoy's critique in *War and Peace* of those military experts who predict the outcome of battles by looking only at the quantifiable elements of the strength of the opposing armies, such as the number of men and weapons—Tolstoy stresses fighting spirit and morale as an often more decisive factor. This thought has an obvious relevance here. The ability to inflict deprivation is more easily quantified than the willingness to accept it for the sake of, say, freedom from domination." Hirschman goes on to say that one must never rely completely on either factor. I would add here that one should no less rely on the possibility that further elements will modify, for a period of time, the principle and determining direction, one way or another, of the relationship. (See, for example, Marx's argument on the tendency of the rate of profit to fall in book 3 of *Capital*.)

26. Of the same period is "On Hegel, Imperialism, and Structural Stagnation" (1976). Hegel, Hirschman explained, had sketched out an economic theory of imperialism (like the one proposed later by John Hobson and Rosa Luxemburg) in his *Philosophy of Right* based on the unequal distribution of income, delayed consumption compared to production, and the search of capitalist countries for new markets. "The sharpness of the Hegelian formulation lays bare the structure of a certain type of theory which is still very much with us" (1981a, p. 172). Hirschman is talking about the theses of structural stagnation claiming that the only way out is an egalitarian distribution of income once the easy stage of industrialization has been overcome. Regarding these, and

all other doctrines dominated by anxiety about change, Hirschman remembers Lenin's words (1920, now in 1967, p. 216): "Revolutionaries
sometimes try to prove that there is absolutely no way out of a crisis
[for the ruling class]. This is a mistake. There is no such thing as an
absolutely hopeless situation." (These are however innovative elements
that coexist with more orthodox points in Lenin's theory, Meldolesi,
1981, parts 2 and 3).

27. Take, for example, the fact that the Italian federalist proposal
written in the early 1940s considered the U.S. "little more than an
appendix of England." In the *Manifesto di Ventotene* Spinelli explains,
"we had in no way foreseen that the Europeans, at the end of the war,
would no longer have been masters of themselves in looking for their
own future. We did not think that, having ceased to be the center of the
world, they would be so heavily conditioned by extra-European powers"
(Spinelli, 1984, pp. 311–12, 317).

28. Paradoxically, these Keynesians were more influential in those
countries where the U.S. had (relatively) less power, because in those
situations they were able to have the last word on economic policy.
In Germany and Japan, on the other hand, governments were directly
dominated by American officers, entrepreneurs, and managers who were
on the whole not Keynesian (1989h, pp. 351–52).

29. Over forty texts, most of which appeared in the *Review of Foreign Developments,* an internal publication of the International Division
of the Federal Reserve Board.

30. Immediately after the war, as we have mentioned, innovative
economists claimed that U.S. support for the balance of payments of
European countries was the only answer to the structural changes that
had taken place. But when in 1947 European recovery suffered a relapse
(and the balance of payments equilibrium appeared further away than
ever), discussion turned to other aspects of the problem such as the
evolution of the terms of trade, the possible use of devaluation of European currencies, and the relationship between inflation and external
disequilibrium. The latter in particular animated the debates of those
involved in reconstruction.

31. Hirschman comes up with a logical construction that will
become familiar to him, for example, in "Invitation to Theorizing About
the Dollar Glut" (1960) that goes over arguments advanced for dealing with the previous shortage; or in "The Welfare State in Trouble:
Structural Crisis or Growing Pains?" (1980) that carves a path between
the two positions in which economists have been entrenched for so long
(complacents on one side, structuralists on the other) and maintains
that the difficulties of the welfare state could be solved with a period
of mutual adaptation between citizens and public power structures. It

is also the case in "In Defense of Possibilism" (1980b, now in 1986b). Here, looking for democratic outcomes of revolutions, Hirschman tries to identify a narrow path between a low level of coercion and substantial realizations. (This capacity to find a middle way between opposing points of view is in fact incipient in *National Power* when Hirschman's reasoning develops, taking into account the arguments of both free trade and protectionist economists.)

32. Critics of European integration, Hirschman adds with a nice *reductio ad absurdum*, claim that the progressive disintegration of customs barriers would bring about even greater shortage of dollars. Logically speaking, then, they should support the increase of barriers and further fragmentation of Europe. "It is doubtless true," he writes (1950a, p. 17), "that if the province of Champagne were separated by high tariffs from the rest of France, some champagne that is now consumed in Paris would be shipped to New York." However, the destruction of the previous integration would damage the area much more than the value of the extra champagne rerouted to New York. ("I have never stopped working for Europe," Hirschman was to say later [1987a], "like my brother-in-law, Altiero Spinelli [his sister Ursula's second husband]. Ever since I was a young official working on the Marshall Plan trying to convince the Americans that the Common Market was not a threat to peace.")

33. In the first group we may include: "Trade and Credit Arrangements between the 'Marshall Plan Countries'" (with M. J. Roberts) (1947h), "Trade Structure of 'The Marshall Plan Countries'" (1947i), "Payments and Trade between ERP Countries in 1947" (with C. Lichtenberg) (1948f), "The New Intra-European Payment Scheme" (1949l), "Country Notes on Recent Currency Adjustments" (1949n), "The European Payment Union—A Short History" (1950d, reprinted in a revised version, 1951a). In the second group we may include: "Note on Offshore Procurement in Europe" (1948e), "Intra-European Payments: A Proposal for Discussion" (1949f), "Proposal for a European Monetary Authority" (1949a), "Liberalization of the ECA Dollar" (1950b), and "European Payment Union: a Possible Basis for Agreement" (1950c). Apart from "Proposal for a European Monetary Authority," the other texts are part of the search for "partial improvements" that can reasonably be followed by others.

34. See "The European Payment Union—A Short History" (1950d), and "The European Payment Union Negotiations and Issues" (1951a).

35. As we have just mentioned, this does not stop him from taking part in completely realistic negotiations. This behavior provoked surprised comment by Milward (1984, p. 296).

36. "Industrial Nations and Industrialization of Underdeveloped Countries" (1951d) and "Effects of Industrialization on the Markets in Industrial Countries" (1952).

37. To this end, Hirschman uses a statistical index (see appendix A in *National Power*, 1945, pp. 157–62) devised in order to study concentration on the basis of a limited number of subjects and unequal distribution. (In a note in 1946, later included in the 1980 edition, Hirschman vigorously defends the "paternity" of his index of concentration that he invented in 1940 while crossing the Atlantic as an exile from Lisbon.)

38. The "traditional type of exchange" amounted to a little less than a third of total foreign trade between the two wars. The exchange of manufactures against manufactures never reached more than a fifth or a sixth of the total, while the exchange of primary against primary products—a category almost entirely ignored in discussions regarding foreign trade—oscillated between two-fifths and one-third. Exchange between manufactures represented about half of total foreign commerce in manufactures.

39. "This belief," claims Hirschman, alluding more in general perhaps to the pessimistic literature concerning the future of international commerce (see Asso and de Cecco, 1987, pp. 26–30), "has found its most articulate expression in the so-called 'law of the declining importance of export trade' which Sombart formulated at the beginning of the century. Sombart claimed that the gradual industrialization of agricultural countries would lead to a reduction of the growth of foreign trade with respect to the growth of internal trade and production. But Sombart's law prophesised only a relative decline of foreign trade and was therefore a rather modest expression of a preoccupation which pervaded Germany at the turn of the century" (1945, p. 146).

40. The last chapter of *National Power* was published as an article in 1943 (slightly abbreviated). It already included the following extract: "An encouraging aspect of present thought on postwar reconstruction is therefore the radical change from the traditional outlook in this respect. Today, schemes for the future industrialization of underdeveloped countries, such as China and those in southeastern Europe, are proposed and discussed in many quarters; and the future economic mission of the older industrial countries is conceived less as the mechanical workshop of the world than as the initiator and educator in industrial processes" (1943a, p. 595, and 1945, pp. 150–51). (From this point of view, the question of the methodological gap discussed above looks notably reshaped; likewise in time another better known "coupure": I am referring of course to that between the younger and the older Marx. See Althusser 1965, and Althusser and Balibar, 1965.)

41. "I had participated in one conference on development," Hirschman remembers, " . . . which was notable primarily for the active participation of some eminent anthropologists, and because this was the occasion for Alexander Gerschenkron to unveil his masterpiece, 'Economic Backwardness in Historical Perspective' . . . The conference stimulated my interest in the problems of development" (1986b, p. 5).

42. Apart from *National Power*, Hirschman cites here Frankel (1943, pp. 188–201) according to whom many countries export and import commodities that end up in the same categories but are in fact different in terms of quality, price, design, etc. As regards the relation between the increase in per capita income and increased imports of manufactures, Hirschman showed, citing data on eight developed countries taken from the League of Nations report on "Industrialization and Foreign Trade" (1945), that imports of manufactures tend to increase more in those countries where the process of development is more rapid.

43. Note that in *National Power*, by contrast, Hirschman wrote that concern and alarm for other countries' industrialization is "a feature of all countries which have arrived at industrial maturity" (1945, p. 150).

44. The favorable attitude of the United States towards the industrialization of other countries, the text clarified, was revealed above all by the policy of aid to Western European and Japanese industrialized countries that created the conditions for potential competition from these countries a few years later. It is curious to note that it was a European agency filled primarily with European economists—the Economic Commission for Europe—that called attention to the fact that by reconstructing European industry the United States was "possibly doing a slightly foolish thing," "in spite of the Economic Commission for Europe." Hirschman prophesied, "the latest period of transfers of capital among the industrial countries will perhaps leave an imprint even on those countries that have traditionally shown most concern about industrialization abroad" (1952, pp. 282–83).

2. HOW TO COMPLICATE ECONOMICS

1. Thus, due to the effect of a paradoxical argument, complicating economics can be equivalent to making it less simplified but simpler. "Le simple," Bachelard once said, "n'est jamais que le simplifié," as L. J. D. Wacquant reminds us (1987, p. 432). Perhaps this was already implied by Gerschenkron when he wrote that "the actual situation . . . is more complex than would appear on the basis of simple models" (1952, p. 7).

2. Hirschman, 1977b, pp. 100–116. The idea that the economic discipline came about as a result of its separation from political science at the end of the eighteenth century is supported by the work of the French anthropologist Louis Dumont (1977). (For a comparison between Hirschman and Dumont's contributions, see Rosen, 1978.) A solution to the "Smith problem" proposed by Hirschman is further elaborated in Meldolesi (1990a).

3. For example, it is clear from *National Power* that Hirschman appreciates the "grain of salt" contained in the classical theory of foreign trade, but at the same time levels criticism against it. This theory, he argues, has not properly studied asymmetries. Smith, Macauley, and others did not "ignore entirely the power aspect of international economic relations. . . . It was rather their belief that the political or power aspect of foreign trade could be *neutralized* efficiently by a universal free trade system, because the trade of every country would be so widely spread over various markets that it need not worry about the interruption of trade with any particular country." However, Hirschman continues, "the conditions which were supposed to lead to a neutralization of the power aspects of international economic relations are not merely 'unrealistic' but entirely fantastic. They presuppose, indeed, a multitude of states of approximately equal importance each with approximately the same volume of foreign trade, the trade of each country being spread equally over all the other countries and no country possessing a monopoly with respect to any particular skill or natural endowment" (1945, pp. 74–75). As for neoclassical theory, Hirschman uses, as we have seen, the economic analysis of asymmetries, including some aspects of the subjectivist analytical apparatus. This does not mean he adhered to the theorems or to the general philosophy of this view.

4. Paradoxically, contributions can even be made to economic theory as such. See, for example, "Devaluation and the Trade Balance: A Note" (1949c) which Hirschman considers (1986b, p. 6) the "late fruit" of his reflections on the economic policies in France and Italy during the 1930s. The origins of this late fruit lay in Hirschman's experience as an employee of the Federal Reserve Board in late 1946. While working there, he wrote a comment in the *Review of Foreign Developments* on a statement made by the French Finance Minister, Robert Schuman, to the effect that "it would be folly to devaluate the Franc in view of the huge excess of imports over exports in France's balance of payments." Working on this theme in general terms and in terms of national currency he came to the conclusion at first that Schuman's thesis should not be discounted. He soon changed his mind, however. In early 1947 he wrote a "mathematical note" dealing with the problem of re-equilibrating the balance of payments in terms of foreign currency,

as one indeed must. He demonstrated the (fortunately) encouraging proposition that the higher the trade deficit the more likely it is that devaluation will bring about positive results. This mathematical note first appeared in the *Review of Foreign Developments*, and then, after rewriting, it was published in the *Review of Economics and Statistics* in 1949. Thus Hirschman's healthy respect for the market born from his experience in the 1930s brought him to an original analytical conclusion: despite the scope of the literature on the subject, economic theory had not yet studied the effects of devaluation on the trade balance when total imports and exports are not equal (or it had only dealt with the matter in terms of national currency: see J. Robinson, 1947, pp. 142–43). Hirschman's result did not go unobserved: see G. Haberler (1949) and J. Meade (1951). It was recently taken up again by H. W. Arndt (1988a, 1988b) in discussing the problem of the surplus in the Japanese balance of payments.

5. This expression, together with development and democracy, forms the title of the Festschrift for Hirschman edited by A. Foxley, M. McPherson, and G. O'Donnell (1986).

6. At this point it would be interesting to consider why economics took to the deductive rather than the inductive-experimental method (or rather, why the discipline did not seek a reasonable compromise between the two approaches). One soon realizes that traditional interpretations do not offer a solution and that the problem of explaining the two periods of the rise of marginalist economics at the end of the last century (Schumpeter) has not yet been settled. This corroborates Hirschman's hypothesis: faced with the extraordinary infatuation with the nonrational pervading culture at the time, marginalist economics launched what was in effect a very successful survival strategy: progressively diluting key concepts (such as interest, utility, value), which, together with a marked push toward formalism, allowed it to distance itself from Benthamite psychological assumptions and to cultivate its own "splendid isolation" from the other social sciences (Hirschman, 1986b, p. 51; Meldolesi, 1987b).

7. Corresponding to this "invasion" today there is a proposal for a general paradigm of social sciences. The guiding idea advanced by Hirschman, L. J. D. Wacquant claimed in the above-mentioned review (1987, p. 432), was that "the (micro)-economic approach so boasted about today that some people do not hesitate to present as an unchallenged paradigm for all social sciences (see the imperialist proliferation of the theories of rational action in sociology and the political sciences, in their conservative forms such as Becker's economic approach, or Coleman's rational choice, or those theories that define themselves as

Marxist such as Roemer and Elster's Analithical Marxism) presents a mutilated view of reality that is ready soon to be complicated."

8. In a recent interview (1990b, p. 159), Hirschman recalled that according to *Exit, Voice, and Loyalty,* one has to recur to both economic and political considerations (i.e., to exit and voice) in order to make a contribution to the workability of social institutions; and that in a review article of the book, Brian Barry (1974) criticized this outlook for not taking sufficiently into account the argument of Mancur Olson. However, Olson, Hirschman says, "argues for the impossibility—not the logic but the illogic—of collective action. According to him, collective action should never happen since people act like rational actors: they always want a free ride and so on. Since my own experience of having participated in collective action was such that I found it very important, this construct of Olson just struck me as obviously absurd. There is of course some amount of evidence in favor of Olson's thesis, but there is also a great deal of evidence to the contrary. And over the years I have tried to develop, in various forms, a counter-explanation." *Shifting Involvements,* then, could be considered "a kind of dialogue with Mancur Olson," in the sense that Hirschman's elaboration unravels itself by taking into account the opposite point of view.

9. See note 2.

10. In a preface to the German edition of *Exit, Voice, and Loyalty,* Hirschman recounts that the "fountainhead of the book may well lie in some carefully repressed guilt feelings" about abandoning Germany and the gravely weakened Jewish community in 1933, though this is "absurd from the point of view of any rational calculus." Reflecting on the success of the book, he came to the conclusion, however, that "it was probably fortunate that I was *not* aware of those deeper moral stirrings; . . . otherwise the presentation of my arguments might have been less general, less balanced . . . and less scientifically persuasive" (1981a, p. 305).

For the origin of this point of view, see (1968a) where Hirschman, referring to a book by Judith Tendler, claims that interdisciplinary research seems to improve if it is undertaken unconsciously. (It is likely, however, that Hirschman is also communicating another message: it is better to act than to talk, to commit oneself to complicating economics rather than stating the need to do so, to promote interdisciplinary, moral, or other analyses, and—even better—to do so without thinking about it too much.)

11. See Hoselitz, 1952, p. v. "True," wrote Hirschman later (1979a, p. xvii), "the success of the Marshall Plan deceived economists, policy makers and enlightened opinion in the West into believing that the problem of underdevelopment was roughly of the same nature as

that of postwar reconstruction, that an infusion of capital helped along by the right kind of development planning would grind out growth and welfare all over the globe. . . . But was that not perhaps a good thing? Had the size and toughness of the problem been correctly visualized from the outset, the considerable intellectual and political mobilization around it would most likely not have occurred and we would have been further away from an acceptable world."(A similar argument regarding Keynesism and development economics is contained in Hirschman, 1989h, pp. 358–59. See also 1981a, pp. 13–14; 1986b, pp. 30 and 33–34; and note 19 below.)

12. In this field, too, the 1951–52 texts take up the inspiration contained in *National Power* and try to use it to work out the problems left unsolved in the book. Later his hopes were reshaped, but the general sense of the argument is not modified: Hirschman continued on his quest for a way to achieve orderly progress in international trade in the interests of all countries concerned; the regular rerouting of riches towards less developed countries; the rapid development of these countries within the world economic system; and a gradual reduction in economic and political asymmetries.

13. This is the "turn of mind" Hirschman was to talk about later, i.e., the "desire to speculate and search in a certain direction, rather than the application of any infallible and objective technique" (1971a, pp. 12–13).

14. Just one example: in the conclusions to "France and Italy: Patterns of Reconstruction" (1947c) we read: "It may be that the idea of a national economic goal appeals strongly to the French people because of the frustrating lack of direction from which they suffered during the interwar period. Italy, on the contrary, emerged cruelly disillusioned from a long period of excessive 'dynamism' and the considerable progress achieved in Italian reconstruction has resulted largely from the confluence of individual ventures, with or without encouragement from the State." Isn't this a first sketch of the *Shifting Involvements*?

15. For the appraisal of economists, see, for example, G. M. Meyer and D. Seers, 1984, and T. Cozzi, 1987; for that of sociologists, A. Pizzorno, 1987, and L. Gallino, 1988; for that of political scientists, see J. Q. Wilson, 1986, and S. Kelman, 1987.

16. "When I do an analysis myself," Hirschman explained in an interview (1990b, pp. 157 and 164), "I never think of economics as a whole and of sociology as a whole and how the two can meet. . . . I do it in connection with specific phenomena. And almost inevitably I find ways in which it is *the intermingling* that explains." In many topics, he added, "you find the need to combine approaches. . . . Again there is

the question of how far you can get with one type of approach and how far with another. And again I think that you have to keep your mind open to precisely *complicating* your analysis rather than pretending to understand everything and explain everything."

17. Private conversation, November 1986, Princeton, N.J.

18. This historical context has been underscored by a group of young, Colombian historians: Carlos Ortiz, Gonzalo Sanchez, Ricardo Panaranda, and Arturo Alape (see E. J. Hobsbawm, 1986, and the books reviewed there).

19. In a Turin conference on his work (November 13–14, 1987), when he received an honorary degree in political science, Hirschman described how when he decides to undertake a new project, he is often protected by a "hiding hand" that is an impression (partly illusion) that the idea he is working on is very different from those that came before. This helps him in his work because what has been done before does not get in the way and because he is stimulated towards new frontiers. When he has obtained the results he was looking for, he realizes that a part of the idea is not original, and that a part is and can be connected to other ideas that came before. As we have already said, through the repetition of this process (conscious and unconscious), gradually a far-reaching intellectual structure emerges which turns out *(ex-post)* to be surprisingly coherent. (An example of a collective "hiding hand" is contained in note 11. The concept was theorized by Hirschman in the first chapter of *Development Projects Observed*, 1967b. See also chapter 5.)

20. From a private conversation with Miguel Fadul in Bogotá (August 1990). The Hirschmans thought at the time they would settle in Colombia.

21. An illuminating example is included in "Petit discours de Nanterre" (May 1993). "In the many discussions I had with the country's policy makers and entrepreneurs," Hirschman said, "I learned much about the way industrial and infrastructure investment decisions were taken and how they moved up and down the Colombian territory, with its striking topography and distinct development poles, to use the language of François Perroux." This recollection is linked to that of Albert Demangeon's lectures in economic geography at the École des Hautes Études Commerciales. "Here we learned a great deal about the location of economic activities and its determinants, about the economic importance of rivers and natural resources for industrial development and on shifts in the flow of commerce between regions (I recall a superb lecture entitled 'La concurrence entre Anvers et Rotterdam'). The vigorous green, brown and blue colors of the geographical maps he displayed enhanced the effectiveness of his teaching." The conclusion is: "Perhaps it was the interaction of the Colombian experience of the

fifties with the still alive Parisian memories of the thirties that made me hit on the notion of backward and forward linkages as an important force in the dynamics of the development process."

22. "Apparently there now existed adequate knowledge," or so it was believed at the time, "even without close study of local surroundings, of the likely ranges of savings and capital-output ratios, and those estimates, joined to the country's latest national income and balance of payments accounts, would yield all the key figures needed" to indicate how much foreign capital would have been necessary to achieve the desired rate of increase of national income per head (1986b, p. 8).

23. Moreover, his dissent from prevailing doctrines—in part carried over from his past and in part the fruit of his readings in development economics on his return to the United States—had become a "natural concomitant" of this effort. "If I may indulge for a moment in some introspective analysis, it was the experience of finding myself instinctively so much at variance with this theory that made me aware of having acquired a distinct outlook on development problems which it might perhaps be worth while to explore systematically" (1958a, p. 50).

24. "Political scientists," writes Hirschman in his introduction to *Journeys* (1963a, p. 5), "typically view good government as resulting from certain institutions and capacities such as an adequate bureaucracy, public participation in the governmental process, legitimacy, ability of a political elite to mediate conflicts and so on. Hence the political scientist's advice to countries with a defective political process is to acquire these institutions and capacities much as economists advise them to step up capital formation or to generate a group of entrepreneurs."

25. The Monnet Plan, Hirschman explained, (1947c, pp. 364–65) when he was working at the Federal Reserve, "is the result of a cooperative effort on the part of the French Government, industry and labor. It does not detail a rigid program for every branch of economic activity . . . but rather sets goals for such aggregate magnitudes as national income, investment, labor force, and required foreign aid." Furthermore, it plans the expansion and modernization of transport, coal, electricity, steel, cement, and agricultural machinery. Apart from the latter, the main thrust of the plan is directed towards nationalized or highly concentrated sectors. "In spite of the difficulties and possible departures from original schedules, the Monnet Plan will leave its mark on the economic structure of France and of Europe."

3. HOW ONE THING LEADS (OR DOES NOT LEAD) TO ANOTHER

1. "Your formative years, dear Professor Hirschman," wrote Jean-Claude Casanova in his *laudatio* (1990, p. 10 and chapter 1), "were

tempestuous. Your spirit was forged in those years and bears the brand of the time; it is both flexible and rigorous. It is flexible because one must untangle the multiplicity of possibilities and choices; it is rigorous because one must stick to one's commitments. You are without illusions; you know perfectly well that the world could have been saved long ago if, as the saying goes, 'men shone with as much virtue as their theories.' But you desire with determination to advance everyone's life."

2. I refer here to the eight monographs and the three collections of essays by Hirschman published in English in the years between 1958 and 1991.

3. A few friends, including Thomas Schelling, Robert Triffin, and Henry Wallich, supported his nomination. The position was annual and was later renewed. The volume that followed opened the doors of the university to Hirschman, who thus changed profession, as he himself underscores.

4. By stressing the practical experience that led to writing *The Strategy*, in fact, Hirschman emphasized that he had chosen a more open viewpoint than the prevailing one, more determined to grasp the specific lessons that arise from everyday reality. This was probably the meaning of the "Colombian story" and of its "riddle" that so puzzled Hirschman's interlocutors.

5. Spinelli wrote in 1984, pp. 289–90:

What impressed [Colorni] most about psychoanalysis . . . was not so much the enormous importance that Freud attributed to psychological conflicts with sexual origins, but the notion that underneath that thin layer of ourselves of which we are conscious, lies an infinite tangle of the repressed unconscious that nevertheless plays a vital role in our personal lives. He had experimented for himself the fact that if one digs into one's own unconscious with enough intelligence and ability, and if one looks at what one has discovered with sufficient courage, one can master it to a fair extent, and generate in one's soul real revolutions. . . . Spurred by a half Socratic, half Mephistophelic demon, he enjoyed . . . uncovering the deeply unconcious motivations for every kind of behavior, and exposing them for what they were. . . . His reasons for doing so were not dictated by skepticism, but by the desire—both for himself and for others—to leave behind as far as possible all certainties based on the mysterious quicksands of the unconscious, and reach others based on the solid rock of awareness.

6. From a conversation at a conference in Turin, November 13–14, 1987.

7. This assumes a cautious and measured personal attitude. As we have seen (chapter 2, note 10), Hirschman goes so far as to claim that on some occasions it is better not to be aware of the ultimate reasons for one's actions, and therefore—by extension—it is better not to be too conditioned (consciously) by one's own subconscious.

8. *Tre continenti. Economia politica e sviluppo della democrazia in Europa, Stati Uniti ed America Latina* is the title of a collection of Hirschman's writings published by Einaudi in 1990.

9. This thesis evidently questions a notion central to economics (from classical to marginalist, Keynesian, and Marxist economics) according to which, given a high level of demand, the economic system tends towards a condition of full employment of productive resources (with the exception in underdeveloped countries of the labor force). On the other hand, Hirschman took it upon himself later to amplify and generalize his point of view. In *Exit, Voice, and Loyalty* (1970a, p. 6; see also chapter 6), he maintained that the existence of a surplus above subsistence allows most human societies to tolerate a certain level of deterioration of their productive efficiency and thus to live beneath the full employment of resources. Moreover, in *A Dissenter's Confession* (1986b, pp. 13–14), looking back over his experience, Hirschman spoke of the "slack paradigm," valid in different forms for both developed and underdeveloped countries, which was developed gradually in the work of a group of researchers: Cyert and March, Simon, Rosenberg, Leibenstein, and himself.

Economic analysis thus recoups greater room for freedom. For example, Hirschman claims in *The Strategy* that the difference between the cyclical unemployment of developed countries and the structural unemployment of underdeveloped countries has been overemphasized. "True," he added (1958a, p. 6), "in an underdeveloped economy we have no idle capital or trained labor resources that cry out to be utilized; but we do have . . . unutilized ability to save, latent or misdirected entrepreneurship, and a wide variety of usable skills, not to mention the modern industrial techniques that are waiting to be transferred from the advanced countries. The task here is to *combine* all these ingredients, a task far more difficult than, but not entirely different from, the *recombining* of idle factors of production that must be accomplished to end a depression." Seen from this point of view (as he himself maintained in 1981a, p. 8), Hirschman's analysis looks like a generalization of the issue raised by Keynes. From the point of view of theoretical foundations, however, his analysis distances itself from Keynes's.

10. This is the "inverted sequence" Hirschman spoke of later (1971a, p. 30) to show the existence of a high level of affinity (unconscious to start with) between *The Strategy* and the theory of cognitive dissonance. On the other hand, he added, those that lag behind are led to accusing the nouveau riche and unconsciously increasing their resistance to changes in behavior that are in fact necessary. Here too a reinforcing inverted sequence is detected, but it is of a negative nature. Hence the text includes, in a nutshell, the problem of how to escape from the cumulative repetition of dissonance which we deal with later. See chapter 3 and chapter 5.

11. This means *(coeteris paribus)* that those policies that increase, in terms of quality and quantity, the number of these occasions and that more than others disseminate behavior and attitudes favorable to development and democracy should be implemented. *The Strategy*'s quest for hidden rationality could be taken up again in order to evaluate the behavioral impact of the various inducement mechanisms and pacing devices.

On the other hand, a country that progresses towards modernization by means of a process where changes in behavior lead to changes in attitude, concludes Hirschman (1971a, p. 326), "will show a personality rather different from the country whose elite right at the outset of the development journey is imbued with the Protestant ethic and saturated with achievement motivation." This does not, however, have univocal implications on future prospects. The ambivalence of cultural conditions (to which the so-called obstacles to development are often linked) is such that "feudal blessings" can help explain the success of Japan, of the smaller Asiatic "tigers," and even of those industrial districts of central and northeastern Italy, while the absence of feudal blessings, Hirschman claimed following Louis Hartz (see chapter 1), can help us understand some of the political and cultural difficulties experienced by the United States. ("Some of the elements in feudalism," Gerschenkron had already written [1962, p. 94], "may be neutral as far as capitalism is concerned; others may be outright favorable to it.") Once again there is ambivalence in the concrete conditions that may, in a continually changing world, either sustain or disadvantage—unfortunately not always in alternation—one population or another.

12. According to the theory of cognitive dissonance, Hirschman reminds us (1982b, pp. 15–17), for peace of mind anyone who has made a purchase or a commitment will suppress contradictory information. But here too there are limits to self-illusion: once they are surpassed, we are forced to admit that we are disappointed and will express our disappointment. The reasoning behind *Exit* regarding loyalty and severe

initiation is thus represented in the experience of disappointment. The results of the theory of cognitive dissonance are reinterpreted as naive shrewdness and procrastination in order to avoid disappointment. In the end, precisely because it has been postponed, disappointment can be perceived without inhibitions.

13. These included (among others) Arthur Lewis, Ragnar Nurkse, Paul Rosenstein-Rodan, Walter Rostow, and Tibor Scitovsky. In this debate Hirschman was in the company of Erik Dahmén, Francois Perroux, Ian Svennilson, and Paul Streeten. In particular, in a letter written to Perroux dated February 20, 1959, that I was able to see courtesy of the author, Hirschman declared that he was "struck by the similarity, from various points of view," between chapters 2–4 of volume 2 of *La coexistance pacifique* (pp. 284–349) and chapters 2, 4, 6, and 10 of *The Strategy*. "I find this," he continued, "even more remarkable because the starting points of our works are obviously quite different. Your treatment is more generalized than mine which arises wholly from the need to maximize what I call the induced decision-making process of underdeveloped countries. If, nonetheless, our analyses reach such similar conclusions, it may be because this necessity exists to a greater or lesser extent in all countries, whether they are industrialized or not." This is the first time, if I am not mistaken, that Hirschman alluded to this correspondence and therefore to the possibility of transferring some of the results of the analysis of underdeveloped countries to that of developed countries.

14. My personal experience as a young student at Cambridge University in the early 1960s is witness to this.

15. On the other hand, Hirschman used the opportunity of the debate to clarify his own point of view. Unlike Marshall's partial analysis, he explained in a conference at the time (1959–60, pp. 17–18, cited in 1961a), those who have supported balanced growth have always quite rightly claimed that the various investments are dependent on each other. "I propose that we take advantage of it, that we probe into the structure that is holding together these interrelated activities. As in the atom, there is much energy here that can and is in fact utilized in building up economic development nuclei. *Later on* these nuclei look as though they could never have been separated even for a single instant when in actual fact they might never have been assembled had not a sequential solution . . . been found by accident, instinct, or reasoned design." "I am in favor," he wrote to André Gunder Frank on August 18, 1959a, quoted in 1986b, p. 27, "of utilizing the energy which holds together economic nuclei of given minimum size in the *building* of these nuclei."

16. This "peroration" was not heard. The evaluation given in a review of the Italian edition is typical in this regard. "Hirschman," Ariotti wrote (1968, p. 278), "complains that his reviewers tend to focus in particular on the chapters devoted to balanced and unbalanced growth, rather than extending themselves to other parts of the book. This tendency, in my view, responds to the way the book actually unfolds. . . . The middle chapters in fact put forward the fundamental arguments, while the early ones seem no more than an introduction, and the later ones look like exercises to verify the correspondence of the central thesis to the various themes usually included in the debate on economic development." (It was from this very restricted viewpoint that the Italian edition of *The Strategy* was linked to the policies of development poles and "programmed bargaining" for the south of Italy: Ariotti, 1968, di Fenizio, 1968.)

17. Despite this, Chenery clings to the idea that a scarce factor can still exist in underdeveloped countries, i.e., the ability to invest. This is a rather weak defense because the scarcity of entrepreneurial skills is repeatedly excluded by the text (see for example, 1958a, pp. 40–41 and 49). Rereading these pages, Hirschman wrote to Chenery on August 8, 1959 (in a letter I was able to read courtesy of the author together with the letters quoted in the following two notes), "you will find that I conceive of the ability to invest as a floor and am most interested in the forces, inducement mechanisms, pressures, pacing devices (these concepts are all more important and recur throughout the book) that permit the economy to develop at a faster rate than would result from the growth of what I define rather restrictively as the 'ability to invest.' "

18. Hirschman himself pointed out these interpretative oversights to the two reviewers, in two letters dated August 8, and July 27, 1959.

19. "I found it," Harrod wrote to Hirschman regarding *The Strategy* on September 8, 1963, "the most interesting book that I have read in economics for years, perhaps the most stimulating book that I have read on any subject for some time."

20. I think that this attitude is reflected today in John Sheahan's criticism of Hirschman (in 1992, pp. 22–23) for not having dealt with the "total neglect [on behalf of the theory of balanced growth] of more orthodox notions of the significance of costs."

21. For example, to show on a theoretical level the logic of Braudel's thesis of world economy and long-term history, which could, in my view, be dialectically connected to Hirschman's idea of event and possibilism. See Meldolesi, 1984, 1992b, 1994b, and above, and chapter 5, note 18.

22. The most suitable seat for reflecting on these peculiarities is probably "Economic Development, Research and Development and Policy Making: Some Converging Views" (1962) written together with Charles Lindblom. This essay compares the ideas of Hirschman, Klein, Meckling, and Linblom (conceived independently in the three fields indicated) in order to both study their correspondences and contrast them to the traditional concepts of "equilibrium," "coordination," "comprehensive vision," etc. Together with an interesting discussion on the *forma mentis* behind each of the three contributions, we find a concise and stylized representation of the alternative between balanced and unbalanced growth. Compared to the optimal balanced growth of a two sector model, unbalanced growth reveals its initial comparative inefficiency by means of a different allocation of resources, losses in some productive activities and super profits in others, and relative price variations. However, the reactions of economic and political operators arising from this set in motion further resources and productive skills thus allowing ground to be recovered and the rate of development of balanced growth to be surpassed. "On the assumption of a given volume of resources and investment, it may be highly irrational not to attempt to come as close as possible to balanced growth; but without these assumptions there is likely to exist such a thing as an 'optimal degree of imbalance,'" the one that generates the highest average rate of growth (1971a, p. 65). The Pareto optimum of traditional economics is thus substituted by the notion of optimal disequilibrium (Meldolesi, 1994a), in which the fruitful use of disequilibria does not depend simply on the actions of market forces but on their way of interacting with the reactions of the interested public and private parties.

As far as verifying the thesis of unbalanced growth is concerned, Moshe Sirquin, in his survey of linkages presented at the Buenos Aires Symposium (1992, p. 115), claimed that "an unbalanced outcome is not an indication of an *ex ante* strategy of planned imbalance. Furthermore, the whole point of creating imbalances is to create tensions that will spur agents to react in the direction of restoring balance at a higher plane. If successful, the strategy will show a high degree of balance even in a comparatively short period of time."

23. Andrea Ginzburg (1986, p. 135, p. 163, and note 4) called attention to François Simiand's notion of development as being the overall result of phases of expansion and stabilization, and to the "similar idea, differently motivated" of Hirschman's sailing against the wind. Simiand was a French sociologist and economist, for a long time a point of reference in the "history of prices" and in the *Annales,* who taught political economics at Paris's Conservatoire des Arts et Métiers during

Hirschman's formative years. What is more, in contrast to traditional economics, he thought that growth was characterized by a "series of imbalances." In a paper given at the 1908 Third International Congress of Philosophy held in Heidelberg (1912, p. 182), he declared, for example, "If, as I think I am right in thinking, the study of facts leads us not only to recognize that our societies live in a kind of perpetual imbalance, but also to present as an aim of the economic art the *organization of imbalance,* can anyone doubt that the theory of organization of this imbalance is a quest of art or of applied science, and not, per se, of science itself?"

We cannot exclude the possiblity, then, that at some point in his research the issues raised during his Paris years came back to Hirschman's mind (unconsciously, or from a different viewpoint). If, however, we go beyond the observation (and terminology) of imbalances and fluctuations and look at Simiand's work more closely, apart from the many important contributions, we find a naturalistic, almost biological, pre-Keynesian view that has little to do with Hirschman's theses (Meldolesi, 1991a).

24. If we follow the former we could even claim (Chenery, 1959, p. 1065) that *The Strategy* "has performed a real service in going beyond the conventional acknowledgement of the importance of external economies and probing the implications for investment behavior of interdependence in production"—a perfectly correct but rather narrow proposition considering how much the text has to offer. As for the latter, we can go back to Hirschman's statement in *The Strategy* (1958a, p. 63) that "Classical economics, while not taking so positive a view of the imbalances of the growth process, at least was never particularly concerned about them because it relied on prices to signal, and on the profit motive to eliminate rapidly and reliably, any structural disequilibria that might arise in the course of growth." This could lead to an interpretation of the text as an independent contribution within the framework of classical logic, as long as the many noncorrespondent analytical aspects are muted.

25. Perhaps also regarding the overall point of view of several supporters of unbalanced growth. For example, this "clash of mentalities" can also be seen in the remarkable incomprehension of Hirschman's approach shown by Paul Streeten in his comment to "A Dissenter's Confession" (1984, pp. 115–17).

26. This also happened with regard to issues on the agenda at the time. For example, according to Javier Villanueva, the book was naturally received in Argentina because its ideas on unbalanced growth and on linkages corresponded to the need to build modern firms locally, as in the case of a few car factories. Furthermore, Aníbal Pinto claims,

by stressing the scant utilization of existing resources and the linkages between economic sectors and geographic areas, *The Strategy* rallied Chilean (and Latin American) economists into considering the relationship between industry, agriculture, and mines. The latter two sectors, in fact, had always been set aside—due to the presence of landowners, and foreign firms' interests, and because they represented important sources of public income—as if they were sinful (observations from conversations, August 1990).

27. Take, for example, Cardoso, Cortés Conde, di Tella, Jaguaribe, Pinto, Rosenthal, Urquidi, Villanueva; or Barros de Castro, Bazdresch, Berlinsky, Foxley, O'Donnell, Serra, Urrutia; or Arida, Cardenas, Ffrench-Davis, Lustig, Malan, Muñoz. This is the conclusion I reached after an intense series of meetings (July–September 1990). As far as Latin Americanists are concerned, I would like to point out Judith Tendeer's view that *The Strategy* taught them to look where they would never have looked in order to go further into the issues of development. The book, she wrote (1968, p. xi) "is a preventive against the economic researcher's variety of 'cultural shock.' Upon first encountering the frenzy of development, the researcher almost naturally backs away from his subject, seeing everything as unrelieved chaos and disorganization. A prior reading of *The Strategy* impels him into the midst of these events with the feeling that, if he is patient enough, he will find a rich complexity of both success and failure, efficiency alongside incompetence, order cohabiting with disorder."

28. Furtado told me (August 1990) he had many things in common with Hirschman: a similar background—France, an interest in Schumpeter, history, and economics. They also shared an analogous orientation. Development is for us, he said, a process of evolution and transformation. The concept of strategy of development implies human action, and indicates the search for a logic to guide this action. In this way development becomes a process of choice. But the mechanism of *The Strategy* is a travesty of these ideas, Furtado claimed, a fantasy linked to the circumstances in which the book was written. "Albert is a great writer, and a noble man; but as far as the problems of development are concerned, we often disagree: he is too elegant, too optimistic."

29. It is important, however, to keep in mind that the notions in *The Strategy* regarding balance of payments and inflation have their own specificity, linked to Hirschman's concept of unbalanced growth. (For more on inflation see 1963a, p. 213 and 1981a, p. 179.)

30. As well as indicating a middle way between futility and brutality, the book opened a path between two currents of thought (as Hirschman succeeded in doing with other writings [see chapter 1 and

note 31]). On the other hand, the fact that ECLA had at times found itself in agreement with the economists of the "new orthodoxy" (1971a, pp. 306–7) might help explain the path taken by the book (and help document the way in which the commission's self-deprecation gave the visiting economist the opportunity to exploit it).

31. In this article, Hirschman concentrates on the doctrine of ECLA and summarizes its essential ingredients: the unequal distribution of the gains from trade and the increasing tendency of the terms of trade to penalize primary commodities; the asymmetry between the income elasticities of demand for (respectively) imports from the center and those from the periphery; the need for industrial protectionism in the periphery from the point of view of resource allocation; import restriction as a means of redirection of the imports themselves (and not of reducing trade). These propositions, Hirschman argued, have two features in common: they supply an answer to the basic question of the cause of Latin American backwardness in the international trading system, and they underscore the need for public intervention in order to correct the negative consequences of this system and to encourage industrialization (through an accelerated process of import substitution). These concerns are reflected in the annual reports published by the Commission that try to deal with the more obscure sides of the economic situation. "Even though numerous Latin American countries achieved considerable economic progress during the postwar period, the successive annual reports frequently read as though things were tolerable enough until a few months ago, but have *now* started to take a definite turn for the worse. In this fashion Latin America's situation was dramatized with the aim of stimulating both national and international action." (1971a, p. 284).

32. While Hirschman was writing the book, his wife Sarah, who was enrolled in a few courses in social science at the time, made a positive contribution on this matter (1958a, p. vi). "The efficient guidance she provided to the anthropological literature permitted some forays into a territory whose rich resources are too often left unutilized by economists."

33. "Even when I lived mainly among economists," Hirschman recently stated (1990b, p. 158), "I always had a strong urge to escape from 'pure' economics and to explore the connections between economic and political phenomena."

34. Compared to the more general term "political economy," "political economics" seems to emphasize the analytical aspect of a research that is not strictly speaking economics or political science. In France and Italy, in fact, the corresponding terms (*économie politique* and *economia*

politica, respectively) preceded the advent of economics as such, and ended up being considered one and the same thing. The terms can however be resuscitated in order to designate an independent point of view announcing "a future with an ancient heart" (see chapter 2, and Meldolesi, 1990a).

35. Coming back to the logic of the preface to *The Strategy*, it can be noted that once again, retrospectively, a series of observations and annotations in the book must have looked to Hirschman like variations on a common theme—that of the interaction between economics and politics—now explicitly theorized.

36. To attribute new contents to already known forms of thought can be a way of circulating one's ideas. Take, for example, the concept of "investment in individual and group identity" introduced by Hirschman to cover, in economic terminology, both Alessandro Pizzorno's view according to which political participation often springs from the need to reinforce one's sense of belonging to a group and his own view that noninstrumental action makes the individual feel more human (1986b, p. 151). The language belongs to the economics of human capital, but Hirshman's message is different.

37. Thus when Hirschman claims that the detailed identification of specific agents of change allows one to be rid of the notion of a "single, homogeneous vanguard group" (a feature of Marxism to be found in many authors), one gets the impression of a true understatement.

38. This is a crucial point in a long journey. Back in 1948, commenting on the Italian economy, Hirschman had recognized "the combination of a general deflationary policy with expansionist measures in specifically selected fields" applied at the time in Italy as positive. But he had also claimed that the existing imbalance had not been correctly exploited. Redressing the balance of payments had been achieved "too soon" and had "actually out-paced basic economic recovery" (1948h, p. 604, and 1948n, pp. 16 and 17). Instead of aiming simply for equilibrium (as the traditional theory of the Pareto optimum would have prescribed), Hirschman grasped the validity of alternating between equilibrium and disequilibrium in the balance of payments, and the utility of oscillations that could have given better results.

The idea was taken up again in two articles written during the period of *The Strategy*. As we have already mentioned (chapter 2), from the first essay (1957b) the idea of oscillation emerges from a political point of view when Hirschman claims that governments in underdeveloped countries should cultivate a propensity to experiment as well as a propensity to plan. The second essay (1959e) takes the thesis from the point of view of the economy: while the importance of reequilibrating adjustments produced by price changes in primary commodities should not be underestimated, it must also be recognized that fluctuation in these prices may be excessive, especially when they encourage irreversible productive substitutions in importing industrial countries (1971a, pp. 165–66).

In *The Strategy*, furthermore, the principle of oscillation is put forward explicitly in a section of chapter 9 subtitled, "Growth-inducing effects of fluctuations in foreign-exchange earnings": "After a period of comparative foreign exchange *affluence* that causes certain consumption habits, based on imports, to take root, the experience of foreign exchange *shortage* has often set in motion industrial developments designed to produce the previously imported goods that are now sorely missed." This observation was first put forward in a 1957 conference on Latin American development (1986b, p. 25, and note 25) and led the author to claim that a certain alternation between good and bad years as far as foreign-exchange availability was concerned can actually encourage industrial growth. A similar argument can be found in chapter 10 of *The Strategy* where, in order to reinforce trickling-down as opposed to polarization effects, Hirschman suggests looking for "optimal institutional arrangements."

Finally, the idea is taken up later with regard to trade and foreign investments. "In order to maximize growth," Hirschman wrote (1971a, pp. 25–26), "the developing countries could need an appropriate alternation of contact and insulation, of openness to the trade and capital of the developed countries, to be followed by a period of nationalism and withdrawnness. In the period of openness, crucial learning processes take place, but many are of the latent kind and remain unnoticed and misperceived. They come to fruition only once contact is interrupted or severely restricted: the previous misconceptions are then forcibly swept away. Thus both contact and insulation have essential roles to play, one after the other." See also 1971a, pp. 229–30.

39. Instead of the criteria based on the cost-benefit relationship, Hirschman suggests distinguishing between substitution and postponement choices, adding in a note that this distinction had not been made in "Economics and Investment Planning" (1954b: see chapter 2). As we have mentioned, this article supports drafting sector projects based on significant generalizations: through the effort of identifying these generalizations, concepts of latitude for poor performance and of backward/forward linkages were reached. Typically, having suitably generalized these basic observations, there is a retroactive effect on the arguments that once supported them, thus opening the way for the construction of *The Strategy*. The first observation, in fact (see

chapter 6), allows for the qualification of substitution choices, while the second helps identify postponement choices, and therefore distinguish between the two kinds of choice. This, as far as I can see, is where the sequentialism of *The Strategy*'s central chapters comes about (just as the very topic of unbalanced growth comes about).

Thus, observing retrospectively the argument put forward in "Economics and Investment Planning," Hirschman claims that postponement choices "must be made at two different stages of the process of development planning: first, before it is decided in which sector or sectors substitution choices are to be studied, for the decision seriously to study alternative means of fulfilling a given need usually already implies a decision to give priority to this need; and second, after substitution choices have been completed in several different sectors" (1958a, p. 78, note 5).

40. "Often designated as 'infrastructures,' " Hirschman wrote later, referring to numerous public goods and services (1981a, pp. 80–81), "as though they were preconditions for the more directly productive activities, these goods have more usually been provided in response to urgent demands emanating from such activities and from their need for consolidation, greater profitability and further expansion." (The surprise sequences in this thesis, which Hirschman used in his university courses—as he did in *The Strategy*—to launch the part dealing specifically with economic policy in underdeveloped countries, were what probably earned him the nickname of "tricky Albert" among his Harvard students.)

41. Concluding a far-reaching collective study of the economic history of his country, the Colombian economist José Antonio Ocampo recently claimed that Colombia's economic development from the 1920s on was generated by three powerful forces. Firstly, the integration of the domestic market that (due to the extraordinary geography of the country and its economic structure that concentrated on gold and coffee exports) had previously been evanescent; secondly, the linkages (in particular backward linkages) generated by industrialization; thirdly, fluctuations in the price of coffee, and the effects of the Depression and World War II. If one bears in mind that "the (rather slow) development of an integrated modern transport infrastructure was largely possible thanks to the interregional trade generated by industrial development" (1990, p. 29), the reference to Hirschman's analysis should be more far-reaching than the one proposed by Ocampo with reference to linkages. In fact, the inverted sequence (like the one just mentioned above) between social fixed capital and directly productive activity is a vital aspect of the strategy of unbalanced growth. To this, fluctuations in price, in trade,

etc., pertaining to the principle of oscillation, must be added (see note 38 above).

42. The unbalanced growth policy, Hirschman explained in "A Dissenter's Confession," is only proposed in *The Strategy* when, given the interdependence of the economic system, one can count on the fact that the expansion of production, sectors, or regions set in motion economic and political forces that tend to eliminate the initial imbalance. The emphasis therefore lies on the specific features of the reaction mechanism: "it is illegitimate to invoke the unbalanced growth idea when there are no compelling reasons why an advance in one direction and the ensuing imbalance should set counterveiling forces in motion" (1986b, p. 27).

43. The declared genesis of this thesis can be traced to chapter 4 of *Rhetoric of Reaction* (1991). However, as I shall argue later, it is probably an idea Hirschman had been developing for some time.

44. Industrialists fear, often with reason, that they will have to use a lower quality product with less uniformity than the imported equivalent; that they will lose their freedom to shop around the world and become dependent on a single domestic supplier; that they will be subjected to competition from other domestic producers encouraged to enter the market by the availability of local means of production, and that they will lose the advantages in location once the sources of input supplies have been moved elsewhere (1958b, p. 118). These are real concerns, probably observed on the field during Hirschman's Bogotá years. Again, this is the first step on a long path that leads us to the present day.

45. If, on the other hand, Hirschman continued, exceptional circumstances, such as the Depression or the World War, sanction the introduction of a welfare state, the tension between a liberal tradition and the ethics of solidarity still remains and can successively come to the fore with the negative consequences we have before our eyes. Note that, in this case, sequentialism does not meet with difficulties due to structural interdependence (as a supporter of balanced growth would have argued); on the contrary, it does so because the two tasks are all too easily separable, to the extent that it is tempting to pursue one until the other is (more or less willingly) undermined.

46. This aspect is dwelt on in more detail later, in order to qualify the analysis of linkages. Whereas in *The Strategy* Hirschman stressed the relationship between the amplitude of the market and the efficient size of the plant, later he takes other variables into consideration, such as the level of strangeness or alienness of the new economic activities. If the productive process and technology required by these new activities are unknown to the industrialists already installed, their linkages will be very

weak, since the technological leap required will present many problems. (Historically, this has proved particularly serious for those producers of primary export commodities whose linkages have induced activities in the hands of others or in another country [see 1981a, pp. 71–72].)

47. "Their entrepreneurs, domestic and foreign," he explained later (1986b, p. 15), "had apparently hit upon a good number of *sequential* rather than *simultaneous* solutions to the problem of industrialization, but the more typical sequences were often unusual by the standards of experience in the more advanced countries."

48. "This basic difference," Hirschman added (1981a, pp. 63–64), "has bedeviled various ingenious attempts at comprehensive cross-section measurement of linkages and thereby 'testing the linkage hypothesis.'" (This does not mean, of course, that this literature does not contain significant contributions [see 1981a, p. 64, and 1986b, p. 59].)

49. Note, moreover, how in *The Strategy* (1958a, pp. 144–45, note 13) and later (1971a, p. 20 and pp. 318–19), Hirschman's aversion to the relationship between challenge and response proposed by Toynbee that Gerschenkron for his part uses: "the challenge, that is to say the 'tension' [between backwardness and growth potential]," writes Gerschenkron (1952, p. 9), "must be considerable before a response in terms of industrial development will materialize."

50. Gershenckron opposed the idea of phases or stages of development (such as Walt Rostow's [see 1962, p. 335]). He "showed, to the contrary, how the industrialization of the late-coming European countries such as Germany and Russia differed in fundamental aspects from the English industrial revolution, largely because of the intensity of the 'catching up' effort on the part of the latecomers" (Hirschman, 1981a, p. 11). Moreover, a review by Gershenkron probably signaled to Hirschman the work of the Swedish economist Erik Dahmén—a coauthor of the thesis of unbalanced growth (see 1958a, p. 43, and note 14 above).

51. Rosenstein-Rodan, Hirschman explained, for example, in *The Strategy* (1958a, p. 51), linked the theory of balanced growth (in the demand side version) to that of the big push (in the version characterized by "a large number of projects of varying size that dovetail with one another").

52. With the passing of time, these points have proved their validity independently of the problem from which they arose—to the extent that today one can read *The Strategy* without even referring to the matter. From one point of view this may seem inadvisable because links with economists' theses and with Gershenkron's work are lost;

246 NOTES TO PAGE 81

from another, however, it seems almost to follow Gershenkron's own indications when he claimed at the end of his book (1962, pp. 363–64) that the accumulation of the advantages of backwardness could be accompanied by an accumulation of disadvantages and that this fact might suggest a different organizing principle from the one (of the different level of backwardness) so far used in historical research until that time. "This would mean," he wrote in a memorable passage, "the end of an approach. But farewell to it would be said in a grateful mood. For what more can be expected of any historical hypothesis than to have stimulated research to the point of becoming the stepping stone to a new hypothesis and to new research?"

53. "For the historically oriented," Hirschman explained retrospectively (1981a, p. 11), "Gershenkron's work supplied the same kind of reassurance Keynesianism had given to the analytically minded: he showed once and for all that there can be more than one path to development, that countries setting out to become industrialized are likely to forge their own policies, sequences and ideologies to that end."

54. Hirschman claimed (1958a, p. 124) that "there is no real alternative between export promotion and import substitution. The former may often be the only practical way of achieving the latter." He also spoke (1958a, p. 169) of the exportability of rapidly growing productions as a condition for external equilibrium. In a process of rapid development, if new products are not very exportable (in terms of price, quality, and kind), a recurrent tendency to excess imports generally takes place. Suppose, for example, that the country's economy is made up of two interdependent sectors (with fixed coefficients) that grow at different rates. The sector that grows faster will only be able to maintain its rate with recourse to necessary imports: this implies corresponding growth in exports. Since traditional exports usually grow at a lower rate, the need to expand into new exports is presented as a "compulsive sequence" in the model (Berlinski, 1992, p. 325).

55. If we compare this analysis with the one presented in the 1951–52 articles (see chapter 1), we can see that while in the latter, the contradictory—but ultimately positive—effects of the industrialization of underdeveloped countries on the markets of industrial countries are studied, in the analysis upon which the first section of chapter 7 in *The Strategy* is based, the same question is treated from the other end of the scale: that is, developing backward countries by exploiting the opportunities offered by the international market. Notice, moreover, that Hirschman returns here to his critique (first expressed in the two articles and in *National Power* [1945, p. 146 ff.]) of those who oppose the industrialization of backward countries. They should concern themselves—

he adds (1958a, p. 123)—with exporting manufactures (and not just machinery) because the purchase of some manufactured goods can be compared to "the imparting of a lesson which is finally learnt as home production is started in the heretofore importing country."

56. Typically, Hirschman explained, import-substituting industrialization is characterized by productive processes entirely based on imported materials and machinery, while imports of the substituted consumption goods are effectively blocked. This gives rise to an exuberant atmosphere (in which the demand is easily overestimated) and to risky, flamboyant public policies. Once the substitution cycle has run itself down, a certain excess capacity, a fall in the rate of growth, followed by disappointment and recrimination are likely to emerge. But the process of development can be started up again by inaugurating new phases through backward linkages. Hirschman, of course, does not deny the existence of "bottle-neck industries," but he claims that these suggest adopting "special protection, or direct promotion, and even better, efforts to export the industry's output that cannot be accomodated by the domestic market" (1971a, p. 105). Later he wrote (1987b, p. 14): "in the ideologically charged debates of the time, no one asked whether the assorted problems of import-substituting industrialization were conceivably growing pains which could be overcome in due course by adroit, incremented policy-making."

57. It is interesting to see how Hirschman's point of view develops through historical experience. It represents an alternative for those countries that have been unsuccessful in dealing with the transition toward a more open economy and have therefore locked themselves into a semi-autarchic system (Berlinski, 1992). It also opposes ultra-liberal monetarist policies used by the military dictatorships in Chile and Argentina at the end of the 1970s which led to "eliminating hundreds of industrial firms for the sake of the 'law of comparative advantage' " (as it opposes the policy of currency overvaluation that led to import desubstitution in Mexico). It points in the direction, rather, of those experiences (in Brazil, Colombia, and Frei's Chile) where "a gradual transition was managed from exclusive reliance on the domestic market to substantial exports of manufactures by means of various devices such as crawling pegs for currency devaluation, progressive reduction in protection, and policies of export promotion" (Hirschman, 1987b, p. 15; see also 1981a, p. 115; Teitel and Thoumi, 1986; and Ocampo, 1990).

58. The explanation of a phenomenon long considered with perplexity (see Hirschman, 1957b, now in 1971a, pp. 264–65)—that of permanent exchange controls and currency overvaluation produced by inflationary pressures and by fixed exchange rates—is emblematic in

this regard. Rather than taxing the traditional export sector to subsidize new industries, Hirschman explained (1971a, pp. 117–19), many Latin American countries found it expedient to transfer resources indirectly, by means of currency overvaluation (penalizing export sectors) and of quantitative controls on imports (usually favoring inputs and machinery for industry). The reason is political. While interests vested in traditional exports would not have tolerated direct taxation, the indirect mechanism was presented under the respectable guise of defending the national currency. Nevertheless, this "hidden rationality" in the industrialization process met with increasing difficulties as time went by (because it increasingly jeopardizes traditional exports, hinders both the development of new exports and the energetic exploitation of backward linkage dynamics). "It could thus be suggested that, at a certain point, overvaluation of the currency turned from a stimulus to industrial progress into a drag on it" (see too, 1971a, p. 12, and 1981a, pp. 82–83).

59. "It is always possible," Hirschman has claimed (1990b, p. 155) "that what is good is not new, and what is new is not good."

60. Comparing temperate and tropical climates, feudal and capitalist production, agriculture based on rainfall and that based on irrigation, or the age of printing and that of electronics, "these 'macrotechnological' theories," Hirschman wrote (1968a, p. ix), "cut history and human experience in general into huge slices." Since the 1930s Hirschman had been familiar with Karl Wittfogel's work on hydraulic societies, and how water conditioned social, political, and cultural life in the East. It is likely that he had little sympathy for the deterministic tone of the research and for the sweeping generalizations made. He did, however, appreciate the analytical thrust of the book, and later considered it one of the factors that inspired his ideas on linkages (from a private conversation, autumn 1989). (As far as Wittfogel's specific interpretative hypothesis is concerned, Hirschman typically belittled its effect [see 1981a, p. 81].)

61. Take, for example, *Formaçao econômica do Brasil* (1958), "Furtado's outstanding book" (Hirschman, 1971a, pp. 303–4, note 54).

62. Both because the work force moves on to producing the staple, and because imports of consumption goods enter into competition with them. In *The Strategy* the possibilities of a negative outcome are left to unbalanced developments, disturbances (in inflation, balance-of-payments, population), or too strong polarization effects. Now the concept of linkages is extended to allow for a clearer focus. For a peripheral country, contact with the capitalist center may well exhaust natural resources and create impoverishment by means of an adverse combination of the bundle of characteristics of the product, just like

when production of an unreproducible staple generates weak or null production linkages, negative consumption linkages, and irrelevant (or wasted) fiscal linkages.

63. As long as only backward and forward linkages are taken into account, Hirschman declared later (1986b, pp. 66–67) development strategy will probably have a pro-industry bias because traditional agriculture uses a low level of industrial inputs. (This is basically the point of view expressed in *The Strategy*, 1958a, pp. 109–10.) "Once agricultural techniques evolve, however, and particularly when consumption linkages are given their due, the expansion of agricultural incomes can be just as stimulating for overall growth as an industrial spurt. Precisely on this ground, recent reappraisals of development strategy favor a tilt of investment priorities toward agricultural improvement."

64. Hirschman connects this notion to that of the "quality bundle" of the product contained in consumption theory, to that of the "property bundle" of metal in metallurgy, and that of a few classifications made by economic geographers and other social scientists. It is a matter of looking beyond the single staple and identifying the linkages that characterize them and that condition the growth of the relative countries. The consequent interpretation of development also raises problems of economic policy linked to the various dislocations of these linkages.

65. This is probably implicit in the microtechnological choice of the analysis. As we have already seen, by transposing onto a smaller scale the thesis of the interaction between productive forces and relations of production, Hirschman modified Marx's argument in small doses, almost as if he wanted to steer the inadvertent reader beyond the Marxist Rubicon and lead him instead towards the logic of the principle of oscillation, and hint at its causes: having to share one's time between public and private, and the misperceptions of opportunities by economic decision makers. In this way, thanks to the conviction resulting from the repetition of the analysis, the micro dimension allows an important intellectual reform to be started. In fact, though it is possible to draw far-reaching consequences from specific features of production, it is, however, probable that the further one goes into the concrete reality of determined productive processes, the less plausible it becomes that their influence on the social-political environment is a determinant. From this point of view, Hirschman's solution brings to mind the path followed (but not completely understood) by the Italian *operaismo* or "workerism" in the 1960s, when Raniero Panzieri and his friends proposed specific, often lucid, analyses of the social and political consequences of technological changes that had taken place

in several big companies (for example, the effects of the production line on the automobile industry). Their difficulty, however, was convincing the general public of the "determining" nature of these relationships.

66. This is also useful for clarifying a fortiori the relationship between Hirschman's work and the materialistic view of history. In the few places where the oscillating sequence of economics and politics appears in Marx's work, it is subordinated to a finalistic pattern (i.e., socialism). A closer observation of oscillations in economic-political processes can be seen in Lenin, though also subordinated to an omnipresent concern with the revolution and the building of socialism (Meldolesi, 1981, 1989). Comparing them, it becomes clear that Hirschman's research worked towards freeing himself from their approach by modifying the logical pattern. In the Marxist approach, the interaction between political and economic forces has a dominant direction, leading to a determined socio-political change after which the process starts all over again. In Hirschman's approach, on the other hand, political and economic forces are considered on the same level and their interaction manifests itself in the temporary supremacy of one over the other, and therefore in the alternate non-predetermined prevalence in the oscillation (see also 1981a, p. 296).

67. A staple, he explained, does not determine the social-political environment "in any unique or exhaustive way." It is true, rather, that it imprints certain patterns of its own on its surroundings, and that it is interesting to study this "imprinting" process. We are talking about the influence of a production process or technology on various socioeconomic configurations that is not one way. At times it is sensible to turn the argument around and ask oneself, for example, whether a certain regime can show a marked preference for a certain activity. Thus, just as sugar-cane production lent itself to the exploitation of slaves, so the standard of living that the conquerers of the New World wanted to achieve led them to take up sugar-cane cultivation in tropical countries. The linkage concept, Hirschman claimed later (1986b, p. 74), invites us to focus on the different productive conditions of economic activities as a means of discovering how one thing leads (or does not lead) to another. "But this focus does not prejudge either the nature or the principal direction of the causal links involved in the complex interactions among technology, ideology, institutions, and develoment." This only allows a certain number of interesting observations and challenges other approaches (such as the "thick description" of his friend Clifford Geertz) to propose alternative or complementary interpretations.

68. Looking back, it is not difficult to see that it is really the logical outcome of our story. The caesura (and continuity) between *National Power* and Hirschman's later production (see chapter 1 and note 40) already implies the "un-Marxist turn" which we have finally reached and is moreover consistent with Hirschman's view of ideology which we shall be examining in chapter 4.

4. *JOURNEYS* AND REFORMS

1. "It seems to me," Hirschman wrote (1971a, p. 311), "that Latin Americans still have not fully emerged from the stage of self-denigration; they are far too ready to issue blanket condemnations of their own ways and to escape to a dream world of ever-new laws, perfectly designed institutions or scientifically calculated plans. Frequently they do not realize how much they could learn if only they scrutinized the growth that is taking hold here and there. Instead of yearning for an unattainable simultaneous solution of their problems they should, in my opinion, train themselves to perceive and evaluate the various possibilities of sequential decision making and problem solving."

2. Two kinds of books exist on economic and social problems: those based on an answer that is applied to a great number of questions and those where there is a question without an answer. When one concentrates on the latter, one's mind cannot rest until a variety of answers have been found. In the case of *Journeys* the question is modulated by a series of objectives and concerns. In addition to asking himself about the process by which politicians arrive at vital decisions for a country's development, Hirschman addressed his concern about Latin American self-denigration, which seems to negate the existence (and even the possibility) of cumulative processes of understanding. He also aimed to identify (and reevaluate) some aspects of the Latin American style of policy making and perorate its reform, fighting a battle on two fronts because he also wished to demonstrate to the North Americans the limits of their attitude. Finally, he addressed the intellectual need to document the claim made in *The Strategy* that nonmarket forces are not necessarily less automatic than market ones.

3. And with increased interest. This clarifies one of the reasons for the durability of Hirschman's works (see chapter 1). It is not only a question of the permanent nature of the problems dealt with: the books are read in today's context and historical oscillations put them into new perspectives.

4. Private discussion, August 1990. The same attitude emerges

clearly in *A Bias for Hope*, translated appropriately in Spanish *Obstinación por la esperanza*.

5. "With its discussion of 'reform-mongering' "—wrote Alejandro Foxley, Michael McPherson, and Guillermo O'Donnell in their introduction to the Festschrift in honor of Hirschman (1986b, p. 2)— "*Journeys* was not only a contribution to studies in policy-making. It was also a crucial contribution to *democratic* policy-making. But for about two decades, the *esprit de géomètrie* that Hirschman's Pascalien mind attempts to temper by the *esprit de finesse* led reactionary technocrats, arrogant planners and self-righteous revolutionaries to ignore or dismiss that contribution. Today, when those and other *systémes* have failed so patently, and democracy is again a vital issue in Latin America, *Journeys* is more relevant and contemporary than ever. It is one of the few intellectual guides available for searching the narrow paths that may allow some fragile democracies to survive in the midst of, and to do something about, the socio-economic crisis Latin America has ever suffered."

6. It is characteristic—I think—that two influential economic journals, the *American Economy Review* and the *Economic Journal*, in their review of *Journeys*, criticized Hirschman for not having paid enough attention to the economic aspects of the countries in question: see, respectively, the favorable review by D. Seers (1964) and the critical one by T. King (1965). David Felix's review in the *Economica* (1964) should also be mentioned. *The Strategy* and *Journeys*, Felix wrote (p. 202), "leave one with a sense of delight, some novel insights, and a feeling of disbelief. Delight not only because Hirschman writes well, but because his Stendhalian view of economic development as a devious process, full of unexpected ironies and paradoxical byways, is a welcome and stimulating diversion from the earnest programming and plodding testing of hypotheses by which economists attempt not very convincingly to earn their passage from ideology to science." But, "rather than merely modifying economists', perhaps excessive, concern with the efficient husbanding of resources and maximum growth paths by introducing a useful dose of political and social realism, Hirschman winds up discarding the economists' standard preoccupations completely. *The Strategy of Economic Development* might well be subtitled 'Economic Development with Unlimited Supply of Labour, Foreign Exchange and Everything Else except the Will to Invest'. . . . Similarly, *Journeys Towards Progress* could be subtitled, 'Social and Economic Reform with Unlimited Amounts of Time.' "

7. This is an example of Hirschman's inductive and micro logic. Note too, Hirschman's ability to participate independently in an ongoing discussion (preferably, not very structured), bringing his ideas

and reinterpreting the theme of the debate from his own point of view.

8. Typically, Hirschman's argument proceeds backwards. Obstinate political problems which seem refractory to any kind of treatment hide a long history that can teach us many things. This blessing in disguise found throughout the entire volume has a series of implications. "Considerable value," Hirschman wrote (1963a, p. 232), "attaches for a society with a poor or one sided signalling system to having a recalcitrant, or recurring attention-receiving problem which stimulates a search for other problems that would otherwise go unrecognized and unremedied, perhaps until it is 'too late.' As in the Arabian tale about the non-existent treasure thought to be buried in a fertile field that has long lain fallow, unexpected benefits are here yielded as a result of the activity connected with the search."

9. In part, the distinctions that follow take into account the reformulation contained in the first part of "Policymaking and Policy Analysis in Latin America—A Return Journey" (1975).

10. In Chile, repeated and not very successful attempts to fight inflation led the authorities to question the underlying causes. In this way, attention was focused on the structural problem of landed property. In Brazil, the fact that dams alone could not resolve the drought problem gave impetus to the examination of other problems in the region. In Colombia, worries over the balance of payments reinforced the search for adequate measures to increase agricultural production. Associations of this kind generally mean that the privileged problem continues to be, for the authorities, a hard nut to crack. Hence it is tempting to maintain that the problem can be resolved by indirect means; that is, by dealing with another issue that had been neglected for some time (and, hopefully, by using different and more adequate methods).

11. The plan, rejected by Hirschman as an external imposition and accepted as a self-disciplinary measure by the governments of underdeveloped nations (see chapter 2), becomes, in this case, an instrument of useful ideological mediation; of an ideology which is designed in such a way as to produce a plausible causal link between distinct problems.

12. "The latter situation . . . is characteristic of Latin American countries to the extent that they import 'solutions' from the outside in the form of the most up-to-date central banking legislation, economic planning agencies, or common market schemes. This typically 'dependent' behavior results, of course, in frustration precisely because these institutions are often established without the necessary minimal understanding of the problems they are set up to resolve" (1981a, p. 152). But the motivation that outruns understanding—Hirschman

goes on to say—may also arise out of an excessive faith in being able to solve all problems. From the time of the Kennedy Administration this hasty style of impulsive decision making became dominant in the United States, to the extent that Anthony Downs was able to create from it an "issue attention cycle" in American policies (1972). Initially, a problem exists but receives little attention. Then it is discovered and it is believed easy to solve. Later on, it is recognized that the solution would be costly and would affect some vested interests; after which public interest lessens and another problem is brought into the limelight. In the end, the energies (and institutions) which have been brought into play are able to survive, and some results are achieved.

13. This expression of Flaubert's (correspondence, 1929) is "marvelously appropriate" to Hirschman's argument and untranslatable into English. During the nineteenth century—as the author clarifies later on (1971a, p. 349)—reacting disconcertingly to the rapid growth of the industrial countries, many thinkers affected by the Flaubert syndrome, established socio-economic laws. This phenomenon repeated itself in the Third World where underdeveloped countries "have become fair game for the model builders and paradigms molders, to an intolerable degree" (and where the intellectuals' compulsion to theorize meets, unfortunately, with the politicians' compulsion to act).

14. Recognizing an answer generally stops the search for solutions. Later on, the policy can easily be exchanged for another (just as ambitious) policy, particularly if both were borrowed from abroad (see 1958a, pp. 138–39). "Nevertheless," Hirschman continued (1963a, p. 241), "the abandoning of a policy which once was hailed as a guarantee of salvation is quite a different matter from a change in fashions. . . . When such a policy has proven disappointing, it will be emphatically cast off, ridiculed, described as an utter failure and abomination; and the denial that it was ever anything but a palliative and a muddle, if not a conspiracy, may well set the stage for the commitment of policy-makers to the next Comprehensive, Fundamental, Integral Solution."

15. A second objective was to identify a few rationalities hidden in such behavior regarding the understanding of problems and of their solutions. The failure complex cuts off ties with emerging intuitions and inhibits the growing trust in their own abilities that would have otherwise been manifested. And even when positive results have been achieved, the country will need time before being able to recognize them (and fall, perhaps, into an exaggerated phase of self-gratification). Hirschman recently reviewed the matter, making particular reference to the Law 200 of 1936 on land reform in Colombia (see note 31 below). Here he recognizes that the cultural interpretation of such behavior in

terms of the failure complex (or fracasomania) is in reality too narrow and that "arguing along the lines of the perversity thesis, as was done so insistently by the Colombian commentators on Law 200, appears to have many attractions for parties who are not necessarily affected by fracasomania" (1991, p. 33).

16. Probably, Hirschman argued (1992b, pp. 1230–31), such disenchantment has historical and cultural origins as did German anxiety at the end of the century (see chapter 1). For Argentina, for example, he wrote, the political scientist Juan Carlos Torre "has suggested that the contempt for what local industries there is, expresses a hidden nostalgia for the good old days of the 'belle époque' at which time Argentina's role in the world economy—to supply England and other industrial countries with livestock products and other unchanging agricultural materials—was felt as both brilliant and nature-given. . . . In other cases the critical attitude towards industrialization can be traced to half-nationalist and half-marxist images of what a 'true,' 'complete,' or 'integrated' industrialization should look like". The aim of the analysis is to demonstrate that these ways of thinking are devoid of meaning, through a comparison (both surprising and topical) with the ex-socialist countries and with the past of some developed countries. This implies, probably, that such dissatisfactions are the offspring of industrialization, in as much as they accompany it in time until society finds a new social-economic adjustment.

17. This reality moved out of phase with the doctrinairialism of conservative North American thought in the 1980s. At the end of "Ideologies of Economic Development in Latin America" Hirschman contrasted the ideological attitude of Latin Americans with the pragmatic attitude of their cousins from the north. He later resumed his argument in an article appropriately entitled "Out of Phase" (1965) where he criticized the orgy of misinterpretations and misunderstandings brought about by this being out of phase. Moreover, in 1986, he published in the *New York Times Review of Books* "Out of Phase Again," (abbreviated version of "The Political Economy of Latin American Development: Seven Exercises in Retrospect") where, referring in particular to the problem of Latin America's foreign debt, he notes once again such a *desencuentro* (failure to meet), but in reversed roles between the two hemispheres. "I almost wonder," the author asked himself ironically, "whether I might have stumbled on some law."

18. Two years later, King observed in his review in the *Economic Journal* (1964, p. 436), it was clear that Hirschman's optimism was premature. "The rate of inflation in Chile in 1963 and 1964 had been circa 40 percent per year, progress in land reform in Colombia has

been by all accounts but very slow and, while it is perhaps too early to judge the success of regional development efforts in north-east Brazil 'master reformmonger' Celso Furtado was deprived both of his position as head of SUDENE and of his political rights after the April 1964 revolution." In fact, it was this coup d'état that inaugurated the turn to authoritarianism in Latin America.

19. In order to get an idea we can refer to the table presented in "The Semantics of Problem-Solving" (1963a, pp. 247–49). "The literature attacking past and advocating new policies," Hirschman maintained, "is extraordinarily rich in laudatory and denigrating epithets." Their choice can be quite revealing for the style used in handling a given policy problem. By distinguishing between those who presume that a definitive solution exists (ideological approach) and those who do not (remedial approach), and between laudatory epithets and derogatory ones, one obtains the four-fold arrangement of the table. And it is possible to identify a cycle that begins, in effect, with destructive criticism of policies (branded as stop gap, haphazard, makeshift, etc.), and goes on to propose an integrated, fundamental, revolutionary, coherent, balanced policy. If the new policy represents progress (however limited), it will then be adapted to the circumstances through realistic, flexible, or pragmatic change. If, on the other hand, it is considered unsatisfactory, it will be unmasked as being dogmatic, doctrinaire, cure-all, utopian. If in the end, it turns out to be only a disappointment, it will be attacked as a palliative, patchwork, or bungling in order to propose once again a systematic, comprehensive, coordinated, planned policy.

20. To them, the author connected "the routine of present-day international experts in blandly proposing year in, year out essentially antagonistic measures of every description regardless of political realities. . . . After having absorbed a critical amount of frustration, frequently become converts to the view that, in this or that country, 'everything' has to change before any improvement at all can be introduced" (1963a, p. 254).

21. "All we are asked to imagine," Hirschman added ironically (1963a, p. 255), "by the revolutionary is the tumbling down of the old regime in a total upheaval which will give birth to the new order. Revolution thus conceived is essentially a quite brief, though cataclysmic interlude between two static societies: one, unjust and rotten, which is incapable of being improved, and the other, rational and harmonious, which has no further need to be improved upon."

22. "The kind of wily and complex tactics the pro-reform forces will have to engage in to be successful," he clarified in "How Policy is Made" (1963b, p. 40), "I call reformmongering to contrast it with the

idea that reforms can be introduced in a perfectly smooth and orderly fashion, as a result of our experts' recommendation backed up by some offers of financial aid." This was, as we shall see further on, the point of view of the administration of the United States.

23. "When the state," Hirschman explained (1963a, p. 258), "believes it important that uncertainty be removed, but does not wish to use force to evict the peasants, it may buy the property from the owner and then attempt to sell it back to the peasant who already holds it, but still is ready to pay something for the much-coveted title which, among other advantages, makes it possible to obtain credit." This is—in my experience—a valid sequence for house squatting as well (see Comitato di Quartiere della Magliana, 1976).

24. Such key observations are later developed in "The Social and Political Matrix of Inflation: Elaboration on the Latin American Experience" (1981).

25. The injection of pressure and tension generated by crisis contributes to speeding up routine tasks, but could also be an impediment to the actual problem-probing because it narrows the ability to reflect and identify alternatives. On the other hand, the crisis summons new forces, which before had been indifferent or hostile. Besides, aggravation of the problem might make wide collective understanding of the problem possible; when (for example) increased inflation discredits the procrastinators' proposals, or when the reappearance of drought conditions shows the inadequacy of past efforts. Hence motivation, forces, and knowledge often move together in favor of change, one influencing the other.

26. At this point, I would like to add two observations (for the future manual). In the first place: the myth probably arises from the individual awakening and projecting onto others (they should all wake up). It is reinforced through the awakening of others and by personal investment in the enterprise (that would hopefully be extremely useful and productive). Moreover, precisely because it seems to materialize, this myth turns out to be initially compatible with a flexible tactic, which shrewdly exploits existing opportunities.

27. This is the reason why the concluding parts of the stories have such breadth and prominence. These episodes of *Journeys,* treating the history of economic policy, have influenced the political historiography of Gabriel Almond and the working party that he organized at the Institute of Political Studies at Stanford in 1968. *Crisis, Choice, and Change,* born from that experience, referred to the work of Hirschman (who read the manuscript critically: cf. G. Almond, S. C. Flanagan, and R. J. Mundt, editors, 1973, pp. 22 and vi). Among other things, the book contained an essay by Wayne Cornelius on the policy of social

reform in Mexico in 1935–40 that referred to the reformmongering of *Journeys* and to the development of this thesis proposed by Anderson in 1965 (see p. 394).

28. Among the other reformmongers that fill other pages of *Journeys*—such as the Brazilian José Américo de Almeida (Minister of Public Works of the Vargas administration during the thirties) or the Chileans Felipe Herrera, Jorge Prat, and Oscar Herrera (Ministers of Finance during the fifties)—attention may be focused on Alfonso Lopéz, the Colombian president of the Land Law of 1936 (and of many other important measures). He belonged to a group of highly intelligent members of the traditional ruling families who intended to modernize the country's economic and social structure. "Lopéz," Hirschman wrote (1963a, p. 108), "was immensely enjoying his own radicalism and the way in which he shocked Bogotá society . . . by siding with striking workers and squatting peasants. Left-wing writers later accused him of 'revolutionary exhibitionism' and deceitful demagoguery, but he seems rather to have had a realistic understanding of the combination of pressures and promises needed to push through measures that went against the class or immediate pecuniary interests of those who were called upon to vote for them."

29. This is one of the political processes studied in "Models of Reformmongering," a digression that concludes the volume (see chapter 8).

30. The reader may ask if candor (or rather that which initially appears to be a naive behavior) is a necessary part of the possibilist mental inclination. Possibilism presents its own recipes in a concrete and reasonable fashion in order to create the illusion that they can be used without delay, without considering the intentions (interests) of the ruling political forces. The same deliberately naive attitude presents itself again in the possibilist search for a way out, an exit that can be found only by looking for it (learning by doing). It seems to me that this naivety is part of the inclination to speculate and to inquire in a particular direction (instead of applying an infallible technique) that Hirschman points out as being characteristic of his own research.

31. It must be kept in mind that Law 200 of 1936, adopted during the progressive administration of Alfonso Lopéz, was later unjustly criticized (see the recent reinterpretation of these vicissitudes in terms of rhetoric of perversity: 1991, p. 33; and note 15 above). The law attempted to dispel uncertainty about land ownership through realistic systems of presumption, documentary evidence, and legal procedures. It also tried to confer legal force to the notion that ownership brings with it the obligation of economic use of the land, with the forfeiture of

land that had not been cultivated for over ten years. But the changes in political and social climate that followed did not favor its application. During the postwar period, renewed violence in rural areas did not interfere with industrial growth; if anything it facilitated it by supplying the labor force of refugees in the city and the investments that would have otherwise traditionally been made in the haciendas. Later on, however, the need for higher agricultural productivity began to be felt. A second phase of the problem was characterized by the use of the fiscal weapon and inaugurated by a World Bank Mission in 1949. The profuse efforts, the difficulties encountered, and the relative disappointments opened the way to land reform.

32. *Come far passare le riforme (How to Pass Reforms)* (1990) is the title of the Italian edition of a group of political texts by Hirschman (above all from *Journeys* and about *Journeys*). I make use of it here to point out a line of research which plays an important role in Hirschman's work.

33. To overthrow the military dictatorship of Rojas Pinilla, Colombia's two main political parties—the Liberal Party and the Conservative Party—signed a pact, known as the National Front, that made the presidency alternate between representatives of each party for four terms and demanded bipartisan governments (with an equal division of seats). The first president to be elected under this system was the liberal, Alberto Lleras Camargo, while Carlos Lleras Restrepo was vice president.

34. The order was as follows: accessible, uncultivated land publicly managed, then privately managed, still poorly-cultivated land, and finally cultivated land. The aim was to extend the *minifundio,* to allow tenants and sharecroppers to take over the land from absentee owners, and to hand over land in the plains to the farmers from the eroding slopes. From a legal point of view, the progressive coalition referred to the 1936 legislation. Since Law 200 ordered the confiscation of land that had been left uncultivated for over ten years (see note 31), it was claimed that it was reasonable to apply milder penalties, such as expropriation paid in bonds, to those who were responsible for less serious forms of neglect. Finally, the Constitution of 1936 permitted expropriation without any compensation for reasons of equity through a majority vote of the House and Senate. Lleras maintained that a law for confiscation of land with a fixed compensation could be approved.

35. This point of view clearly goes against those who, like Lauchlin Currie, considered reform to be a nonexistent problem. After having led the World Bank Mission in 1949 (and having maintained that Colombian agriculture was managed in an absurd and unjust way), he changed his view to the point of asserting that the agrarian revolution

had already silently taken hold in the countryside and the only solution for the peasants of the mountainous areas was urbanization. "While the extravagant notion," Hirschman commented (1963a, pp. 154–55), "that the problem of the idle or underutilized *latifundio* had suddenly gone up in smoke was of course avidly espoused by the still powerful *latifundistas,* its intellectual origin is elsewhere: in our opinion, it stems from the inclination to consider a problem as solved, hence as uninteresting and no longer worthy of official attention and action, once spontaneous and decentralized forces making for a solution are perceived to be at work. Perhaps the basis of this strange misunderstanding of the role of centralized state action is . . . that the state is typically expected to majestically reorder reality, unaided and unassisted, by the sole virtue of its power and sovereignty." The issue regards two concepts of the state: opposing traditional étatism, Hirschman accentuated the need for the institutional structures to deal with the problems as they crop up and, hence, the possibility for the state to play an active role supporting the progressive forces within society.

36. All this seems to suggest a broadening of Hirschman's point of view. As we have seen in chapter 2, he recently maintained that at the origin of many of his works there was an observation provoked by a surprise and to this end it is necessary to be ready to receive the impulses of surprising facts. "I still maintain," he wrote (1975, now in 1981a, p. 159), "that the 'capacity to be surprised' considered by Raymond Poincaré to be the essence of scientific genius, needs to be cultivated by the policy analysts as well." This ability may be held back by the desire not to upset one's own comfortable intellectual schemes: surprising facts can activate research only if we develop the ability to learn from them. Besides which, we can casually run across them or we can go out and search for them where they manifest themselves. This is not as easy as it might appear because when they are observed in retrospect, those events usually appear obvious, hardly questionable, and therefore lacking in interest. The mere fact that a reform has been approved (and therefore not opposed sufficiently enough by those forces that theoretically should have blocked it) makes it appear to have been an easy choice, while in fact it required an entire constellation of favorable circumstances.

5. POSSIBILISM AND SOCIAL CHANGE

1. See the third part of *The Passions and Interests* (1977), and the last chapters of *Shifting Involvements* (1982) and of *The Rhetoric of Reaction* (1991).

2. The existence of another (less known) interlocutor to add to those openly declared, might contribute to the explanation of this conclusion. (Hirschman often claims he had in mind a "battle on two fronts"; the revolutionary one and the reformist one [see chapter 4] or the Latin American one and that of the United States.) I refer in particular to his sister Ursula and his brother-in-law Altiero Spinelli who were involved at the time in European agitation. Between 1954 and the end of 1960, Spinelli wrote (1987, p. 18), "I have worked on the hypothesis that it would be possible to mobilize Europeanism, now diffused, in a widespread growing protest—The European People's Congress—aimed against the very legitimacy of the national states." It should not, therefore, be ruled out that Hirschman may have wished to influence the activities of his Roman relatives in the direction of reformmongering. "Later on," he told me in a conversation in 1986, "even Altiero became possibilist."

3. "In the first place," Hirschman argued (1971a, p. 338), "leadership may be achieved by those who hold to the average perceptions with an uncommon degree of 'passionate intensity,' who articulate them most forcefully, and who best reflect and express what is in everybody's heart and mind." Hirschman's emphasis is on correct perceptions as well as on misperceptions. But charisma is often accompanied by the ability to perceive change before others, so that a leader often appears to create opportunities (rather than bluntly exploiting them).

4. "That leadership," Hirschman wrote (1971a, p. 340 and note 15), "often requires this successive display of contrasting characteristics by the same person has been noted by several authors. . . . I would add that, in many cases, the required switch from one set of qualities to another must take place not after the conquest of power, but at some point prior to it, when agitation and mobilization give place to negotiation and partial winning over of the existing powerholders." (In my turn, I feel it necessary to point out that it is only the prevalence of one kind of quality over another that is at stake; and that, for example, a remarkable degree of skill was required to manage the "red bases" or to develop the political and military tactic of the Chinese Revolution.)

5. In two passages, Hirschman pointed out, Womack implies that the outcome of the revolution was not only attributable to the presence of Magaña, but might also have been due to the absence of Zapata. It is easy to surmise that the theses of alternate leadership, as a significant element of the success of the Morelos insurrection, must have come to his mind.

6. One may note at this point that our original discussion of Hirschman's "passion for the possible" was linked to his work in the

early postwar period (see chapter 1) as a consequence of his manner of proceeding, that begins with specific observations and then goes on to "forge continuously ahead," dealing with different research projects and creating logical devices that correspond to them. The links (conscious and unconscious) that are thus formed among the subsequent contributions allow one to move back in time to trace the origins of his ideas.

7. As I have already mentioned (chapter 1), Hirschman does not share the traditional view, according to which analyses must be conducted on rigorously objective (and therefore "scientific") grounds so that their results become a solid basis for politics. The two parts of the introduction, in fact, do not refer to this view; they respond to the idea, typical of the author, of studying different aspects of reality—in the present case political economics and possibilism—held together by two-way relationships, and therefore by interactions. ("The Count of Saint-Simon's meditation," . . . Fernand Braudel wrote [1969, p. 16], "originates from the torment of the French Revolution, then followed by that of his adversary disciples, Auguste Comte, Proudhon, and Karl Marx, who since then have never ceased to torment the souls and reflections of men." Note that the opposition between Saint-Simon and Comte—to which a good part of the French economic-political and sociological traditions refer—regarded whether economics or social physiology was to become the foundation of politics, but *not* the idea that politics should be founded—by one or by the other science. "Will our social scientists—may I ask—eventually be able to hoist these time-honored anchors to larboard?")

8. While unexplained phenomena in natural sciences are important as a starting point for the search for new theory able to explain them, in the social sciences it is not at all clear which is the means and which the end. "True," Hirschman went on to say in an ironic tone (1971a, p. 27), "most social scientists behave in this respect as if they were natural scientists; but they would be more surprised than the latter and, above all, considerably distraught if their search for general laws were crowned with total success. Quite possibly, then, all the successive theories and models in the social sciences, and the immense efforts that go into them, are motivated by the noble, if unconscious, desire to demonstrate the irreducibility of the social world to general laws!"

9. "The seven essays published since 1965," Hirschman wrote in the preface to *A Bias for Hope*—which make up "over one-half of the book—were written so closely together in time that one often starts where the other leaves off; increasingly they became chapters of a book in formation."

10. As we have seen, the notion of a "blessing in disguise" is initially connected to that of "hidden rationality" which occupied a central role in *The Strategy*. A part of this rationality leads to the blessing (as, for example, in "Obstacles to Development" when the obstacles turn into advantages). It is simply a label for a certain class of data. Thus, the search for a more satisfying methodological foundation of possibilism continued in Hirschman's use of the theory of cognitive dissonance. Hirschman broadens his argument with the intention of widening the number of known sequences but not—he stressed—of claiming primacy for inverted sequences over orderly ones. The importance of redressing the balance between indirect and direct relations, as I observed in chapter 4 when I dealt with fracasomania, thus emerged.

11. Hirschman appraised his text thus: "an attempt to delineate common themes and to discover an underlying methodology and perhaps philosophy" in the essays contained in *A Bias for Hope* (1971a, p. ix).

12. The officers, to whom it had been taught that "it was their mission to forge a united Peru which could be a true fatherland for all of its sons including the most miserable Indian, were suddenly placed in the position of napalming the villages of those very Indians and of killing them, as well as young poets and intellectuals from the cities who had taken seriously those very teachings. As a result, the tension between ideology and actual behavior as imposed by the environment was exceptionally wide and painful. On the other hand, the military had bred into them a high degree of confidence that the environment is subject to change at their hands. Jointly, then, that painful tension and that confidence may account for their reforming zeal" (1971a, p. 33).

13. It is not a matter of maintaining that this point of view has to replace that of desired consequences but rather to document its importance in order to increase our ability to visualize social change. This is made clear by the example of the lungfish which, while trying to get back into the water and remain amphibians, strengthened their fins (transformed in time into legs that eventually allowed them to invade land). Hirschman further clarified his point with the example of population growth in rural areas which, under certain conditions, gives way to development; of the attempt to restore maritime contact with India that led to the discovery of America; and of the interruption of normal trade flows which can lead to important inventions (and innovations) and even to industrialization.

14. "Womack," Hirschman later added (1971a, p. 349), "draws conclusions with the utmost diffidence and circumspection. His respect

for the autonomy of the actors . . . is what gives the book its special appeal. . . . For it is today a most unusual restraint." Carlos Fuentes also commented (1963):

> Womack marshals the military, economic, political and psychological evidence of the significance of Zapata and his movement. Let me pay passing homage to the author's extraordinary sensibility regarding things Mexican. We are exceptionally and refreshingly far from the exotic point of view that makes so much of North American writings on Mexico so remote from its subject or, worse still, tinges it with a mawkishness, ignorance, or condescension masquerading as sympathy. Womack has an uncanny feeling for the infinitely complex strains of Mexico as a *civilization.* . . . He understands *Zapatismo* as the history . . . of *campesinos,* people from the fields who did not, in the larger sense of the term, feel *culturally* deprived but, rather were conscious that a social and political opportunity was given them to realize, in actuality, the latent promises of their local culture.

15. We have already seen this view of the inventiveness of history and possibilism at the end of his 1971 introduction to *A Bias for Hope.*

16. This is the third illustration that follows the one on why a gloomy vision (fortunately transitory) constitutes the first stage of any reflection about a backward reality and the one about why, in evaluating the broadest consequences of an outgoing event, we must be suspicious of paradigms that give a clear-cut and definite answer.

17. Obviously, it is not a question, to echo Gino Luzzatto (1901, now in 1967, p. 59), of reevaluating the traditional historian of kings and of battles who, had he been asked "to write the history of a peaceful Kingdom, . . . would have felt miserable just like Caligula who complained that during his empire no major calamity had occurred" (see also Braudel, 1969, part 1).

18. This occurs in the works just quoted where passages and chapters of long term history alternate with detailed analyses on certain periods and concepts. The same can be said, perhaps, even for *La Mediterranée* by Fernand Braudel (1949)—the *livre de chevet* of long-term historians—which also reconstructs the history of the period of Philippe II (see Paule Braudel, 1992, p. 243).

19. Whether it is a matter of United States' railroads (Fishlaw, 1965) or electric energy production in Brazil (Tendler, 1968), of the fishing industry in Peru (Roemer, 1970) or petroleum in Nigeria (Pearson, 1970), the importance of this kind of work lies in the ability

of the concept of linkages to clarify the variety of solutions that exist "in nature" and the choices of economic policy connected to them.

20. Here, as elsewhere in Hirschman's work, Lenin's writings are recalled in an antidoctrinarian vein (1971a, pp. 340 and 358–59; 1981a, pp. 175–76; and note 26 of chapter 1). For another side of the Lenin question, see Meldolesi, 1989, part 2. Hirschman has recently suggested the idea that Lenin was influenced by reactionary theses on the futility of democracy (1991, pp. 147–48).

21. See Schlesinger, Jr. (1965), and Packenham (1973, chapter 2). "Castro's rise to power," Hirschman explained (1971a, p. 177),

> made the United States favor a more intensive use of public funds as a principal instrument of foreign policy. At the same time, it compelled a reexamination of what we wanted to achieve through an increase in U.S. aid. The Cuban revolution could not have occurred had there not been basic faults in the organization of Cuban society and legitimate, highly exploitable popular grievances. Thus, it was argued, if a new Cuba was to be prevented in Latin America, every effort should be made to correct similar faults and prevent similar grievances. Put your house in order suddenly acquired a different content. Even in the last months of the Eisenhower administration, it came more and more to mean, "Improve your land tenure system, distribute your tax burden more equitably, erase slums and illiteracy."

22. In the book, this comment follows a note signed "Ypsilon," because of Hirschman's official role. "Perhaps the most controversial idea in any of the essays [on *Latin American Issues*]," William Carr wrote in *World Affairs* (1963, p. 222),

> occurs in a short statement modestly entitled "A Note on Inter-American Relations," signed by an unidentified member of the study group [i.e., "Ypsilon"]. He believes that inter-American relations may be improved by deemphasizing the special nature of the inter-American relationship and by placing United States dealings with Latin America in a broader context. To play down "hemisphere solidarity" is, as the author recognizes, counter to deep-rooted traditions, assumptions, and vested interests in both Americas. Nevertheless, the author insists that the existing intercontinental relationship is ambiguous and frustrating. He makes a persuasive case for bringing international investment, technical

and financial aid, and many other matters into a more widely representative forum in which not only North and South Americans, but also Europeans, Asians and Africans would be represented. Anyone who has had to deal with the intense and sometimes irrational regionalism of Latin Americans is likely to find himself hoping that this analysis may prove to be workable.

23. "Frequently," wrote Hirschman in "Second Thoughts" (1971a, p. 180),

> we "discover" problems that have a long history. . . . Recently, for example, we have "discovered" the urgency of doing something about Brazil's northeast, largely because the peasant leagues that have sprung up in that area and have taken over a few half-abandoned sugar estates are obvious points of penetration for "Fidelismo." But the northeast, with its periodical droughts and its failure to participate in the general progress of the country, has been troubling Brazil for almost a century. . . . Similarly in Colombia, land reform has been "around" as an issue and object of policy making for decades. Advances in some directions have been achieved, and delicately balanced alliances are constantly forming and breaking up. In this kind of situation, uninformed pressure from us to "get going," far from playing a decisive part, may well cast us in the role of bull in the china shop.

24. This is a recurring idea in Hirschman's work (chapter 1, note 31; chapter 3, note 31). Even *Development Projects* may have been conceived as a battle on two fronts; the 1963 decision to focus on a group of development projects perhaps incorporated the desire to give authority to alternatives to the program approach suggested by North American scholars at the time. (If nothing else, from the viewpoint of development aid, the closer evaluation of projects that this work demands would not only be in the interest of the recipient country, but would also increase the guarantees offered to the donor country.)

25. This criticism finally becomes a real indictment. "To recapitulate," Hirschman concluded (1971a, p. 210),

> the program approach will accentuate old and create new discord within the recipient country and it will erode the government's support; it will lead to attempts of backsliding and reneging on the commitments that have been entered into; it will have a hidden cost for the donor and will diminish public support for aid programs

in the donor countries as it impels the recipient to assert his independence by moving away from the donor in areas not covered by the aid agreement; and the negotiations leading to program aid will prove highly irritating to the recipient, both because he will not recognize the claim of the donor to superior knowledge of the questions that are typically the subject of program aid negotiations and because the gap in the respective levels or ranks of those who do the actual negotiating between donor and recipient is painfully wide.

26. "The explicit or implicit conditioning of aid on changes in policies of the recipient countries," Hirschman added (1971a, p. 211), "should be avoided." This thesis, which has recently been reproposed (1989f, p. 11), is very much in tune with the spirit of the brief articles of 1961–62. It implies taking every precaution to separate discussions between partners from aid: this will increase "the educational virtues" of such discussions.

27. Regarding the first point, Hirschman was thinking about foreign investment that is keener than national investors to innovate and to take the first unsettling steps in growth sequences, i.e., about a kind of capital that can overcome indecision and reluctance, and induce further investments (Malan, 1989, p. 4). Regarding the second, he recalled later (1986b, p. 24) that "at some stage the need of the expanding economy for imported inputs outpaces its ability to increase exports, unless the country is lucky enough to produce some items that are in rapidly expanding demand on the world market." Finally, regarding the third, the role of foreign capital is to permit more rapidly growing sectors to overcome certain difficulties and pressures that would be imposed upon them by the development of slower growing sectors. This is particularly significant in the case of exportable goods, since their production will relax constraints on the balance of payments.

28. A first group of proposals concerned the creation of an inter-American divestment corporation, an agency that acquires at fair prices foreign owned assets of corporations indicated by the government of the host country. It could be financed by various sources (including the government and foreign corporations that have an interest in dissolving existing conflicts and trouble spots) and could even pursue other ends such as employees' ownership or the "Latinamericanization" of corporations. A second group dealt with schemes on programmed divestment of new investments, such as the transfer of firms to local entrepreneurs who participate in the initiative according to a fixed schedule, the extinction of property rights at the end of a preestablished period, the setting of a

mandatory limit to profit remittances that creates incentives to reinvest in loco. Finally, a third group combines divestment with other objectives such as exports, regional integration, etc.

29. See Packenham (1973), Devine (1972), and Huntington (1968a).

30. "The Charles River economists," Schlesinger wrote (1965, p. 590), "had their more direct influence on Kennedy who was, after all, their Senator and accustomed to consulting them on other matters. As the decade progressed, Kennedy's interest in aid problems had repeatedly increased. His concern with India soon led him to larger reflections about the challenge of modernization. He readily accepted the Cambridge thesis that the American interest would be best served by the development of strong and independent states." (On the other hand, this raises the question of the relationship between the mental attitudes prompted respectively by economics and by liberal absolutism and, therefore, between democratization of the discipline and overcoming that absolutism.)

31. In Argentina and Peru in 1962; in Guatemala, Ecuador, the Dominican Republic, and Honduras in 1963; and in Brazil in 1964.

6. VOICE AND LATITUDES

1. The wide circulation of Hirschman's most recent work means that our discussion can be more concise.

2. Enrique Gil Calvo (1992, p. 56) recently spoke of Hirschman's second career: "initially an economist, expert of international trade and economic development and later a well-known essayist and expert in history of ideas and social analysis." It is a career that "does not presuppose a break off from the previous one; actually, on the contrary, it [requires] a second reading, more screened and essential, but at the same time more penetrating, ambivalent and suggestive." This observation proposes a two-way reading of Hirschman's texts: from past to present, and vice versa.

3. And there was also discontent as to how the ongoing discussion was proceeding (see Hirschman, 1981a, pp. 14–24). The decline of development economics, as Hirschman recently reiterated in a letter to Lal Jayawardena, April 22, 1992, is not only due to the failures of its proponents, as claimed by Krugman (1992) in his rehabilitation of these ideas. Development economics and Latin American *desarrollismo*

were attacked not only from the Right, by Brazilian and Argentine generals and the neoclassicals, but also from the Left, the dependencia theorists and other "impatient" critics . . . , even from within the World Bank—see Mahbub ul Haq's well-known paper "Employment and Income Distribution in the 1970s" which played an important role in the new emphasis the World Bank tried to give to redistribution, under McNamara and Chenery, quite some time before it turned zealously neoclassical.

See the well-known texts by Johnson (1967); Little, Scitovski, and Scott (1970); Balassa et al. (1971), etc.

4. This is exactly why it has been able to suggest relevant guidelines on how to complicate economics. Conversely, in chapter 2, this allowed us to introduce the period of development economics.

5. Thanks to the initiative of Gabriel Almond, who was at the time involved in a political and historical research project related to *Journeys* (see chapter 4, note 27), Hirschman was invited to spend a sabbatical year at the Center for Advanced Study in the Behavioral Sciences of Stanford University. He used most of his time there to compose *Exit:* the analytical and technical structure of the text undoubtedly reflects the favorable environmental conditions (see the preface).

6. "I rather became concerned," Hirschman recalled in his preface (1970a, p. vii), "that the concepts of 'exit' and 'voice' might be too broad as my writing expanded with surprising ease into ever new territories. The principal concession I made to these worries was to keep this book short." This is probably what astonished readers. "Drawing on an extremely broad range of empirical knowledge," Jon Elster wrote, for example (1982, p. 8) "sifted, purified and rearranged by an acute and imaginative analytical mind, it generated a state of almost intolerable intellectual excitement in the reader. For many of us it provided a durable model of what a work in the social sciences should be like."

7. "It is perhaps because," he explained (1970a, p. 4, note 1), "the whole range of phenomena here described has no place in the perfectly competitive model that it has not been paid attention to by economists."

8. As I said in chapter 3, note 9, this presentation draws already on the work of Simon, Cyert, March, and Leibenstein, who will be mentioned later to support the "slack paradigm" (1986b, pp. 12–14). It also contains two quotations from Steuart and Nieto Arteta according to whom economic progress is thought to restrict the discretionary powers of policymakers; quotations which play an eminent role in respectively *The Passions and the Interests* and "The Turn to Authoritarianism in Latin America" (1977b, pp. 84–85; 1981a, p. 101). Together with the model of perfect competition, they ironically illustrate in *Exit* the presence of man's ambivalent attitude towards surplus—a wish combined with the

fear that he will have to bear the cost of it—which might be the root of the myth of perfect competition and of paradise as well.

9. However, if the firm acquires new customers while losing its old ones, the mechanism jams. This happens in those cases in which competition produces collusive behavior: in the simultaneous deterioration of product quality, in products found to be faulty during use, in customers falling prey to the illusion that they are avoiding deterioration by turning to another manufacturer in the same conditions, in political or labor organizations that get involved in rebate-oriented competition, etc. In arguing against these aspects of competition, *Exit* immediately challenges some of the key verdicts of American social life. "The ideology of exit," Hirschman explained (1970a, p. 112), "has been powerful in America. With the country having been founded on exit and having thrived on it, the belief in exit as a fundamental and beneficial social mechanism has been unquestioning. . . . As long as one can transfer his allegiance from the product of firm A to the competing product of firm B, the basic symbolism of the national love affair with exit is satisfied."

10. Note how in *Exit* complementarity plays a secondary or ancillary role. Only later on—as we shall see repeatedly—will it undergo a gradual rehabilitation process.

11. "The two [voice and exit] were not viewed as mutually exclusive; while they were alternatives, they could in some situations be combined for best results; moreover, the exit-voice polarity did not yield a systematic, instinctive preference for one mechanism over the other, in contrast to more traditional, not unrelated dichotomies . . . such as Gesellschaft vs. Gemeinschaft, or universalism vs. particularism" (Hirschman, 1981a, p. 212; see also 1981a, pp. 236–37).

12. For example: in his introduction to the conference on "Economics and Cultural Models in Comparative Policy-Making" organized by the International Social Science Council in 1973, Stein Rokkan, then president of the International Political Science Association, stated that "the exit-voice polarity found echoes across the entire range of the social sciences, from psychology across anthropology and sociology to linguistics and the study of religion, from the analysis of personality across the study of marriage, family and kinship towards the investigation of complex organizations and systems of communication and belief" (1974, p. 28).

13. Despite this, there was some expectation at the time as to how Hirschman would pursue his path. When he published "The Changing Tolerance for Income Inequality in the Course of Economic Development" (1973, see chapter 7), some wondered what connection this

had with *Exit.* "They are two different things," he answered (private conversation, September 1988).

14. See chapter 2. This solution was obviously made possible by Hirschman's familiarity with economist circles but also by his critical— ironic and (perhaps) half-conscious—detachment from this milieu, which he was cultivating at the time. In fact, after "the exit effect" opened the doors to his new career, Hirschman only occasionally found the desire and patience to recreate a close dialogue with some aspects of economic theory.

15. While multi-party systems can be affected by collusive competition (see note 9 above), "the best possible arrangement for the development of party responsiveness to the feelings of members may then be a system of just a very few parties, whose distance from each other is wide, but not unbridgeable" (1970a, p. 84). The theme was further developed by Hirschman in 1974 (now in 1981a, pp. 228–31).

16. "The critique of the optimal mix concept thus leads to a triple suggestion," he wrote in conclusion to his book (1970a, p. 126). "In order to retain their ability to fight deterioration those organizations that rely primarily on one of the two reaction mechanisms need an occasional injection of the other. Other organizations may have to go through regular cycles in which exit and voice alternate as principal actors. Finally, an awareness of the inborn tendencies toward instability of any optimal mix may be helpful in improving the design of institutions that need both exit and voice to be maintained in good health."

17. He explained to me (September 1989) that for quite some time he almost felt spurred forward by this work: the exit-voice duality continued to move ahead under its own impetus. Undoubtedly, it is also thanks to this complex internal dialogue that Hirschman's work is so unpredictable and original (also in relation to the general evolution of social thought—as pointed out to me by Barros de Castro).

18. "It took the explosion of protest activities after the invasion of Cambodia and the Kent State shootings," Hirschman wrote for the meetings with political scientists recalled in note 12 (now in 1981a, p. 212), "to remind me that, in certain situations, the use of voice can suddenly become one most sought after, fulfilling activity, in fact, the ultimate justification of human existence."

19. The thesis was further elaborated in his following work: see chapters 2 and 7.

20. This theme was recently picked up by Louis Lowenstein (1988), who has repeatedly argued in favor of institutional proposals and inventions aimed at activating the voice mechanism in financial markets.

21. In this context, he refers to the work of Richard Nelson and Michael Krashinsky (1974), Kenneth Arrow (1973), and the three contributions made by Richard Freeman, Oliver Williamson, and Dennis Young at the session "Political Economy: Some Uses of the Exit-Voice Approach" of the 1975 annual meeting of the American Economic Association.

22. The exit-voice polarity develops as a result. Whereas in *Exit* (1970a, p. 40) he stated that "in comparison to the exit option, voice is costly and conditioned on the influence and bargaining power" that customers and members can respectively exercise on the firm or on the organization, in the paper prepared for the meeting with a group of economists (see the previous note), Hirschman underscored four characteristics of voice that distinguish it from exit: "voice is rich and modulated" because "it conveys more information than exit"; voice is "exuberant" because "it is more apt than exit to become an end in itself," which goes unrewarded, especially when it is perceived as an action in the public interest; voice is "hazardous" because it can be fought with a carrot and a stick; voice is "treacherous" because the changes achieved can prove to be in the principal interest of the people representing the members (1981a, pp. 236–45).

23. Of course, it also has a great objective influence: by representing what people think, it is a point of reference in the management of numerous economic and political activities.

24. The other two are "The Concept of Interest: From Euphemism to Tautology" and "Linkages in Economic Development" (see chapters 2 and 3). Hirschman also wrote for the dictionary "A Prototypical Economic Advisor: Jean Gustave Courcelle-Seneuil." (All these entries are now in 1986b.)

5. See the preface to the paperback edition of *Rival Views* (1992e). In addition to these, Hirschman also referred to the stock market (see note 20) and to employee responses to dissatisfaction. Discussion on this last topic (developed at a meeting edited by David Saunders in 1992) continues the preexisting debate on trade unions and industrial relations (Freeman, 1976; Freeman and Medoff, 1984).

26. But of course it might: in the face of high exit (or transaction) costs, vertical integration might become convenient. Hirschman himself, who had not discussed exit costs in *Exit*, recalled Williamson's work on this point (1974, now in 1981a, pp. 222–23).

27. "The argument for hierarchy in cases where resort to voice must be frequent," Hirschman continued (1986b, pp. 86–87), "probably arises from thinking of market relationships only in terms of an ideal, highly competitive, anonymous market where exit is all-powerful

and voice wholly absent." Once again, we see Williamson's inability to grasp the perspective underlying *Exit*.

28. This implies different degrees of empathy among the people involved: from aspiration, to understanding, to interest in results, to active participation in the debate. The extraordinary character of the achievement thus obtained (no matter how small it may be), compared to the normal development of things, a priori appears to be outside one's scope of action, and therefore creates a pleasant surprise in the participant. But once the most intense phase of the discussion is over, it also gives the whole business a vaguely enigmatic taste which may be mitigated over time through the repetition of the cultural miracle of the new construction.

29. "For many economists," Hirschman explained (1986b, p. 20),

competition is the all-powerful social institution bringing pressures for efficiency. Strangely and somewhat inconsistently, some of these economists seem intent on granting competition a monopoly in this endeavor. But, with competition being so often quite feeble and with the battle against inefficiency and decay being so generally uphill, why not search and be grateful for additional mechanisms that, to paraphrase Rousseau, force man to be efficient? [In *The Strategy*] lack of latitude seemed to me to hold considerable promise in this regard. Twelve years later I stressed another such mechanism: voice. It so happened that both consciously and unconsciously, an elementary observation on the Colombian reality gradually turned into a specific category and subsequently into a more general theory.

30. This confirms the function of "analytical overture" performed by this essay (see chapter 2). Thomas Schelling, who was among the first to realize the importance of the ideas it contained, encouraged Hirschman to continue his work and supported his candidacy as visiting research professor at the University of Yale (see chapter 3, note 4). A long-lasting friendship thus arose between the two authors, both of whom are endowed with a particular talent for originality.

31. In connection with this, the 1954 article already compares Colombian airways and roads: in the former, the lack of maintenance leads to disaster; in the latter, it produces a long deterioration that comes to an end only with the disappearance of the road. Consequently, Hirschman stated, underdeveloped countries can actually be more successful with complicated technology industries that require high levels of maintenance than with industries based on simple operation and

machinery. This criterion can also be useful in selecting the technical processes for a given industry. This is followed by an example (taken from a letter by Forrest Green) of roads built with a bitumen surface rather than stone or gravel, as the former are characterized by a narrower latitude. This letter is picked up again in *The Strategy* and in "A Dissenter's Confession" with growing consideration; in the first case, as "a striking example of reliance on nonmarket forces . . . for corrective action in a disequilibrium situation" and in the second case to link latitude to voice (see 1958a, p. 143 and 1986b, pp. 20–21). Hirschman's repeated reference to this example in his texts, suggests that it may have played a role in the identification of the initial surprising observation on the "defective maintenance" issue.

32. In other words, Hirschman concluded, maintenance is essentially an administrative process. Already in his article of 1954 he had observed that the absence of adequate maintenance can be a particularly important aspect of a more general difficulty. "I believe," he observed (1971a, p. 59), "that quite frequently the technical operation of industry is fairly competent but that much is left to be desired in accounting, full use of cost—and quality—control methods, training and organization of the labor force, and utilization of raw materials and by-products."

33. Lastly, the latitude thesis probably has a remote (inverted) connection with book 1 of Marx's *Capital*. It also has a partial but significant correspondence with some of Gerschenkron's propositions. The latter had in fact opposed simple models on the connection between capital and labor in backward countries and had claimed that "industrial labor, in the sense of a stable, reliable, and disciplined group that has cut the umbilical cord connecting it with the land and has become suitable for utilization in factories is not abundant but extremely scarce in a backward country. . . . Under these conditions the statement may be hazarded that . . . it was largely by application of the most modern and efficient techniques that backward countries could hope to achieve success" (1952, p. 7).

34. This makes it possible to enhance the capacity to explain and predict project successes and failures and also to consider a country's development experience as essentially conditioned by the type of projects implemented. In his introduction to the text, Hirschman responds in advance to the concern that might arise with respect to the significance and the explanatory value of the structural characteristics analyzed (i.e., their relative number and variety: a problem that should perhaps be extended to their complexity and ambivalence). The point at issue is that these categories "are meant for selective use, rather than for mechanical application all the way through to any and every project" (1967b, p. 6).

They are aimed at learning to analyze projects and do not constitute "an elaborate check-list." In this sense, this point of view is consistent with the contemporary statement contained in the preface to *Electric Power in Brazil* by J. Tendler (1968), according to which the main contribution to understanding development should now come from detailed studies. (Focusing on some specific aspects of socio-economic change, Tendler succeeded in explaining how Brazil was able to realize a prolonged industrial expansion without a high rise in electricity bills and without nationalizing the sector. This provides us with some sound clues as to the typical structure of these microtechnological solutions.) Finally, another important goal of the book is to "complicate the cost-benefit analysis"—this, at least, appears to be the sense of the conclusion of the introduction, where Hirschman states that he had wanted to reclaim to the normal rule of *la raison raisonnante* at least part of the vast field left to intuitive discretion (Meldolesi, 1990b).

35. It is in fact probable that, similarly to what happened to the most deep-rooted motivations behind his work (see chapter 2, note 10), this partial loss of contact with his previous work actually enhanced the book's innovative message by facilitating the expression of that "theoretical thrust" so typical of the text.

7. PASSIONS AND INVOLVEMENT

1. This inevitably presupposes familiarity with the text (an outline of which is sketched in chapter 2). It also means I overlook other aspects of *The Passions* such as the question of the spirit of capitalism, which disclose further developments; see for example, Meldolesi, 1991–92.

2. This is the source of Steuart's watch metaphor applied to the economy: it is immediately destroyed unless it is handled by the gentlest of hands and in order to stay in proper working condition it requires frequent and delicate operations (1977b, pp. 86–87).

3. More precisely, between *The Strategy*'s discussion on the comparative analysis of Colombian airlines and roads (see chapter 6, note 31) and the principal theme of *The Passions*.

4. "In other words," Hirschman later corrected himself (1978b, now in 1981a, pp. 259–60), "exit and a certain kind of voice increased hand-in-hand, even though, at the same time, exit lowered the volume of another more militant kind of voice. These two developments may be causally connected: because a number of disaffected people had departed, it became comparatively safe to open up the system to a larger number of those who stayed on."

5. This ultimately led us to a theorem according to which the state can control two of the three variables: repression, exit, voice (1981a, p. 227).

6. This of course is far less true for larger and more powerful countries in which the low feasibility of capital outflows spurs capitalists to concentrate their efforts on voice, thus fostering an ideology that is favorable to them. Furthermore, Hirschman later explained, referring to European integration (1981a, pp. 377–78), when large economic and political unities are established, the flight of capital is made less attractive, which improves the prospects for reform.

7. Extending this argument further, it is not difficult to think of mixed cases in which the flight of capital is simultaneously provoked by the government's passions and by the fear of reform. Nor is it difficult to imagine a voice made up of Unions which combines legitimate with less legitimate claims.

8. This is the opposite of exit for voice: typical examples, as Offe explained, would be going on strike or voting against one's party in order to teach the leadership a lesson.

9. See Rebecca Scott (1986) on the Cuban slaves' process of emancipation at the end of the last century. She showed that slaves sometimes adopted a strategy of "voice to pursue exit" using the statute that imposed a number of constraints on landowners from 1880 onwards.

10. In addition to real income, Hirschman argued, individual well-being also depends on expected income. To start with other people's advancement is gratifying because it boosts our expectations; but when this confidence is not confirmed by facts, tolerance soon becomes indignation. The detail of Hirschman's argument, compared to the theories on relative income, relative deprivation, and envy developed respectively by economists, sociologists, and anthropologists is worth noting. The "tunnel effect" works because other people's advancement provides information about the outside environment that is more favorable than expected. This is gratifying and outdoes, or at least suspends, our envy. The fact that many social scientists insisted on envy may have distorted their view of events. To shed further light on his insight, Hirschman proposed turning the phenomenon around: If my neighbor is fired, he argued, it is unlikely that I will rejoice: "Once again I shall take what is happening to my neighbor as an indication of what the future might have in store for me, and hence I will be apprehensive and worried. . . . This reaction is well-known from the onset and spread of depressions" (1981a, pp. 42–43).

11. As far as his thesis of narrow latitude is concerned, the idea of the transition from one condition to another introduces an important novelty that was developed further in *Shifting Involvements*, 1982.

12. "As everyone knows," Hirschman wrote (1981a, pp. 107–8), "purely political factors, and in particular the reactions to the Cuban revolution . . . have contributed mightily to the installation of authoritarian regimes." This political constraint should be relaxed in the light of recent changes on the international scene. "During the forty-five years of the cold war," Hirschman later added (1990a), "the United States has been intensely, almost obsessively, concerned that social and political policies and experiments in Latin America might cause this or that country to 'fall' into the expansionist Soviet orbit. . . . With the end of the cold war, with the disintegration of the Soviet 'bloc' and the failure of whatever appeal it had, the North American propensity to intervene should be considerably reduced and Latin America should enjoy correspondingly more room for manoeuvre for social experiments." This might give rise to a situation in some ways similar to that defined by Burke as England's "wise and salutary neglect" that, in his view, facilitated the rise of the North American colonies in the eighteenth century.

13. "Some of the trouble that can arise," Hirschman continued, "is no doubt traceable to characteristics of the two functions taken in isolation. But the present formulation intends to draw attention to their perhaps more crucial interaction." (Significantly, "The Changing Tolerance" and "The Turn to Authoritarianism" are later included in *Essays in Trespassing* in the section entitled "Around *The Strategy of Economic Development*.")

14. In his introduction to *A Bias For Hope* (1971a, pp. 7–8), Hirschman left aside the macroscopic economic spinoffs onto politics. The intellectual opportunity opened up by *The Passions* enabled him to tackle a general issue of this sort, though he is obviously "far from any unified theory" (1981a, p. 133).

15. Furthermore (and not by chance), "In Colombia, there is a tradition of self-conscious intellectual isolation from outside ideological currents and a conviction that the country's problems can somehow be handled by home-grown, savvy members of the country's political elite" (1981a, p. 122).

16. Hirschman had been thinking about this theoretical development for some time. Hirschman recalled an official of Argentina's authoritarian government headed by Ongania claiming in 1968 that they were applying his theory of unbalanced growth, that it was their intention to redress the economic situation, and that they would then address the issue of social equity and the reinstatement of civil liberties. The reference is undoubtedly illegitimate (see chapter 3, note 42) as Hirschman's theory postulates that if one function expands before another, this expansion should activate compensating forces that tend to

offset the initial equilibrium. This observation, however, does not alter the fact that this grotesque claim had a two-fold function: it raised the problem of a broader scope for the model put forward in *The Strategy* which, until then, had only been used for economic relations between sectors and regions, and it focused attention on antagonism. Hirschman recalls having later studied tolerance to some antagonistic implications through the tunnel effect. The issue comes to the fore in the "Turn to Authoritarianism" where he claims that alternation between the entrepreneurial and reforming functions should not lose sight of overall development, which means (as it is now necessary to add) accepting also a temporary reversal back to either one of the functions, as the overall process requires. This is not how things went in Latin American countries. In order to explain the positive effects of alternating efforts, Hirschman turned his attention to advanced Western countries and to a study by Douglas A. Hibbs Jr. (1977).

17. Montesquieu's and Steuart's doctrine, Hirschman explained (1981a, pp. 100–1), is surprisingly mirrored by some Colombian writers of this century. It should also be noted that it is qualitatively much richer than the thesis (of alliance for progress and of development economics) according to which "all good things go together" (Packenham, 1973, chapter 2; Hirschman, 1981a, pp. 142–43 and pp. 20–21).

18. From a private conversation held in October 1986.

19. Inherent in human nature, disappointment and dissatisfaction are peculiar to modern society. Hirschman analyzed them from the viewpoint of some elementary features of consumption (1982b, pp. 11–13).

20. In *Shifting Involvements* (1982b, pp. 25–26), Hirschman claimed that consumer experience reflects on that of work (see note 35). This relationship can also be reversed, however, in the sense that work experience—whether it is interesting, repetitive, hard-going, etc.—can affect and condition consumption. He later considered work experience to be pervaded by the tension between instrumental and noninstrumental activities (1984d; see chapter 2).

21. Moreover, the endogenous option relentlessly separates those who focus on external factors (consider the Vietnam War). This is probably a basic reason for the attitudes of some of his critics who—to a varying extent—were uneasy about the book; see, for example, S. Axinn (1983), C. E. Greek (1983), J. Smith (1983), S. M. Moser (1984). On the other hand, the decision to start the social cycle with private consumption favors the 1950s generation over that of the 1960s. It is also self-evident that the book both suggests and requires some degree of ironic aloofness concerning private and public involvement; this attitude is not always easy to come across.

22. This notion is part of an important approach to money (generally neglected by economists) that could be combined with the contemporary point of view advanced by François Simiand (Meldolesi, 1985a).

23. There are a multitude of reasons. Newly acquired wealth can threaten social order or, on the contrary, widen the gap between the rich and the poor; it can lead to the purchase of insignificant commodities or have harmful side effects; it can give rise to a will-o'-the-wisp.

24. Hirschman's characteristic microapproach helps him to identify a few ladders that make it possible to climb gradually from private to public life and back down again. But like micro-Marxism (see chapter 3, note 65), in my view the topicality of the private (consumer) or public (corruption) experience referred to by Hirschman (see 1982b, pp. 65 and 123–25), notwithstanding its importance, does not succeed single-handedly in explaining the change. This lends support to the idea that anybody who attempts to assign a determining role to a specific aspect of experience—such as consumption or production, family or gender relations—ends up pursuing a mirage. The reason is that the various disappointment experiences are actually interrelated. The complementary microapproach could thus shed light on some of these interrelations, and help us to explore and gradually master sizable areas of the vast world of disappointment.

25. As a result, pleasure penetrates cost and suffuses it with its own experience. Anyone experiencing this phenomenon can thus enhance his pleasure by increasing his contribution. This is particularly true for those experiencing it as a revelation of a forthcoming change which had previously been considered outside their scope of action. It is also true for those who perceive it as part of their own individual development, an aspect of their personality that the previous private experience had atrophied.

26. This is achieved by focusing on the shift from one to the other, and observing the trajectory from different angles—almost like the cycles of monetary, productive, and commodity capital described by Marx in volume 2 of *Kapital.* In this respect, Hirschman stated that he refrained from fully endorsing a particular life style so that he could concentrate on the shift. "I have tried to cultivate," he added (1982b, p. 131), "an empathy for both the weaknesses and the strengths of opposite styles and, as a result, my point of view has been shifting as my story moved along: first I marshaled the strongest argument I could find in favor of a turn to public action on the part of previously private-consumption-oriented citizens, and later I did the same for a turn in the opposite direction."

27. "A Dissenter's Confession" was published in English in 1984; in Italian, in 1983.

28. In contrast to what took place in the Third World, the alternation between long privatization phases and short-lived spasmodic outbursts did not prevent the boat of developed countries, Hirschman suggested (1984d, now in 1986b, p. 31, note 33, and note 16 above), from sailing in a generally acceptable way throughout the postwar period.

29. The reference to Newton's laws underlying this principle—according to Michael McPherson (1986, p. 307)—"serves both to capture an important finding in a memorable phrase and, implicitly, to remind us how much more limited and context-dependent such a finding is compared to the laws of classical mechanics." Apart from the ironic aspects of the story, this does not belie the fact that, as we shall now see, the principle might even have broader implications.

30. According to a study by Jacques Guyaz (1980)—Hirschman continued (1984, pp. 43–44)—some of the most successful entrepreneurial ventures in postwar France, especially in the service sector, were promoted by people who had been previously involved in left-wing activities. This brings to mind the episode of a few followers of Count Saint-Simon who embarked on a series of large-scale industrial and banking activities after their movement had petered out. Much was said on "whether the capitalistic activities of the Péreire brothers and other Saint-Simonians under Napoleon III constituted an application or a betrayal of the master's doctrines; the correct answer is probably a bit of each. What is undeniable is that the early propagandistic efforts and the later entrepreneurial ventures are activities of a very different kind, yet with a strong internal link." (A reconstruction of Saint-Simon and his school's main ideas can be found in Meldolesi, 1982; other similar examples are in "'68-type capitalism" by Alain Minc, 1984, chapter 11, and in Andrea Graziosi's description of the behavior of a few Bolshevik chiefs who later became corporate managers under Stalin's industrialization process, 1986).

31. This can be obtained by further developing the critique contained in the book (1982b, p. 70) according to which *The Logic of Collective Action* by Mancur Olson and most exponents of mainstream theory assume that individuals be free of a personal history (see Meldolesi, 1987a).

32. If I am allowed a personal remark, I joined Javier Villanueva and Miguel Urrutia in praising Albert Hirschman's work on the day he was awarded an honorary degree in Economic Sciences at the University of Buenos Aires, two days after the fall of the Berlin Wall. I could not

help noticing, before an enthusiastic but concerned audience, that such a significant event for the entire world was particularly meaningful for the newly-declared Laureate. A year later, in fact, he reopened his "Chapter on Berlin" and started concentrating his efforts on the study: a topic, he wrote (1993b, p. 175), that "provided me with a point of reentry into German politics and history after an absence of over half a century from the country where I had spent my first eighteen years."

33. The dissolution of the G.D.R. is attributed both to the selective expulsion policy applied to the opponents that prevented an alternative option from coming to the fore, and to the extraordinary force of the exit-voice combination; i.e., recovery mechanisms that are too strong for the existing structure of the state (this idea had already been advanced in *Exit*).

34. Once again Hirschman traces his way out of contrasting viewpoints: on the one hand, the exaggeration of the differences; on the other, the particular gift of the German language for compact terms which makes these linguistic constructions appear realistic, such as "the negation of the negation," and similar "mysterious, if preordained, processes which dissolve all contrasts and reconcile all opposites" (1993b, p. 202). He kept away from the second danger but not from the first.

35. At the end of *Shifting Involvements,* Hirschman wrote (1982b, p. 133): "The divorce of the private and the public as a characteristic feature and a problem, even an affliction, of modern society is only one of several such splits. It has much in common, for example, with that between work and love. . . . Industrial society has tended to empty work of affective and expressive elements and to make it into a purely instrumental relationship. . . . Love, on the other hand, stands in the dichotomy for the affective relationships that are ideally thought to be . . . undertaken for their own sake with no thought of any utility beyond the one to be gotten out of the act of loving." On turning back, however, he now realizes that the contrasting of public and private categories is exposed to the danger of "making too much of a theoretical construct," and that, with respect to the thesis of the fundamental antagonism between the two realms, the German history of 1989 reminded him that this is not how matters necessarily stand: "a principle in theoretical modesty that social scientists disregard at their peril" (1993b, pp. 201 and 202).

36. The central theme of *Shifting Involvements* thus appears to have fulfilled its specific function. On the one hand it makes the reader aware of the reality of shifting involvements (as compared to other exogenous or finalistic literature). On the other, it needs to be reconsidered from within a more complex reality. To go back to where we started: the

destiny of this notion seems to be analogous to that of the economic cycle theory of the 1930s and 1940s. It is enlightening with regard to the existence of cyclical social oscillations and to the need to master them, but it fails to convince us that they should occur at predetermined deadlines and uniquely through the mechanism described. Therefore, following for a moment my own *Bildungsroman*, I am led to think that the propensity to shift from public to private domains, typical of our societies, is fortunately revealed in a multitude of ways that are more complex and less antagonistic than would be expected from an overly rigid theoretical structure of the cyclical repetition based on disappointment.

8. DEMOCRACY: DOUBTS AND INTRANSIGENCE

1. Hirschman provides an explanation in chapter 1 of the term "reaction" (its genesis, the negative connotation it assumed during the French Revolution, the nonpejorative sense he would like to use it in), but not "rhetoric." In his acknowledgments he does, however, recognize the generative influence of Donald McCloskey's work, a "spirited rehabilitation of rhetoric as a legitimate branch of inquiry for economists" (1983, pp. 482–83). Hirschman uses "rhetoric" to mean argumentation, and declares that the main arguments of reaction are sometime confirmed by facts. Thus the aim of the book is not so much to establish which arguments are right and which are wrong, but to reveal the repetitive nature of basic arguments. He hopes thereby to establish a certain presumption that standard reactionary arguments are often defective, intellectually suspect, routinely invoked to deal with a vast range of disparate situations, and that their remarkable attraction is based on powerful myths, influential interpretative formulas, and on the fact that they are a source of self-satisfaction. Later, in answer to Raymond Boudon, who had accused him in a 1992 book review of knowing nothing about the "new science of rhetoric" (as developed above all by Chaim Perelman) and of basing his argument on a "brutal and naive" opposition between rhetorical effects and scientific arguments, he wrote (1992d, p. 104): "I don't understand where Boudon has found evidence of this, for there is nothing further from my way of seeing things. On the contrary, it is in the spirit of Perelman that I use the word *rhetoric* to mean argument, to the extent that I use the two terms synonymously. . . . All my efforts have been directed at showing not that certain arguments must be excluded ('forbidden' as Boudon puts it) with the excuse that they might reveal who knows what kind of 'a-scientific rhetoric,' but that they must not be embraced too precipitously."

2. Picking up a few themes discussed in chapter 4 (also note 16), the concept of fracasomania is here revisited as a form of progressive rhetoric. The interpretation of Law 200, moreover, is extended to reach the perverse effect, while Hirschman's thoughts on ideology are explicitly echoed in those regarding the weak point of the futility thesis— i.e., that it is proclaimed too soon, in a preconceived fashion without taking into account the process of social learning and the incremental and corrective character of public policy (1991, pp. 162, 33, 78–80). As far as the unintented consequences are concerned (see chapter 5), Hirschman stresses three important "finds" in a later article: the brusque turnabout in the development of the concept—from a positive to a negative connotation—during the French Revolution; the clear separation between unintended and perverse effects; and the distinction between actions with unintentional consequences, and actions with no consequences which are therefore futile (1993e, pp. 293–96).

3. It becomes clear as one reads that Hirschman accepts the broad canvas of Marshall's analysis only as a starting point. In fact he shifts Marshall's angle of observation and concentrates rather on the complexity and difficulties of advancement. This allows him to avoid the slippery retrospective illusion of a path, generally supposed to be historically necessary, on which some progressive rhetoric is based (see note 14) and to retrieve that feeling of uncertainty and discretionality at the heart of human experience.

4. These three categories, Hirschman explains (1991, pp. 136–37), are "more exhaustive than meets the eye." A negative appraisal of a public policy can only be attributed to two reasons: because it has not accomplished its mission, in which case, "perversity and futility are two stylized versions of this turn of events"; or because the costs incurred and the consequences set off by the reform outweigh the benefits, in which case, "a good portion of this (vast) territory is covered by the jeopardy argument." The fact that costs outweigh benefits is highlighted in Hirschman's answer to Boudon (1992d, pp. 106–7) "is clearly the most generalized accusation that can be advanced against a public policy. In any case, I do not maintain that only these three theses are important; I also undertake a series of historical inquiries in order to demonstrate that these arguments have in fact been evoked in a wide range of crucial debates and that they do take into account the principle conservative points of view formulated in the last two centuries. If Boudon does not appreciate my triad, or finds it defective, it is up to him to prove that my demonstration is insufficient."

5. From Hirschman's personal papers.

6. The concerned and heated tone in which much of the book is written, Hirschman glosses, explains the vehement reaction with which it was received. I would say rather that it is a lucid analysis conducted with the author's usual mastery and driven by a discernible moral indignation.

7. The patron saint of the whole enterprise is undoubtedly Flaubert. Concluding his answer to Boudon's criticism (1992d, p. 108), entitled not by chance "Intransigent argument as a received *(reçue)* idea," Hirschman writes: "I have been an avid and passionate reader of Flaubert's *Dictionnaire des idées reçues* for a long time. His declared aim was to make the future use of a number of clichés and banal metaphors impossible. My objective is much more modest: I would simply like to nourish the hope that my book will contribute to making room for a *moment's reflection* before people evoke once again the reactionary and progressive stereotypes I have analysed there." (One can see that the same objective is considered here, compared to the Tanner Lecture which I shall deal with in note 8, less rather than more ambitious than Flaubert's. Could this change be the result of a further consultation of Flaubert's *Dictionnaire?*)

There is, in addition, a precursor: F. M. Cornford's brochure *Microcosmografia Academica* (1906), unfailingly referred to by members of the audience at his conferences on *The Rhetoric* with an Oxbridge background. "Cornford," Hirschman writes (1991, p. 82), "seems to be unique among analysts of conservatism in sharing my interest in the *rhetoric* of opposition to reform, rather than in the underlying philosophy or *Weltanschauung*. I differ from him in that I convinced myself that the subject deserved more than a purely jocular treatment."

8. Hirschman writes in his conclusion to the Tanner Lecture (that is, before the about-face that led to writing chapter 6): "I hope that I will have convinced the reader that it is worthwhile to trace these theses through the debates of the last 200 years, if only to marvel at certain invariants in argument and rhetoric, just as Flaubert liked to marvel at the invariant *bêtise* of his contemporaries." However, he adds, "To show how the participants in these debates are caught by compelling reflexes and lumber predictably through certain set motions and maneuvers—this is perhaps fulfilling enough for the historian of ideas," but not for the "unreconstructed, if modest, *Weltverbesserer* (world improver)" Hirschman believed himself to be. His objective, already expressed at the end of *The Passions* is more ambitious: to "raise the level of the debate," to make the people who use these set arguments "a bit reluctant" to do so, and "inclined to plead their case with greater originality, sophistication, and restraint." "Secondly," he adds, "my exercise could have an

even more useful impact on reformers and sundry progressives. They are given notice here of the kinds of arguments and objections that are most likely to be raised against their programs. Hence, they may be impelled to take extra care in guarding against conceivable perverse effects and other problematic consequences." This is the argument which (referring to the reduced version of the text and becoming self-critical) Hirschman claims today he uses only as "somewhat gratuitous advice" for users of reactionary rhetoric. It is true, on the contrary, that in the original version, advice to reformers is already included.

9. The pairs are as follows: (1.) The contemplated action will bring disastrous consequences; Not to take the contemplated action will bring disastrous consequences. (2.) The new reform will jeopardize the older one; The new and the old reforms will mutually reinforce each other. (3.) The contemplated action attempts to change permanent structural characteristics (laws) of the social order; it is therefore bound to be wholly ineffective, futile; The contemplated action is backed up by powerful historical forces that are already "on the march"; opposing them would be utterly futile. (1991, p. 167).

10. This attitude can already be seen in Hirschman's reply to readers of the *Atlantic* (September 1989d, p. 14): "It seemed to me worthwhile to demonstrate the extent to which discussions of the most varied proposals and programs evoke identical knee-jerk responses. I am naive enough to believe that exposing such rigidities on all sides (there will be a chapter on 'progressive' stereotypes in my book) can make a contribution toward more productive discussions in a democracy."

11. Objections from the reactionary camp, Hirschman comments (1992c, p. 10) picking up from his concluding argument in the Tanner Lecture, must be taken seriously because reformers should be prepared for the attacks likely to be leveled against their proposals, and because they should look out for the real dangers of these proposals. "I believe," he adds, "that my chapters on the perversity, futility, and jeopardy theses will be useful to reformers on both these counts, as they provide them with a conceptual guide to the principal counter-arguments as well as to the several actual pitfalls any proposed reform must face."

12. This is a short story by Jamaica Kincaid published in the *New Yorker* (June 26, 1989), almost certainly discussed with Sarah Hirschman ("For fifty years the first reader and critic of my 'ghiribizzi'" reads the Machiavellian dedication to the Italian edition of *The Rhetoric*.) It is not at all easy to overcome incommunicability and diffidence; Ignazio Silone evokes this, for example in *Polikusck'a* (1965).

13. In doing so, however, Hirschman adds, they must not become overtimorous or concerned with avoiding the numerous possible

objections, such as in the case of some American proposals to provide more aid for its child population. It is important to remember that the mere identification of possible negative reactions says very little about their likely effects. Moreover, many unintended consequences are not at all perverse and therefore a balanced view must include the probable total impact of positive and negative effects alike.

14. In fact, Hirschman comments, this thesis is very close to the previous view. "While I was at pains to point out in my book the considerable differences between the perversity and the futility theses, the 'progressive' counterparts to these two arguments turn out to have much in common. In both cases an appeal is made, not to human reason and judgment, but to anxiety and fear. And both views share the characteristic that, as a result of recent historical experience, they are highly discredited at the present time" (1992c, p. 15). In my opinion, this does not mean that less emphasized forms of "being on the side of history" are not common today, as, for example, in T. H. Marshall, Hirschman's starting point for *The Rhetoric* (see note 3; 1991, p. 86).

15. These texts play a part in the curious rule of three that permeates the whole of *The Rhetoric:* a problem regarding three centuries marked by three important thrusts, followed by three counterthrusts, characterized by three main rhetorical arguments, from which three counterarguments can be derived, thus forming three rhetorical couples, leading to three conclusions and three paths to follow including that of the three articles written in parallel to the volume that we will deal with.

16. On the other hand, comparing the behavior of French, German, and Anglo-American democracies, various authors remain perplexed. The problem of the origins of democracy, Rustow concludes, "has greater pragmatic relevance than further panegyrics about the virtues of Anglo-American democracies or laments over the fatal illnesses of democracy in Weimar or in several of the French Republics" (1970, p. 340).

17. "No two existing democracies have gone through a struggle between the very same forces over the same issues and with the same institutional outcome. Hence it seems unlikely that any future democracy will follow in the precise footsteps of any of its predecessors." "Hirschman and other economists," Rustow continues, "have argued that a country can best launch into a phase of growth not by slavishly imitating the example of nations already industrialized, but rather by making the most of its particular natural and human resources and by fitting these accurately into the international division of labor. Similarly, a country is likely to attain democracy not by copying the constitutional laws or parliamentary practices of some previous democracy, but rather

by honestly facing up to its particular conflicts and by devising or adapting effective procedures for their accommodation."

18. Moreover, "in India and in the Philippines the prolonged contest between nationalist forces and an imperial bureaucracy over the issue of self-government may have served the same preparatory function," while in Lebanon the struggle was (at the time) between denominational groups over government offices. In these cases, as in those of Turkey and Sweden discussed by Rustow, economic factors certainly play a part. These are more pronounced in Sweden and in Turkey than in India, the Philippines, and Lebanon; nowhere however, do they have a determining role. Contrary to what is commonly held, there is no evidence that a predetermined minimal level of per capita income is a necessary condition for the transition. As a matter of fact, Rustow deliberately leaves open the possibility of "properly so called" democracies in "premodern, prenationalist times and at low levels of economic development" (1970, pp. 352–53).

19. In Turkey, the article explains, a series of democratic practices are being developed, but this was not the case in the past with regard to the Armenians or the Greeks. Perhaps in the future—one might add—the same will be said for the fratricidal enemies in the former Yugoslavia.

20. "Since precise terms must be negotiated and heavy risks with regard to the future taken, a small circle of leaders is likely to play a disproportionate role. Among the negotiating groups and their leaders may be the protagonists of the preparatory struggle. Other participants may include groups that split off from one or the other side or new arrivals on the political stage," as in the case of Sweden. "The formula that carried the day in 1907," Rustow adds, "included crucial contributions from a moderately conservative bishop and a moderately liberal farmer, neither of whom played a very prominent role in politics before or after this decision phase" (1970, pp. 356–57).

21. Rustow mentions the following: the fear on the part of Conservatives to lose even more ground in the end (as in the case of the British Whigs in 1832 and of Swedish Conservatives in 1907); the desire to live up to long-proclaimed principles (as in the case of 1945 Turkey); the acceptance on the part of radicals of a first installment, confident that time is on their side and that future installments are bound to follow; the exhaustion of both sides after a long struggle or the fear of a civil war, especially if the country has been through such a war recently, as in the case of the English civil war in the seventeenth century or—one might add—in the case of the Spanish Civil War after the death of Franco.

22. Thus in Sweden the Social Democrats surrendered their early pacifism, anticlericalism, and republicanism, as well as their demand for

nationalization of industry, while the Conservatives endorsed Swedish participation in international organizations, and accepted government intervention in the economy and the social welfare state.

23. Ingredients and tasks of the transition-to-democracy model must be assembled one at a time thus forming a sequence. "The model thus abandons the quest for functional requisites of democracy; for such a quest heaps all these tasks together and thus makes the total job of democratization quite unmanageable." The argument, Rustow comments, "is analogous to that which has been made by Hirschman and others against the theory of balanced economic growth." These economists, he goes on, do not deny that development requires changes on all fronts, but they insist that any country that attempted all these tasks at once would find itself totally paralyzed. Hence, the problem in their view is one of finding a manageable sequence of tasks. "The model does suggest one such sequence" (1970, pp. 361–62).

24. In Rustow's opinion, the basis of democracy is not consensus, neither in the form of a common belief in certain fundamental values, nor in that of procedural consensus over the rules of the game; and it is not even the capacity for empathy or the desire for participation, these characteristics are proposed whether individually or combined with others. Nor can one say that the decision to install a democratic regime derives from consensus. It can be instrumental for achieving other goals; in as much as it is compromised it will appear to the contenders as a second best, and it will not represent an agreement on fundamental values; it will not cancel differences, not even as far as procedures are concerned; it will represent initially only a limited agreement between few leaders. "Consensus on fundamentals," Rustow writes (1970, pp. 362–63), "is an implausible condition. A people who were not in conflict about some rather fundamental matters would have little need to devise democracy's elaborate rules of conflict resolution. And the acceptance of these rules is logically a part of the transition process. . . . The present model transfers various aspects of consensus from the quiescent state of preconditions to that of active elements in the process." "The essence of democracy," Rustow concludes, "is the habit of dissension and conciliation over ever-changing issues and amid ever-changing alignments."

25. Rustow's analysis, Hirschman writes in a note, could be said to be a rediscovery of Machiavelli's famous statement that "the 'perfection' of the Roman Republic and 'all the laws that were made in favor of liberty' were due to the so often lamented 'disunion between the Plebs and the Senate' (*Discorsi*, book 1, chapters 2 and 4)."

26. "Albert," Fernando Henrique Cardoso told me in August

1990, "was very impressed by the Brazilian political reawakening. I remember, for instance, a vast demonstration in São Paolo. We too were surprised by the participation." For a survey of the debate on democracy in Latin America, see Norbert Lechner (1986).

27. "Neither Reforms, Nor Revolution" is the title of René Remond's review of *The Rhetoric* published by *Le Monde* in 1991. It can also be seen as an enviable continuity in Hirschman's inspiration, although, of course, starting with reformmongering in *Journeys*, overcoming this antinomy has been later transferred to the problem of rhetorical argumentation and the improvement of political deliberation.

28. The history of northeastern Brazil contains examples to illustrate both models. Published separately in the *Quarterly Journal of Economics*, his "Models of Reformmongering" enters into dialogue with several significant works, such as Kenneth Arrow's *Social Choice and Individual Values* and James Buchanan and Gordon Tullock's *The Calculus of Consent*. These models belong to the very few that stem from a careful and systematic reconstruction of concrete situations rather than from the more common summary observations, as François Simiand put it (see 1912, chapter 1).

29. "In a society where decision-makers are 'toderos' rather than sectionalists," Hirschman points out further on (1963a, p. 292), political behavior "is not amenable to majority formation through logrolling. . . . This is an interesting result: the more uncompromising, ideological, strongly committed the individual decision-makers are, the more likely it is that the government will have to draw in turn on different groups for support." This does not mean, however, that one has to accept the existing division of intellectual labor. To the contrary, Hirschman's experience shows that it is possible to be highly specialized in closely linked matters which appear to contemporary culture to be miles apart. To develop one's intellectual curiosity without erecting barriers, and know a bit of everything in fields other than one's own—if this is tempered by the knowledge of one's own limits—does not mean having the mentality of a "todero." Rather, it allows one easier access to the "culture of doubt" (see below).

30. He had, furthermore, referred to Latin America in contrast to the United States. But, as I have already noted, (chapter 4, note 18) the situation evolved to the point of inverting the terms of the *desencuentro*. This had the indirect effect of allowing *The Rhetoric* to be written in general terms, referring above all to the more advanced democratic societies.

31. These honorary degrees were conferred on Hirschman in Europe, following, he comments (1993c), "an interesting pattern: the

degrees I received retrace, with remarkable fidelity, my largely involuntary wanderings during the eight long years from 1933 to 1941, from my native Berlin to France, from there to Italy, then back to France and then, via Spain and Portugal, to America. It is perhaps because of this emergent pattern that I wrote, for each of those occasions, a brief autobiographical memoir relating to the period which I had spent in the respective location."

32. "Even though his writings are anything but mainstream," Hirschman writes about Schelling, with a judgment that fits the world of ideas we have evoked (1989a, pp. 162–63), "he hardly ever writes in an adversarial, disputatious tone. . . . Tom refrains from the imprecations because he has absolutely no use for the related activity: the construction of an alternative paradigm. He does not want to fall into the trap of exchanging one straitjacket for another."

33. This is perhaps where the confluence of the "production line" of *The Rhetoric* and that of the three short articles lies. Hypothetically, evidence of this can be found in Hirschman's letter to Offe dated September 15, 1988, in which he writes, "Talking with you I had the idea of adapting for the occasion a paper I am writing for the American Economic Association annual meetings on the individual and collective utility of having opinions. I suddenly realized that, almost providentially, that theme would be quite appropriate." This sudden realization could well be linked to the work in progress that led to writing chapter 6. On the other hand, if we are to give space to the unconscious and the unexpected in Hirschman's development, we should also talk about the conscious and intelligent efforts made in that direction. It is highly likely that the two paths—*The Rhetoric* and the three short articles—both originated in the idea that progress in political deliberation and the democratic personality is more likely to be achieved through indirect rather than direct analysis. These are ultimate objectives which, as Hirschman writes (1988b, p. 9), "it can only be obtained, as Jon Elster has underlined as a *by-product* of activities whose proclaimed and conscious aims are quite extraneous to that objective." All this notwithstanding, Hirschman had the idea to jot down what he considered achievable through direct analysis. Therefore, it cannot be excluded that Hirschman cultivated the hope from the start that the two parts of his work in progress would interact and that this was one reason why he pursued the analytical path that would lead to chapter 6 of *The Rhetoric* and the constructive conclusions of the book.

Compared to Hirschman's work on *The Strategy* (see the beginning of chapter 3), here we cannot trace any note of caution or reticence. Reading "*The Rhetoric:* Two Years Later," it is clear that Hirschman made every effort to clarify matters and open up a channel of communication for those who had not understood (or misunderstood) the book. This effort is described in an answer to Boudon (1992d, p. 108): "While writing his work, has Boudon never met with arguments in disagreement with his own original convictions, with the result that he has been obliged to modify or temper the point of view he initially thought he would have to defend? Of all the experiences open to a writer, this is one of the most exciting."

34. More exactly, the American and German texts are about the same length. The middle part is the same, while the beginning and the end have a different readership in mind. The American text contains an interesting hint at the end about the possibility of importing political theses on deliberation in the analysis of consumer tastes and the functioning of the market.

35. A further consequence is of course the open construction of the analysis, the multiplicity of approaches and generalizations, the denial of the existence of a unique path, etc. Referring, for example, to the concept of linkages, Hirschman recently stated (1993d) that this is a generalization of an intermediate level conceived as an alternative to macroeconomic models that had always seemed to him too abstract, mechanical, and lacking that dramatic quality that was characteristic of Professor Demageon's geography lessons. "In dealing with the multiple and complex problems of development we have learnt that we must fashion generalizations at all kinds of ranges and be deaf, like Ulysses, to the seductive chant of the unique paradigm."

36. The conclusion, of course, is that the individual and social utility function of opinions is "backward sloping" when these opinions vary in number and firmness. That is, when there are too few or too many opinions, or when they are under- or overemphasized, the individual and society not only do not benefit from the formative and deliberative process, but might even get in its way or prevent it from taking place properly. There is, however, a middle way: limited and incompletely formed opinions can be advantageous both to the individual and to society. The problem then becomes how to encourage this attitude, transforming it into a clear commitment to individual political satisfaction and to the functioning of the deliberative process.

37. With these danger signals directed at our democratic travelers, the long list of motivations and objectives comes to an end. Hirschman flanked his original criticism of reactionary rhetorics—dictated by the desire "to help stem the conservative tide of the 1980s" (1993e, p. 314) —with additional aims such as: raising the level of the debate on rhetoric; offering advice to his users; "suggesting a new style and rhetoric around

'progressive' policy-making," making space for a moment's reflection before pronouncing for the umpteenth time one of the criticized stereotypes; exposing and loosening the servitudes of argumentation by using irony in order to reinstate communication between the different camps and make their debate more genuine; and, finally, liberating oneself from the counterposed intransigent rhetorics in order to promote a political and cultural climate that allows one to escape from permanent belligerence. Thus, in analogy with what Hirschman wrote in *Journeys,* we can conclude that the main preoccupation in *The Rhetoric* with the development of democracy—this question without an answer—has finally led to a variety of objectives and results.

38. Rereading today some of Colorni's political writings from the period 1934–38 brings Hirschman's possibilism to mind. As far as his practical commitment was concerned, being "without a homeland" as his sister Ursula put it in her book of memoirs (1993), Albert played a supporting role in antifascist activities, which he later developed in Marseilles working with political refugees with Varian Fry. "We had three problems to solve," writes Fry (1946; new ed. 1992, p. 39), "all at the same time. One was to locate new sources of false passports. The second was to get false identity cards that would pass for real. The third was to find some way to get large sums of money into France from New York without the police knowing about it. Beamish solved all three of these problems."

39. Considering the complexity of this process it is easy to understand why Hirschman attributed a primary role to learning in his work but did not indicate a general model for learning, (as Donald Schön—see Rodwin and Schön, 1994, ch. 4—would have liked). Take, for example, the many similarities that I have pointed out. Take the Colornian conclusion to "Notes" which states, in the Spanish edition: "Providentially, to borrow Marx's famous word on Feuerbach, to refine our interpretation of the world signifies, in this case, to start changing it." Take the Colornian roots of *The Rhetoric* and the work that followed it with its far-reaching polemic over intransigence. Take, finally, the "propensity to self-subversion" (1994a) which picks up and modifies a concept of Nietzsche's. Evidently, in addition to the criticism of "one thing at a time" and the writing of chapter 6, the chapter in *The Rhetoric* on the jeopardy thesis launched a broader awareness of the construction of thought which Hirschman attributes today to various aspects of his works.

Bibliography

ALBERT O. HIRSCHMAN'S WORKS

Entries marked with an asterisk (*) are included in A. O. Hirschman, *A Bias for Hope: Essays on Developments and Latin America* (New Haven, Conn.: Yale University Press, 1971). Entries marked with a dagger (†) are included in A. O. Hirschman, *Essays in Trespassing: Economics to Politics and Beyond* (Cambridge: Cambridge University Press, 1981). Entries marked with two asterisks (**) are included in A. O. Hirschman, *Rival Views of Market Society and Other Recent Essays* (New York: Viking/Penguin, 1986).

1937. "La fecondità della donna italiana secondo l'età e il numero dei figli avuti: Osservazioni critiche." Typescript.

1938a. "Note su due recenti tavole di nuzialità della popolazione italiana." *Giornale degli economisti* (January).

1938b. "Les finances et l'économie italiennes: Situation actuelle et perspectives." *Supplément su buttletin quotidien* 123, no. 1 (June): 1–22. Paris: Société d'études et d'information économique.

1938c. "Il franco Poincaré e la sua svalutazione." Dissertation. University of Trieste, Faculty of Economics and Commerce.

1939a. "Mémoire sur le contrôle des changes en Italie." Paper presented at the 12th session of the Conference permanente des hautes études internationales, League of Nations, Paris, June. Italian trans. in *Potenza nazionale e commercio estero: Gli anni Trenta, l'Italia e la ricostuzione,* ed. Asso and De Cecco, 161–255.

1939b. "Italie." *L'activité économique* 15 (January 31): 353–57; 16 (April 30): 29–34; 17 (July 31): 137–42.

1939c. "Statistical Study of the Trend of Foreign Trade toward Equilibrium and Bilateralism." Typescript. Original in French. English trans. P. F. Asso, *Political Economy* 4, no. 1 (1988): 111–24.

1943a. "The Commodity Structure of World Trade." *Quarterly Journal of Economics* (August): 565–95.

1943b. "On Measures of Dispersion for a Finite Distribution." *Journal of the American Statistical Association* (September).

1945. *National Power and the Structure of Foreign Trade.* Berkeley, Cal.: University of California Press, 1945. Reprint, 1969. Paperback ed. with new introduction, 1980.

1946a. "Bilateralism and Proportionalism—Two Aspects of Trade Structure." *Review of Foreign Developments* (December): 1–7.

1946b. "Schuman's Devaluation Paradox." *Review of Foreign Developments* (December): 1–3.

1947a. "Conditions and Tests of Successful Devaluation: A Mathematical Note." *Review of Foreign Developments* (January): 1–6.

1947b. "Exchange Control in Italy, I." *Review of Foreign Developments* (March): 11–17.

1947c. "France and Italy: Patterns of Reconstruction." *Federal Reserve Bulletin* 33, no. 4 (April): 353–66.

1947d. "Exchange Control in Italy, II." *Review of Foreign Developments* (May): 1–4.

1947e. With F. M. Tamagna. "British-Italian Financial Settlement." *Review of Foreign Developments* (May): 14–17.

1947f. "Swiss Foreign Economic Policy." *Review of Foreign Developments* (June): 13–20.

1947g. "Public Finance, Money Markets, and Inflation in France." *Review of Foreign Developments* (July): 8–14.

1947h. With M. J. Roberts. "Trade and Credit Arrangements between the Marshall Plan Countries." *Review of Foreign Developments* (August): 1–4.

1947i. "Trade Structure of the Marshall Plan Countries." *Review of Foreign Developments* (August): 1–5.

1947l. With C. Lichtenberg. "French Exports and the Franc." *Review of Foreign Developments* (September): 11–15.

1947m. With C. Lichtenberg. "French Foreign Trade: Customs vs. Exchange Control Statistics." *Review of Foreign Developments* (December): 4–9.

1947n. "Italian Exchange Rate Policy." *Review of Foreign Developments* (December): 6–11.

1948a. "The French Monetary Move." *Review of Foreign Developments* (February): 1–7.

1948b. With F. Nixon. "Types of Exchange Rate Discrimination." *Review of Foreign Developments* (February): 4–6.

1948c. "*Franco Valuta* Imports in France." *Review of Foreign Developments* (March): 7–8.

1948c. "Credit Restrictions and Deflation in Italy." *Review of Foreign Developments* (April): 5–9.

1948e. "Note on Offshore Procurement in Europe." *Review of Foreign Developments* (June): 6–9.

1948f. With C. Lichtenberg. "Payments and Trade between ERP Countries in 1947." *Review of Foreign Developments* (June): 1–12.

1948g. "Inflation and Balance of Payments Deficit." *Review of Foreign Developments* (August): 6–8.

1948h. "Inflation and Deflation in Italy." *American Economic Review* 38, no. 4 (September): 598–606.

1948i. "Dollar Shortage and Discrimination." *Review of Foreign Developments* (September): 1–4.

1948l. With R. V. Roosa. "Some Recent Developments in French Finance and Credit Policy." *Review of Foreign Developments* (November): 20–25.

1948m. "Disinflation, Discrimination, and the Dollar Shortage." *American Economic Review* (December): 886–92.

1948n. "Economic and Financial Conditions in Italy." *Review of Foreign Developments* (December): 1–17.

1949a. "Proposal for a European Monetary Authority." Typescript. Italian trans. in *Tre continenti: Economia politica e sviluppo della deomocrazia in Europa, Stati Uniti e America Latina,* ed. Meldolesi, 7–18.

1949b. "The OEEC Interim Report on the European Recovery Program: A Summary." *Review of Foreign Developments* (January): 1–15.

1949c. "Devaluation and the Trade Balance: A Note." *Review of Economics and Statistics* 31, no. 1 (February): 50–53.

1949d. With R. V. Roosa. "Credit Controls in the Postwar Economy of France." *Review of Foreign Developments* (February): 1–13.

1949e. "Relaxation of Exchange Controls in Belgium and France." *Review of Foreign Developments* (February): 13–15.

1949f. "Intra-European Payments: A Proposal for Discussion." *Review of Foreign Developments* (March): 1–3.

1949g. With R. V. Roosa. "Postwar Credit Controls in France." *Federal Reserve Bulletin* (April).

1949h. With L. N. Dembitz. "Movement toward Balance in International Transactions of the United States." *Federal Reserve Bulletin* (April).

1949i. "International Aspects of a Recession." *Review of Foreign Developments* (June): 1–9.

1949l. "The New Intra-European Payment Scheme." *Review of Foreign Developments* (July): 1–5.

1949m. "The U.S. Recession and the Dollar Position of the OEEC Countries." *Review of Foreign Developments* (September): 1–5.

1949n. "Country Notes on Recent Currency Adjustments." *Review of Foreign Developments* (October): 1–19.

1950a. "Approaches to Multilateralism and European Integration." Typescript. Washington, D.C.: Department of State, Foreign Service Institute. Italian trans. in *Tre continenti: Economia politica e sviluppo della deomocrazia in Europa, Stati Uniti e America Latina,* ed. Meldolesi, 19–34.

1950b. "Liberalization of the ECA Dollar." *Review of Foreign Developments* (January): 1–10.

1950c. "European Payment Union—A Possible Basis for Agreement." *Review of Foreign Developments* (February): 1–8.

1950d. "Annex I: The EPU—A Short History." *Review of Foreign Developments* (June): 1–6. Expanded and revised version pub. under the title "The European Payments Union: Negotiations and Issues" [Hirschman 1951a].

1950e. "The Influence of U.S. Economic Conditions on Foreign Countries (Draft for Discussion)." *Review of Foreign Developments* (June): 1–20.

1951a. "The European Payments Union: Negotiations and Issues." *Review of Economics and Statistics* 33, no. 1 (February): 48–55.

1951b. "Types of Convertibility." *Review of Economics and Statistics* 33, no. 1 (February): 60–62.

1951c. "Size and Distribution of the Public Debt in Selected Countries." *Review of Foreign Developments* (February): 1–8.

1951d. "Industrial Nations and Industrialization of Underdeveloped Countries." *Economia internazionale* (August): 606–18.

1951e. "Note on Hinshaw's Article on Currency Appreciation." *Review of Foreign Developments* (September): 1–5.

1951f. "The Problem of the Belgian Surplus in EPU." *Review of Foreign Developments* (September): 1–4.

1952. "Effects of Industrialization on the Market of Industrial Countries." In *The Progress of Underdeveloped Areas,* ed. Hoselitz, 270–83.

1954a. "Guía para el análisis y la confección de recomendaciones sobre la situación monetaria." *Economia Colombiana* 1, no. 2 (October): 531–40.

*1954b. "Economics and Investment Planning: Reflections Based on Experience in Colombia." Typescript. In *Investments Criteria and Economic Growth.* Cambridge, Mass.: M.I.T., Center for International Studies, 1995. Pub. New York: Asia Publishing House, 1961.

1955a. Diary of Survey Trip through Central America. Typescript. March 5–April 6.

1955b. "Study of the Present and Prospective Financial Position of the Empresas Municipalities of Cali, with Recommendations." Typescript.

1955c. With G. Kalmanoff. "Colombia: Highlights of a Developing Economy." Pamphlet. Bogotá: Banco de la República Press.

1956a. "Survey of Executive Salaries in Colombia." Typescript.

1956b. "The Market for Paper and Pulp in Colombia." Typescript.

1956c. "La demanda para gas en Cali y en el Valle del Cauca." Typescript.

1956d. With G. Kalmanoff. "Demanda de energia eléctrica para la C.V.C." *Economia Colombiana* 3, no. 9 (June): 507–19.

1957a. With G. Kalmanoff. "Investment in Central America: Basic Information for United States Businessmen." Washington, D.C.: U.S. Department of Commerce.

*1957b. "Economic Policy in Underdeveloped Countries." *Economic Development and Cultural Change* 5 (July): 326–70.

1957c. "Investment Policies and 'Dualism' in Underdeveloped Countries." *American Economic Review* (September): 550–70.

1958a. *The Strategy of Economic Development.* New Haven, Conn.: Yale University Press. Reprint, New York: W. W. Norton, 1978.

1958b. With G. Sirkin. "Investment Criteria and Capital Intensity Once Again." *Quarterly Journal of Economics* (August): 469–71.

1959a. Letter to François Perroux. February 20.

1959b. Letter to Hla Myint. July 27.

1959c. Letter to Hollis Chenery. August 8.

1959d. Letter to André Gunaer Frank. August 18.

*1959e. "Primary Products and Substitutes: Should Technological Progress Be Policed?" *Kyklos* 7, fasc. 3: 354–61.

1959–60. "The Strategy of Economic Development." *Farm Policy Forum* 12:15–21.

1960. "Invitation to Theorizing about the Dollar Glut." *Review of Economics and Statistics* 42, no. 1 (February): 100–102.

1961a. *The Strategy of Economic Development.* New preface to papberback ed.

1961b. "Exchange Controls and Economic Development: Comments." In *Economic Development for Latin America,* ed. Ellis, 457–65.

*1961c. "Second Thoughts on the 'Alliance for Progress.'" *Reporter,* May 25.

1961d. *Latin American Issues: Essays and Comments.* Ed. Hirschman. New York: Twentieth Century Fund.

*1961e. "Ideologies of Economic Development in Latin America." In *Latin American Issues: Essays and Comments*, ed. Hirschman, 3–42.

*1961f. "Abrazo vs. Co-existence: Comments on Ypsilon's Paper." In *Latin American Issues: Essays and Comments*, ed. Hirschman, 59–63.

*1962a. "Analyzing Economic Growth: A Comment." In Asher et al., *Development in the Emerging Countries.*

*1962b. With C. E. Lindblom. "Economic Development, Research and Development, Policy-Making: Some Converging Views." *Behavioral Science* 7 (April): 211–22.

1962c. "Critical Comments on Foreign Aid Strategies." In Asher et al., *Development in the Emerging Countries.*

1963a. *Journeys toward Progress: Studies of Economic Policy-Making in Latin America*. Twentieth Century Fund. Reprint, New York: Norton, 1973.

1963b. "How Policy Is Made." *Américas* 16 (August 16): 39–41.

1963c. "Models of Reformmongering." *Quarterly Journal of Economics* (May).

*1964a. "The Stability of Neutralism: A Geometrical Note." *American Economic Review* 54 (March): 94–100.

1964b. "The Paternity of an Index." *American Economic Review* 54 (September): 761–62.

*1965a. "Obstacles to Development: A Classification and a Quasi-Vanishing Act." *Economic Development and Cultural Change* 13 (July): 385–93.

1965b. "Out of Phase." *Encounter,* special issue on Latin America (September).

1967a. "The Principle of the Hiding Hand." *Public Interest* 6 (winter).

1967b. *Development Projects Observed.* Washington, D.C.: Brookings Institution.

1968a. Foreword to J. Tendler, *Electric Power in Brazil.* Cambridge Mass.: Harvard University Press, vii–x.

*1968b. "The Political Economy of Import-Substituting Industrialization in Latin America." *Quarterly Journal of Economics* (February).

*1968c. With R. M. Bird. "Foreign Aid: A Critique and a Proposal." *Princeton Essays in International Finance* 69 (July).

*1968d. "Underdevelopment, Obstacles to the Perception of Change, and Leadership." *Daedalus* 97, no. 3 (summer): 925–37, estate.

*1968e. "Industrial Development in the Brazilian Northeast and the Tax Credit Scheme of Article 34/18." *Journal of Development Studies* 5 (October): 5–28.

*1969. "How to Divest in Latin America, and Why." *Princeton Essays in International Finance* 76 (November).

1970a. *Exit, Voice, and Loyalty: Responses to Decline in Firms, Organizations, and States.* Cambridge, Mass.: Harvard University Press.

*1970b. "The Search for Paradigms as a Hindrance to Understanding." *World Politics* 22, no. 3 (March): 329–43. Reprinted in *Interpretative Social Science: A Reader,* ed. Rabinow and Sullivan, 257–79.

1971a. *A Bias for Hope: Essays on Development and Latin America.* New Haven, Conn.: Yale University Press. Reprint, Boulder, Colo.: Westview Press, 1985.

1971b. "Ideology: Mask or Nessus Shirt?" In *Comparison of Economic Systems: Theoretical and Methodological Approaches,* ed. Eckstein, 289–97.

1973a. Preface to the Norton ed. of *Journeys toward Progress: Studies of Economic Policy-Making in Latin America.*

†1973b. "The Changing Tolerance for Income Inequality in the Course of Economic Development." *Quarterly Journal of Economics* 87 (November): 544–62.

†1973c. "An Alternative Explanation of Contemporary Harriedness." *Quarterly Journal of Economics* 87 (November).

†1974. "Exit, Voice, and Loyalty: Further Reflections and a Survey of Recent Contributions." *Social Science Information* 13, no. 1 (February): 7–26.

†1975. "Policy Making and Policy Analysis in Latin America—A Return Journey." *Policy Sciences* 6 (December): 385–402.

†1976a. "On Hegel, Imperialism, and Structural Stagnation." *Journal of Development Economics* 3 (March): 1–8.

†1976b. "Exit, Voice, and Loyalty: Comments." *American Economic Review, Papers and Proceedings* 66 (May): 386–89.

†1977a. "A Generalized Linkage Approach to Development, with Special Reference to Staples." *Economic Development and Cultural Change* 25, supplement (essays in honor of B. F. Hoselitz): 67–98.

1977b. *The Passions and the Interests: Political Arguments for Capitalism before Its Triumph.* Princeton, N.J.: Princeton University Press.

†1978a. "Beyond Asymmetry: Critical Notes on Myself as a Young Man and on Some Other Old Friends." *International Organization* 32, no. 1 (winter): 45–50.

†1978b. "Exit, Voice, and the State." *World Politics* 31 (October): 93–107.

1979a. Foreword to *Toward a New Strategy for Development,* ed. Hill.

†1979b. "The Turn to Authoritarianism in Latin America and the Search for Its Economic Determinants." In *The New Authoritarianism in Latin America,* ed. Collier, 61–98.

**1980a. "The Welfare State in Trouble: Systemic Crisis or Growing Pains?" *American Economic Review, Papers and Proceedings* 70, no. 2 (May): 113–16.

**1980b. "In difesa del possibilismo." In *I limiti della democrazia,* ed. Scartezzini, Germani, and Gritti, 88–91.

1981a. *Essays in Trespassing: Economics to Politics and Beyond.* Cambridge: Cambridge University Press.

†1981b. "The Rise and Decline of Development Economics." In Hirschman, *Essays in Trespassing: Economics to Politics and Beyond,* 1–24.

†1981c. "The Social and Political Matrix of Inflation: Elaborations on the Latin American Experience." In Hirschman, *Essays in Trespassing: Economics to Politics and Beyond,* 177–207.

†1981d. "Morality and the Social Sciences: A Durable Tension." Paper presented upon accepting the Frank E. Seidman Distinguished Award in Political Economy, P. K. Seidman Foundation, Memphis, Tenn., October 1980. In *Social Science as Moral Inquiry,* ed. Haan.

**1982a. "Rival Interpretations of Market Society: Civilizing, Destructive, or Feeble?" *Journal of Economic Literature* 20, no. 4 (December): 1463–84.

1982b. *Shifting Involvements: Private Interest and Public Action.* Princeton, N.J.: Princeton University Press.

1983a. "The Principle of Conservation and Mutation of Social Energy." *Grassroots Development (Journal of the Inter-American Foundation)* 7, no. 2: 3–8.

1983b. *Ascesa e declino dell'economia dello sviluppo e altri saggi.* Ed. A. Ginzburg. Torino: Rosenberg and Sellier.

1984a. "University Activities Abroad and Human Rights Violations: Exit, Voice, or Business as Usual?" *Human Rights Quarterly* 6, no. 1 (February).

1984b. *L'économie comme science sociale et politique.* Ed. F. Furet. Paris: Gallimard/Le Seuil.

1984c. *Getting Ahead Collectively: Grassroots Experiences in Latin America.* New York: Pergamon Press.

**1984d. "A Dissenter's Confession: Revisiting *The Strategy of Economic Development.*" In *Pioneers in Development,* ed. Meier and Seers.

**1984e. "Against Parsimony: Three Easy Ways of Complicating Some Categories of Economic Discourse." *American Economic Review* 74, no. 2 (May): 7–21. Rev. versions in *Bulletin of the American Academy of Arts and Sciences* (1984) and in *Economics and Philosophy* 1 (1985).

1984f. "Erinnerungen an das Französische Gymnasium." Typescript.

1984g. "Grassroots Change in Latin America." *Challenge* 27, no. 4 (September–October).

†1985. "Inflation: Reflections on the Latin American Experience." In *The Politics of Inflation and Economic Stagnation*, ed. Lindberg and Maier. Washington D.C.: Brookings Institution.

**1986a. "On Democracy in Latin America." *New York Review of Books* (April 10).

1986b. *Rival Views of Market Society and Other Recent Essays.* New York: Viking/Penguin, Elisabeth Sifton Books. Paperback ed., with new preface, Cambridge Mass.: Havard University Press, 1992.

1986c. *Vers une économie politique élargie.* Paris: Editions de Minuit.

1986d. "Out of Phase Again." *New York Review of Books* (December 18): 53–54.

1986e. Preface to *Potenza nazionale e commercio estero: Gli anni Trenta, l'Italia e la ricostruzione,* ed. Asso and de Cecco.

1986f. "Felicità doppia formula." *l'Unità* (November 13).

**1986g. "Linkages in Economic Development." In *Rival Views of Market Society and Other Recent Essays,* 56–76.

**1986h. "Exit and Voice: On Expounding Spheres of Influence." In *Rival Views of Market Society and Other Recent Essays,* 77–101.

**1986l. "The Concept of Interest: From Euphemism to Tautology." In *Rival Views of Market Society and Other Recent Essays,* 105–41.

1987a. "Ora pensiamo alla pace." *Il Corriere della Sera* (January 3).

1987b. "The Political Economy of Latin American Development: Seven Exercises in Retrospection." *Latin American Research Review* 22, no. 3: 7–36.

1987c. "Io 'detective' dell'economia fascista." *Il Corriere della Sera* (November 13).

1987d. *L'economia politica come scienza morale e sociale.* Ed. L. Meldolesi. Napoli: Liguori.

1987e. *Potenza nazionale e commercio estero: Gli anni Trenta, l'Italia e la ricostruzione.* Ed. P. F. Asso and M. de Cecco. Bologna: Il Mulino.

1988a. Preface to *Entwicklung, Markt und Moral* [1989l].

1988b. "Berlin Festvortrag." Speech delivered upon receipt of honorary degree from the Freie Universität, Berlin. Typescript. Italian trans. in *Come far passare le riforme,* ed. Meldolesi, 343–51.

1988c. Letter to Claus Offe. September 15.

1988d. *Come complicare l'economia.* Ed. L. Meldolesi. Bologna: Il Mulino.

1989a. "Thomas Schelling," In "Distinguished Fellow: Reflections on Thomas Schelling," ed. R. Zeckhauser. *Journal of Economic Perspectives* 3, no. 2 (spring): 162–63.

1989b. "Having Opinions: One of the Elements of Well-Being?" *American Economic Reviews, Papers and Proceedings* 79, no. 2 (May): 75–79.

1989c. "Two Hundred Years of Reactionary Rhetoric: The Case of the Perverse Effect." In *The Tanner Lectures in Human Values,* vol. 10, 1–32. Salt Lake City, Utah: University of Utah Press.

1989d. "Reactionary Rhetoric." *Atlantic* 263, no. 5 (May): 63–70.

1989e. "Opinionated Opinions and Democracy." *Dissent* (summer): 393–95.

1989f. "Statement of Dissent." In *The Road to Economic Recovery: Report of the Twentieth Century Fund Task Force on International Debt,* ed. Dornbusch, 11.

1989g. "Comment on Chapter 6." In *The Political Economy of Argentina 1946–83,* ed. di Tella and Dornbusch.

1989h. "How the Keynesian Revolution Was Exported from the United States, and Other Comments." In *The Political Power of Economic Ideas,* ed. Hall, 347–59. Princeton N.J.: Princeton University Press.

1989i. "Reactionary Rhetoric: A Reply." *Atlantic* 263, no. 9 (September): 14.

1989l. *Entwicklung, Markt und Moral.* München: Hauser.

1990a. "Good News Is Not Bad News." *New York Review of Books* (October 11).

1990b. "Albert O. Hirschman" (interviews with). In *Economics and Sociology,* ed. Swedberg, 152–66.

1990c. "Tribute to Charles P. Kindleberger On His Eightieth Birthday." Typescript. September.

1990d. "The Case Against 'One Thing at a Time.'" *World Development* 18, no. 8: 1119–22.

1990e. "Remerciements." Speech delivered upon receipt of honorary degree from the Institut d'études politiques de Paris. In *Doctorats Honoris Causa,* pp. 14–16. Paris: Institut d'études politiques.

1990f. *Come far passare le riforme.* Ed. L. Meldolesi. Bologna: Il Mulino.

1990g. *Tre continenti: Economia politica e sviluppo della deomocrazia in Europa, Stati Uniti e America Latina,* Ed. L .Meldolesi. Torino: Einaudi.

1991. *The Rhetoric of Reaction: Perversity, Futility, Jeopardy.* Cambridge Mass.: Harvard University Press.

1992a. Letter to Lal Jayawardena. April 22.

1992b. "Industrialization and Its Manifold Discontents: West, East, and South." *World Development* 20, no. 9: 1225–32.

1992c. "La rhétorique progressiste et le réformateur." Paper presented at the Colloque justice sociale et inégalités, Commissariat générale du plan, November 12–13, Paris, pp. 1–18. Abridged version in *Commentaire* 62 (summer, 1993): 303–9.

1992d. "L'argument intransigeant comme idée reçue: En guise de réponse à Raymond Boudon." *Le Débat* 69:102–8.

**1992e. Preface to the paperback ed. of *Rival Views of Market Society and Other Recent Essays*.

1992f. "Does the Market Keep Us out of Mischief or out of Happiness?" *Contemporary Sociology* 21, no. 6: 741–44.

1993a. "Varien Fry in Marseilles." Preface to Fry, *Assignment: Rescue* (rev. ed. of Fry, *Surrender on Demand*).

1993b. "Exit, Voice, and the Fate of the German Democratic Republic: An Essay in Conceptual History." *World Politics* 4–5, n. 2 (January): 173–202.

1993c. "Coimbra Talk." Typescript.

1993d. "Petit Discours de Nanterre." Typescript.

1993e. "The Rhetoric of Reaction—Two Years Later." *Government and Opposition* 28, no. 3 (summer): 292–314.

1994a. "A Propensity to Self-Subversion." *Common Knowledge* 3, no. 2.

1994b. "The On-and-Off Connection between Political and Economic Progress." *American Economic Review, Papers and Proceedings* (May).

1994c. "Social Conflictes as Pillars of Democratic Market Society." *Political Theory* (June).

1994d. "A Hidden Ambition." New Preface to *Development Projects Observed*.

OTHERS' WORKS

Alape, A. 1986. *La paz, la violencia: Textigo de exception.* Bogotá: Planeta.

Almond, G., S. C. Flanagan, and R. J. Mundt, ed. 1973. *Crisis, Choice, and Change: Historical Studies of Political Development.* Boston, Mass.: Little, Brown, and Co.

Althusser, L. 1965. *Pour Marx.* Paris: Maspero.

Althusser, L., and E. Balibar. 1965. *Lire "Le Capital."* Paris: Maspero.

Anderson, C. W. 1965. "Reformmongering and the Uses of Political Power." *InterAmerican Economic Affairs* 19, no. 2.

Ariotti, R. 1968. Review of Italian ed. of Hirschman, *The Strategy of Economic Development (La strategia dello sviluppo economico). Statistica* (April–June): 277–79.

Arndt, H. W. 1988a. "Yen Appreciation, J-Curve, and Valuation Effects." *Pacific Economic Papers* 156 (February).

———. 1988b. "The Valuation Effect of Changes in Exchange Rates." *Banca Nazionale del Lavoro Quarterly Review* (December).

Arrow, K. 1951. *Social Choice and Individual Values.* New York: Wiley.

———. 1973. "Social Responsibility and Economic Efficiency." *Public Policy* 21 (summer): 303–18.

Asher, A. E., et al. 1962. *Development in the Emerging Countries.* Washington, D.C.: The Brookings Institution.

Asso, P. F. 1988. "Bilateralism, Trade Agreements, and Political Economists in the 1930s: Theories and Events Underlying Hirschman's Index." *Political Economy* 4, no. 1: 83–110.

Asso, P. F., and M. de Cecco, ed. 1987. Hirschman essays. *Potenza nazionale e commercio estero: Gli anni Trenta, l'Italia e la ricostruzione,* 7–38. Bologna: Il Mulino.

Axinn, S. 1983. Review of Hirschman, *Shifting Involvements: Private Interest and Public Action. Annales of the American Academy of Political and Social Science* 467 (May): 241–42.

Baffi, P. 1985. "Via Nazionale e gli economisti stranieri, 1944–52." *Rivista di storia economica* 2, no. 1: 1–45.

Balassa, B., et al. 1971. *The Structure of Protection in Developing Countries.* Baltimore, Md.: Johns Hopkins University Press.

Banfield, E. 1958. *The Moral Basis of a Backward Society.* Glencoe, Ill.: Free Press.

Barry, B. 1974. Review essay on Hirschman, *Exit, Voice, and Loyalty: Responses to Decline in Firms, Organizations, and States. British Journal of Political Science* 4, part 1 (January): 79–107.

Bell, D. 1984. "The American Academy of Arts and Sciences." Typescript. March 14.

Berlinski, J. 1992. "Trade Policies and Industrialization." In *Towards a New Development Strategy for Latin America: Pathways from Hirschman's Thought,* ed. Teitel, 323–36.

Bertelli, S. 1980. *Il gruppo: La formazione del gruppo dirigente del PCI, 1936–1948.* Milano: Rizzoli.

Blaug, M. 1986. *Great Economists since Keynes: An Introduction to Lives and Work of One Hundred Modern Economists.* London: Harvester Press.

Bobbio, N. 1975. Introduction to Colorni, *Scritti,* v–xlii.

Boudon, R. 1992. "La rhétorique est-elle réactionnaire?" *Le Débat,* 69: 92–101.

Braudel, F. 1949. *La Mediterranée et le monde méditerranéen a l'époque de Philippe II.* Paris: Colin.

————. 1969. *Ecrits sur l'histoire.* Paris: Flammarion.

Braudel, P. 1992. "Un témoignage." *Annales* 47, no. 1: 237–44.

Brehm, J. W., and A. R. Cohen. 1962. *Exploring the Cognitive Dissonance.* New York: Wiley.

Buchanan, J., and G. Tullock. 1962. *The Calculus of Consent.* Ann Arbor, Mich.: University of Michigan Press.

Caporaso, J. A. 1978. Introduction to special issue on Dependence and Dependency in the Global System. *International Organization* 32, no. 1 (winter): 1–12.

Cardoso, F. H., and E. Faletto. 1969. *Dependencia y desarrollo en América Latina.* Mexico City: Siglo XXI. English ed. with new introduction, Berkeley, Cal.: University of California Press, 1979.

Carr, W. 1963. Review of Hirschman, *Latin American Issues: Essays and Comments. World Affairs* 126, no. 3 (fall): 220–22.

Casanova, J. C. 1990. "Eloge du Professeur Albert Hirschman." Presented upon Hirschman's receipt of honorary degree at the Institut d'études politiques de Paris. In *Doctorats Honoris Causa,* pp. 8–13. Paris: Institut d'études politiques.

Chenery, H. 1959. Review of J. Timbergen, *The Design of Development,* and Hirschman, *The Strategy of Economic Development. American Economica Review* (December): 1063–65.

Collier, D., ed. 1979. *The New Authoritarianism in Latin America.* Princeton, N.J.: Princeton University Press.

Colorni, E. 1937. "La spontaneità è una forma di organizzazione." *Nuovo Avanti,* Paris, June 12. Reprinted in Solari, *Eugenio Colorni,* 115–24.

————. 1938–1942. Letters. In *Lettere di antifascisti dal carcere e dal confine,* ed. G. Pajetta, 411–20. Roma: Editori Riuniti, 1962.

————. 1944. Preface to E. Rossi and A. Spinelli, *Il Manifesto di Ventotene.* Reprinted in *Quaderni federalisti europei* 26 (March, 1979): 17–22.

————. 1975. *Scritti.* Firenze: La Nuova Italia.

Comitato di Quartiere della Magliana. 1976. *La Magliana: Vita e lotta di un quartiere proletario.* Milano: Feltrinelli.

Condliffe, J. 1940. *The Reconstruction of World Trade: A Survey of International Economic Relations.* New York: Norton.

Congresso Nacional. 1959. Veto presidencial. Mensagem no. 192, 1959, Rio de Janeiro: Imprensa Nacional.

Cooper, R., ed. 1969. *International Finance.* London: Penguin, 1969.

Coppa, C. 1992. "La ricerca socio-economica come scoperta: Albert O. Hirschman ed Eugenio Colorni." Dissertation, Napoli, Facoltà di economia e commercio.

Cornelius, W. A. 1973. "Nation Building Participation and Distribution: The Politics of Social Reform under Cardenas." In *Crisis, Choice, and Change: Historical Studies of Political Development,* ed. Almond, Flanagan, and Mundt.

Cornford, F. M. 1908. *Microcosmografia Academica.* 2d ed. Cambridge: Bowes and Bowes, 1922.

Coser, L. A. 1984. *Refugee Scholars in America: Their Impact and Their Experiences.* New Haven, Conn.: Yale University Press.

Cozzi, T. 1987. "Albert Otto Hirschman, scienziato sociale." *La Stampa* (November 14).

Crick, B. 1964. *In Defense of Politics.* Rev. ed. Baltimore, Md.: Penguin.

Cyert, R. M., and J. C. March. 1963. *Behavioral Theory of the Firm.* Englewood Cliffs, N.J.: Prentice-Hall.

Desrosières, A. 1985. "Histoire des formes: Statistique et science sociale avant 1940." *Revue française de sociologie* 26, no. 2 (March–April): 277–310.

Devine, D. J. 1972. *The Political Culture of United States: The Influence of Member Values on Regime Maintenance.* Boston: Little Brown.

di Fenizio. 1968. "La contrattazione programmata." *La Stampa* (April 16).

di Tella, G., and R. Dornbusch, ed. 1989. *The Political Economy of Argentina 1946–83,* London: Macmillan.

Dornbusch, R., ed. 1989. *The Road to Economic Recovery: Report of the Twentieth Century Fund Task Force on International Debt,* New York: Priority Press.

Dostoyevski, F. 1864. *Zapiski iz podpol'ja (Notes from the Underground).*

Downs, A. 1974. "Up and Down with Ecology: The 'Issue-Attention Cycle.'" *Public Interest* 5, no. 4 (December): 375–414.

Dumez, H. 1985. *L'économiste, la science et le pouvoir: Le cas Walras.* Paris: PUF.

Dumont, L. 1977. *Homo aequalis.* Vol. 1, *Genèse et epanouissement de l'idéologie économique.* Paris: Gallimard.

Eatwell, J., M. Milgate, and P. Newman, ed. 1987. *The New Palgrave: A Dictionary of Economic Theory and Doctrine.* London: Macmillan.

Eckstein, A. 1971. *Comparison of Economic Systems: Theoretical and Methodological Approaches.* Berkeley, Cal.: University of California Press.

ECLA. 1990. *Transformación productiva con equidad.* Santiago: UN-ECLA.

Eisenstadt, S. 1980. "Gli esiti delle rivoluzioni: Società autocratiche e democratiche post-rivoluzionarie." In *I limiti della democrazia: Autoritarismo e democrazia nella società moderna.* ed. Scartezzini, Germani, and Gritti, 53–78.

Ellis, H. S., ed. 1961. *Economic Development for Latin America*. New York: St. Martin's Press.

Elster, J. 1982. Review of Hirschman, *Essays in Trespassing: Economics to Politics and Beyond* and *Shifting Involvements: Private Interest and Public Action*. *London Review of Books* 4, no. 17 (September 16): 8–10.

Febvre, L. 1922. *La terre et l'évolution humaine*. Paris: La Renaissance du livre.

Felix, D. 1964. Review of Hirschman, *Journeys toward Progress: Studies of Economic Policy-Making in Latin America*. *Economica* 31, no. 122 (May): 201–3.

Ferguson, A. 1767. *Essay on the History of Civil Society*. Ed. D. Forbes. Edinburgh: University of Edinburgh Press, 1966.

Ferraresi, F. 1990. "Laurea honoris causa al prof. Albert O. Hirschman." In Hirschman, *Tre continenti: Economia politica e sviluppo della deomocrazia in Europa, Stati Uniti e America Latina*, ed. Meldolesi, xxiii–xxix.

Festinger, L. 1957. *A Theory of Cognitive Dissonance*. Stanford, Cal.: Stanford University Press.

Fishlow, A. 1965. *American Railroads and the Transformation of the Ante Bellum Economy*. Cambridge, Mass.: Harvard University Press.

Flaubert, G. 1869. *L'éducation sentimentale: Histoire d'un jeune homme*. Paris: Garnier Frères, 1964.

———. 1881. "Dictionnaire des idées reçues." In G. Flaubert, *Bouvard et Pécuchet*, 485–555. Paris: Gallimard, 1979.

———. 1929. *Correspondence*. Paris: Conard.

Forte, F., and E. Granaglia, ed. *La nuova economia politica americana*. Milano: Sugarco.

Foxley, A., M. S. McPherson, and G. O'Donnell, ed. 1986. *Development, Democracy, and the Art of Trespassing: Essays in Honor of Albert Hirschman*. Notre Dame, Ind.: University of Notre Dame Press.

Frank, A. G. 1960. "Built in Destabilization: A. O. Hirschman's Strategy of Economic Development." *Economic Development and Cultural Change* 8, no. 4 (July): 433–40.

Frankel, H. 1943. "The Industrialization of Agricultural Countries." *Economic Journal* 53, nos. 210–11 (June): 188–201.

Frankfurt, H. G. 1971. "Freedom of the Will and the Concept of a Person." *Journal of Philosophy* 68, no. 1 (January): 5–20.

Freeman, R. B. 1976. "Individual Mobility and Union Voice in the Labor Market." *American Economic Review, Papers and Proceedings* 66, no. 2: 361–68.

Freeman, R. B., and J. L. Medoff. 1984. *What Do Unions Do?* New York: Basic Books.

Friedman, M. 1962. *Capitalism and Freedom.* Chicago: University of Chicago Press.

Fry, V. 1945. *Surrender on Demand.* New York: Random House. 2d ed., pub. as *Assignment: Rescue,* New York: Scholastic, 1993.

Fuentes, C. 1969. "Viva Zapata: *Zapata and the Mexican Revolution,* by John Womack, Jr." *New York Review of Books* (March 13).

Furet, F., ed. 1984. Hirschman essays. *L'économie comme science sociale et politique.* Paris: Gallimard/Le Seuil.

Furtado, C. 1959a. *Formaçao economica do Brasil.* Rio de Janeiro: Editoria Fondo de Cultura.

———. 1959b. "Grupo de Trabalho para o desenvolvimento do Nordeste." In *Uma politica de desenvolvimento para o Nordeste.* Rio de Janeiro: Imprensa Nacional.

———. 1969. Review of Hirschman, *The Strategy of Economic Development. Economica Brasileira* 5, nos. 1–2: 64–65.

Galbraith, J. K. 1961. "A Positive Approach to Foreign Aid." *Foreign Affairs* 39, no. 3 (April): 445–46.

Gallino, L. 1988. "Hirschman, le scienze sociali: Tra lealtà e critica." *La Stampa* (January 6).

Geertz, C. 1963. *Peddlers and Princes: Social Change and Economic Modernization in Two Indonesian Towns.* Chicago: University of Chicago Press.

———. 1973, *The Interpretation of Cultures.* New York: Basic Books.

Gerschenkron, A. 1943. *Bread and Democracy.* Berkeley, Cal.: University of California Press.

———. 1952. "Economic Backwardness in Historical Perspective." In *The Progress of Underdeveloped Areas,* ed. Hoselitz, 3–29.

———. 1962. *Economic Backwardness in Historical Perspective.* Cambridge, Mass.: Harvard University Press.

———. 1971. "Ideology as a System Determinant." In *Comparative Economic Systems: Theoretical and Methodological Approaches,* ed. A. Eckstein, 269–89. Berkeley, Cal., and Los Angeles: University of California Press.

Gide, C., and C. Rist. 1910. *Histoire des doctrines économiques.* 7th ed. Paris: Sirey, 1959.

Gil Calvo, E. 1992. "El arte de navigar contra el viento: La traversía de Albert Hirschman." *CLAVES Ciencias Sociales,* pp. 56–62.

Ginzburg, A. 1986. "Dependency and the Political Solution of Balance of Payments Crises: The Italian Case." In *Development, Democracy, and the Art of Trespassing: Essays in Honor of Albert Hirschman,* ed. A. Foxley, M. S. McPherson, and G. O'Donnell, 133–66.

Ginzburg, A., ed. 1983. *Ascesa e declino dell'economia dello sviluppo e altri saggi.* Torino: Rosenberg and Sellier.

Gluckman, M. 1965. *Politics, Law, and Ritual in Tribal Society.* Chicago: Aldine.

Granovetter, M. 1985. "Economic Action and Social Structure: A Theory of Embeddedness." *American Journal of Sociology* 91, no. 3 (November).

Graziosi, A. 1986. "A. O. Hirschman e l'URSS, ovvero le trappole dello sviluppo." Typescript.

Greek, C. E. 1983. Review of Hirschman, *Shifting Involvements: Private Interest and Public Action. Contemporary Sociology* 12, no. 6 (November): 671.

Gutmann, A., and D. Thompson. 1989. "The Place of Philosophy in Public Affairs." In *The Public Turn in Philosophy,* ed. J. Lichtenberg and H. Shue. Totowa, N.J.: Rowman and Allanheld.

Guyaz, J. 1980. "Innovation dans le secteur des services: Du militant à l'entrepreneur." In *Français qui etes-vous?* ed. J. D. Reynand and Y. Gafmeyer, 191–201. Paris: La documentation française.

Haan, N., et al., ed. 1983. *Social Science as Moral Inquiry.* New York: Columbia University Press.

Haberler, G. 1949. "The Market for Foreign Exchange and the Stability of the Balance of Payments: A Theoretical Analysis." *Kiklos* 3:193–218. Reprint in *International Finance,* ed. Cooper, 107–34.

Hall, P. A., ed. 1989. *The Political Power of Economic Ideas.* 347–59. Princeton, N.J.: Princeton University Press.

Harrod, R. 1963. Letter to Hirschman. September 8.

Hartz, L. 1955. *The Liberal Tradition in America: An Interpretation of American Political Thought since the Revolution.* New York: Harcourt.

Heckscher, E. 1963. Preface to Hirschman, *Journeys toward Progress: Studies of Economic Policy-Making in Latin America,* iii–v.

Hegel, G. W. F. 1807. *Phänomenologie des Geistes.* Hamburg: Heiner, 1937.

———. 1821. *Grundlinien der Philosophie des Rechts.* Hamburg: Meinez, 1955.

Helper, S. 1991. "How Much Really Changed between U.S. Automakers and Their Suppliers?" *Sloan Management Review* 32, no. 4 (summer).

Hibbs, D. A., Jr. 1977. "Political Parties and Macro Economic Policy." *American Political Science Review* 71, no. 4 (December): 1467–87.

Hill, K. Q., ed. 1979. *Toward a New Strategy for Development,* New York: Pergamon Press.

Hirschmann, U. 1993. *Noi senzapatria.* Bologna: Il Mulino.

Hobsbawn, E. J. 1986. "Murderous Colombia." *New York Review of Books* (November 20): 27–31.

Hoselitz, B. F. 1960. "Balanced Growth, Destabilizers, and the Big Push." *World Politics* 12, no. 3 (April): 468–77.

———. 1952. Preface to *The Progress of Underdeveloped Areas*, ed. Hoselitz.

Hoselitz, B. F., ed. 1952. *The Progress of Underdeveloped Areas.* Chicago: University of Chicago Press.

Huntington, S. 1965. "Political Development and Political Decay." *World Politics* 17, no. 3 (September): 386–430.

———. 1968a. *Political Order in Changing Societies.* New Haven, Conn.: Yale University Press.

———. 1968b. *Military Intervention, Political Involvement, and the Un-lessons of Vietnam.* Chicago: A. Stevenson Institute of International Affairs.

Inkeles, A., and D. H. Smith. 1974. *Becoming Modern.* Cambridge, Mass.: Harvard University Press.

Johnson, H. G. 1967. *Economic Policies toward Less Developed Countries.* Washington, D.C.: Brookings Institution.

Kallscheuer, O. 1992. Review of Hirschman, *The Rhetoric of Reaction: Perversity, Futility, Jeopardy. Die Zeit,* supplement on the Frankfurt Book Fair (October 2).

Kaplan, R. 1989. *The Exiles.* Documentary film.

Kelman, S. 1987. *Making Public Policy: A Hopeful View of American Government.* New York: Basic Books.

Keynes, J. M. 1936. *The General Theory of Employment, Interest, and Money.* London: Macmillan.

Kincaid, J. 1989. "Mariah." *New Yorker* (26 June): 32–37.

Kindleberger, C. P. 1959. "For Unbalanced Growth." *Yale Review* 48, no. 3 (March): 440–42.

King, T. 1965. Review of Hirschman, *Journeys toward Progress: Studies of Economic Policy-Making in Latin America. Economic Journal* 75, no. 298 (June): 435–37.

Knox, A.D. 1960. Review of Hirschman, *The Strategy of Economic Development. British Journal in International Affairs* 30, no. 1 (January): 99–100.

Krugman, P. 1992. "Towards a Counter-Counter-Revolution in Development Theory." World Bank Annual Conference, April 30–May 1, Washington, D.C., pp. 1–33.

League of Nations. 1945. *Industrialization and Foreign Trade.* Princeton, N.J.: League of Nations.

Lechner, N. 1986. "De la révolution à la démocratie: Le débat intel-lectuel en Amérique du Sud." *Esprit* 116, no. 7 (July): 1–13.

Leibenstein, H. 1966. "Allocative Efficiency versus X-Efficency." *American Economic Review* 56, no. 3 (June): 392–415.

———. 1976. *Beyond Economic Man.* Cambridge, Mass.: Harvard University Press.

Lenin, V. I. 1920. "Report on the International Situation and on the Fundamental Tasks of international Communism" (in Russian). *Pravda*, no. 162 (July 24). Reprint in vol. 31 of V. I. Lenin, *Opere complete* (Roma: Editori Riuniti, 1967), 205–23.

Lewis, A. 1954. "Economic Development with Unlimited Supplies of Labour." *Manchester School of Economic and Social Studies* 22, no. 2 (May).

Lindbeck, A. 1988. "Individual Freedom and Welfare State Policy." *European Economic Review* 32, nos. 2–3 (March): 295–318.

Lindberg, and C. S. Maier, ed. 1985. *The Politics of Inflation and Economic Stagnation.* Washington, D.C.: Brookings Institution.

Little, I. N. D., T. Scitovski, and M. Scott. 1970. *Industry and Trade in Some Developing Countries.* Oxford: Oxford University Press.

Lluch, E. 1992. "Alabanza de Albert O. Hirschman." Typescript.

Lowenstein, L. 1988. *What's Wrong with Wall Street: Short-Term Gains and the Absentee Shareholder.* New York: Addison Wesley.

Luzzatto, G. 1901. "Storia individuale e storia sociale." In G. Luzzatto, *La scienza sociale* (Palermo), 198–212. Also in G. Luzzato, *Per una storia economica d'Italia.* (Bari: Laterza 1967), 57–80.

Machiavelli, N. 1531. *Discorsi.* Roma: Blado, and Firenze: Giunta. Firenze: Le Monnier, 1887.

Mahbul ul H. 1986. "Employment and Income Distribution in the 1970s: A New Perspective." In *Employment, Distribution, and Basic Needs in Pakistan: Essays in Honour of J. Azfar,* ed. Mahbul ul Haq and M. Baqai.

Malan, P. 1989. "Hirschman on Foreign Capital and External Finance in Latin America: A Bias for Hope?" Typescript.

Manin, B. 1985. "Volonté générale ou délibération? Esquisse d'une theorie de la délibération politique." *Le Débat* 33 (January): 72–93.

Mansbridge, J. J. 1980. *Beyond Adversary Democracy.* New York: Basic Books.

Marshall, A. 1923. *Money, Credit, and Commerce.* London: Macmillan.

Marx, K. 1867. *Das Kapital.* Vol. 1. Hamburg: Heissner.

McCloskey, D. 1983. "The Rhetoric of Economics." *Journal of Economic Litterature* 21, no. 2 (June): 481–517.

McPherson, M. S. 1986. "The Social Scientist as Constructive Skeptic: On Hirschman's Role." In *Development, Democracy, and the Art of Trespassing: Essays in Honor of Albert Hirschman,* ed. Foxley, McPherson, and O'Donnell, 305–15.

Meade, J. E. 1951. *The Theory of International Economic Policy.* Vol. 1, *The Balance of Payments.* London: Macmillan.

Meier, G. M., and D. Seers, ed. 1984. *Pioneers in Development.* Oxford: Oxford University Press.

Meldolesi, L. 1981. *La teoria economica di Lenin: Imperialismo e socialismo nel dibattito classico 1914–1916.* Roma and Bari: Laterza.

———. 1982. *L'utopia realmente esistente: Marx e Saint-Simon.* Roma and Bari: Laterza.

———. 1984. "'Economica critica' e 'Storia della lunga durata': Un'introduzione." *Inchiesta* 14, nos. 63–64 (January–June): 68–86; English trans., *Review* 9, no. 1 (summer): 3–55.

———. 1985a. "Georg Simmel e la filosofia del denaro." *Studi economici* 27, no. 3: 123–28.

———. 1985b. "America, America: Note su Hirschman, Hartz e Braudel." *Inchiesta* 15, no. 69 (July–September): 1–15.

———. 1987a. "Economia e politica vent'anni dopo." *Inchiesta* 17, no. 78: 39–55.

———. 1987b. "Per una nuova ipotesi interpretativa sulla storia del pensiero economico moderno." *Quaderni di storia dell'economia politica* 5, no. 1–2: 281–89.

———. 1989. "Inevitabilità del socialismo o crisi dell'antico regime?" In *Teoria dei sistemi economici,* ed. B. Jossa, 295–322. Torino: UTET.

———. 1990a. "Il futuro ha un cuore antico?" *Economia Politica* 7, no. 2 (August): 191–217.

———. 1990b. "Come complicare l'analisi costi-benefici." *Amministrare* 20, no. 1 (April): 127–35.

———. 1991a. "Durkheim, Simiand e la riforma dell'economia." In F. Simiand, *La moneta realtà sociale ed altri scritti,* ed. L. Meldolesi, xiii–xlvi. Napoli: ESI.

———. 1991b. "Economia e democrazia: A proposito di Vilfredo Pareto." In *Pareto oggi,* ed. G. Busino, 159–65. Bologna: Il Mulino.

———. 1991–1992. "Gli spiriti del capitalismo." *Modernizzazione e sviluppo* 2, no. 3: 24–37; 3, no. 1–2: 36–41.

———. 1992a. *Spendere meglio è possibile.* Bologna: Il Mulino.

———. 1992b. "Braudel e un 'post scriptum.'" *Il Ponte* 48, no. 10 (October): 74–83.

———. 1994a. "La nozione di ottimo squilibrio." In *Teorie dell'equilibrio,* ed. G. Caravale, 229–32. Bologna: Il Mulino.

———. 1994b. "Economia-mondo." *Enciclopedia delle scienze sociali* (forthcoming).

Meldolesi, L., ed. 1987. Hirschman essays. *L'economia politica come scienza morale e sociale.* Napoli: Liguori.

———. 1988. Hirschman essays. *Come complicare l'economia,* Bologna: Il Mulino.

———. 1990a. Hirschman essays. *Tre continenti: Economia politica e sviluppo della democrazia in Europa, Stati Uniti e America Latina,* Torino: Einaudi, 1990.

———. 1990b. Hirschman essays. *Come far passare le riforme.* Bologna: Il Mulino.

Millikan, M. F., and W. W. Rostow. 1957. *A Proposal: Key to An Effective Foreign Policy.* New York: Harper.

Milward, A. S. 1984. *The Reconstruction of Western Europe 1945–1951.* Methuen: London.

Minc, A. 1984. *L'avenir en face.* Paris: Seuil.

M.I.T Center for International Studies. 1955. "Investment Criteria and Economic Growth." Typescript of papers presented at a conference, October 15–17, 1954.

Montesquieu, C. L. de Secondat, Baron de. 1748. *De l'esprit des lois.* Paris: Flammarion, 1979.

Moser, S. M. 1984. Review of Hirschman, *Shifting Involvements: Private Interest and Public Action. American Political Science Review* 78, no. 2 (June): 590–91.

Mueller, D. C. 1979. *Public Choice.* Cambridge: Cambridge University Press.

Myint, H. 1960. "The Demand Approach to Economic Development." *Review of Economic Studies* 27, no. 33 (February): 124–32.

Nelson, R., and M. Krashinsky. 1974. "Public Control and Economic Organization in Day Care for Young Children." *Public Policy* 22 (winter): 53–76.

Ocampo, J. A. 1989. "The Economic Development of Colombia." Typescript.

O'Donnell, G. 1975. "Reflexiones sobre las tendencias generales de cambio en el estado burocrático-autoritario." Buenos Aires: Centro de Estudios do Estado y Sociedad. English trans. in *The New Authoritarism in Latin America,* ed. Collier, 285–318.

———. 1986. "On the Convergence of Hirschman's *Exit, Voice, and Loyalty* and *Shifting Involvements.*" In *Development, Democracy, and the Art of Trespassing: Essays in Honor of Albert Hirschman,* ed. Foxley, McPherson, and O'Donnell, 249–68.

Offe, C. 1988. "Notes for Hirschman Colloquium (Introduction)." Typescript. September 1.

Oliver, H. 1946. Review of Hirschman, *National Power and the Structure of Foreign Trade*. *Southern Economic Journal* 12: 304–5.

Olson, M. 1964. *The Logic of Collective Action: Public Goods and the Theory of Group*. Cambridge, Mass.: Harvard University Press.

Ortiz Sarmiento, C. M. 1986. *Estado y subversion in Colombia: La violencia en el Quindio Anos 50*. Bogotá: Fondo Editorial CEREC.

Packenham, R. A. 1973. *Liberal America and the Third World: Political Development Ideas in Foreign Aid and Social Science*. Princeton, N.J.: Princeton University Press.

Panaranda, R., and G. Sanchez, ed. 1986. *Pasado y presente de la violencia in Colombia*. Bogotá: Fondo Editorial CEREC.

Parsons, T. Prize. 1983. *Bulletin of the American Academy of Arts and Sciences* 37, no. 1 (October): 5–8.

Pascal, B. 1670. *Pensées*. Port Royal. Paris: Gallimard, 1977.

Payne, J. L. 1968. *Patterns of Conflict in Colombia*. New Haven, Conn.: Yale University Press.

Pearson, S. R. 1970. *Petroleum and the Nigerian Economy*. Stanford, Cal.: Stanford University Press.

Perelman, C. *Rhétoriques*. Bruxelles: Editions de l'Université de Bruxelles.

Perroux, F. 1958. *La coexistence pacifique*. 2 vol. Paris: PUF.

Piatier, A. 1940. *Exchange Control: A General Survey*. Paris: League of Nations.

Pizzorno, A. 1986. "Sul confronto intertemporale delle utilità." *Stato e mercato* 16 (April): 1–25.

Przeworski, A. "Ama a incerteza e seras democratico." *Novos estudos* 9 (July).

Rabinow, P., and W. M. Sullivan, ed. 1970. *Interpretative Social Science: A Reader*. Berkeley, Cal.: University of California Press.

———. 1979. *Interpretive Social Science: A Second Look*. Berkeley, Cal., and Los Angeles: University of California Press.

Rémond, R. 1991. "Ni réforme ni révolution." *Le Monde* (April 19).

Rist, C. 1934. "L'institut scientifique de recherches économiques et sociales." *Revue d'économie politique*, pp. 1769–74.

———. 1935. "Avant-propos." *L'activité économique* 1, no. 1: 1–2.

———. 1945. *Précis des mécanismes économiques élémentaires*. Paris: Sirey.

Robinson, J. 1947. *Essays in the Theory of Employment*. 2d ed. Oxford: Oxford University Press.

Rodwin, L., and D. A. Schön, ed. 1994. *Rethinking the Development Experience: Essays Provoked by the Work of Albert O. Hirschman.* Washington, D.C.: Brookings Institution.

Roemer, M. 1970. *Fishing for Growth: Export-led Development in Peru 1950–1967.* Cambridge, Mass.; Harvard University Press.

Rokkan, S. "Introduction to *Economics and Cultural Models of Comparative Policy-Making.*" *Social Science Information* 13.

————. 1975. "Dimension of State Formation and Nation-Building: A Possible Paradigm for Research on Variations within Europe." In *The Formation of National States in Western Europe,* ed. C. Tilly, 562–600. Princeton, N.J.: Princeton University Press.

Rosen, S. 1978. "Louis Dumont from Mandeville to Marx." *Economic Development and Cultural Change* 27, no. 1 (October): 206–14.

Rosenberg, N. 1969. "The Direction of Technological Change: Inducement Mechanismis and Focusing Devices." *Economic Development and Cultural Change* 18, no. 1 (October): 1–24.

Rosenthal, G. 1990. "Las ciencias sociales en el proceso de democratización." *Micronoticias* (Santiago: NU-CEPAL, 16 November), 1–4.

Rossi, E. 1975. *Un democratico ribelle.* Ed. G. Armani. Parma: Guanda.

Rossi, E., and A. Spinelli. 1944. *Il manifesto di Ventotene.* Reprint, *Quaderni federativi europei* 26 (March, 1979).

Rostow, W. W. 1958. "The National Style." in *The American Style,* ed. E. E. Morison. New York: Harper.

————. 1960. *The Stages of Economic Development: A Non-Communist Manifesto.* Cambridge: Cambridge University Press.

————. 1960. *The United States in the World Arena.* New York: Harper.

Rothschild, M. 1973. "A Mathematical Appendix" to Hirschman, "The Changing Tolerance" (1973b). *Quarterly Journal of Economics:* 562–66.

Rustow, D. A. 1967. *A World of Nations: Problems of Political Modernization.* Washington, D.C.: Brookings Institution.

————. 1970. "Transitions to Democracy: Toward a Dynamic Model." *Contemporary Politics* (April): 337–63.

————. 1990. "Democracy: A Global Revolution?" *Foregn Affairs* 69, no. 4: 74–91.

————. 1992–1993. "Democracy: Historic Essentials and Future Prospects." *Harvard International Review* (winter).

Rustow, D. A., ed. 1968. "Philosophers and Kings: Studies in Leadership." *Daedalus* 97, no. 3: v–vi and 683–1081.

Sabel, C. J. 1992. *Work and Politics: The Division of Labor in Industry.* Cambridge: Cambridge University Press.

Samuelson, P. 1948. "International Trade and the Equalization of Factor Prices." *Economic Journal* 58, no. 230 (June): 163–84.

———. 1952. "International Equalization Once Again." *Economic Journal* 62, no. 246 (June): 278–304.

Saunders, D. M., ed. 1992. "Symposium on *Exit, Voice, and Loyalty*." *Employee Responsibilities and Rights Journal* 5, no. 3.

Scartezzini, R., L. Germani, and R. Gritti, ed. 1985. *I limiti della democrazia: Autoritarismo e democrazia nella società moderna.* Napoli: Liguori.

Schelling, T. 1980. "The Intimate Contest for Self-Command." *The Public Interest* 60 (summer): 94–118. Reprint in T. Schelling, *Choice and Consequence: Perspectives of an Errant Economist* (Cambridge, Mass.: Harvard University Press, 1984), 57–82.

Schlesinger, A. M., Jr. 1965. *A Thousand Days: John F. Kennedy in the White House.* Boston: Houghton Mifflin.

Schön, D. 1992. "Hirschman's Elusive Theory of Social Learning." In *Rethinking the Development Experience,* ed. Rodwin and Schön, 1–46.

Schumpeter, J. 1911. *Theorie der wirtschaftlichen Entwicklung.* 6th ed. Berlin: Duncker and Humblot. English trans., Cambridge, Mass.: Harvard University Press, 1951.

Scitovsky, T. 1976. *The Joyless Economy: An Inquiry into Human Satisfaction and Consumer Dissatisfaction.* New York: Oxford University Press.

———. 1977. Preface to the paperback ed. of *The Joyless Economy.*

Scott, R. J. 1986. "Dismantling Repressive Systems: The Abolition of Slavery in Cuba as a Case Study." In *Development, Democracy, and the Art of Trespassing: Essays in Honor of Albert Hirschman.* ed. Foxley, McPherson, and O'Donnell, 269–81.

Seers, D. 1964. Review of Hirschman, *Journeys toward Progress: Studies of Economic Policy-Making in Latin America. American Economic Review* 54, no. 2: 157–60.

Sen, A. K. 1960. Review of Hirschman, *The Strategy of Economic Development. Economic Journal* 70, no. 279 (September): 590–94.

———. 1977. "Rational Fools: A Critique of the Behavioral Foundations of Economic Theory." *Philosophy and Public Affairs* 6 (summer): 317–44.

Serrano Sanz, J. M. 1991. "La riforma economica en la España de la transición." Typescript.

Sheahan, J. 1992. "Development Dichotomies and Economic Strategy." In *Towards a New Development Strategy for Latin America: Pathways from Hirschman's Thought,* ed. Teitel, 22–45.

Silone, I. 1933. *Fontamara*. Zürich: Oprecht. English trans., London: J. Cape.

———. 1965. "Polikusc'ka." In I. Silone, *Uscita di Sicurezza*, 43–53. Firenze: Vellecchi.

Simiand, F. 1912. *La méthode positive en science économique*. Paris: Alcan.

———. 1991. *La moneta realtà sociale ed altri scritti*. Ed. L. Meldolesi. Napoli: ESI.

Simmel, G. 1900. *Philosophie des Geldes*. Leipzig. In vol 6 of G. Simmel, *Gesamtausgabe*. Frankfurt am Main: Suhrkamp, 1989.

Simon, H. A. 1955. "A Behavioral Model of Rational Choice." *Quarterly Journal of Economics* 49, no. 1 (February): 99–118.

Sirquin, M. 1992. "Linkages and the Strategy of Development." In *Towards a New Development Strategy for Latin America: Pathways from Hirschman's Thought*, ed. Teitel, 103–35.

Smith, A. 1759. *The Theory of Moral Sentiments*. In A. Smith, *Works* (pub. 1811–12). Reprint, London: Aalen, 1963.

———. 1776. *An Inquiry into the Nature and Causes of the Wealth of Nations*. In A. Smith, *Works* (pub. 1811–12). Reprint, London: Aalen, 1963.

Smith, J. 1983. Review of Hirschman, *Essays in Trespassing: Economics to Politics and Beyond* and *Shifting Involvements: Private Interests and Public Action*. *American Journal of Sociology* 89 (June): 225–28.

Solari, L. 1980. *Eugenio Colorni*. Venezia: Marsilio.

Spinelli, A. 1984. *Come ho tentato di diventare saggio: Io, Ulisse*. Bologna: Il Mulino.

———. 1987. *Discorsi al Parlamento Europeo 1976–1986*. Ed. P. V. Dastoli. Bologna: Il Mulino.

Staley, E. 1944. *World Economic Development*. Montreal: ILO.

Steuart, J. 1767. *Inquiry into the Principles of Political Economy*. Ed. A. S. Skinner. Chicago: University of Chicago Press, 1966.

Stinebower, L. D. 1946. Review of Hirschman, *National Power and the Structure of Foreign Trade*. *American Economic Review* 36, no. 3 (June): 418–20.

Streeten, P. P. 1959. "Unbalanced Growth." *Oxford Economic Papers* 2 (June 11): 167–90.

———. 1984. "Comment." In *Pioneers in Development*, ed. G. M. Meir and D. Seers, 115–18. Washington, D.C.: World Bank.

Swedberg, R. ed. 1990. *Economics and Sociology*. Princeton, N.J.: Princeton University Press.

Taylor, L. 1994. "Hirschman's Strategy at Thirty-Five." In *Rethinking the Development Experience*, ed. Rodwin and Schön.

Teitel, S., ed. 1992. *Towards a New Development Strategy for Latin America: Pathways from Hirschman's Thought.* Washington, D.C.: Inter-American Development Bank.

Teitel, S., and F. Thoumi. 1986. "From Import Substitution to Exports: The Manufacturing Exports Experience of Argentina and Brasil." *Economic Development and Cultural Change* 34, no. 3: 455–90.

Tendler, J. 1967. *Electric Power in Brazil.* Cambridge, Mass.: Harvard University Press.

Tiebout, C. M. 1956. "A Pure Theory of Local Expenditure." *Journal of Political Economy* 64 (October): 416–24.

Tillich, P. 1952. *The Courage to Be.* New Haven, Conn.: Yale University Press.

Tocqueville, A. de. 1835–1840. *De la démocratie en Amérique.* Paris: Gallimard, 1961.

Tucker, R. 1968. "The Theory of Charismatic Leadership." *Daedalus* 97, no. 3: 731–56.

Tullock, G. 1970. Review of Hirschman, *Exit, Voice, and Loyalty: Responses to Decline in Firms, Organizations, and States. Journal of Finance* 25, no. 5 (December): 1194–95.

Wacquant, L. J. D. 1987. Review of Hirschman, *Vers un'économice politique élargie. Cahier internationaux de sociologie* 83 (July–December): 421–24.

Watkins, M. H. 1963. "A Staple Theory of Economic Growth." *Canadian Journal of Economic and Political Science* 29, no. 2 (May): 141–58.

Whitehead, A. N. 1930. *Process and Reality.* New York: Macmillan.

Williamson, O. 1975. *Markets and Hierarchies: Analysis and Antitrust Implications.* New York: Free Press.

———. 1976. "The Economics of Internal Organization: Exit and Voice in Relation to Markets and Hierarchies." *American Economic Review, Papers and Proceedings* 66, no. 2 (May): 369–77.

Wilson, J. Q. 1985. "The Rediscovery of Character: Private Virtue and Public Policy." *Public Interest* 81 (fall).

Womack, J., Jr. 1967. *Zapata and the Mexican Revolution.* New York: Knopf.

Yamey, B. S. 1960. Review of Hirschman, *The Strategy of Economic Development. Economica* 27, no. 105 (February): 82–83.

Young, D. R. 1976. "Consolidation or Diversity: Choices in the Structure of Urban Governance." *American Economic Review, Papers and Proceedings* 66, no. 2 (May): 378–85.

Ypsilon. 1961. "A Note on Inter-American Relations." In *Latin American Issues: Essays and Comments,* ed. Hirschman.

INDEX OF NAMES

319

INDEX OF SUBJECTS

Doux commerce: 32, 151, 164, 166, 168, 181
Downs, A.: party convergence, 149; issue attention cycle, 254 (12)
Dumont, L.: separation of economics from politics, 220 (23), 226 (2)

ECLA: 66–67, 239–40 (30, 31)
Economic history: Latin-American industrialization, 75–76, 80; "staple," 84–87. *See also* History
Economic policy: 70, 247 (57); some key features, 81, 149
Economics: 16, 20, 43, 146, 149, 233 (9); paradigm, 31–32, 226 (2); complicating economics, 30–42, 65, 225 (1), 227 (7); a new hypothesis, 33–34, 227 (6); slack, *see* invisible hand, 38, 152; scarcity, 62, 252 (6); partial equilibrium, 65, 235 (15); general equilibrium, 65, 238 (24); input-output, 77–78; classical economics, 38–39, 238 (24); preferences, 37, 61, 122; external economies, complementarities and linkages, 78; perfect forsight vs. learning, 80; neighboring, 78, 149
Economics and politics: 7, 59, 67–70, 240 (33), 241 (35); separation, 70–71, 226 (2), 231 (24); economics as basic, 16, 220 (23), 262 (7); economic theory of politics (public choice), 33, 36, 152; politics-economics, 50; political economics, 70, 240 (34); automatism of market and non-market forces, 45–46, 68–71, 73; transition points, 53, 69, 89; interaction, 18, 20, 70, 136–37, 152, 262 (7); pro-market vs. pro-planning, 20, 67–70; fine dimensions, 71, 148, 277 (14)

Eisenstadt, S.: revolution and democracy, 127
Elster, J.: *Exit*, 269 (6); ultimate objectives, 290 (33)
European economic integration: market, 21–22, 223 (32); monetary, 22, 223 (34, 35), 261 (2)
Exit: 144–49, 228 (10), 270 (11, 12), 275 (35); recovery issue, 145, 147, 184; hydraulic model, 144, 147, 165, 168; feeding on exit and voice, 147, 155, 165, 168, 179, 184-85, 186, 270 (10), 271 (33); loyalty, 149; with severe initiation, 67, 149; cognitive dissonance, 60–61, 234 (12); competition, 146, 149, 269 (7), 270 (9), 273 (29); economics, 146, 149, 271 (14); political system, 149, 271 (15); education, 148; stock market, 148, 271 (10); industrial relations, 272 (25); market and hierarchies, 153–54, 272 (26, 27); emigration, 154–55, 275 (4); voice for exit, 166, 276 (9); exit for voice, 276 (8), *see also*, 186; conclusion, 149, 271 (16)

Federalism: 14–15, 40–41, 223 (32), 229 (12), 222 (27)
Felix, D.: *The Strategy* and *Journeys*, 252 (6)
Ferguson, A.: critique of doux commerce, 167
Festinger: cognitive dissonance, 200
Flaubert, G.: 124; idées reçues, 194, 284 (7, 8); syndrome, 93, 254 (13); narration, 114, 192
Foreign policy: 47, 128–37, 277 (12)
Formative experiences: 4–9, 18, 218 (12)